Preventing Failure in the Primary Grades

Preventing Failure

in the

Primary Grades

SIEGFRIED ENGELMANN

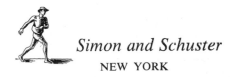

Simon and Schuster
NEW YORK

SBN 671-20368-1
Manufactured in the United States of America
SECOND PRINTING

70-03528
T
372.241
E 577p

The author, editor, and publisher wish to express their gratitude for the courtesy and cooperation shown by the authors and publishers who were kind enough to grant permission for the quotations used in this book.

Pages 3 and 4: Reprinted from "Sociological Perspective on the Education of Culturally Deprived Children," by Eleanor P. and Leo Wolf, in *The School Review*, Winter 1962. Copyright 1962 by the University of Chicago and used by permission of the authors and publisher.

Page 7: Reprinted from "The Overlooked Positives of Disadvantaged Groups," by Frank Riessman, in *Journal of Negro Education*, Summer 1964. Used by permission of the publisher.

Page 63: Reprinted from "The Contingent Use of Teacher Attention and Praise in Reducing Classroom Behavior Problems," by Becker, Madsen, Arnold, and Thomas, in *Journal of Special Education*, Vol. 1, 1967. Used by permission of the publisher.

Page 64: Reprinted from "Behavior Modification in an Adjustment Class: A Token Reinforcement Program," by K. D. O'Leary and W. C. Becker, in *Exceptional Children*, May 1967. Used by permission of the authors and publisher.

Acknowledgments

I am particularly grateful to the people with whom I have had the pleasure of working—Elaine Bruner, Jean Osborn, Valerie Anderson, and Greta Hogan—for ideas solidly demonstrated in the classroom. I am indebted to Wesley Becker for documenting specific relationships between teacher behavior and the behavior of the children. Finally, I am grateful to Carl Bereiter for making this book possible.

SIEGFRIED ENGELMANN

Author's Note

Although the title of this book refers to children in the primary grades, the tasks that are outlined in the reading and arithmetic sections are designed for children who have not mastered the basic skills, whatever their age or grade level. Segments of the program were used initially in work with tenth-grade disadvantaged children. Others were developed expressly for primary children.

Not every part of the program will be right for a particular child. If he has mastered some of the skills that are presented in a sequence, it is wasteful to work on those skills. If a child has serious problems in reading, language comprehension, or arithmetic, however, he should be tested on tasks from the book that appear to be related to his deficiencies. His performance will enable the teacher to pinpoint what he does not know, so that she can take him to the beginning of particular task sequences and teach him the basic skills he has failed to learn.

The program presented here, by a judicious selection of task sequences and a system of reinforcement appropriate to the older child, can be adapted to the needs of a sixteen-year-old who has gone through school without learning basic skills.

Contents

Preventing Failure in the Primary Grades

Introduction

If you pick up a handful of sand at an ocean beach and look at the grains, you will probably be impressed by their apparently uniform size. Yet if you sort the grains according to size, you will find that some are bigger than others. Most will be average size, and about 15 percent of the grains will be noticeably smaller than average. As it is with grains of sand, so it is with any population. If you give all children an IQ test, you will find that about 15 percent of them are substantially below the average. Historically, the children in this 15 percent have been regarded in much the same way as the below average grains of sand in your collection. They have been classified as mentally retarded, slow learners—they have been adorned with labels—and they have been treated accordingly. The assumption has been that it is no more possible to change them than it is to change a small grain of sand into a big grain of sand.

A great deal of research evidence, gathered over the past two decades, has cast serious doubt on the traditional view of the slow learner. Experimental programs have demonstrated that IQ can be changed, and that the achievements of slow learning children can be substantially increased. Observers have noted that a large proportion of slow learners and school failures come from home environments in which little is taught. However, little has been done to help the slow-learning child catch up instead of merely becoming a happy slow learner.

This book details a catch-up program for the child who is seriously behind in basic arithmetic and reading skills. It does not contain detailed descriptions of culturally disadvantaged and slow-learning children. It is not designed for those who look at these children from the often remote viewpoint of the school administrator, psychological diagnostician, or social reformer. Rather this book is

1

designed for the teacher who watches these children fail year after year and has never learned to live with such failure. This book promises that teacher nothing but hard work—an effort far in excess of that implied by the size of her paycheck. However, she will probably receive another reward through her hard work. She may save a great many children from special classes, from school failure, and from ignorance. It can be done.

The Need for an Engineering Approach

All children who fail in school have one thing in common. They are all products of prior teaching that has failed. The reason for failure is irrelevant. Perhaps the teaching was below average in intensity; perhaps it was above average in intensity. In either case it has failed. The child has not been taught skills that are essential to success in school. The job facing the educator is therefore similar to that of what we might call a remedial engineer, that is, an engineer who is charged with the job of correcting defective products as economically and painlessly as possible. The educator must bring the child up to the level of standard performance for children of his age. He must do so quickly and efficiently. He must take the problem that is given to him and solve it. Although the role of the remedial educator is quite similar to that of the remedial engineer, the educator has somehow failed to use the kind of hard-nosed, product-oriented reasoning that characterizes the engineer. The difference in approach is most apparent when the educator talks about the culturally disadvantaged or educationally disadvantaged child.

Engineer vs. Educator

If the remedial engineer is faced with the problem of correcting the performance of a certain model of automobile that has faulty brakes, he first decides whether there is actually a problem, whether the model in question actually falls below performance standards of the average car. Similarly, the first step in educating a group such as the disadvantaged is to note whether there is a real problem. Educators have done a commendable job on this phase of the engineering problem. Although there are some who object to the terms *culturally deprived* and *disadvantaged* (just as there may be an occasional remedial engineer

2

who objects to the term *faulty brakes* and wants to argue about whether there is such a thing), most investigators probably agree that the disadvantaged child fails to meet the performance standards of the average child in all academic areas, with relatively severe performance deficits in language, reading, logical reasoning, and arithmetic. The tests used to reach this conclusion are the same kind as those used by the remedial engineer—performance tests in relevant situations. The remedial engineer takes a sample of the particular model in question and tests the brakes of each car under various conditions. He then compares the performance of the cars tested with the performance of other models and makes. The educational investigator tests samples of culturally disadvantaged children in various academic areas and compares their performance with that of average children.

In approaching the second phase of the problem, let us say that there is a severe problem with the brakes of the cars tested (just as there is a severe problem with the school-age culturally disadvantaged children tested). The engineer must now seek causes. He seeks causes for two reasons: his findings will facilitate the production of future models; and understanding the defect will enable him to correct it with a minimum effort. Unless he analyzes causes, the engineer has no way of knowing how specific the cause of failure is. Without specific knowledge he may be obliged to scrap the entire brake system—the hydraulic lines, the cylinders, the drums, and so on. A thorough investigation of causes therefore represents an economy in effort.

At this point the line of investigation adopted by educators departs dramatically from that of the engineer. While the engineer looks for clues that lead to the specific causes of failure—testing the variables that come into play *the educator seeks nonspecific causes*, often ones that cannot be demonstrated to have any immediate bearing on the problem.

Wolf and Wolf provide this summary of the position: "Some of the talk heard at conferences and meetings is a bit glib and overly optimistic. Father images are not supplied by contacts with men teachers; self-conceptions are not re-formed by words of praise, nor is a sense of emotional security restored by a friendly smile. All these are desirable in and of themselves, but the school is not a primary group, and thus far there is little evidence that teachers can, in a school setting, restructure basic personality."[1] Wolf and Wolf conclude that the sensitive teachers avoid slum schools because they feel inadequate.

"We need to remember the magnitude of problems they face and not add to these burdens by excessive expectations. Rather, as educators who can also act vigorously as citizens, we must redouble our efforts to improve the social and economic conditions under which slum children live and which so profoundly affect their learning."[2]

This type of causal analysis is relatively safe. If one changes the total environment in which these children grow up, one will probably correct the cause of school failure, along with many other aspects of the culture that had little to do with failure. Let us suppose that the remedial engineer adopted the same line of attack as the educator who expects little from teachers and recommends that the learning problems of disadvantaged children be attacked through economic and social reform. The engineer would then say, after performing his tests, "You don't expect us to be able to correct this defect, do you? After all, consider the adverse conditions under which this model was manufactured. The machines that install the window wipers are forty years old. The designers are unimaginative. The workers are indifferent. You cannot expect much in the way of performance from this model. The only way to correct the situation is to *work on the factory*. Change its entire structure. *Then* we won't have to worry about such problems as these." This engineer may be correct and his suggestions may have some long-term merit, but they are not very closely related to the problem at hand. Instead of explaining the failure in specific terms, he took the easy way out. He set up his argument so that he could relate *any fault in the factory* to the present brake failure. Everything became a cause. And as a result he has no remedy for the failure except to change the structure of the factory.

One can always find general causes. The trick is to find the causes that are relevant to the present problem. The remedial engineer who suggests changing the entire brake production facility to remedy the brake problem could go to seven plants and perhaps find a number of things that are not good in each. And it is quite possible that all seven plants are turning out cars that measure up to expected performance standards, in which case the engineer has causes for problems that don't exist. Similarly, if we provided educational cause finders with a complete protocol of a child, *any child*, they could explain why the child should fail in school. They could find many things that aren't good in the child's background or present conditions. However, not all these children will be failures, which means that the cause finders will

4

have causes for failures where there are no failures. Such explanations, like others that are derived after the fact, are not very persuasive.

A major problem associated with gross cause finding is that there is little hope of identifying specific causes if one makes gross changes. Let's say, to pursue our engineering example, that the cause of brake failure has to do with the manner in which a small pin has been installed. If management follows the suggestion of changing the entire brake production facility, the fault will be corrected. The engineer's conclusions about what had been wrong will be substantiated. He will be able to say, "See, I was right," and in a sense he *will* be right. But his remedy is indeed costly, compared to changing procedures for installing the pin. The engineer should specify the minimum action necessary to correct the problem; he should identify the pin as the cause of failure. Once he has done this, he can add suggestions dealing with preventive measures and indirect causes. *But he must first specify the most economical solution to the problem* so that management can act intelligently.

Educators often violate the principle of the minimum remedy and do so from their armchairs, not from the testing grounds. For example, Helene Lloyd, in discussing what can be done to improve the reading performance of disadvantaged children, suggests that there are "at least eight avenues of attack":

1. New types of tests will be developed.

2. All-out efforts will be made to encourage earlier language development and to build the necessary language concepts.

3. The development of urban-oriented materials will be accelerated.

4. The preservice and inservice education of teachers will be improved.

5. There will be an increase in the quality and the quantity of the special personnel provided for upgrading reading in schools in areas in which there are large numbers of disadvantaged citizens.

6. The reading program will be stabilized by the use of adequate records describing children's progress in developing reading skills.

7. There will be a special focus on more and improved research studies in beginning reading.

8. Ways will be found to stretch the school day and school year to provide the required reading instruction time for disadvantaged children.[3]

5

These remedies may work, but there is no reason offhand to suppose that they will. They are based on a purely rational hope that through more research the specific causes will be uncovered and that by changing all the "appearances" associated with reading, reading achievement will be improved. It is somewhat paradoxical that the call for research should be included in the list of solutions to the problem. It is as if the engineer said, "We must change the entire brake production facility and, by the way, we should hire somebody to research this problem and discover why the brakes failed and what can be done to correct them."

The model builders represent another strange breed of educator. Their efforts are premised on the idea that the causes of failure can be best explained not in more specific terms, but in more general terms. A remedial engineer who followed the model-building solution might identify the failure of the pin as the cause of brake failure, but he would not stop there. He would work out a method of classifying pin failures. His suggestion might go something like this: "Pin failure is a type of failure which we could call steel-member failure. The way to avoid pin failure is to select steel members randomly (fenders, bumpers, and so forth) and replace them."

Not only is the procedure expensive, but there is no assurance that the faulty steel member will be replaced through the procedure. Although nobody would accept such a solution from an engineer, many teachers find themselves accepting perfectly analogous explanations from educators. Frostig and ITPA remedial programs are based on a perfectly analogous approach. If the child fails in a particular task, his failure is classified in a broader category. The proposed remedy for the category of failure is to teach the child tasks selected from the category. If a child cannot read, his failure may be classified as "perceptual," or "sequencing." Then he is given exercises in "perception," or "sequencing." That the remedies will correct the specific skill deficit is about as probable as the success of the sampling remedy offered by the engineer. And the educational remedy is just as expensive. Although some of the tasks may solve some of the child's specific problems, most will probably be no more effective than trying to fix a brake pin by replacing a bumper.

The "definitional" approach, which is perhaps the most interesting of all attacks, involves first acknowledging that there is a problem and then, when the remedy is offered, trying to redefine the problem

6

in such a way that it either evaporates or doesn't seem as serious. The engineer using this approach might say, "I know this car has poor brakes, but look at the things that are good about it; look at its strong points. It has nice ashtrays, and it gives a nice, smooth ride—even when you're trying to stop." Or the engineer might try this tack: "Does this car *actually* have poor brakes? It appears to, but closer analysis shows that this is a false impression. The brakes are perfectly adequate, just slightly different from those on the other cars. The difference is this: our model requires a greater *distance* to stop at highway speeds. This makes our car *appear* as if it has faulty brakes."

The educational engineers that use the redefining approach try to convince us that the problem is not as severe as it really is. Some investigators solve the problem of cultural deprivation by noting that it is not as severe today as it was twenty years ago. Educational redefiners say that the disadvantaged appears to be disadvantaged only because we use middle-class norms by which to evaluate his achievement or IQ. Yet they cannot seem to produce any other norms to demonstrate that the problem is illusory. Riessman is a strong proponent of the redefining approach. He stresses the strengths of the poor, noting that they have "hidden verbal ability" and have a "physical" style of learning, which "has many positive features hitherto overlooked." Regarding slowness Riessman states, "A child may be slow because he learns in what I have called a one-track way. That is, he persists in one line of thought and is not flexible or broad. He does not easily adopt other frames of reference, such as the teacher's, and consequently he may appear slow and dull."[4] Not many engineers would assert that the car appears to have poor brakes because it requires more distance to stop at a given speed, but in education such statements are often met with cheers.

Another variation of the redefinition approach has to do with adjusting the goals of the curriculum to the "needs of the child." The remedial engineer who used this approach would perhaps say, "Look, these brakes are bad, but only if you're driving fast. We've discovered that if you change driving habits to suit the personal style of this model, you won't have any trouble. This means that you should never exceed fifteen miles an hour." Although some educators use euphemisms when talking about how the problem of poor performance should be handled, their implication is clear: There is no way to salvage educationally deprived children. We must gear the curriculum to their needs—water it down, reduce the abstract to the concrete, the distant to the immediate, the cognitive to the kinesthetic, and the difficult to the easy. We must take it slowly, recognizing the child's "slow learning" style. We must set our sights lower and satisfy ourselves with performance far below that of the middle-class child.

The approaches characterized above represent no small segment of the approaches to the disadvantaged; they virtually exhaust our "best thinking." And our best thinking has neither the diagnostic focus, the knowledge of how to find causes, nor the inference-drawing capability required to provide the teacher with more than general inspiration (or perhaps general despair). Books of readings on the disadvantaged and his education stress the broad economic and social causes, the lack of early stimulation, the attitudes of failure that result from slum living. From these causes come sweeping, nonspecific conclusions about how to educate the disadvantaged. They don't tell us why JC can't read. They cannot express his failure in terms of the causes over which the teacher in a remedial program has control—the subskills he has failed to learn. They do not tell the teacher how to program the teaching of these subskills.

The approach outlined on the following pages attempts to identify *specific causes* that result in the disadvantaged child's failure in reading, arithmetic, and language skills, and it attempts to provide the *minimum solution*, the very least that must be done to correct the deficits. There is a great deal more that can be done, but the essential part of the remedy is the minimum solution. To have a great deal more without having the minimum solution is to have nothing. To have the minimum solution and nothing more is adequate if not fully satisfying.

Limiting the Teacher's Role

Nothing can be achieved by relating the specific causes of a child's failure to his home background or "learning style" (especially since nobody seems to be very clear about what "learning style" means). The first and most important step in cause finding is to discover *what* the child has failed to learn. Which fundamental procedures associated with reading has he failed to learn? Which arithmetic operations has he failed to learn? Which behavioral rules has he failed to learn? This step is the counterpart of discovering the faulty pin in the engineering

8

analogy. Once the specific defect has been discovered, the engineer can ask the question "Why?" and trace the defect to its origin in the manufacturing process. But first he has to discover the pin. Similarly, the educator and teacher must discover the "pin" before they start trying to discover causes in the background of the child.

In dealing with the immediate problem of fixing automobiles that have faulty pins, the engineer does not have to ask questions of origin; he simply identifies the specific defect and offers the most economical solution available to him. Nor are questions of background causes basically relevant to the job of the classroom teacher. These are questions that are relevant to agencies and organizations in the community that have the responsibility for improving living conditions, solving problems of job opportunity, or building community morale. But the teacher must recognize that she is providing a service that will not be provided by anyone else in the community. Her primary job is to teach the children in her classroom specific skills. As an interested citizen she may want to become involved in issues that go beyond the relatively narrow scope of her profession. As a teacher, however, her primary responsibility is to teach—to identify the specific defect and offer the most economical solution.

This point is often not appreciated by educators and teachers. They seem to think that one cannot have an intelligent grasp of a problem without understanding its broad, causal background. As a matter of fact, such a broad view usually inhibits attempts to solve learning problems. Knowing a child's history in detail will not give the teacher any advantage in dealing with him. If he has specific problems, they will show up in the classroom. If they are health problems, the teacher should call them to the attention of the school nurse or principal. If they are learning problems or behavior problems, she should handle them. If his problems—whatever they may be—do *not* show up in the classroom, they are not the kind of problems to which the teacher can address herself. She must limit herself to those problems for which she can provide a remedy. She must limit her attention to specific skills the child has and doesn't have, because she can work only on the child's performance, not on his history or his home.

1 The Causes of Failure and a Remedy

An eighth-grade teacher passes out a relatively simple test. The instructions at the top of the sheet read, "CIRCLE THE CORRECT ANSWERS." After handing out the tests, the teacher says, "Follow the instructions. You have twenty minutes." The children in the class pore over the tests for a few moments; some of them start to work. Others don't. One who doesn't finally raises his hand. "Yes, John," the teacher says.

"What are we suppose do?"

"Read the instructions and do what they say."

John returns to his test, looking a little uncomfortable. Another hand goes up. "Are we supposed to write in the answers?"

"Follow the instructions, JC. Do what they tell you to do."

Another hand goes up. "Do da mean we suppose do da circle for each one?"

"Well, what does it tell you to do?"

"It say, 'Circle the correct answer.' "

John, the first boy to raise his hands, looks relieved at this pronouncement. A girl raises her hand. "It says, 'Circle the correct *answers*.' That mean if it's correct you circle it."

"I know da, girl. Da what I say."

"You did not. You said circle the correct *answer*."

The teacher interrupts. "Now, does everybody know what to do?"

John raises his hand. "Teacher, what di word? I caa member it." He brings his test to the teacher. She reads the second word of the first item.

"Farm."

This is a class of school failures. It moves like a hippopotamus —with a pathetic lumbering gait, little animation, no tiptoes, no impala-like moves. It's no great wonder that the teacher (who was once enthusiastic and dedicated) is disheartened. What she had been able to accomplish with a few words in another school she must now do with many words and more demonstrations. Telling one child is not enough; the same question will be asked by four or five children, even when each answer is addressed to the class.

A teacher does not have an easy job at best. She must carry out a host of housekeeping functions—keeping the bulletin board current, adjusting the shades, collecting money for the United Fund, attending meetings, preparing the Thanksgiving decorations, assisting in intra-mural activity. She has social worker or counselor duties; she visits homes, arranges for medical attention, calls parents about chronically absent children, examines children for impetigo and lice. In addition she is supposed to teach. Teaching, however, is not easy. She has Mary and John in the same class. Mary reads slightly above her grade level. She wants to be a teacher when she grows up. At the last testing, John scored slightly below second-grade level in reading. He doesn't seem to hear what is said, and he generally acts like a brain-damaged child (which is the label the school psychologist gave him). Between John and Mary is the full range of motivation. The teacher often asks herself, "How can I do it? If I teach to Mary, I lose everybody else. If I teach to John, I bore everybody else. If I teach to the children in the middle, I lose those on both ends."

The teacher faces an almost impossible problem. The children lack comprehension and interest. They can't generalize. They can't follow instructions. They are about two full years retarded in major academic areas. But why? What are the causes in the school that lead to such intellectual poverty? What did the school do and what did it fail to do? How did the school teach these children the behavior they exhibit?

The Causes

1. Basic language skills were not taught. John and some of the others in his class struck out in the first grade. The school, the primary teachers, and the publishers of materials for the disadvantaged were primarily at fault. In the first grade, John's teacher tried to teach him how to read. She began with readiness tasks, giving John such instructions as "Cross out the number that is not like this one" as she pointed to the numeral 2. When John failed to respond, she told him, "John, please do what you're supposed to do. Follow the instructions." At other times she would ask, "Did you hear the question, John? Do you want me to repeat it?" During social studies she would try to get John to participate by asking him, "Would you rather be a fireman or a policeman?" She tried to explain things to John, but she apparently never asked herself whether he could understand the words she used. As a matter of fact, he didn't understand most of them. He didn't understand *or, hear, repeat, question, it*. He didn't grasp the points the teacher was trying to make with most of her teaching demonstrations. These demonstrations succeeded in teaching John one basic rule: *Don't rely on the teacher's statements to help clarify the task*. John learned that if he waited, the talk would stop and the teacher would show him how to do the task. Occasionally demonstrations would help. At least they were better than the barrage of words that preceded them.

John struck out because he didn't have the basic language skills, but John could have been taught. Before he was told to draw a line around the top man, he could have been taught the meaning of the words *draw*, *line*, and *top*. The teacher could have demonstrated how words such as *not* and *or* function before including them in instructions. She could have begun by presenting simple objects that were known to the child and telling what they were *not:* "This is a shoe. This is *not* a rabbit; this is *not* a hot dog; this is *not* a car; this is *not* a —come on, John, not what?" Then she could have proceeded to more complicated tasks in which *not* is used to describe actions. "Watch me and tell me what I am doing. . . . Yes, I am clapping. Am I tying my shoe? No, I am not tying my shoe. Am I driving a car? No, I am not driving a car. Am I eating a hot dog? No, I am not eating a hot dog. Am I clapping? Yes, I am clapping." After programing a basic vocabulary for instruction, she could have *confined herself* to the words she knew he understood. In this way she could have demonstrated to John that language is precise and that a change of one word makes a monumental difference in the meaning of a statement.

Next, John's teacher could have made him aware of the difference between familiar words and unfamiliar ones. She could have programed a series of exercises in which she gave instructions containing an unfamiliar word. The child could not carry out the instructions *unless he asked about the word*. "O.K., John, touch your cranium. . . .

Wait a minute John. Do you know what a cranium is? . . . No? Then ask me. Say, 'What's a cranium?' " Through such a program she could have shown John the difference between knowing and not knowing. She could have given him a method both for identifying unfamiliar words and for inquiring about them. She could have taught him that every word is important and that unless you understand every word in a statement you may not know what to do: "How can you touch your cranium if you don't know what it is?"

Finally, John's first-grade teacher could have taught John how to follow instructions. She could have introduced a variety of simple instructions *for the same presentation*, thereby making it quite clear that he couldn't handle the task simply by examining the presentation. For example, she could have presented John with a picture of a ball and a bat, and said, "Draw a circle around the ball. Draw a circle around the bat. Draw a circle around the ball and the bat. Cross out the bat." And so forth.

But she didn't. As a result John developed an experimental approach. John's standard operating procedure became one of examining the material, trying to figure out how it should be handled, moving ahead, and waiting. If his impression of how to handle the task was right, the teacher would sometimes smile and pat him on the shoulder, saying something about "paying attention." If he was wrong, she would show him how to handle the task.

In every grade since the first, John's initial impression of learning has been reinforced. His second-grade teacher didn't test him to see whether he knew fundamental language concepts. She, too, proceeded to talk, assuming that he could follow what she said. But he couldn't. And when she taught, she never did so in a way that provided her with much feedback from John. She would give an explanation to the class that might take several minutes. When she walked around the class to see what the children were doing, she would find John doing nothing. He would look completely blank, and she would be at a loss. She knew John wasn't doing his work, but she didn't know why. She could have found out. Instead of giving two-minute explanations, she could have broken the explanation down into components and asked the class questions about each component, using a series of questions for each statement. In this way she could have discovered which statements John did not understand. She could then have taught John the specific things he did not know. Not only would this procedure have provided the teacher with feedback about John (and a lot of the other children in the class), it would also have provided John and the others with some clear idea of what it was they were trying to learn. They would have been able to know when they had learned it; they would have learned a strategy for learning. They would have seen how much effort and concentration it takes to learn, and they would have seen how the new learning was to be used in various situations. Whenever they encountered something they had learned, they would have recognized it: "I know that. I know what it means."

But John's second-grade teacher didn't use this approach. She lectured; she shrugged her shoulders when John responded with that I-know-you-want-me-to-do-something-but-I-don't-know-what-it-is look; and she confided to some of the other teachers, "John's one of the worst I've ever had."

John's tendency to experiment and learn in a semiconscious, uncontrolled manner continued through the third grade. He learned that if you keep going over a task, alternately trying to listen to what is said and trying to ignore it, something gradually happens. That something is learning. It is fragile and it never quite emerges from the shadows. John was never quite aware of what it was he did when he was successful that was different from what he did when he was unsuccessful, because he hadn't learned a precise strategy for attacking tasks.

In the third grade John finally learned to ask questions, but they were not information-seeking questions that are asked when not enough information is provided. They were demonstration-seeking questions asked about the instructions. His questions were designed to get help, not information.

John struck out in the first grade because he didn't learn enough of the basic skills on which instruction is based. And John, although he was the most dramatic, wasn't the only strikeout victim.

2. Teachers dealt in learning tendencies, not in absolute performance. JC, the boy who sits next to John, was reasonably verbal when he entered school. His home environment provided him with a fair background in basic concepts. For JC the first grade was not a total mystery, as it was for John, but he had problems in learning how to read. In fact, he knew only two words with any degree of certainty by the end of first grade—*he* and *little*. At the end of the year JC was given a standardized achievement test in reading, along with the other

14

members of his class. The children were told to circle the appropriate words. For each item there were four words to choose from. JC could not read any of the words, but he managed to circle one word in each row. His guessing ability was about average, which meant that he got about one out of four words correct and scored at the 1.7 grade level (getting 7 words correct, including *property*). JC (and the other guessers) were promoted to the second grade. After all, JC performed at almost the second-grade level. By the end of the second year, however, his performance had not improved. JC again scored at the 1.7 grade level (this time missing the word *property*).

The use of tests to evaluate performance is commendable, but the type of achievement test normally used to evaluate children like John and JC is often deceptive. The test items are usually cluttered, containing a variety of comprehension and decoding skills, with the result that the teacher (or test interpreter) is often unable to pinpoint what a child like JC does and does not know. Often the tests provide nothing more than a vague impression that the child "tends" to read, or "tends" not to. Since JC's teachers weren't aware of the precise causes of failure, they shifted the emphasis from discovering what JC had failed to learn to finding out what outside factors could account for his poor showing after a relatively strong start. Perhaps he needed glasses. Perhaps some outside event traumatized him, resulting in dyslexia.

JC was taught carefully (although inadvertently) that the school dealt in tendencies to learn, not in skills that are either mastered or not mastered. By the end of the third grade JC had been taught that—

a. Even if you don't fully understand what's going on in school, you'll get a passing grade, because you tend to perform adequately.

b. If you get lost trying to learn something, be patient, because it will go away.

JC's impressions were reinforced by many experiences. He was shown that he could receive a passing grade in science, even though he never understood what the atmosphere was or why candles sometimes burned and sometimes didn't. He learned, through the spiral curriculum, that he wasn't actually expected to master a skill; he was to dabble in it. The atmosphere and burning candles would go away if he were patient. Perhaps they would be replaced by something just as puzzling, but at least it would be something new—and this too would go away.

15

JC's third-grade teacher had what was considered a good science series. The series dealt with air and water at four grade levels, starting with the third. At the third-grade level the children were introduced to a few facts about the atmosphere—not general principles, but miscellaneous facts. The purpose of this introduction was to stimulate curiosity and set the stage for abstract principles. The next year the facts were handled a bit more systematically. The following year more system was introduced, until finally the children were exposed to the abstract principles that related all they had learned. By the time the series got around to the principles—which should have been presented first—JC had long since given up any hope of unifying the bits of information that had been hurled at him over the years. He had learned an effective way of handling these—to try to recite them at the appropriate time. His experiences in science demonstrated again that learning is conceived of in terms of tendencies and not skills that are either mastered or not mastered.

JC also learned that speed is more important than understanding. There was a great emphasis on speed in JC's school, especially on speed reading, which crippled several of the children in the class. They were encouraged to speed, to skim, to get the general impression of the ideas contained in the books. The teachers, particularly those in the fourth and fifth grades, thought that speed was especially important. They had been taught that if children read faster, they will read better and tend to comprehend more. These teachers didn't know that this educational "fact" is pure fiction. When a child (or an adult) is forced to read at a rate faster than the one that is natural for the material, comprehension drops. The original studies on which the speed-reading fad was based showed that faster readers comprehended more than slower readers. The studies did not show that if the slower readers were *made to read faster* their comprehension would increase. JC's teachers adopted the maxim: make children *behave* like faster readers and they will *comprehend* like faster readers.

Most of the children in JC's class were taught that it is not important to understand every word and every statement, but to pick out the familiar and rush past the unfamiliar. They were taught that the aim of reading is to sort of get the message, not to get it in a very precise way.

3. The teachers shifted the focus of the learning situation from solving problems to learning certain behaviors. Mary will probably finish high school, and she certainly knows a great deal more about what learning is than John does. But she too has acquired some serious misconceptions about the nature of satisfactory performance. In the second grade Mary learned very little, because her teacher managed the children in such a way that she wouldn't have to teach too much. She succeeded in keeping the class in a state of semidisruption, with a great deal of talking and movement going on. In this way she could spend most of the school day working on behavior—admonishing the children to sit quietly, chasing around the room after first this child and then that one to make them sit down. Mary was a good student. She very quickly learned that the objective of instruction was *to teach the appropriate appearances*. Mary, who was always a joy to her teachers, learned to print fast and neatly. Neat printing must be very important, Mary concluded, or else why is so much time spent teaching it? Mary learned how to look busy, how to handle school material in the proper way, how to sit quietly and pore over the material that had been assigned. Mary learned all these behaviors because she was taught that they are the important ones.

But Mary never learned an effective *solution strategy*. A solution strategy begins with understanding that the goal is to solve the problem confronting you, not to go through a behavioral ritual. To solve a problem, you must know both where you are starting from and where you would end if you discovered an adequate solution. In the problem $2a + 1 = 7$, the goal is to find out what $1a$ is. The problem, however, tells what $2a + 1$ is, not what $1a$ is. There are obstacles that must be removed before a solution can be reached. How do you proceed from $2a + 1$ to $1a$? You follow the rules. The rules are important for one reason only. They allow you to dispose of the obstacles. First you get rid of the $+ 1$: $2a = 6$. Then you convert the $2a$ into $1a$. Solution: $1a = 3$. When a solution strategy is employed, rules take on a special meaning, because they specify the types of moves that can be made in attacking a problem. An arithmetic problem is not an individual thing that demands a certain rotelike set of steps. It is a member of a class, and it admits of the same rules as the other members. To learn a rule is to learn how to attack a whole class of problems. Mary was never taught this. She was taught the terms *commutative* and *distributive*, but again the teaching focused on the behavior of memorizing and reciting. For her a math problem was something to be handled by trying to remember a problem that was similar. "It's like the problem on page 40," she would say to herself. Removing the obstacles was not her goal. Her goal was to give the appearance of learning. So she took notes when the teacher talked; she behaved. And Mary's teachers accepted her performance.

These teachers could have saved Mary from her robot approach by requiring Mary to specify *why* she was making each move she made. For example:

$$2a + 1 = 7$$
$$2a = 7 - 1$$

What step was taken? How did it help her reach the goal of stating what $1a$ equals? Just as each word in a clear set of instructions has a function, each step in the solution of an algebra problem has a function—to remove an obstacle.

In English, as in mathematics, the instructional emphasis was on the superficial rather than the basic. The children in Mary's class studied grammar, but they were never taught basic language strategies. They did quite a bit of dictionary work, but they never really understood what definitions were. Their teacher never had them perform exercises in which she defined a word such as *fram* and had them figure out from the definition what a *fram* was. ("Listen, a fram is a vehicle used to transport people and freight. It runs on tracks. What's a *fram?*") The teachers never assigned the children the tasks of defining a *vink* in such a way that others in class would know what familiar thing was being referred to as a *vink*. Their teachers never showed them the ambiguity that resulted from an inadequate definition. They never presented definitions as problems that can be solved only by taking certain steps, just as a math problem is solved only by taking certain steps. They didn't try to show the children that descriptions followed the same problem-solving model as definitions. They never assigned construction tasks, saying, for example, "Describe this desk so that I would be able to pick it out from among all the desks in the world. First put it in a classroom, so I'll know where to begin looking, and then tell me enough about this desk so that I'll know it's not any other desk in the world."

To remove the obstacle in the problem $2a = 6$, you must convert the 2 into a 1. In solving the problem of becoming a doctor or lawyer, you must remove the obstacles that stand between you and a sheepskin. JC wants to be a doctor, but he doesn't have the faintest idea of how to go about achieving his goal. He doesn't know what the

18

obstacles are or how to remove them. He may not understand the steps that are involved any better when he is fifteen years old than he does now, because he hasn't been taught to think of a problem in terms of the steps essential to its solution.

4. The teachers did not teach basic principles. A teacher once objected to a demonstration of how to teach children the concept that liquids don't expand or contract when transferred from one vessel to another. "You are teaching untruth," she protested, "by saying that the amount remains the same when the contents are transferred from one glass to another. There is always a residue, a drop in the bottom of the glass, that is not transferred." This objection illustrates a problem involved in teaching. Where do you start, with the drop in the glass or the general principle? If Newton had been concerned with accounting for the fact that feathers drop more slowly than rocks, he might never have worked out his laws of motion. If we follow the principle of teaching what is hairsplittingly true in the classroom, we won't teach a child that red objects are red, that some things are big, that the letter *a* has the short-*a* sound as in *and*, that three is more than two, that a circle has a line around it, or that George Washington was the father of our country. But we have to start somewhere. We have to begin with the principle that covers most of the cases (all the cases that will be dealt with in the immediate future). This principle holds for teaching the color red, the *a* sound, and scientific pinciples. If you don't teach the child the general idea of what red is, he may never learn the basic rule. Similarly, if you don't teach the child the basic principles of science, he may never learn them. They are the most logical starting point. The argument that they are not meaningful to the child is as preposterous as saying that the color red is not meaningful to him. It is not meaningful to him until he learns it. When the child learns the color red, he can do things that he couldn't do before. He can describe a host of objects using a new conceptual dimension. He can sort objects according to the criterion of redness. Similarly, when a child learns a scientific principle, he can use it—if the program is adequate. He can use it to handle problems that he could not handle before. He can use it as a criterion for distinguishing between different kinds of problems.

When basic scientific principles (including those in geography, geology, and social studies) are not programed in this manner, the child is not being taught what he must learn. The child must be shown

19

speed, and so on. Why, these educators ask, shouldn't the differences in performance of tasks that involve thinking or remembering be treated in the same way—as a developmental characteristic? Doesn't the child develop intellectually at his individual rate, just as he becomes taller at his individual rate? By answering these questions in the affirmative, educators equate ability to learn with the ability to grow tall. The emphasis is placed *on the child, not on what the child is taught.*

Having adopted this interpretation of aptitude, educators and psychologists were hard put to it to explain the disadvantaged syndrome when faced with a large group of children who lacked aptitude. Some chose to interpret this phenomenon in genetic terms. The disadvantaged child, they concluded, is genetically inferior to the average, middle-class child. Others focused on the environmental conditions that affect aptitude. Again, basing their analogy on physical characteristics, they noted that certain environmental conditions stunt physical growth. They began the search for conditions that account for the disadvantaged child's lack of aptitude. Investigators began analyzing performance and noting what went on in the disadvantaged community, in an attempt to find something that functioned like a vitamin deficiency. They did not search for *specific causes,* expressed as deficiencies in skills, that would account for a child's failure to learn arithmetic, because they saw his failure in arithmetic as a manifestation of a general aptitudinal failure (in much the same way that small hands are a manifestation of general physical stunting). They were hoping to find the key that would change the child's entire mental stature.

These investigators went down the wrong road because they expressed the problems in terms of "aptitude" and "aptitude stunting." By focusing on aptitude, they virtually closed the door on education, because they saw the child's failure to learn not as a function of what he had been taught, but as a function of his aptitude. The remedies they sought, therefore, did not have to do with teaching him the concepts he had failed to learn but with finding ways to boost or restore his aptitude.

The aptitude interpretation cannot yield an educational remedy, because "aptitude" describes a characteristic of the child. Teaching, on the other hand, is an activity concerned with modifying the child's behavior so that he meets certain criteria of performance. The assump-

22

tion on which teaching is based is that it is possible to program the presentation so that the child will learn. If the child does not meet certain performance criteria, the cause must be expressed in terms of what he doesn't know, because these are the only causes over which the teacher has any control.

If the child cannot read the word *cat* because he cannot blend the sounds *cu–ah–tu*, he may possibly lack aptitude, but he certainly lacks the knowledge of how to telescope letter sounds into a word. The teacher can do nothing about the child's aptitude, but the general assumption of teaching is that she can do something to teach the child how to blend the sounds (if she knows how to demonstrate the operation).

In the classroom of middle-class children the aptitude assumption usually goes unquestioned. If three children out of a class of twenty fail to learn a given skill, the teacher can say, "Oh, they're immature," and point out that the seventeen more mature members of the class managed to learn the skill. In this situation the teacher's presentation seemed adequate for all but those who lacked the aptitude to learn. The possibility that the teacher's presentation was in fact not adequate to teach the concept to a child unless he had learned many of the components outside school, and that the child who failed to learn had not learned these components, is not usually given serious consideration. In the classroom for the disadvantaged, however, this possibility must be considered. Most disadvantaged children lack aptitude. In a disadvantaged classroom perhaps only one-third of the children will learn from the same presentation that seemed adequate in the middle-class classroom.

There are individual differences between children, but these differences must be expressed in such a way that the teacher can do something about them. The alternative to the aptitude explanation is to translate the child's performance into statements about what he has been taught. One must first assume that what the child has learned, the child has been taught. His instruction has either succeeded or failed in teaching him basic skills. The "smart" middle-class child has had relatively good teachers. These teachers (as well as all the influences that have succeeded in teaching him—his parents, his peers, his experience with the world) have successfully brought the child to a level of satisfactory performance on a great number of specific performance criteria. They have taught him language operations, reason-

23

ing operations, and behaviors that help him in any new learning situation. This child can be expected to achieve in a school situation more rapidly than a child who has not been taught as many relevant skills. The disadvantaged child, on the other hand, can be viewed as a child who has had poor teachers. These teachers have not taught him the skills that other children are assumed to have mastered when they enter school. Therefore his performance in a learning situation in which these skills are called for will not be as good as that of the average or above-average child *because he needs to learn more to master the task.*

For example, before he learns how to blend sounds into words like *fat, hat, sat, bat,* the advantaged child has already learned (among other things) how to rhyme. He can therefore hear that these words rhyme. He knows (either consciously or unconsciously) that for words to rhyme, the ending of each word must be the same. As he focuses his attention on the word endings, he notices that they contain the same letters, and he is led to the conclusion that the same letter groups make the same sound. Many disadvantaged children, on the other hand, cannot draw this conclusion from the teacher's demonstration because they do not know how to rhyme. (Not uncommonly, fifteen-year-old disadvantaged children cannot rhyme, even after repeated demonstrations.) Since they don't know that the word endings sound the same, they cannot grasp the relation between the sounds and the letters. The disadvantaged child, therefore, has a great deal more to learn than the advantaged child. *But the difference between the two children can be explained solely in terms of the difference in their knowledge.*

The advantage of expressing their differences in terms of what they have been taught (rather than in terms of their aptitude) is that the teacher can do something about a deficiency in knowledge. She can proceed to teach the child what he doesn't know. If the differences are expressed in terms of specific skills, the teacher knows what to do. (As a matter of fact, there is no reason to believe that *any* child will learn without being taught, regardless of his aptitude. Children who learn quickly in school have received the necessary foundation elsewhere.) The aptitude explanation cannot stand alone. Teaching is essential to performance, regardless of the child's aptitude.

Do children learn without being taught? We don't expect African aborigines to learn calculus. Why? Because they have not been taught

24

the skills necessary for learning calculus. Psychologists sometimes express this idea by saying that the aborigine child has not received adequate learning opportunities, but exactly what does this expession mean? Certainly many situations in his life are examples of calculus, yet he hasn't learned from them, just as he may not have learned from examples of color, triangularity, porosity, and transitivity. It follows that examples are not enough. A learning opportunity includes more than simply presenting examples. The examples must be systematized and differentially reinforced. In other words, *they must be taught.*

Developmental psychologists such as Piaget see learning as an interaction of the organism with the environment.[5] The child learns by developing cognitive structures that allow him to process various operations. That this is an unproductive analysis (at least from the educational standpoint) can be demonstrated by pointing out that unless the child acquires certain kinds of knowledge, he cannot possibly handle operations based on such principles as the conservation of the amount of liquid when it is transferred from one vessel to another. Unless the child knows that liquids do not expand or contract, there is no way that he can learn this principle. Similarly, the adult who is asked how much water will be displaced from a tank if a muscular man standing in the tank (*a*) takes a deep breath or (*b*) flexes his arm cannot answer correctly unless he knows that the chest is expandable but the arm isn't. Clearly, it is impossible to make the proper judgment unless one understands the properties of the object under examination. If one is taught these properties, however, he can solve a problem without developing a broad cognitive structure. The solution does not depend on an amorphous interaction between the organism and the environment. It depends on the skills that must be mastered to handle the task.

A further teaching assumption is that the more carefully skills are taught, the greater the possibility that the child will learn them. In environments where children are conscientiously taught verbal and reasoning skills, there are very few school failures. The poorest performer from a superior background often performs well above the mean of disadvantaged children.

The Remedy

Teaching at an above-normal rate

The difference between the intelligent and the dull child is the rate at which key skills are learned. Granted, the difference can be expressed in other terms, but from a strict educational view the difference must be expressed in terms of what is taught. Only then is a clear remedy implied. The rate of the normal child in learning skills, as measured by an intelligence test, is usually designated as 100. This means simply that concepts are being taught to him at the average rate. If the child has an IQ of 75, his environment has taught him at only 75 percent the normal rate. If he has an IQ of 150, his environment has taught him one and one-half times the number of concepts the average environment teaches during the same time.

The environment of the child who fails in school teaches him at a rate slower than that of the average child's environment. In school as well as at home, he typically learns only about eight concepts in the time the average child learns ten. The advantaged child therefore has a greater repertoire of skills to use in any given learning situation. The learning deficit of the disadvantaged child is cumulative. By the time the advantaged child has learned a hundred concepts, the disadvantaged child has learned only eighty, giving him an absolute deficit of twenty concepts, compared with a deficit of two when the advantaged child had learned only ten concepts.

The only way the disadvantaged child can catch up, at any grade level, is to be taught at a faster-than-normal rate. Teaching at a normal rate is not sufficient. If the disadvantaged child has accrued a deficit of twenty concepts and is then taught at the same rate as the advantaged child for an indefinite period, he will still have a twenty-concept deficit at the end of the training period. The only way to wipe out the deficit is to teach the child at a faster-than-normal rate. Unless this principle is adhered to, the dull child will remain dull.

But can dull children be taught thoroughly and rapidly enough for them to catch up? While data are relatively scarce, the work that Carl Bereiter and I have done with preschool and kindergarten children is relevant, although not definitive. Our 1967 "graduating class" completed two years of instruction (preschool and kindergarten) with an average Stanford-Binet score of 121. The group had entered two years before with an average IQ of about 96. The range of IQs upon graduation was from 137 to 103. In reading achievement the average grade level for the group (as measured by the Wide Range Achievement test) was 2.6. Arithmetic performance (also measured by the Wide Range) was 2.6. According to both measures of IQ and measures of achievement, these children graduated as intellectually superior children. It is often asked whether these children will be able to maintain their gains. This question is not really relevant. They have achieved criteria of performance in reading and arithmetic that were set as goals of instruction. Having achieved these criteria of performance, the children are ready to move to a more advanced phase of instruction. A lack of basic skills will not be responsible for failure on a more advanced level, if they do fail. Failure, rather, will result from deficiencies in the instruction they receive in elementary school.

Steps in developing an effective program

The most important rule for solving educational problems is to describe every phase of the teaching procedure—from the establishment of objectives to the teacher's presentation—*in terms of specific concepts*. Any departure from this rule results in varying degrees of chaos. The objectives must be set up in terms of the specific concepts the child is expected to master; the analysis of the tasks must be made in terms of specific concepts; the teacher's presentation must be planned in terms of specific concepts; and the performance of the children must be evaluated in terms of mastery of specific concepts. The entire process, in other words, must be expressed in terms of what the children are expected to know, and what they learn (as inferred from their behavior).

STEP ONE: OBJECTIVES. The first step in constructing a program is to specify the objectives. An objective is an *absolute criterion of performance* that is to be achieved by the children through training. In other words, after training they are supposed to be able to do things they couldn't do before—very specific things. If the objective is to teach certain communication skills, the children must be taught these skills. And the program is a failure if these skills are not mastered. If a program to teach certain communication skills fails to teach these skills, the program failed to do what it set out to do and must be considered a failure, even if it succeeds in teaching the children how to do freehand sketches. Look at the matter in another way. Suppose that every child in the class learned something, but no two children learned the same thing and none of the children could demonstrate at the end

27

of the program that he had learned the skills he was supposed to have been taught. The program is a failure because, if the objectives of the program are legitimate, the children will be expected *to use* the skills in working future problems. If they haven't been taught these skills, they will not be able to use them, and *will not be able to meet the next set of educational objectives.*

Since objectives must be absolute, they cannot possibly be derived from a study of the child. *They are imposed as statements of what we want all children to do.* The word *all* must be emphasized. We cannot have one objective for some children and another objective for others. It is possible that some children will not achieve all the educational objectives that are established and, since children differ in their repertoire of skills, it is axiomatic that a greater amount of teaching will be required to bring some children to the desired level of performance. But the objectives hold for all children. We want to teach disadvantaged Negro children the same set of skills we expect middle-class white children to acquire.

Goals and objectives should not be confused with techniques. Sometimes educators imply that there should be a different set of objectives for the slow learner or the disadvantaged child. But this cannot be what they mean. An educator cannot seriously maintain that there should be different educational *objectives* for disadvantaged children. By admitting a different set of educational objectives, the educator is not only acknowledging that education cannot succeed with all people; he is sanctioning a vicious cycle of poverty and ignorance. If education does not succeed, the disadvantaged child of today will be the disadvantaged parent of tomorrow. He will not have been taught the same set of skills the middle-class child has been taught. And he therefore will not be in a position to take advantage of the social-mobility potential of education. His children will be disadvantaged and will receive the education designed for disadvantaged children. This is a clear case of educational prejudice. The only way to avoid it is to maintain the same long-range objectives for all children and to use techniques that are successful in transporting them from where they are to the educational level they should reach. Children differ, but an educational program must acknowledge these differences without penalizing slower children with watered-down educational objectives.

For educational objectives to be acceptable, they must be stated in terms of specific tasks that children should be able to handle after

28

training. This stipulation is introduced to avoid confusion. Let us say that the objective is presented as a general statement rather than a series of specific tasks: "The objective of this program is to teach children basic communication skills." The person who is charged with developing a program to meet this objective may interpret the objective in many ways. He may interpret it in terms of communication as used in social interaction. He may interpet it in terms of communication skills used in the primary grades. He may interpret communication broadly, taking it to mean behavior in any interpersonal situation, and he may provide instruction in general interpersonal behavior—verbal and nonverbal. These are a few of the options that are open to him. When objectives are stated in general terms, it is always possible to argue that the instruction failed, that it did not teach a certain kind of communication skill. One can always construct a "communication" problem that would be failed, but one has no way of knowing whether a given test provides a fair evaluation of the program. He knows only that the program should teach communication skills.

These and other difficulties can be avoided if the objectives of a program are expressed as specific tasks. For example: "The child should be able to answer the question 'Is this a ———?' in connection with familiar objects. This answer should be expressed correctly as either 'Yes, this is a ———' or 'No, this is not a ———.' "

A given program may have many such objectives, as many as are needed to show what the program is to teach. By detailing the objectives in this manner, the educator makes it possible for the program to be rigorous. The objectives serve as the basis for developing the curriculum. Analysis of the objectives articulates the subskills that are necessary for successful performance of the criterion tasks. The objectives serve as the basis for testing children to see whether or not the instruction has succeeded. And the objectives serve as a basis for directing the activity of the teacher. She knows what the end product of her teaching is supposed to be and she can measure the mastery of her children by comparing their performance with the performance called for by the criterion tasks.

Objectives that cannot be translated into specific tasks cannot be allowed in program construction. Teaching the whole child, stimulating self-realization, and providing readiness can be accepted as objectives only if they can be translated into specific tasks. The argument is sometimes presented by educators that not everything can be measured and that one cannot reduce such concepts as the "whole child" to a series of tasks. This argument is not convincing. Without specific performance tests, the educator is never quite sure whether the program he advocates is actually the one that achieves the desired learning. *It is quite possible, in the absence of specific measures, that the program he most strongly opposes is actually the most effective in teaching the whole child.* In fact, unless specific measures are provided, every program can claim that it teaches the whole child. Similarly, the objective "providing meaningful experiences" can be claimed by any program, unless this objective is translated into a series of specific tasks.

Educational objectives must be demonstrably consistent with the priorities of skills valued in our society. Educators must recognize that they are not policymakers. They cannot make up objectives that are inconsistent with society's general commitment to make children competent in the academic arena. If educators and teachers are allowed to make up policy, it is possible that they will introduce objectives that are not consistent with the general educational values of society, or they may introduce objectives that cannot be realized through education. The objective of teaching the child to cope with his home environment probably cannot be achieved effectively through classroom instruction, simply because instruction is limited to the classroom and does not include the home environment. Therefore many of the problems encountered in the home environment cannot be demonstrated and the rules of behavior for handling certain situations cannot be reinforced. It would be possible to teach the child *facts* about how to cope with his home environment, but one cannot effectively teach the *behaviors* that constitute effective coping. Formulating objectives related to dancing and basket weaving is not consistent with society's general commitment to competence. The skills learned in dancing and basket weaving are not *used* in higher-order tasks, such as writing expositions at the college level, solving quadratic equations, or doing assignments in history.

Two questions must be answered affirmatively about any objective of an educational program.

1. Does it provide a precise standard for evaluating the performance of the children?
2. Does it specify skills that will be used in future educational tasks?

Although there is a great deal of concern about the long-range objectives of early and remedial education, the problem is rather simple. All children should learn a set of skills sufficient to allow them admittance to college. If they do not go to college, it should not be because they have failed to learn the appropriate skills.

STEP TWO: ANALYSIS. If the objectives are stated as legitimate tasks, the next step follows naturally. That is the step of breaking down the objectives into the constituent concepts (the concepts that are *used* in performing the criterion task). When the objective is broken down into tasks, the concepts involved in these tasks can be rigorously analyzed. For example, following the instruction "Draw a straight horizontal line on your paper" may be one of several hundred criterion tasks for a unit in following instructions.

To determine conceptual components of this task, one simply specifies the concepts that are needed for the task. If a concept is to be used, it must first be taught. It is prerequisite to performance of the task. This is not a mere empirical fact; it is a logical necessity.

The major concepts or operations involved in the task above are these:

- The child must understand the word *draw;* he must know the kind of behavior that is required by the signal "Draw ————" and be able to demonstrate his understanding by following such instructions as "Draw a circle," "Draw a boy," "Draw a line."
- The child must understand the word *line;* he must be able to identify things that are lines and distinguish between lines and things that are not lines (such as ropes, sidewalks, and other objects that may look like lines when they are represented in a drawing).
- The child must be able to demonstrate that he understands what the words *a line* mean. He must demonstrate that he can discriminate between the singular "a line" and the plural "lines," "three lines," "some lines," and so on.
- The child must understand what *straight* means. He must be able to discriminate between things that are straight and things that are not straight.
- The child must understand that "straight horizontal line" calls for a line that is both straight and horizontal. He must demonstrate that he can discriminate between "straight horizontal lines," "not-straight horizontal lines," and "not-straight not-horizontal lines."

31

- The child must understand the concept "on." He must be able to demonstrate that he can point to things that are on something and things that are not on something. He must be able to tell what object the things are on. (The coat is on [the floor, the table, John, etc.].)
- The child must demonstrate that he understands the instructions "Draw on ———." He must demonstrate that he can distinguish between "Draw on ———" and "Sit on ———," "Put your hand on ———" and "Push on ———," and the like. He must also demonstrate that he can handle the instructional form "Draw ——— on ———," in which different object words appear in the blanks.
- The child must understand the meaning of the word *paper*.
- The child must demonstrate that he understands the word *your*.
- He must be able to discriminate between instructions containing *your, my, his, the, a, all, some, any,* and so on.

While the procedure of analyzing the criterion task (objective) in terms of its constituent operations may seem laborious, it is necessary if the program is to be solid. Instruction is based on analysis. *Unless the analysis brings out each skill required to handle the criterion problems, the analysis will not lead to adequate instruction.* Without adequate instruction, a child may fail the criterion task for any of a number of reasons. He may not understand the word *straight*, for example. He may not understand what the teacher means by "Draw a line." He may not know what "your paper" refers to. The training the child receives must systematically eliminate each of the possible causes of failure. The training will do this consistently only if *all possible causes of failure are identified.* They will be identified if the criterion task is carefully analyzed in terms of the concepts involved in it.

The analysis is only partly completed with the identification of the concepts that are used in the criterion task. To teach each of these constituent concepts, the teacher must use concrete demonstrations. That is, she must present specific objects and specific statements. However, specific tasks do not necessarily follow from the procedure of identifying constituent concepts; it is possible for one to make up more than one presentation for teaching the meaning of *straight*, *horizontal*, and so forth. Furthermore, each of these presentations may contain words and operations that are not included in the criterion task. For example, in teaching the word *straight*, the teacher might use

32

the instructions "Show me the lines that are not straight." New concepts are introduced in this task: "Show me," "that," and "not straight." Provision must be made for teaching each of these concepts.

Since the teacher must demonstrate each of the constituent concepts, *the curriculum designer must present every constituent concept as a task*—a demonstration complete with the statements and objects that are to be presented. In this way he will be able to see whether any concepts that do not appear in the criterion problem must be included in the program. In this way he will be able to provide for the teaching of these new concepts. He will be able to analyze the constituent tasks in the same way he analyzed the criterion tasks. The ordering of the tasks comes about naturally from the kind of concept analysis that is conducted. If an operation or skill is needed for the performance of a complex task, that operation precedes the complex task in the presentation sequence.

To assure that each constituent concept will be taught, *each presentation specified in the analysis must be designed so that it is consistent with one and only one interpretation*. If the presentation could possibly admit of more than one interpretation, it will probably fail to teach *all* children the desired skills, which means that the presentation is not adequate. If only one object is presented in teaching the concept "red," the child may conclude that red refers to the color of the object, but he could legitimately conclude that red is another name for that particular object or that red has something to do with the shape or texture of the object. Unless the presentation rules out all possible incorrect interpretations by demonstrating with a variety of objects that the invariant referred to as "red" is the color and only the color, the presentation is not adequate. If appropriate statements have been programed, some incorrect interpretations may be ruled out with statements. However, physical demonstrations are usually necessary, especially when the curriculum designer is dealing with basic sensory concepts.

The specification of tasks that are to be presented to the children should be governed by the principle of *presentational economy*. According to this principle, some operations are essential to the understanding of concepts and others are not. For example, the ability to *use* syntactical forms is essential to successful performance on communication tasks; however, the ability *to explain the usage in terms of syntax or grammar* is not. The former ability would have to be covered in a

33

program designed to teach communication skills; the latter would not, because it is possible to teach all relevant skills needed for the criterion task without referring to grammar or syntax.

Also, the principle of presentational economy dictates that any procedure that can increase the rate of new learning is preferable to slower techniques. Presentational economy is achieved by treating identical aspects of a task in the same way. For example, the negative of the opposite is the same as the original statement, in terms of the kind of reasoning that is involved here. If one is told that something is not wet, he knows that it is dry. He can draw this conclusion from the *not* statement. Since all opposites share this characteristic, they can be presented with variations of the same statement forms and variations of the same basic demonstration procedures.

Using the procedure of analysis outlined above, one can work from any complex task down to the level where the most naive child can start on the program. Furthermore, it is possible to determine precisely how close any individual is to meeting the performance criterion and to specify precisely what he must learn in order to handle the criterion task. In other words, precise testing and teaching are implied by this method of analysis.

STEP THREE: TRYOUT. The analysis of the objective or criterion task provides one with a list of prerequisite skills and the specifications of tasks designed to teach each skill. However, the analysis does not tell anything about the relative psychological difficulty of the tasks. It does not predict which tasks will be relatively easy for the children and which will be relatively difficult. The degree of difficulty is discovered when the tasks are presented to the children. What often happens is that the children will go through an entire sequence of tasks in a few minutes only to bog down on the next task for a few days—or weeks. When such rough spots are encountered, the investigator should first assume that his analysis is inadequate. He should *blame himself* and assume that the children are having difficulties because he is asking them (*a*) to learn more than one new concept at a time or (*b*) to take more than one small step at a time.

Here is an example of the problems that may be encountered: The program calls for the teacher to teach number identification using the statement form "This number is ———." Young disadvantaged children, however, may fail to learn numbers simply because the task is requiring them to learn a new way of identifying things and at the same time to learn the names of the new objects. As a result the children may not realize that the task calls for the same identification process they use in other situations. They may conclude that the statement is somehow a part of the identification procedure and that the exercise is a word game, not an identification task. This programing error can be corrected by changing the identification procedure so that it is more like the procedure the children are accustomed to using. Instead of saying "This number is ————," the teacher can ask "What is this? . . . Three." Now the children can concentrate on the identification of the object without at the same time having to produce an unfamiliar statement.

Through tryout the investigator is able to give his program the refinements that cannot come from the analysis of constituent concepts alone. If the children find the tasks dull, he must do something to liven them up, perhaps changing the pace of tasks in the program so that children are not operating on the same level of intensity at all times. If the children aren't serious about what is being taught, he must devise exercises in which there is a strong positive payoff for using the skills being taught and a negative payoff for failing to use them properly. It may be that the investigator has failed to figure out how to lead children to grasp a concept without difficulties or excessive drill. And although another investigator might be able to devise a series of tasks that work, for the present the investigator might have to work with the program as it is, recognizing its shortcomings.

STEP FOUR: PRESCRIPTIONS. The next step in the development of a program will ensure that the teacher can present concepts effectively and diagnose the children's responses in terms of precisely what they have been taught and what they have not been taught. If the teacher asks a child, "Are there more red beads in this box, or are there more beads made of wood?" she may think that she is testing the child's understanding of class inclusion, but unless the child understands every constituent concept in the question—the concepts "more," "beads," "or," "made of wood," and so on—the child may fail the item for reasons that have nothing to do with the concept she is trying to teach. If she proceeds on the assumption that the child failed the item because he does not understand the concept of class inclusion, she is operating from a position of ignorance.

The adequate program is buttressed against such errors because the concepts are programed one at a time, so that the teacher knows that the children understand all the concepts in her statements except *one*—the one she is currently teaching. However, no program is ever perfect, and the teacher must be able to diagnose the performance of the children in terms of what they don't know. She needs more than quantitative data. She must be able to infer from a child's responses to a series of questions *what he thinks the concept is*. For example, if his behavior is consistent with the interpretation that he thinks *red* is another word for *ball*, she must quickly demonstrate that things that cannot be called balls can be called red and that not all balls are red. Inferring concepts from children's performance is not easy; it requires a great deal of practice in formulating hypotheses, providing appropriate questions to test these hypotheses, and then providing the demonstration that corrects the misinterpretation.

To teach properly, the teacher must hold her intuition in check. She may have learned in teacher training that she should do what comes naturally to her. Nothing could be further from the truth. She must satisfy the requirements of the program, although she can do it in a way that comes naturally to her. However, she must stifle the impulse to refer to operations and to use words that have not been programed. She must learn to work fast, so that the children can receive as much practice as she can cram into a session, and so that the point is obvious when she is treating things in an analogous way. If the elements in a series are spaced several minutes apart, it may be some time before the child is able to get the point. If the elements follow each other at an interval of only a few seconds, however, the point is more obvious. There is less intervening noise for the child to deal with. Most important, the teacher must realize that those children she is working with—those complex beings—*must be considered in terms of precise statements of what they know*. Such statements are necessary if she is to bring every child to the desired level of performance in the least time. In summary, the teacher must be a highly trained technician, not a combination of educational philosopher and social worker. She must recognize that she is responsible for a unique contribution to the child's welfare—that of teaching him essential concepts and skills. If she fails to satisfy this need, she will have failed, regardless of how well-meaning she is or how many visits to the home she makes. If *she* doesn't teach relevant skills, nobody will.

STEP FIVE: EVALUATION. The final step in constructing a program is to evaluate the results of the program. The most significant measure from an educational standpoint is the measure of whether the children meet the desired criteria of performance. Such a detailed achievement evaluation is of primary importance because it shows what the children know and therefore provides a clear basis for formulating the next set of educational objectives. If children have mastered basic algebra by the end of the second grade, tasks in which basic algebra concepts are used can be introduced.

Evaluation of the program in terms of IQ gain or general achievement levels is interesting but not particularly pertinent to the problem of teaching children, because it does not relate the performance of each child to the specific criteria of instruction that have been established. The most useful measure evaluates the instruction in terms of the criteria of performance that grew out of the objectives.

Summary on constructing a program

Rules for constructing a program have been detailed because without them, confusion results. The primary rules are these:

1. Educational objectives must be stated as a series of specific tasks.

2. Everything that follows—the analysis, the development of specific teaching presentations, and the teacher's behavior—must derive from the objective tasks.

3. The analysis must be made by noting every concept needed for successful performance of the tasks.

4. Tasks that teach these concepts must be specified.

5. Each presentation designed to teach a given concept must admit of one and only one interpretation.

6. For clarity and maximum feedback of information from the performance of children, the program should be designed so that the child learns one new concept at a time.

7. The teacher must infer from the children's performance whether they have mastered a concept; she must provide appropriate remedies for children who have developed misconceptions or inadequate formulations of a given concept. She must recognize that she deals only in concepts and that the child's responses must be interpreted in terms of concepts.

8. The program must be evaluated in terms of whether the children meet the various criteria of performance specified by the objectives.

37

Compensatory education will have direction and focus only if the specific causes of failure are identified. Specific causes, however, must be expressed in such terms that teaching is implied. They must therefore be expressed in terms of what the child has not been taught. The statement "John reads at the 1.5 grade level" describes John, but not in a way that gives a teacher any specific direction. Why? Why does he read at only the 1.5 grade level? The answer to this question must be expressed in terms of the skills John has not been taught—not in terms of his home life, his brain injury, or his general aptitude for learning. The teacher has little if any control over John's brain injury, but she has a great deal of control over what he is taught. The answer to the question "Why?" must indicate what he should be taught. "He cannot rhyme; he cannot produce words that alliterate; he cannot identify words that are presented verbally as a series of discrete sounds —*mmm–aaa–nnn*." This kind of answer provides the teacher with specific direction. It specifies the steps that must be taken to correct the child's skill inadequacy. It specifies the real causes of failure.

Specific statements of what the child has not been taught represent a sufficient diagnosis in the educational setting. If such statements are not presented, the teacher is not told specifically what to do. Statements about the child's brain injury do not alter one fact about what the child must be taught if he is to achieve specific criteria of educational performance. A diagnosis expressed in terms of the child's perceptual deficiency, his immaturity, or his lack of integrated self-image does not guide instruction. It is therefore virtually useless in solving the teaching problem. The only facts that are really helpful are facts about performance. Why does the child fail a complex task? Because he hasn't been taught certain skills required by that task.

2 Teaching Techniques

To prevent the buildup of school failure that culminates in indifference and school dropouts, solid education should begin in the primary grades. This education should start at the level of the children and proceed systematically. Teachers should not assume that first-grade children or third-grade children should be operating at grade level. By going through the motions of teaching at a particular grade level, a teacher will not necessarily succeed. She must first teach the child the skills prerequisite to handling grade-level tasks, taking the time required to do a thorough job. The teacher should not panic at the thought of teaching first-grade material to third-graders. There is enough time to catch up, and there are methods that will allow her to economize time and teach skills more rapidly than they are normally taught. The first step, however, involves an honest appraisal of the children's ability. Only through such an appraisal will the teacher know where to begin.

After the appraisal has been made, the teacher should take advantage of all the techniques that allow her to speed the teaching process. These do not involve teaching children to skim or avoiding important educational objectives. They are procedures that will give the teacher the greatest amount of information about the progress of the children and the greatest opportunity to present concepts in a manner that will motivate the children and clearly demonstrate what the concepts are. These procedures are outlined in this chapter.

The Teacher's Responsibility

The premise from which all the procedures derive—either directly or indirectly—is that the teacher is responsible for the learning and performance of the children. Although this premise may strike some teachers as being too tough on the teacher, it is essential to any kind of systematic attack on problems of teaching children. That the premise must be accepted can be demonstrated by considering what may happen if it is ignored. Let's say that none of the children in a particular classroom learn to read after a year of instruction. And let's say that the teacher does not assume responsibility for the children's performance. She may maintain that the children are immature, or that they are not ready for formal instruction. She may say that they lack aptitude for learning or that they are brain-damaged. Furthermore, her description may be accurate. Perhaps every child in the classroom is brain-damaged. Regardless of how accurate the description is, however, it is not allowable. When the teacher blames the children for not having learned, she automatically excuses herself from teaching. The onus for the failure is not on her, but on them. She did not fail. They failed. There is no reason for her to examine her procedures, to make changes and try to do a more effective job, because she has not failed. Her practices may have been inefficient, her demonstrations inadequate, but so long as she does not take responsibility for the performance of the children, the effectiveness of her techniques is not questioned. Only by saying "I'm responsible for the performance of these kids" can the teacher follow the argument to its logical conclusion: "The children did not perform adequately at the end of the year; therefore my techniques are not effective. I must examine them to see where they are weak. I must improve upon them."

The focus is now where it should be—on specific techniques that promote better learning. The focus cannot be on techniques if the teacher begins with the idea that the children are responsible for what they learn and that the teacher is simply a supplier of "learning opportunities."

According to the basic teaching premise, the teacher cannot have a floating standard. She cannot take credit for those children who learn from her demonstrations (insisting that she taught these children) and deny responsibility for those children who did not learn (insisting that they lack aptitude). She must take responsibility for the performance of all the children. She should recognize that if one child does not learn, she failed to teach that child. And she should try to find out where and why she failed. It may be that she will encounter some children who fail despite her best efforts. She should not feel unduly guilty about these children—no more than a surgeon feels unduly guilty if, after using the best techniques at his disposal, a patient dies. However, the teacher should assume professional responsibility for the child's failure. Only if she does will she be prompted to examine what she did and consider alternatives.

In summary, the stipulation that the teacher is responsible for the performance of the children is introduced not to punish the teacher but to provide her with the outlook necessary to improve her techniques. Only if she blames herself for children's failures does she have any reason for making better use of the teaching variables over which she has control.

Fourteen Teaching Techniques

1. Group the children in a way that will make it possible to work with them effectively. Obviously, the teacher cannot address herself to a group that varies from the fourth-grade level of performance to the first-grade level in every major subject. It is unproductive to try, because John must learn principles that have long since been mastered by Mary. The secret of teaching John is to group him with others who are on a similar level.

Try to form three groups. Group the lowest-performing children in a group of four-to-seven children. Group the middle children in a group of seven-to-twelve children, and put the best-performing children in the remaining group. The size of the group is not nearly as important for the highest performers as it is for the low-performing children, because the need for feedback—for responses from which inferences can be drawn about what the children are learning—is far greater with the children who are lacking in basic language skills. Although feedback is important in a higher-performing group, it is easier to get, because the problems the children encounter are usually specific, and the children know how to ask questions relevant to their problems.

After grouping the children, plan to work with each group thirty minutes a day on reading and language concepts and thirty minutes a day on arithmetic, in small-group sessions.

While the teacher is working with the children in the small group, the others in the class have to be occupied. Ideally, an aide should be available to handle the children who are not participating in small-group work, but an aide is often not available.

An alternative solution to the grouping problem is for two teachers at the same grade level to pool their children. One teacher manages the children who are not in small-group activity and the other teacher works with the small groups (which may have to be somewhat bigger than the ideal so that the small-group teacher doesn't work six hours in small-group instruction). This alternative is actually quite good, because the small-group teacher can give the children arithmetic and reading assignments at the end of the period, and the assignments can be carried out under the management teacher's supervision. If the children have questions or encounter difficulties, a teacher will be available to help them, which is not possible under the one-teacher arrangement.

If neither pooling nor an aide is available, the teacher should not give up. Although she faces the problem of controlling the children who are not engaged in small-group work, she can solve this problem to a degree by giving children assignments at the end of each small-group session. The assignments should be on material that has already been taught. If the children have mastered the algebra form $a + 4 = 7$, the teacher can give them a sheet of perhaps twenty such problems which they can work at their seats. This assignment will keep them occupied for perhaps twenty minutes, after which they can begin a writing assignment. Writing assignments, if they are interesting, can keep children occupied for an hour or more. For example, the teacher can have them tell about a time when they were brave or a time when they were really scared. "Make it interesting. Tell me what happened and why you were scared. Remember, I don't know; you have to tell me." During the final half hour of unsupervised activities, the children can study. After the small-group activities are finished, the teacher can talk about the writing assignment to all the children and discuss what it means to be scared and how one goes about writing about it.

Another alternative is working with the entire class at one time. This approach is quite effective for middle- and upper-range children, but weak for the very low-performing children, who need the chance to respond to each of the teacher's questions.

In summary, the teacher aide is the best solution to the grouping problem, but the two-room pool is more likely to be feasible. If neither is possible, the one-teacher situation can be effective if the teacher is relatively strong and makes the rules governing the situation quite clear.

42

2. Teach children in a way that provides maximum feedback on what they are learning and where they are having difficulty. The maxim that a good classroom is a quiet classroom doesn't hold where children are learning and the teacher knows what they are learning. In order to adjust her presentation to the level of the class, the teacher must constantly test the children.

She tests by asking questions and by requiring simple motor responses: "Find the triangle that is on the line." If the teacher lectures, a relatively complicated test is called for. For example, the teacher may say, "There's a big difference between temperature and heat. Temperature measures how hot something is, but when we talk about heat, we're referring to how much heat energy it has. The concept of heat is useful if we want to know how much energy it's going to take to cool something or heat it up. We use the concept of heat when we talk about air conditioners and . . . what else?" If one of the children answers, the teacher may get the impression that all the children are following her presentation. However, she has introduced a host of concepts without testing to see whether the children understand. To test a lecture unit of this length, the teacher could spend five minutes testing understanding without having a clear idea of what the children know. The unit is too complex to admit of a precise test. The teacher should have tested the children a statement at a time:

"How do we measure how hot something is?" No answer. "O.K., let's try something else. How do we measure time? . . . I'll tell you one way: in minutes. Give me another way. . . . And how do we measure distance?"

This presentation makes no assumptions. If the children don't respond to the first statement, it is possible that they do not understand what is meant by *measure*. The teacher should start here, because everything that follows hinges on the understanding that temperature is a measure of one thing and heat is a measure of another.

In order to conduct such a presentation effectively, the teacher must be able to receive immediate feedback from the children—not after every paragraph, but after every statement. Such feedback, however, is not possible if the children are quiet or if they must raise their hands before they are allowed to talk. The teacher should know how all the children are responding all the time. This means that the number of questions she asks should be increased by a factor of about twenty over the question output of the average teacher. It also means that she must be able to parlay her questions. "Distance: how far I am from you, that's distance. How can we measure it? . . . Good, let's say that: a foot is a measure of distance. Come on, JC, talk. A foot is a measure of distance. Is a foot a measure of time? . . . Well, what is a foot a measure of? . . ." The proceedings will often become very loud. The more information the teacher receives during a given period of time, the louder the proceedings may become.

As a rule, the teacher should never say more than a few sentences without asking a question. If her statements don't admit of relevant questions, she is speaking in fluff and should save it for discussion periods in the teachers' lounge, not use it in teaching periods.

When working with the higher- and middle-performing children, follow the same basic approach. The presentation can be less rigid, because the children will probably be able to see the generalizations or rules through a presentation that is less structured. But the teacher should not make the mistake of assuming that the children have a grasp of all necessary concepts. *She should enter the session prepared to test and remedy.* Remedies are based on the outcome of the tests. If the children pass the tests, proceed to the next task. If they do not pass, then try to pinpoint why and specify what it is they don't know. Even in working with more able groups, always be prepared to work on basic concepts, because you never know in advance when the children will encounter difficulty with something they need to know.

3. Make use of the feedback. Children can't say, "Hey, teacher, you left out an important point in your demonstration, and without it I can't follow what you are trying to get across." If they knew enough to make such observations, they would already know the concept and know how it should be taught. But they don't know the concept, and as a result their difficulty shows only in their performance. The teacher, if she is to be effective, must learn to read the child's performance and infer from it what the child is trying to tell her.

As a rule, if all of the children bog down at a particular point in the presentation, the teacher is asking them to take too many steps all at once. The teacher is asking them to learn a compound task that involves the interplay of different skills. When all the children (or most of them) bog down at the same place, therefore, they are telling the teacher, "You're giving us too many things to learn all at once. Simplify it. Find out where the hidden difficulty is. Maybe it's a word

44

we don't understand. Maybe the operation involves procedures we haven't learned. Test and find out what the trouble is."

When all the children have difficulty, the teacher should either begin testing immediately or move to another task (if she can't think of an appropriate test). After the session, she should try to figure out what she said, how the children responded, what kind of operations were involved, and how one could go about testing to see which operations were giving trouble. This kind of analysis is not easily performed, but with practice a teacher can become very good at it—so good in fact that she can introduce the appropriate tests with scarcely a pause in the presentation. The secret of devising such tests is to take the viewpoint of the children. The teacher should pretend that she knows absolutely nothing except what has been presented in the teaching demonstrations. Is what has been told adequate for handling the operation? What other operations are necessary?

A word of warning: In analyzing performance, don't get side-tracked. Don't stray from the task at hand, and don't become involved in intuitive feelings. If you can't demonstrate the operation clearly or if you can't provide the children with a simple statement that summarizes the fundamental operation needed to handle the task, forget about teaching it. Remember, if it's a legitimate concept, it can be broken down and demonstrated clearly. There are no exceptions. If you can explain what a particular concept means in terms of what a child should be able to do after he has been taught the concept—even a concept as vague as "time"—you can devise the kind of tests that will show whether the children have understood it. You can work from such tests to the component skills. In analyzing why a child didn't pass a given test, ask yourself what the child must be able to do to succeed, and the answer to this question will help pinpoint the various problems children may have.

When only a few children in the group have difficulty, they are telling the teacher, "We can't keep up. We don't know as many of the basic operations or how to use them as the other kids in the group do, and as a result we have difficulties that the other kids don't have." Although children in a relatively homogeneous group will differ somewhat in the amount of demonstration and practice they need to master a particular concept, a child who is constantly behind the others is asking to be put in a different group. You cannot give him the practice he needs without slowing the rest of the group down.

4. Gear the presentation to the lowest member of the group. The teacher's goal is to teach *all* the children, not merely some of them. This means that she must select, as the test of her presentation, the responses of the lowest-performing child in the group. If she teaches him, she will certainly teach all the others. If she teaches to the top of the group, she will not provide the lowest or middle performers with the necessary amount of practice. Teachers, like other people, like to be flattered. The top-performing children tend to flatter teachers the most, responding more quickly and accurately. The natural reaction is to think more of them, talk to them, and take their successes (and learning problems) more seriously than those of the lower-performing child, who doesn't flatter the teacher as much. The tendency to teach to the top of the class is not easy to overcome, but it must be overcome if the teacher is to get adequate feedback. The overlearning that results for the higher-performing children will not harm them or cause them to lose interest (unless the gap between the higher-performing and the lower-performing children in the group is substantial).

The teacher should seek flattery from the lowest-performing children. When they succeed, the teacher should indeed feel that she has received the highest form of professional compliment.

An important part of gearing the presentation to the lowest member of the group involves using appropriate statements. The chapters on reading and arithmetic in this book give a great many examples of statements that allow for a precise presentation. Go over these statements; learn them; memorize them. Although memorizing statements can sometimes make for the worst kind of authoritarianism and rigidity, these statements are designed to help you avoid confusion. They will speed the teaching process and provide you with a handy reference for correcting mistakes. If a child makes mistakes in response to carefully programed statements, you know immediately what his problems are and what he must be taught.

A teacher is not merely the extension of a basic reading series, especially when she works with slower learners. She is a combination motivator, learning diagnostician, and remedial program writer. To be effective at her job, she should rehearse her lines—go over them when she is riding to school or doing the dishes. She should think of herself not as a teacher in the traditional sense, but as an actress who has a difficult part to play. She must give praise when she doesn't feel like giving praise. She must act excited when she feels not the slightest excitement. She must limit her verbal output when she feels like giving a long lecture. And she must teach to the slowest children in the group, making sure that *all* the other children are learning.

5. Don't be afraid of looking bad. A teacher often avoids working on basic concepts because it quickly becomes apparent that drill will be necessary. Until the children have caught on to what learning is about and how to use the operations being presented, they will not look like star students. A teacher knows, furthermore, that visitors, the principal, or another teacher will tend to judge the value of the instruction by a process best described as "instant evaluation." If they walk in and see something immediately pleasing to the eye—children with their hands in the air and the quest for knowledge fairly bursting out of their outstretched arms—they will like what they see. They will conclude that the instruction is a success without asking where the children were when the instruction began, where they are now, or where they are going.

When the teacher pursues a criterion-referenced approach and receives constant feedback from the children, there will be times when the children have difficulties, times when they do not live up to the image of the child who is exploring new horizons. There must be such periods, just as surely as the best children's orchestra in the world does not sound good when trying out a new piece for the first time. Visitors to rehearsals of a children's orchestra are reasonable, however. They realize that they are attending a practice session, not a performance. They know that if they want to find out what the orchestra can do with the pieces assigned, they should attend the performance. Similarly, if classroom visitors want to find out what the children in the class can do, they should wait for the evaluation of the skills the children are practicing.

Perhaps the best approach to handling visitors is to tell them that they are viewing training, not a performance. The teacher may want to have the children show off some of the skills they have already learned, as a kind of reinforcement for the children, but she should not work only on these skills, or she will not do much teaching.

Remember at all times: The teacher who avoids the part of instruction in which the children's deficits will be laid bare, the teacher who is afraid to go back to the beginning, may be able to fool visitors and conduct what seems to be a successful, interested class, but she will be limiting herself to teaching what is easy, not what is essential.

47

6. Make maximum use of study periods; reduce homework to a minimum. The teacher has no control over how the child studies his homework assignments. If he develops a serious misconception, she may not find out about it for days, and in the meantime it has grown roots that may be very difficult to pull out. The child may not have a clear idea of what he is reading, but the teacher is not there to supervise his activities, ask him questions, discover what he doesn't know, and help correct his misunderstanding. Yet the typical teacher has a great deal of faith in that aspect of teaching over which she has the least control—homework. She tends to think that the homework will help the child form good study habits and give him valuable practice, although she may have no idea what kind of habits the child is developing or what he is practicing. He may be practicing skimming operations and guessing procedures that will be extremely difficult to correct.

You cannot teach the disadvantaged child anything unless you have control over the presentation and the child's response to it. The less control you have, the less you know that the child is learning what he is supposed to learn. Instead of banking on the hope that the child will get an amorphous something out of his homework assignment, identify what you want the children to learn, and teach them in a highly structured manner. If you want them to be able to read a passage and understand it, begin with a relatively small passage and go over it intensively. Show them what kind of questions they should ask themselves, what they should do if they are unable to understand statements or words in the passage.

There is actually plenty of time in the school day to schedule everything the child should learn. Homework is legitimate when the children have both the reading and the comprehension ability necessary to understand subject material, for then homework assignments can be programed. Initially, however, the work that is to be done should be handled in school.

To make use of the available time, have specific assignments for the children to handle during study periods. Study periods should not be periods of free-choice activity. A teacher should be on hand to monitor the work of the children, answer their questions, and identify problems quickly so that the remedy will be given immediately. The small-group study sessions should handle the brunt of the teaching attack. Any new concepts, new vocabulary, and new operations should

48

first be introduced in the small-group sessions. As the children demonstrate that they have mastered the tasks presented in the small group, introduce similar tasks as seatwork. Proceeding in this manner, you can control the way a child is introduced to the more sophisticated examples of the concept. The procedure can involve making up daily worksheets for the seatwork sessions, but these are not particularly difficult to work up, since they are essentially the same as the examples presented in the small-group session.

7. *Learn to isolate the concepts.* In presenting new concepts, make sure that your presentation is adequate. *This means that it must admit to one and only one interpretation—the desired one.* If the concept is not isolated in this manner, the child may misinterpret the demonstration. Too often magical thinking takes precedence over the principle of isolating concepts. The teacher knows the concept she wishes to teach. The presentation that she provides is *consistent with* that concept. She therefore concludes that the presentation is perfectly adequate to teach the concept. However, it may not be adequate. It is adequate if the demonstration is consistent with the desired concept and with *none other.*

This point can be illustrated by the following example. The teacher wishes to teach the concept "porous," so she presents a greenish, porous rock, runs her finger laterally over the surface, and says, "This is porous." The demonstration is perfectly consistent with the concept "porous." However, it is also consistent with a number of other concepts, such as rocklike object, greenish, and moving the finger laterally. It is therefore possible for the child to misinterpret what *porous* means. He may conclude from the demonstration that *porous* means a greenish color, for example, or that it means moving the finger laterally, or that it refers to a rocklike object. In this example the teacher can rule out some of these misconceptions by using a verbal explanation, but in many cases verbal explanations become too involved. The children must be *shown* what the concept means. In the example the teacher could have demonstrated that *porous* does not mean greenish by presenting something that is porous and not greenish. She could have demonstrated that *porous* does not mean a rocklike object by presenting objects that are porous but not rocklike. And so forth.

The teacher should never suppose that a presentation is adequate unless she has asked herself, "How could the naive child possibly misinterpret the demonstration?" and then provided other demonstrations that rule out the unintended interpretations.

8. *Don't use complicated demonstrations; always seek the simplest form in which to present a concept.* If the teacher's job is to isolate the concept from the extraneous "noise" that goes with it in any presentation, it follows that her job of presenting new concepts is easier if she limits herself to presentations involving the fewest extraneous variables or the least amount of "noise." Simpler presentations have fewer parts and therefore admit of fewer misinterpretations.

This principle can be illustrated by an example: A teacher wants to demonstrate how story problems can be reduced to the formula $D = R \times T$. She does this by introducing the following story problem: "A man drives his car at an average speed of twenty miles an hour for five hours. How far does he go?" She then attempts to show how the pieces fit into the formula. Her demonstration has many parts and therefore admits of many misinterpretations. To rule all of these out would take some time and lead to a number of similar problems, and by the time the process was finished, the child who was confused to begin with (perhaps thinking that the term *average speed* or the general form of the problem somehow dictated what the teacher should write down) might be more confused.

The confusion can be reduced by working in smaller segments. The teacher can begin by writing the formula $D = R \times T$ on the board. "What does D stand for? What does R stand for? What does T stand for?" Next she can introduce the task: "I'm going to name some measures of distance, rate, and time. You tell me where to put them. If it's a measure of distance, it goes here where the D is. If it's a measure of rate, it goes here where the R is. If it's a measure of time, where would it go?" She then tests the children to make sure that they understand the rules of the game. "If it's a measure of time, where does it go, John?" After the children have demonstrated that they understand the rules of the game, she gives examples. "Fifteen miles an hour. What's that a measure of? What does it tell you? Does it tell you how far you go? . . . No. Does it tell you how fast you go? . . . Yes. What does it tell you? . . . So where does it go? . . . Yes, where the R is. I erase the R and put fifteen. Here's another one: Three days. What's that a measure of?" After the children can handle these tasks, the teacher introduces a simple example: "This is hard: A man goes ten miles an hour for three days. What measures did I say?"

The maxim of taking only one step at a time is based on the reality that the more steps the teacher takes, the greater the number of extraneous variables she introduces, the more difficult it becomes to rule out these extraneous variables, and the less likely it is that the child will focus on the appropriate variables. Cluttered demonstrations encourage the child to think of learning as mysterious rather than as precise.

9. *Don't correct the child by appealing to his intuition or his thinking habits—program rules for thinking.* Teachers of the disadvantaged sometimes imply that there is something obvious about the concept being presented and that the child will catch on if he "applies himself." In the first grade, a teacher may react to the child's response that a blue triangle is red by saying, "Now John, *look at it*. Does it look red to you?" Later another teacher may comment on his confusion of rate with time: "John, you put the fifteen where the time should be in this problem. You know better than that. Fifteen is miles an hour. That's not a measure of time, is it?" The assumption behind such explanations is that the teacher has done a perfectly adequate job of demonstrating the concept and that if the child acts more reasonably, he will perform properly. Actually, however, these explanations do not serve their intended purpose at all. John won't get the right answer if he thinks about it, and this point should be perfectly obvious to the teacher. When she exhorts him, she is simply encouraging him to rely on what she says, not encouraging him to apply a test that will allow him to evaluate whether the object is blue or whether the fifteen goes in the rate slot or the time slot. The teacher should never ask the child to *think* unless she has demonstrated the type of thinking that is necessary—what questions the child should ask himself, what kind of tests he should perform. To violate this principle is to encourage the child to rely on the teacher's authority about things that should be judged not on the basis of authority but on the basis of a specific operation.

If the teacher wants the child to think about whether fifteen miles an hour is a measure of rate or time, she should first have provided the child with an operation that he can refer to. "Here's the rule: If it's rate, it tells you *how fast* you're going. Ask yourself, 'Does it tell you how fast?'" When the child becomes confused, the teacher can then refer back to the operation when she exhorts him to think: "John, you're not asking yourself the right questions. What do you ask if you

51

want to know about rate? . . . Yes, how fast. Does fifteen miles an hour tell you how fast? . . . Does it tell you how far? . . . Does it tell you how long it takes? . . . O.K., so what's fifteen miles an hour a measure of? . . . So where does it go? . . ." When the basic thinking rules have been programed, the teacher has a basis for asking the child to think. When they haven't been programed, her exhortations are empty.

Perhaps the most difficult point for many teachers to grasp is that intuition has no place in teaching. If something must be programed in a way that involves broad intuitive steps, it cannot be taught. Perhaps the child will *learn* the rule, but the teacher cannot be assured of teaching it. Only if the intuitive trappings have been stripped from the concepts and the basic operations programed in the most straightforward way, can the child be taught. This position sometimes strikes "intuitive" educators as being extreme. It is extreme to them only because they have not seriously analyzed the problems associated with teaching. They have taught smarter children, who tend to learn from demonstrations that are inadequate. *Some* smart children don't learn from these demonstrations, and *many* disadvantaged children don't. To teach, the teacher must forget about the nebulous and concentrate on concepts.

10. Preserve the child's self-image, but tell him when his answers are wrong. The best procedure for providing the child with the information he needs in order to know whether he is on the right track or not is (*a*) to repeat his correct answers, perhaps adding "Good," and (*b*) not to repeat his incorrect answers but to say "No," and then give the correct answer.

This procedure should be followed rigorously during the early stages of instruction. Not only does it give immediate feedback to the child who responds; it also reduces the confusion of the other children in the group. Sometimes the child who is responding does not articulate clearly. As a result the teacher may answer "Yes" to a wrong response, and the others in the group may suppose that the wrong response is correct. If she clearly repeats what the child said ("Yes, porous"), the other children in the group will hear the correct response reinforced. A similar problem occurs when more than one child responds at the same time. Perhaps not all of them gave the correct response. If the teacher repeats the correct response, she will be correcting the child who gave the incorrect response and reinforcing the children who gave the correct one.

Some educators who believe that the child needs to experience success in learning have concluded that the way to avoid discouraging the child is not to tell him when his answers are incorrect. In other words, tell the child he is doing a good job, regardless of whether or not he is correct. This method has been accepted by many teachers. If one puts himself in the position of the child, however, the fallacy of the method becomes obvious. Let's assume that after the teacher presents the concept of porous, the child indicates that he thinks porous means greenish by pointing to a green object and saying, "Here's porous." The teacher can respond to the child's attempt positively ("Yes, John, that's porous"), but is she actually making the child feel successful? Is she actually helping the child learn? Or is she reinforcing the wrong concept and setting the stage for a great deal of confusion later on? Clearly, she is doing the latter, and although many mistakes may not be as obvious as the example, the outcome is just as certain. If the child makes a mistake, he is confused. He has mis-learned something. The teacher must let him know at once, in the most lucid manner possible, that he doesn't understand the concept: "No, John, this is not porous. Here, let me show you about porous. See this piece of clay? No holes. Not porous. Now watch. I'm going to make holes in it with this pin. . . . Now the clay is porous. Is the clay green? No. Is the clay porous? . . ."

Those who propose not telling the child that he is wrong and not using the word *no* are basically confused about the function of the words *yes* and *no* (or their equivalents) in teaching. Formulating an idea is an act of creation. The teacher cannot climb inside the child's head, pull a few levers, and materialize an idea. The child must formulate it. All the teacher can do is demonstrate how to use the idea and tell the child when his creation is acceptable. To do this, she uses *yes* (which means "Go—you've got the *right idea*") and *no* (which means "Stop—you've got the wrong idea"). If the teacher says yes when she should say no, she is giving the child unreliable cues. She is not teaching, but confusing. She is telling the child to go ahead when she should be telling him to stop.

Yes-no responses, in other words, have an important function. They provide the child with the information he needs in order to arrive at the goal. However, it must be remembered that yes-no responses can have another function. If the child hears "no" repeatedly, the teacher's presentation is consistent with the interpretation that the child is inadequate—an interpretation that the child is sure to make if the teacher yells "NO" instead of saying it in a matter-of-fact, conversational tone.

In the learning effort, the child must never get the idea that he has done something wrong unless he fails to pay attention or fails to try hard. To avoid conveying the idea that the child is inadequate, carefully structure the presentation.

Continually remind the child that if he keeps trying and working he will learn; let him know both through tone of voice and through verbal reassurance that you are not displeased with him if he is not learning. Reassure him that the concepts are not easy—which must be true or the child would have learned them from more casual presentations. "Don't worry, John. This is tough stuff. But if you just keep working at it, you'll get it."

Arrange the tasks so that at least two-thirds of your responses are yes responses. If you find that the child is simply not learning from the present task and that you are saying nothing but "No, John, that's not right," recognize that you may be teaching the child that he is a failure. Restructure the task in such a way that he will succeed. Simplify the task, or distribute it over a number of teaching sessions, so that he will see your yes and no responses in proper perspective— as sources of information and not as punishment or as proof that he is stupid.

Don't allow any but positive comments from other members of the group when a child is having trouble. Actually, negative comments from other children can be used by the teacher to demonstrate that she has faith in the child who is having difficulties. For example, if someone says "He's a slowpoke," the teacher should not allow the comment to stand uncontested: "I don't want to hear that kind of talk, JC. John is not a slowpoke. He's trying very hard, and he's going to get this stuff. You'll see."

After the child masters the difficult concept, make a fuss over it. It is virtually impossible for a good teacher in the primary grades to be a deadpan. Teachers who try to comport themselves in a well-controlled manner are usually ineffective, because they can never convey to the child that what he has learned makes any difference or that anybody cares. The flat "Very good, John" is not enough. The child has worked very hard to learn the concept, and the teacher must not judge his success by an absolute standard. She should treat his accomplishment as the product of a monumental effort. Unless the teacher shows that she appreciates his effort, she may leave him feeling "All that work for what? 'Very good, John.'" Rather the teacher should be animated: "Good boy! You've been thinking and you've got it. I'm really proud of you, John. You see that, JC? I told you he'd get it." The idea is to provide the child with a payoff and to use his success as a demonstration that he is smart.

In summary, structure the tasks so that the slower-learning child is not failing most of the time. Let him know that your nos are informational, and make it clear that by paying attention to the yeses, he will succeed. By following these guidelines, you will be able to help the child build a self-image based on real success, rather than one artificially constructed of praise for inappropriate behavior.

11. Give the children ample evidence that they are capable of learning. The teacher should become excited when the children succeed, because she is trying to teach them that learning is an important process and that other people think it's important. To do this, the teacher must *show* the children that she treats it as something important. The deadpan teacher's presentation is like a flat contour map, on which one would be hard pressed to find landmarks. There are no obvious landmarks in the presentation and responses of the "well-modulated" teacher. There are no obvious high spots and low spots— no goals to aim for or dangers to avoid.

The teacher must *react* to the child. She must exaggerate, showing excitement when the child succeeds, disapproval when he behaves in a way that will not lead to success, and patience when he is trying to learn.

Always assume that if *you* don't show the children that learning is important, nobody will. You are probably the children's only model for learning. Be a good model. Show them that learning involves working. Do this by working at least as hard as they do. If you work hard, and if the work seems physically demanding, the children won't resent having to work hard themselves.

Point out that each success is consistent with the principle that if you work hard you'll get it: "See, I told you you'd get it!" The hard-work principle is important, because the attitudes the child develops about himself affect his learning. These attitudes become

55

self-fulfilling prophecies in many classrooms. The child who believes that he cannot succeed in learning will use his first false start as evidence to strengthen this attitude. He will give up, concluding that further effort is useless. On the other hand, the child who has the attitude that he can succeed will respond quite differently to obstacles. He will try again, because he believes that if he keeps trying he will succeed. He finally does succeed, and his success serves as further evidence that his attitude about himself was correct. He worked hard and he succeeded. What goes on in the teaching-learning process will strengthen one attitude or the other.

Never forget that you are teaching an attitude toward learning as you teach specific skills. You must let the child know that he is capable of learning. You can best do this by being a strong model and structuring the learning situation to use each of the child's successes as evidence that he can learn: "John's doing a good job. He works hard and he gets it. Let's all clap for John."

12. Structure the teaching sessions so that the children work for no more that five to eight minutes on a particular series of tasks. Teachers often try to teach too much at one sitting. They spend too long on a task, drill too much, and remove whatever reinforcing properties the task might have had for the children.

Prepare lessons so that during a half-hour period you will have a distinct change of pace. Try to schedule at least three different exercises (preferably four). Start with an exercise that is relatively easy for the children. Let them work on it as a group, giving unison responses. Then proceed to material that is new. Plan to spend about eight minutes on this material. Then give the children tasks they can work on individually (worksheets). Always try to end the period on a note of success. To assure success, reserve a relatively easy set of tasks for the last.

Do not follow an exercise that places great verbal demands on the child with a similar exercise. If the material involves complicated verbal chains, follow it with an exercise that is relatively nonverbal.

Use fun tasks as a payoff: "These problems are tough, aren't they? But maybe when we've finished, I'll give you some of those silly multiplication problems." From time to time, remind the children of the payoff: "O.K., this is the last of these problems. Do a job, so we can work those silly multiplication problems."

Sometimes children will plead with you to continue with a particular set of exercises. As a rule, do not yield. Tell them, "We can't do any more of them now, but I'll give you some more tomorrow." The next day, at the beginning of the period, remind the children that you are going to give them the desired problems. "But first, let's do this hard stuff."

Often a teacher relaxes when she has succeeded in doing something that attracts the children's attention, and her pace slows down. She becomes visibly pleased with the attention and takes the opportunity to launch into a leisurely lecture. When the teacher gets solid attention, however, she should *speed up*—not by presenting tasks that the children cannot handle, or forcing them to read problems or instructions at an uncomfortably fast pace, but by setting a pace that will keep the children's attention. "O.K., here's the rule: When the bottom number and the top number are the same size, the fraction equals one whole group. Let's see if it works. Let's try the fraction four over four. . . ."

As a general rule, try to present about ten times as many examples of a concept as you would usually present in the given period of time. Work from diagrams that can be quickly altered to provide a new example. A line on the chalkboard can be erased in a second, creating a new example.

13. Use fun examples and tasks with a payoff. Teaching sessions shouldn't be dull. Keep them lively by introducing tasks that are fun. Use themes that the children like—such as eating, or situations in which people do something wrong. Fun examples can make difficult tasks palatable.

Keep the presentation moving with a series of challenges to the children: "I'm going to give you a problem to work, but I really don't think you'll be able to do it." When the children work the problem, act surprised: "I didn't think you'd be able to do that. How did you get so smart?" When challenges of this kind are met, the children have a basis for believing that they are smart. They are given the sense of pride that comes from accomplishment.

React to silly mistakes as if they were quite amusing. This technique should be introduced only after some of the children in a group (preferably most of them) have mastered a given skill. For example, if most of the children in a group have caught on to the

57

principle that seven equals seven, eight equals eight, and so on, the stage is set for using the technique. One of the children in the group may indicate that seven equals eight. Since you have worked for some time on the principle that a number equals that number, your natural reaction is one of irritation. Stifle the impulse and laugh: "Did you hear what JC said? Oh, that's funny. He said that seven is the same as eight. He said that seven apples is the same as eight apples. He said that seven dogs is the same as eight dogs. . . ." Get the other children laughing. The child who committed the error will probably laugh too. But you have successfully demonstrated to him that there is a reason for remembering the basic rule. The rule must be important, since the teacher and the others in the group find the mistake as silly as the mistake of calling a boy a girl. By simply lecturing the child who makes a mistake, the most you can hope to do is to show him that you think he should learn the rule. By involving the others in the group, you are showing him that perhaps everybody thinks the rule is important.

(NOTE: Do not ridicule *children*. The technique above ridicules a response, but the ridicule must be kept on that level. It must never involve the child, merely what he said—never "JC doesn't know that . . . ," always "JC said that . . .")

On material that is relatively well understood, try to fool the children. For example, if they respond to the problem "twelve plus five" with the answer "seventeen," write a seven on the board. If none of the children catch the error, act amused: "I got you that time. Oh boy, that was fun. I really fooled you." The more you gloat, the more careful the children will be in the future. The next time you try to fool them, they will be ready. The fooler approach has been criticized by some educators, but their criticism is based on a misunderstanding of the function of foolers. The idea behind instruction is to get the children to depend on rules and information, not on the teacher's authority. They should learn that something is true because investigation or experience dictates that it is true, not simply because the teacher says so. The fooler games help free the rules and information from the teacher. If the teacher makes mistakes that are programed, the children can't simply take things on her authority. They learn to rely on the critical information variables. This does not mean that a teacher should try to fool the children when she is teaching them a new skill. It means simply that after they are supposed to have learned

58

a discrimination, they should be able to use it and not rely on the teacher to help them use it.

Let the children take turns at being teacher: "Boy, I'm really sleepy today. I stayed up late and watched TV. I don't think I can do much teaching. That's hard work, you know. We just better sit here and take it easy unless one of you wants to be teacher. I warn you—it's hard work." This technique is very good, because it makes the children aware of the role of the teacher. The children become conscious of the teacher's statements, her method of presentation. In learning the characteristics of her role, they learn a great deal about how to teach. They learn the concepts well enough to explain them to other children.

14. Concentrate on those aspects of the curriculum that can be accelerated. Not much can be done to teach the child multiplication facts. There is no way that the process of learning them can be appreciably speeded. Mnemonics and distributed practice help, but not greatly. Since the learning of multiplication tables represents one aspect of learning that cannot be speeded greatly, the teacher should not concentrate on it. Instead she should concentrate on those aspects of learning that *can* be speeded. The understanding of the process of multiplication, its application to algebraic problems, its application to certain problems in fractions—this learning *can* be accelerated.

If the work on facts is founded on a firm understanding of operations, the learning of facts will be more meaningful to the child. For example, if the child has learned to count by different numbers and has learned how to figure out such problems as $5 \times 6 = ?$, he will also learn a certain number of facts and some of the relationships between facts. He will see for instance that 5×7 has to be greater than 5×6. He will see that facts are not arbitrarily assigned but are actually the product of operations on numbers. When he learns these relationships, he will be in a far better position than the naive child to learn the facts and to understand them as part of a coherent pattern. If the facts come first, he may never fully understand the relation between $5 \times 6 = ?$ and $5 \times 7 = ?$, except to know that the answer to the first is 30 and the answer to the second is 35 (or is it 20?).

The rule you should follow in designing a course of study is not to delay the child until he masters a particular skill, *unless that skill is essential to what is to come.* Furthermore, you must try to reduce the essentials to the minimum. If the facts are of questionable value, omit

59

them. The teacher must recognize that she must do with a minimum of facts what is normally done through the arduous programing of many facts. The reduction of fact learning means not that the child will learn less, but that he will learn more. It means that important learning is not delayed while relatively trivial facts are digested. If the facts are not trivial, but essential to what is to come, they must be mastered.

3   *Classroom Management*

Classroom management involves keeping the children on target, maintaining motivation and interest, and eliminating behaviors that are incompatible with working on the assigned tasks. It is not easy to discuss classroom management in general, because the problems of management are specific. Management problems can begin with the kind of material presented to the children. If material is very dull, with no payoff for the work involved, it will not motivate the children. On the other hand, if material is designed so that it has a payoff, the children may be highly motivated to work on the task. If a child misbehaves, he may do so because the instructional material is too difficult for him, or because the teacher is demanding too high a rate and level of performance. He may misbehave to attract the attention of the other children in the group or the teacher. Each misbehavior implies a slightly different remedy.

To provide the appropriate remedy, *the teacher must first identify the aspect of the situation that is controlling the child's behavior.* She must then devise a program to change that aspect. She might change her behavior by restructuring the tasks she presents, thereby reducing the response demands placed on the child. She might change the tasks so that they have a more effective payoff. To change the child's behavior, she might introduce strong reinforcers for children who are behaving adequately. She might reinforce the offender for behavior incompatible with his inappropriate behavior. (For example, if the child talks during quiet periods, she may give him points for sitting quietly or for engaging in a nonverbal task.)

Although the problems of classroom management are sometimes difficult and often complex, there are effective procedures that a teacher can use to induce appropriate classroom behavior. For a teacher to become effective in classroom management, she must first accept two basic premises:

1. A teacher's *behavior*—not the way she feels—affects the behavior of the children.

2. Simply by reinforcing appropriate behavior, a teacher can control the behavior even of children who have been labeled as serious adjustment problems.

Experimental Support for Basic Premises

Wesley Becker and his associates at the University of Illinois have conducted a number of dramatic studies that support the validity of these premises. The procedure used in their experiments follows:

1. The classroom teacher receives training in basic management principles. The training includes instruction in the use of praise and practice in observing one's own behavior.

2. Base-line data on the children are obtained. The base-line data indicate the number of times the target children in the classroom (the children on whom data are recorded) behave in various ways— the number of times they work on a task, exhibit motor behavior, produce a vocal response, turn around in their seats or look at their shoes, and so on.

3. After base-line performance of the target children has been established, the teacher is instructed to change her behavior. In some experiments the teacher simply praises children who are behaving appropriately while ignoring those who are not. In other experiments the teacher introduces rules of behavior, goes over these with the children, and then relates each child's performance to the rules—usually in a positive manner: "Oh, Harry's really working quietly, isn't he? If Harry keeps working like that, he's going to earn his glider." The changes in the behavior of the children during this phase of the experiment are noted.

4. The conditions are then reversed. The teacher is instructed to behave as she did during the base-line phase. Again the changes in children's behavior are noted.

5. The teacher resumes the experimental behavior.

The reason for having the teacher alternate between two patterns of behavior is to determine whether the behavior of the children is controlled by the behavior of the teacher. If it is, there should be a

62

change in the children's behavior for every corresponding change in the teacher's behavior. And if the children's behavior changes every time the teacher's behavior changes, the teacher's behavior must be what is controlling the children's behavior.

The results of these experiments are dramatic—especially since they were carried out in the classroom with the classroom teacher providing the demonstrations. The experiments were limited to the school setting, with no attempt made to work with the home or to provide the children with psychiatric help. The following comments were taken from the psychological report on a child before he participated in a classroom management experiment.[6]

"Danny's lack of conscience development and other intrinsic controls still presents a serious problem in controlling his behavior. His immediate impulsive aggressive reaction to threatening situations may hamper any educational remediation efforts. The evidence presented still suggests that Danny, in light of increasing accumulation of family difficulties, lack of consistent masculine identification, his irascible and changeable nature, and educational pressures, will have a difficult time adjusting to the educational situation.

"It is our opinion that unless further action is implemented, i.e., school officials should attempt to refer this boy to an appropriate agency (Mental Health, Institute for Juvenile Research) for additional help and correction, he is likely to become a potentially serious acting out youngster."[7]

During the base-line period Danny was averaging 80 percent deviant behavior on workbook assignments (which means he was off task 80 percent of the time). Two months later his deviant behavior had dropped to an average of 15 percent. Danny was now on task 85 percent of the time.

The treatment that accounted for this change in behavior had two components—praise and tutoring. Danny was praised for on-task behavior, and he was tutored in reading. The investigators noted, "In view of the rather dramatic changes Danny made in classroom behavior through a combination of remediation and social reinforcement, perhaps it is necessary to question the assumptions implicit in the quotation from Danny's psychological report given earlier. It should be noted that no attempt was made to work on family problems, his conscience, his masculine identification, or his 'irascible nature' in changing his adjustment to school."[8]

In another study tokens were awarded to seventeen nine-year-old children, described as emotionally disturbed. These children "exhibited undesirable classroom behaviors such as temper tantrums, crying, uncontrolled laughter, and fighting."[9] Under the token system the children could accumulate points for appropriate behavior and exchange these for pencils, clay, gliders, and so on. The deviant behavior dropped almost immediately from a base-line performance of 76 percent off-task behavior to 10 percent off-task behavior during the experimental phase in which tokens were awarded for following the rules. According to the investigators, analysis of behavioral changes indicated that "the treatment accounted for [an estimated] 96 percent of the variance of the observed deviant behavior."[10] What this means, simply, is that for all practical purposes the behavior of these children was being controlled by the environment, not by something within the children. Specifically, it was being controlled by the teacher and her use of positive reinforcement.

One of the most significant experiments in demonstrating the control the teacher's behavior exerts over the behavior of the children in the classroom concerned a teacher who had good classroom control over a class of twenty-eight socially advantaged, mid-primary-grade children. During the base-line phase, children's deviant behavior was less than 9 percent. During the second phase of the experiment the teacher purposely changed her behavior from generally approving (her natural teaching style) to generally disapproving. The deviant behavior of the children rose to 25 percent. After returning to the base-line procedure and demonstrating that the deviant behavior of the children dropped correspondingly, the teacher resumed the experimental behavior, increasing the number of disapproving comments she made to about four times the number she had used during the base-line phase. The disruptive behavior of the children in the class immediately rose to 31 percent When the teacher returned to her base-line procedure (frequent praise and relatively infrequent disapproval), the disruptive behavior dropped to 13 percent.[11]

Implications for teachers

These experiments conducted by Becker and his associates show that the teacher's behavior controls that of the children. They also show that a teacher can learn to be effective in classroom management simply by learning the appropriate set of behaviors. These experiments have another very interesting implication: the children's behavior is controlled by the teacher's behavior whether or not the teacher feels comfortable behaving the way she does. In the experiment with children who were initially well behaved, the teacher felt more natural giving praise than showing disapproval, yet her disapproving behavior *was effective in influencing the children's behavior.* The children responded to her disapproval by becoming disruptive. Similarly, a teacher may feel quite uncomfortable giving praise, and yet the praise will be effective in controlling the behavior of the children. One teacher who participated in an experiment did not know how to give praise. She used either disapproval or barbed praise. ("That's good, for a change"). When she tried to follow the experimental procedure of "catching children being good" and ignoring inappropriate behavior, her attempts seemed unconvincing to classroom observers. Although her attempts at praise were characterized as "phony" by observers, they proved very effective. A classroom that had been poorly managed with great effort was now easily managed with praise. Soon the use of praise and other forms of social reinforcement became natural to this teacher.[12]

Some teachers react to suggestions about ways of behaving in the classroom by saying "Oh, that's not my style," or "I don't feel right doing it that way." Such teachers will probably never become very skillful. The first step a teacher must take in learning to control classroom behavior is to acknowledge that she must adopt techniques that will produce the desired results, regardless of whether they seem natural to her at first. In time they will become natural and her personal style will not be submerged. Four motion picture directors working from the same script will produce four different versions. Yet all will contain the essential ingredients the author wrote into the script —the essential lines and actions. Similarly, four teachers working from the same script will give different interpretations, all of which will be acceptable.

Structuring a Management Program

The purpose of management procedures is to bring the children's behavior under the control of increasingly subtle cues. At first the cues should be very obvious. They should be spelled out in the greatest detail. After the children have learned to perform adequately from this set of cues, the teacher can begin to fade the cues somewhat. Instead of saying "You're working quietly, John. That's good. And what happens when you work quietly? . . . Yes, you earn points," the teacher can now say "Good work, John." In another situation, instead of saying "John, you're making noise and you know what happens if you keep making noise. . . . That's right, no points," the teacher can now say "John . . ." The child has been taught the meaning of this more subtle cue and it can now function in the same way as the more elaborate statement did.

Sometimes teachers proceed in the opposite direction, at first admonishing the children ("John, I think you'd better sit down") and then building up to more vigorous types of aversive control ("SIT DOWN! EVERYBODY, SIT! YOU TOO, JOHN! SIT DOWN!"). This program fails because it teaches the children to ignore the teacher's comments, especially when they are not (or cannot be) enforced. The teacher has no recourse except to escalate her negative comments. She cannot set the stage for positive statements.

Often negative comments reinforce the very behavior the teacher is trying to eliminate. This fact was nicely documented in a study by Madsen *et al.*[13] The teachers in the study were instructed to increase the frequency of the command "sit down" during a period in which the teacher worked with a reading group while the other children were engaged in seatwork activity. The result was an increase in the number of times children *stood up*. When the procedures were changed, and the teachers "caught the children being good" (praising children who were sitting), children stood up only half as often as they had during the disapproval phase of the experiment.

Procedures for most children

Here are the basic procedures for efficiently managing most children:

1. Specify the rules that serve as the basis for positive reinforcement. State the rules *positively*, telling the children what they should do to receive positive reinforcement, not what kind of behavior leads to punishment. The rules may be different for different periods. During intensive instruction periods, the rules are simple—

Work hard.

Talk big.

During seatwork periods, the rules are—
> Work quietly.
> Raise your hand if you have a question.

Additional rules can be introduced if necessary, but no more than five rules should be introduced for a given period.

2. Initially, go over the rules every day. Go over them at the beginning of the period. "Tell me, what are the rules? . . . Yes, work hard and talk big. John, tell me the rules. . . ." Do not present the rules as if they were threats. Present them with the attitude that, as a matter of fact, these are the rules.

3. As the children become familiar with the rules, as evidenced by performance, state the rules less often and become less mechanical in your presentation. After about a month it should only occasionally be necessary to have the children state the rules.

Always relate the performance of the children to the rules. Try to do so in a positive manner. Working hard actually covers a variety of behaviors, and you must relate the various aspects of working hard to the rule if it is to have meaning for the children. Generally, what you mean by working hard is—

- Giving the correct response.
- Following your presentation—looking at the chalkboard, listening to instructions, responding to commands, answering questions.
- Not engaging in behaviors that are incompatible with looking at the chalkboard, listening to instructions, and so forth.

Give the children feedback on each of the component behaviors that enter into "working hard." This means that you should let the children know when they are working hard.

If a child gives the correct answer, relate his performance to the rule: "Good. You're really working hard."

If a child who is having trouble with the task appears to be trying, say, "John's working hard. He'll get it. You'll see."

If a child who used to squirm around frequently is squirming less, say, "Look how nicely Harold is sitting. He's really working hard."

If all or most of the children perform well on a task, say, "Gee, I didn't think you could work that problem. You're really smart. You really work hard."

The best way to demonstrate to a child that he is not following the rules is to make it obvious that you are reinforcing others in the group, but not him. Sometimes simple tangible rewards, such as raisins or bite-size crackers, are effective. If a child is not talking, have the entire group answer a question. Then lavishly praise the children who responded: "Boy, I heard some good big talking." Give each child a cracker or a few raisins, and tell him, "You sure are a good talker." Do not give the offender a reward. If someone mentions that the child didn't receive a cracker or that he didn't talk, say, "Well, that's O.K. He can do this stuff because he's a smart boy. You'll see. He'll be getting crackers before long." Repeat the task so that the offender has another chance to receive a reward. If the child responds, say something like this: "I told you he would get a cracker. He can talk big."

The technique outlined above should be your stock technique. Introduce reinforcers that work, those for which the children will work. If praise isn't effective, introduce something more potent than praise. In summary, make the teaching situation attractive for the children. Make it fun. Show some animation and excitement. If a child is not following the rules, demonstrate to him that those who are following the rules are receiving rewards that he is not receiving. Always voice faith in a child's ability to perform: "John can do it. And he will, you'll see." And always let the children know why they are being reinforced: "That's good talking. I didn't know you could say something that hard."

This approach implies that the teacher must say things that she doesn't feel. She may feel like saying, "Well, it's about time you said the right thing," but instead she says, "Wow! Harold is really working hard. Good work, Harold."

4. Focus behavior on the tasks. When the children are working on a particular task, continually relate their performance to the rules. Do not equivocate. Do not reward a child who is *not* working according to the rules, and make sure that you reward those children who *are* working according to the rules.

When the children are in a small-group session, the work-hard and talk-big rules should be firmly enforced. When you are not presenting tasks, however, do not enforce the rules. After the period is over, you can relax the rules and let your hair down. When children talk to you about miscellaneous subjects, respond to all of them. But make a greater fuss over some observations than over others. If a child tells you that he's been working arithmetic problems at home, make a greater fuss than you would over a child who tells you that his cat had kittens: "You know, I can tell that you've been working at home. It really shows. You're really a smart boy."

During these informal exchanges with the children, do not correct grammar. Comment on every observation the children make. Do not enforce order and quiet too vigorously. Let the children do most of the talking.

The purpose of this behavior is to make it clear to the children that there is a time for hard work and a time for relaxing. The teacher is their model for working hard. If they see that the model is only a machine that corrects and teaches all the time, they will not learn what it means to work hard. Working hard will mean being quiet at all times, speaking correctly at all times, and generally being proper at all times. The teacher should place the focus on the tasks. She should make it clear that when she is on task, certain rules apply; when she is not on task, these rules do not apply. The children can thereby learn to discriminate between working on a task and not working on a task. The teacher demonstrates that when she is not working, she is a person similar to some of the adults the children know. The teacher does not have to maintain a prim distance, nor does she have to try to be friends with the children. She needs only to be more permissive when she is off task than when she is on task.

Whenever the teacher is on task, she should focus on the task rather than on behavior in the abstract. If the children are restless at the beginning of a study session, your impulse may be to work on the children's behavior before presenting the first task. The impulse is to call attention to the misbehavior. Actually, there is no important misbehavior at this point. You haven't asked the children to do anything, so no real offense has been committed, unless a child is being hurt or the noise is deafening. Present the task. Then, if the children don't behave appropriately, they will have broken a basic rule about working hard and you will have some basis for calling their attention to the rule. A good procedure is to announce, "Here's a hard problem and I don't think you'll be able to do it. I can do it because I'm smart." Present the problem without any further introduction. If none of the children can work the problem, do it yourself and reward yourself: "I told you I could do it. I worked hard, so I'm going to give myself a cracker. Boy, this is fun. I love crackers. . . . Here's another problem and I don't think you're going to be able to do it. . . ." The chances are overwhelming that some of the children will do it. If one

69

or two children do work the problem when it is presented the first time, call attention to these children: "Good work, John. I didn't think anybody would be able to work that problem, but John did." Follow the statement of praise with confidential comments to one or two of the children who did not work: "You know, John really surprised me. I didn't think *anybody* could do that problem, but he's really smart. He really fooled me. He's really doing a good job, isn't he?" The child in whom you confided will most probably demonstrate that he can do a good job on the next problem. "Wow! You did that problem. How did you do that? I didn't think you could do that problem."

Another technique to use when only one or two children in the group are paying attention is to indicate they are the only ones who *can* do the problem: "There are only three people in this room who can do the problem—John, Mary, and I. We're really smart. I think we should all have a cracker. . . ."

If the children are unusually rowdy, you may want to quiet them down somewhat before introducing the first task. Give them a signal that it is time to work hard, and then reinforce the children who are ready: "Time to work hard. Look here." Do not give an elaborate warning; just make a simple statement: "Tommy's ready to work. Here's a cracker for Tommy. And Lenord is ready to work. . . . There you are, Lenord. I think Lenord likes to work. All right. Who's ready to work? Look here. . . . *Everybody's* ready to work. Let's start with a hard problem and see who the hard workers are. . . ."

The general rule always applies. Try to catch the children who are following the rules and reinforce them. The others will follow. When they do, reinforce them, too. If they don't, use more lavish reinforcers for those who are performing. If a particular child doesn't respond when the other children receive one cracker, give the children who perform three crackers. If he doesn't respond when the other children receive three crackers, give them something else. Make the act of responding or behaving appropriately attractive to the offender, so attractive that he would rather respond than not respond. Find what it is that the child will work for and use it as a reinforcer. As you do, accompany the reinforcer with plenty of praise.

5. Anticipate behavior problems and use a presentation that avoids them whenever possible. It is much easier to structure the program so that a potential behavior problem will not come up than it is to cope

with the problem after it has come up. For example, if you know that a particular child is reluctant to respond when he is called on to repeat a statement or answer a question, do not start out by asking him a question. Start with a series of tasks that are not as difficult for him: "Everybody, stand up." Reinforce the children who follow the command: "Everybody, sit down. . . . Good sitting. Everybody, stand up. . . . Sit down. Hold hands. Clap. Stand up. . . . Sit down. . . . Good." The children usually enjoy this type of exercise. The child who may not respond when he is called on to answer a question will probably participate in this game without the slightest reluctance. By participating in the game, however, *he is doing what you tell him to do.* If he does what you tell him to do on a dozen commands, he will probably do what you tell him on the next command. You can therefore follow the series of commands with the command, "Everybody, read what I write. . . ." Give praise to the children who perform: "Hey, good reading, Tommy. You're really working hard, aren't you?" Without gloating over your victory, move to the next task: "I can say it with my *eyes* closed. Listen: one plus three equals four." Let the children take turns at saying it with their eyes closed—including the offender. Go on to the next task: "I can say it with my eyes closed while I stand on one foot." Do it and let the children demonstrate, to your apparent dismay, that they can also perform the task. You have thus demonstrated to the offender that he can do things that you apparently think are very difficult. He is now ready for the next task that you consider difficult: "All right. You think you're pretty smart, but you'll never be able to do this. . . ." You are now into the lesson proper. And the chances are that the child who would have presented a management problem is working and is eager to work. Instead of working him through his problem, you prevented the problem. Your prevention probably took no more than one minute, far less time than you would have to spend working the problem through a stubborn, I-won't-talk session.

The best way to prevent problems is to start with tasks that the children can do easily, but that you indicate are difficult. A good technique is to start with a race: "We're going to have a race." Draw a score box on the board:

M	
Y	

"The *M* is for me and the *Y* is for you. Every time I win, I'll put a mark up here. Every time you win, I'll put a mark down here." Begin the race, starting with easy questions: "What's one plus one? . . . Two. I won. Ho, ho! I can see I'm going to get more points than you."

As the race proceeds, let the children win more and more. When they start winning, act as if the race is really important to you: "You were lucky on that one. I'll still beat you. I'm smart." Act somewhat irritated as the children accumulate more and more points: "Well, I'm tired today. I don't want to race anymore. I don't like this game."

After racing with the children at the beginning of one or two sessions, they will always want to start with a race. Do not race with them eagerly: "I don't want to play that game. It's really not very much fun. Besides, everybody knows that I'm really smart and I'd win the race anyhow." From now on the race can function as a part of the lesson. When you wish to work on something new or difficult, introduce some questions about the new material in the race. Use the race to teach the children facts that they have not learned adequately. For example, if the children are weak on 3 + 3, introduce that fact in the race: "I can get you on this one every time. What's three plus three—six. I said it. I win. Oh boy! This is fun. I really like this game." Return to the fact from time to time. Before long the children will know it. When they do, act disgusted: "This game isn't much fun anyhow."

Getting the child focused on a task is one thing; keeping him focused is another. To keep him going, you have to provide continuous support in the way of reinforcement. This support comes in two ways —from the task itself, and in the form of praise or social reinforcement from you. Support comes when the task is designed so that performance brings a payoff. The task of identifying the numbers that the teacher writes on the board, for example, has no payoff unless one is deliberately imposed on it. Even when the teacher supports the children who are working hard and giving correct answers, the task remains barren. The children have no direct demonstration that what they are learning has any particular function. By redesigning the task, the teacher can give it a payoff: "O.K., tell me what number this is and you can erase. Tommy. . . . Yes, it's a seven. You get to erase it." Now there is a point to the task.

Another example: Reading off a series of words is an indifferent task. There is no particular payoff in getting through the task. If the child knows, however, that near the end of the list is a word that tells about the interesting or amusing picture the teacher will show him, the task has a built-in payoff. The children receive support from the teacher as they go through the list of words, but they have an additional reason for working—to get to the word that tells them about the picture. Most tasks can be restructured so that there is a payoff.

Another good technique for demonstrating the payoff for learning a rule is to take a negative approach. First demonstrate with a few examples that a relationship holds. For example, demonstrate that each of the fractions $\frac{3}{3}$, $\frac{2}{2}$, and $\frac{5}{5}$ equals one whole group: "Hey, look! When the number on the top is the same as the number on the bottom, the fraction equals one whole group. I'll bet that doesn't work for all fractions. I'll bet I can find a fraction it doesn't work for." The children may suspect that you are right, or they may believe that you are wrong. In either case they are interested in the tasks that are to come, because there is a potential payoff. Each task will either demonstrate that you are wrong or call for another example to confirm that you are right: "Well, that one worked, but I'll still bet I can find one that won't work." The children have two reasons for working. There is a certain amount of suspense to the presentation, and the children are receiving reinforcement from the teacher.

"O.K., I was wrong. Seven over seven does equal one whole group. You were right and I was wrong. But I'm not through yet. . . ."

If a task is set up in such a way that the payoff follows a great number of indifferent tasks, the teacher must bridge the gap between the payoff and the tasks: "If you work all these problems on your sheet, you can be teacher and write a problem on the board." The children will generally work for such a payoff, but they may also need intermittent support: "Oh, I think John is going to be a teacher. He's really working . . . and so is Tommy. Look at him go. . . . We're going to have a lot of teachers today."

For beginners, you may have to structure all tasks so that the payoff is immediate. As time goes on, gradually delay the presentation of the payoff. Introduce more nonpayoff tasks before presenting the payoff. By systematically increasing the time span between task and payoff, you are getting the children to work for goals that are increasingly distant. Follow the same procedure if the children are working for tokens or points that can be exchanged for toys or other goodies. Start them on a schedule of immediate payoffs. At first, tokens should be exchanged at the end of a short period (fifteen to forty minutes). As the children's performance improves, the amount of time between exchanges can be increased until the children are able to work for perhaps a week before they exchange.

Similarly, the type and amount of support the teacher gives to the children as they work for the goal should not remain unchanged. If a child needs a great deal of support and a great many indirect reminders about following the rules (which reminders are given by praising a child who is performing adequately), give him the support he needs. As his performance improves, cut down on the number of supporting comments. Systematically reduce the number until the child is working with relatively few direct or indirect comments. The goal is to teach him to work under normal school conditions and to have him work as if he were "intrinsically motivated." For him to become so motivated, however, the teacher must start where he is, provide the kind of support that is needed to keep him going, structure the tasks so that they have an immediate payoff, systematically reduce the number of supporting comments, and systematically increase the delay between the beginning of a task series and the payoff. With an effective program, the children will soon be working on their own. The teacher will have demonstrated the social and intrinsic value of working in this way. She will have taken them, a small step at a time, from where they were to where she wants them to be.

The behavior problem

A teacher must be able to take all children where they are, even children with severe problems, and shape their behavior. The teacher is not exonerated from dealing with such children and teaching them appropriate behavior. While a child is misbehaving, he is not learning, and while he is not learning, he is slipping farther behind where he should be. The teacher is responsible for correcting his behavior as quickly as possible. This point is extremely important. There are many techniques that may work with a severely disturbed child over a relatively long period of time, but the teacher doesn't have a relatively long period of time. She must reduce the child's inappropriate behavior as quickly as possible. The following principles apply to working with severe behavior problems:

Do not unintentionally reinforce undesirable behavior. Sometimes children seek the support of their peers. Sometimes they like attention from adults, even if the adults are critical of them while giving attention. Sometimes children are so strongly reinforced by their peers that they do not respond well to mild social and physical rewards. A teacher who is confronted with such a child often finds herself in an awkward position. The child acts up and receives a certain amount of approval from his peers. (Even if his peers don't respond immediately, he may continue to act up because he has learned that his behavior will eventually be reinforced by his peers. He may therefore try harder if his peers do not reinforce him immediately.) If the teacher ignores the child, she will have difficulty presenting tasks to the other members of the group. If she gives the child attention, she may be reinforcing inappropriate behavior. The child wants to attract attention, and that's exactly what he is doing.

In a case like this, (a) don't reinforce the child's behavior, and (b) deprive him of reinforcement from his peers. The child must be effectively punished. Teachers (and educators) are often shocked by the word *punishment*, but it is not a particularly evil word. The most productive way to view punishment is this: When you ask a child to behave in class and work hard, you are asking him to invest a certain amount of energy. The responses you call for cost the child a certain amount. For some children the cost is greater than it is for others (since all children are individuals with individual differences). For the severely emotionally disturbed youngster the cost is extremely high. Basically, you must do two things. You must reinforce the child for appropriate behavior and thereby reduce the cost of behaving appropriately. Before you can reduce the cost of these responses, however, the child must produce appropriate responses frequently enough so that he will receive reinforcement from time to time.

When the child begins producing appropriate responses, he will probably discover that they cost far less than he had imagined. He will find that these responses are supported by attention from the teacher and from his peers: "Let's all clap for Lenord. He's really doing a good job."

If, however, the frequency of appropriate responses is very low, you will not have much opportunity to show the child that you are reducing the cost of appropriate behavior. The child is not responding frequently enough to discover this. There are several possible solutions. First try to reach the child by reinforcing the children who behave appropriately. When you use this approach, you are using the children who behave as models. If this approach doesn't work and if the offender is disruptive, you may have to use punishment.

Punishment is the means by which you make inappropriate responses cost more than appropriate responses. You do this by stripping reinforcing consequences from inappropriate behavior and substituting aversive consequences. Through punishment, it is possible to increase the cost of inappropriate behavior to the point where it is far greater than the cost of appropriate behavior.

Use punishment only when the child behaves appropriately so infrequently that it is difficult to reinforce him for appropriate behavior, or when his behavior affects the performance of the other children in the group. Punishment works, and for that reason it is sometimes dangerous to use. Teachers who discover the power of effective punishment (punishment that makes inappropriate behavior cost more than appropriate behavior) too often learn to rely on it to the exclusion of other techniques. They discover that they can rely almost exclusively on punishment to keep the children in line. They do not use praise. They do not try to restructure tasks to bring a payoff. They do not introduce routines that will get the children in gear for the tasks that are to come. Instead they punish.

The teacher must remember how effective punishment is and always try other means first. If these fail, she should use punishment, but only to get the child started, only to increase the number of times the child behaves appropriately so that she has some basis for reinforcing his appropriate behavior. When the child begins to behave appropriately, the punishment should cease.

Try to punish the disruptive child in the study group. If you send him out of the class, he may be reinforced. Schools usually do not have isolation booths that reduce the possibility of the child's having a good time while he is supposedly receiving punishment. Other teachers to watch the group or the disruptive child are usually not available at the moment they are needed. Furthermore, the child's misbehavior may be strongly reinforced by another teacher who may think that what he needs is to have somebody listen to him, hold him, or be his friend. Often children who are sent out of the room manage to receive further reinforcement from their peers by knocking on the door or distracting the teacher. Even though the offender cannot see into the classroom, he will certainly be able to hear the delighted giggles of his classmates.

By working with the child in the classroom in the presence of his peers, you will demonstrate to the child that (*a*) he is not receiving attention from his peers and (*b*) although he is receiving attention from you, it is far more costly than he had imagined it would be.

For the serious behavior problem, begin with commands that can be enforced. You cannot correct the child who does not say the word *house*, but you can correct the child who does not stand up on command by physically standing him up. Start with a set of simple commands, such as "Stand up" and "Sit down." If the child does not stand up on command, forcefully stand him up. From time to time remind him, "When I say 'stand up,' you stand up." If he manages to make the other members of the group laugh, ignore their responses. If he turns his head away or tries to communicate with other members of the group, forcefully turn his head back. Do not repeat commands. Say, "Stand up"; count to three to yourself and forcefully stand the child up.

Let the child know that you will continue with this punishment until he behaves: "We're going to keep on doing this until you do it right. Stand up. . . . Sit down."

After the period is over and the other children have left for their next class, keep the offender: "Now you're going to do the work you were supposed to do before. We're going to work until it is done." During this period, tell the child when his answers are right, but remember that this is a punishment session. You don't want the child to have so much fun that he will act up in order to have a private session with you. Keep the session strictly work until the very end. Then remind the child that he is smart and that he can do the work if he tries: "You're a smart boy, Lenord. You can do this stuff. All you have to do is work hard. Now, what are you going to do when you come into class tomorrow? Are you going to fool around? . . ." It often helps to be confidential with the offender: "If you promise not to tell. O.K.? . . . You're really one of the smartest boys I know, when you work. And you can work hard. Look at the good work you did just now. You can do it. Now when you come in tomorrow, I want to see you show those other children how smart you are."

You may have to have several sessions with the extremely disruptive child. Design punishment sessions so that—

- The child discovers that he doesn't receive much reinforcement from his peers while he is being punished.

- The child discovers that he has not escaped from the classroom tasks by misbehaving. He still has to do the assigned work during a makeup session.
- The makeup session is scheduled at a time when the other children are engaged in some form of enjoyable activity.
- You are more persistent than he is, and you are firm in insisting that he do his work. (He should learn that when you issue a command, such as "Stand up" or "Sit down," the command must be followed. From this lesson he can easily generalize that all your commands must be followed.)

Through this kind of effective punishment, the cost of the child's inappropriate responses are made very high. He will soon relinquish them in favor of less costly, more rewarding behaviors.

Tokens

Although most children will work well for praise and the payoffs that are built into the various tasks, these motivators may not be effective for a child with a serious behavior problem. The rule about reinforcing children is this: If the children don't work for a particular reinforcer, it is not sufficiently reinforcing for them. You must look for another set of reinforcers. Don't get caught in the trap of assuming that if a reinforcer works for one child it will work for all children. Children are different.

One way to get a child with a serious behavior problem working hard is to let him work for something he really wants.

1. Ask the child what he wants, or note some of the things he seems to be interested in.

2. Purchase something that he likes—perhaps a glider or a water pistol.

3. Explain to him how he can earn points to get the toy: "At the end of each period I'll give you points. If you work very hard, I'll give you ten points. If you don't work at all, I won't give you any points. When you get thirty points, you can have the glider."

4. Award points generously at first. The child should be able to earn his first toy after only one or two days. Don't use an absolute scale for awarding points. Behavior that would warrant only two or three points later in the program should receive eight or nine points initially.

5. Relate the child's performance to the points, both during the study session and when you tally the points at the end of the period:

"Listen to Lenord talk. I didn't know he had such a big, good voice."
When tallying the points: "Let's see, you did a pretty good job today.
You worked pretty hard and you really talked big. You surprised me.
All at once, here's Lenord talking with a great big voice. You earned
eight points."

6. When you give the child the toy that he has earned, remind
him of his performance: "Do you know why you're getting this glider?
Because you worked hard. You're a good worker and you're getting
better all the time. See what happens when you work hard? A glider,
and it's all yours."

7. Tell the child that you're going to have to change the rules for
the next prize: "I'm going to make this next prize tougher for you. I
thought it would take you a long, long time to earn this glider, but
look at what you did. You got it in *one day*. Thirty points in one day.
That's too much. So do you know how many points you're going to
have to earn for this squirt gun (and remember—you can't use it in
school)? One hundred points! Whew, that's a lot! Probably take
you forever to earn that."

8. Award points generously for the second prize. Focus on the
child's improvement: "You're getting better all the time. Imagine—ten
points."

9. After the second prize, see if the child will work effectively for
special privileges: "I'll tell you what I'm going to do this time, Lenord.
I'm going to give you a chance to do something really special. You
know, at the end of the period I need somebody to erase the
chalkboard for me. Now I normally do that myself, because I know
that all the children want to do it and they'll start fighting over who
gets to do it. I don't want to get the other children mad, but here's
what I'll do. If you earn twenty-five points every day, I'll let you erase
the board at the end of the period."

10. Support the child's appropriate behavior with praise as you
introduce prizes of lesser value. As the child progresses, his behavior
should be increasingly supported by the kinds of social reinforcement
that work for other children.

Making the tasks easier

When the tasks presented in the study periods become too
difficult for the children, the children will respond with an increased
output of inappropriate behavior. The child who acts up in a class
quite a bit, although considered intelligent enough by his teachers, may

not have learned a host of essential skills needed for the tasks being presented. For this child, the cost of appropriate responses is increased. He cannot consistently give the right answers. As a result, he does not consistently receive reinforcement from the teacher. Even if he does receive reinforcement from *her*, he receives no reinforcement from *the task*. Working on the task for him is hard and mysterious. The payoffs associated with the task have no value to him.

When working with a child who exhibits a serious behavior problem, always be suspicious about what he actually knows. The chances are good that he knows less than you may imagine.

A child will not feel that he is a success in the new-learning situation if (*a*) the teacher focuses on the child's failures rather than on his successes or if (*b*) he can see by comparing himself with other children in the group that they can handle the tasks and he cannot. A child cannot be supported solely by social reinforcement if he receives no demonstrations that he is succeeding with the work. You cannot convince the child that he is doing well when he receives constant demonstrations that he is not. The misbehaving child may have a history of failure and may be reluctant to engage in the classroom tasks. He may feel that he will perform more poorly than the other children. For this reason, *it is always a good practice to put a misbehaving child into a lower-performing group.* If you put him in with children who probably know less than he does, you are ensuring that he will receive reinforcement.

Again make sure that the curriculum proceeds in small steps. The misbehaving child will probably react poorly to new learning. In the lower group the new learning proceeds more slowly, and he will be less threatened by the performance demands of the new situation. If the tasks are properly structured, he will learn that he can do well—perhaps better than the other children in the group, almost certainly as well. In either case he will succeed part of the time, and you will be able to reinforce him for real success. When you say "Wow! You're really a smart boy," your comment will not be hollow, because the child cannot compare his performance with that of children who are performing better. He will be more likely to believe you, take the praise seriously, and work harder for it.

4   Reading for the Nonreader

A nonreader is a child who cannot read three-letter words that are phonetically regular. Like John, the nonreader may have learned a few words that he recognizes at sight, but generally he will not be able to discriminate between a familiar sight word and another word that is similar in configuration. Although he may always identify the word *little* correctly, he may also call other words *little—letter, light, listen*. The nonreader lacks the attack skills that allow him to derive the sound a word makes from the arrangement of the letters. Regardless of what grade the nonreader is in, he must learn these basic attack skills before he can hope to read. This chapter outlines the approach.

The Form of Instruction for the Nonreader

The act of reading is interesting, so interesting that it has been an obsession of American education for the last fifty years. The amount of research that has been conducted is appalling in terms of its productive yield. The controversy between the look-and-say method and the phonic approach has stimulated an incredible amount of discussion, and most of it has been sterile. The controversy is based on an argument over what reading is. Is it an experience, with the whole child participating in it meaningfully? Is it a mechanical code-cracking skill? There are two ways to resolve the controversy. The first is to conduct experiments with the two approaches and note which approach produces better readers. The second is to analyze the controversy carefully and see which arguments are reasonable.

Jeanne Chall, in her book *Learning to Read*, has provided an eloquent answer to which of the approaches gets better results. Her well-documented analysis shows that just insofar as code cracking is diluted with "sight-reading experience" will the approach be inferior to the intensive code-cracking program. The evidence in favor of the phonic approach is overwhelming.

An analysis of the skills that must be used in reading provides the same answer. The code-cracking, mechanical skills are logically prior to the gross experience of meaningful reading. To see why they are logically prior, consider the child who is asked to read the statement *The horse is on the ridge*. The child may read the statement correctly, or he may not. He may or may not understand what he reads. There are a number of possible combinations. The most publicized possibility is that the child may read the statement correctly and not be able to demonstrate in any way that he understands what he has read. However, an equally interesting possibility is that he may not read the statement correctly and yet demonstrate that he understands what he has incorrectly read. For example, he may read "The horse is on the bridge," and when he is asked to draw a picture of what he has read, he may draw a picture of a horse on a bridge. Does he understand what he read or doesn't he? If we say that he does, we are giving both "reading" and "comprehension" rather strange meanings. If we say that he doesn't, we are admitting that code cracking (the ability to translate written symbols into appropriate word sounds) is logically prior to comprehension. We are saying that the child cannot possibly demonstrate that he understands the statement unless he first reads it correctly. The most basic question is not "Can he understand what he reads?" but "Can he read what is written?" Before he can comprehend, he must correctly identify the words that appear in a statement. The first step in reading, therefore, must be to teach the child how to identify words correctly. This step has nothing to do with meaningful experiences or with total involvement.

A teacher does not make the child's job any easier by teaching reading in connection with meaningful objects and meaningful experiences, because the basic skills that he must learn are *sound skills*, not skills associated with objects. All that he can derive from a series of symbols, such as *glickering* or *door*, is a series of speech sounds, not an object.

Let's look at the problem from another angle. Let's say that we are confronted with a child who correctly reads the statement *The horse is on the ridge*, but cannot demonstrate that he understands the meaning of the statement. If his failure is a reading failure, it should imply a remedy that is unique to reading. But does it? Let's say that we present the statement *The horse is on the ridge* verbally and then ask the child such questions as "What's a horse? What's a ridge? Was the horse under the ridge?" The child may fail some of these tests. Does it follow that we should work on reading? These tests are certainly not tests of reading, and we would be hard pressed to indicate how reading has anything to do with the child's failure. Yet it is almost certain that if a child cannot handle statements presented verbally, he will not be able to handle them in written form. In other words, the child cannot be expected to pass tests of reading comprehension unless he is able to pass comparable tests of language comprehension. But the remedy implied by a child's failure of a language test is *language instruction, not reading instruction.* The most obvious and direct remedy is to teach the child the meaning of that statement—teaching the meaning of each of the words and demonstrating the form of the statement.

In summary, there is one primary type of failure that calls for a reading remedy. That is the type in which the child does not correctly identify the words that are presented. In this situation there is no possibility that the child can comprehend what is written, because he cannot identify what is written. The remedy is to teach him how to translate the written symbols into appropriate sounds. The implication of this situation is that in reading instruction the first step is to teach the child how to identify words correctly. A further implication is that he must master *all the subskills involved in word identification.*

The Basic Reading Skills

The typical school failure is likely to encounter trouble with any of a number of subskills involved in word identification.

1. He may fail to learn the relation between individual letters and verbal sounds, or to learn that, in most words, every letter functions and that the same letter has the same sound-producing function in various words.

2. He may fail to learn how to blend. It is not all uncommon to see third-grade children who cannot read the word *cat.* A child sounds out the word, "*cu, ah, tu,*" and the teacher asks, "What word is that?" The child repeats, "*cu, ah, tu.*" The teacher becomes more insistent. "John, what word is that?" But the child stares at the word a moment before repeating, "*cu, ah, tu.*"

3. He may fail to learn that there are "regular" words and "irregular" words. He may be able to read the word *bat* but fail to read the word *ball* (because the *a* in ball has a different sound from the *a* in bat). And then, when exposed to the idea that words are not always regular, he may conclude that spelling is purely arbitrary and go on a wild guessing spree—perhaps calling the word *many* "people" because the two words had been presented together on a previous occasion.

A carefully worked-out reading program must help the child over these potential trouble spots. If the program is to succeed, it must focus on the hidden verbal skills. Rhyming is a hidden verbal skill. Let's say that a child attempts to sound out the word *fan*, and he knows that the last part of the word is *an*. Unless he can rhyme, however, he may not understand that when *f* is added to *an*, the word will rhyme with *an*. Before the child can be expected to handle this task, he should be required to demonstrate that he can handle a similarly constructed *verbal task:* "O.K., JC, we're going to rhyme with *an*. Listen big: *fff* . . ." Unless the child can complete words by rhyming, he will probably encounter trouble when he tries to sound out words.

Another pair of hidden verbal skills consists of sounding out words that are presented verbally and then telescoping the sounds together. He must learn the relation between the word when it is sounded out and the word spoken at a normal speaking rate. Many school failures are unable to perceive this relation. The teacher may tell the child, "I'm going to show you a picture of a f–a–n. What am I going to show you a picture of?" The child may be unable to answer the question. Or he may be unable to handle the more difficult task of sounding out a word: "Listen, John. I'm going to sound out a word: *fan*. Sound it out: *f–a–n*. Your turn: *fan*. Sound it out." The child may repeat the word at a normal speaking rate.

The reading program outlined in this chapter provides for the teaching of the hidden verbal skills. It is geared to the child who has not been taught these skills at home. It structures tasks so that the children will be transported over the trouble spots of sound and letter correspondence, blending, and irregular words. By following it, a teacher should be able to teach the potential school failure the critical reading skills of code cracking. Chapter 5 extends these skills and integrates them into a realistic comprehension program.

Word counting

The first rule the disadvantaged nonreader must learn is that people talk in words and that words are entities. For the child to understand this, he must be able to count events.

1. Without any great buildup, say, "Listen to what I say: *She is happy.* Say it with me." After the children have repeated the statement a few times, ask, "How many words are there in *She is happy?*" Repeat the statement slowly, pausing between the words: "*She—is—happy.* How many words? Let's count them" (assuming the children understand what this means). Repeat the statement, a word at a time, and hold up a finger for each word: "Three words. *She —is—happy.*" Have the children count the words with you by holding up fingers: "How many words? Three words." Don't attempt to explain what you mean by *word.* The meaning will become clear from your demonstrations.

2. After the children have counted the words successfully, introduce the next task: "Listen to what I say: *Is she happy?* How many words did I say? Listen again: *Is she happy?*" The purpose of following the statement with a question using the same words is to make the children aware that a word is a unit independent of the other words that occur before or after it.

3. After counting the words in the question *Is she happy?* with the children several times (asking the question "How many words?"), introduce a variety of statements for the children to analyze. *Use statements that contain at least one two-syllable word.* Unless two-syllable words are programed from the beginning, the child may get the idea that a word is a syllable, and that to count words, one simply counts the syllables.

Initially introduce only nouns that do not require the articles (*a* or *the*), and only statements that use a form of the verb *to be:*

> Fish are animals.
> We are sitting down.
> John is smiling at me.
> They were driving cars.

After the children have counted the words in a statement, convert the statement into a question: *Are fish animals? Is John smiling at me?* (These statements can be converted into questions merely by changing the order of the words.)

4. After the children have demonstrated that they can count the words in short sentences, introduce statements containing articles (but still using a form of the verb *to be*):

> A dog is an animal.
> The dog is brown.
> He is a happy boy.
> She is a woman.

The children may have some trouble counting articles as separate words. When counting the words with them, say the sentence very slowly and emphasize the articles, so that the children get used to hearing them: "Listen: *She—is—UH—woman*." Do not produce the word *a* as long *a* unless you would normally do so.

Work on the articles (*a, an, the*) until the children have a solid understanding that they are words. You can draw this conclusion when the children consistently count them as words.

(NOTE: In the first set of exercises a word always changed position from statement to question: *These are men. Are these men?* In the second set, most of the words changed position: *This is a man. Is this a man?* The article, however, still preceded the word *man*, which makes it relatively more difficult for the child to learn about articles than about such words as *is* and *man*.)

5. If the child continues to have difficulty recognizing articles as words, introduce a basic statement with different articles, thereby demonstrating that articles can be removed from a statement.

Introduce a statement in which the article is the first word uttered:

> A dog is an animal.

Then, after counting the words, introduce variations:

> The dog is an animal.
> This dog is an animal.

Introduce a series of similar examples.

To demonstrate how the article *an* works, convert the statement into plural:

> These dogs are animals. (The *an* has disappeared.)
> Those dogs are animals.
> Dogs are animals.

Also convert plural into singular:

> Cows are animals.
> A cow is an animal.

If the child does not understand the difference between singular and plural (which is quite possible if he is a disadvantaged Negro), introduce basic language tasks. A procedure for teaching the distinction between singular and plural is outlined in the book *Teaching Disadvantaged Children in the Preschool*, by Carl Bereiter and Siegfried Engelmann.

6. Introduce statements that use verbs other than *to be*. If the child has successfully handled the preceding tasks, he should have no trouble with these. Start with relatively short statements (ideally one-word or two-word statements), and work up to seven- and eight-word statements. First repeat each statement slowly, then have the children repeat it, and finally have them count the words. Here are examples at the different levels of difficulty:

> Stop.
>
> Let's eat.
>
> Slow down.
>
> Let's play ball.
>
> Who likes hamburgers?
>
> Where did John go?
>
> He ran down a big hill.
>
> Earthmen live on the planet Earth.
>
> Don't ask me if you can have a cooky.

If the children have difficulty with a particular word, use the word in various sentences. For example, if the children indicate that *planet* is two words, introduce several other sentences containing *planet*, strongly emphasizing the word:

> Mars is a planet.
>
> Planets do not burn up.

The children may not understand that events as well as objects can be counted. To correct this deficit, show them that you can count the number of times you clap your hands, then the number of times you jump, the number of times you open your mouth, and so on. Also introduce sets of mixed events: clap, stand, stamp. "How many things did I do?"

The children may have difficulty hearing what they say as a series of units that can be counted. The remedy is to give them ample practice. Soon the children should show good progress.

Rhyming

Begin to work on rhyming as soon as the children have finished their first word-counting exercises. This first set of exercises has demonstrated what words are. They provide an operational definition that can be used in talking about words that rhyme.

1. Introduce rhyming with the following instructions: "Listen to this word: *money.* Say it: *money.* Say the word very slowly: *muuuney.* I'm going to say words that rhyme with *money.* Here I go: *honey, funny, bunny.* Listen—they all rhyme: *money, funny, bunny, honey.* If I ask you for a word that rhymes with *money,* you can say *honey,* or you can say—what, John?"

Play a game in which you say only the first part of the word and the children have to complete the word: "I want words that rhyme with *money.* I go first. Then you say *neee. Fu*—say it fast: *funny; bu*—say it fast: *bunny.*"

The children may have trouble at first. If they do, go through each word, breaking it down into syllables and having the children repeat the words with you. Breaking down the words demonstrates that the last part of each word is the same: *fu–ney, hu–ney, bu–ney, mu–ney.* Then return to the game.

2. Start rhyming exercises with words of more than one syllable. The one-syllable word is more difficult for the beginner to handle, because the part of the word that rhymes is small. Words that rhyme with *cat,* for example, have only *at* in common. Here are some of the better words to work on:

> hopping, stopping, mopping, bopping
> mister, sister, blister
> slapping, napping, tapping, capping
> sitting, fitting, knitting, spitting

Go through a rhyme series several times, breaking down each word into syllables.

Have the children repeat each word with you.

Then produce only the first sound and have the children complete the word *mis–.* Don't be dismayed if they fail on this task, perhaps producing bizarre words. If they are unable to complete the words, show them how and put the parts together to form the word: *mis–ter . . . mister; sis–ter . . . sister.*

3. Introduce nonsense words as soon as the children have begun to master the preceding tasks. Start with the word *hamburger:* "I'm going to make up words that rhyme with *hamburger.* Here I go: *famburger . . . ramburger . . . whamburger.*" Point out that these words do not mean anything: "I don't know what a *whamburger* is,

88

but it rhymes with *hamburger*." Have the children repeat the rhyming words with you. Then have them make up words that rhyme with *hamburger:* "Who can do that?" If the children don't respond, say, "Listen: *hamburger . . . ram–*" Encourage the children to provide the appropriate endings: "Here's another one: *fam–*. And another: *sam–*."

4. Follow *hamburger* with other relatively long words, such as *Pontiac, television, crocodile*. Introduce the word with four or five nonsense words that rhyme with it. After going through the series several times with the children, see if they can produce any of the rhyming words. Finally, see if they can complete the words if you provide the first syllable. Always give the model word before asking for the rhyming word: "Rhyming with *crocodile: soc–, noc–, loc–*."

5. Reduce the cue for producing the desired word.

Begin with a relatively long cue: "O.K., I want you to give me a word that rhymes with *Cadillac*. It starts with *fad*. Rhymes with *Cadillac: fad–, mad–, dad–, sad–*."

Cue them with smaller sound units: "I want a word that rhymes with *Cadillac*. Rhymes with *Cadillac: ma–, ba–, sa–*." And so on.

Reduce the cue to a single letter sound: "I want a word that rhymes with *Cadillac: m–*. Rhymes with *Cadillac: sh–*."

Use the procedure outlined above with a variety of longer words. Present two or three words a day.

6. As the children become increasingly proficient with long words, introduce short words.

Use common words that he will encounter in beginning reading materials, such as *dog, have, he, has, me, to, new, who*. Present only the initial sound to be used in rhyming: "It rhymes with *he: r–*."

Use nonsense rhymes liberally. If you only use words, the child may not catch on to the idea that there is a general rule for producing rhymes that applies to any combination of sounds. The child must learn to deal with syllables, and these are often nonsensical: *cred, gov, tion*. He will also deal with parts of words, such as *op* (as in *shop, stop, crop*), *ent* (as in *sent, bent, went*), *oon* (as in *spoon, moon, noon*). These are not meaningful words, but obviously they are important.

Alliterating

Practice in alliteration teaches the child that an initial letter sound can be used to form different words. Alliteration skills are not as important as rhyming skills, and they are not as difficult to teach.

1. Introduce alliteration tasks after the children are able to rhyme from a single-sound cue (a word that rhymes with *batman:* it's *f–*). Present the task of making up words that *start the same way.*

Begin with entire syllables and decrease the cue that is given until the child is able to work from a single sound or a group of difficult consonant sounds (*spl*): "Listen. I'm going to say some words that start the same way as *ice cream.* Here I go: *ice–cube, ice–ing, ice–icle.*" Separate the sounds of the words so that the children can hear clearly what is being held constant.

Have the children repeat the words that start the same way.

2. Give them practice on such series as these:

pa–int, pa–le, pa–ce, pa–per, pa–ste

let–ter, let–tuce, let–ting

in–sect, in–side, in–to, in–ner.

Accent the first part of each word strongly and then add the remainder. Have the children identify the word. They may not be familiar with some of the words. If a child offers a nonsense word, accept it, adding, "I don't know what that means, but it starts the same as *in–sect,* doesn't it?" Repeat the series above until the children have learned them by rote.

3. Move to short words in which you give only a single sound as a cue: "I want words that start the same way as *run: r–.*"

Here are some good words to introduce initially:

f–an

d–og

s–ing

Use other words that have a single consonant before the vowel. Repeat words from time to time until the children can handle them.

4. Now introduce double-consonant sounds. These are more difficult, but it is a good idea to work on them as verbal exercises. Children often have a great deal of trouble trying to read such words as *creep* and *sleep.*

Say, "O.K., here's a tough one. I want some words that start the same way as *st–op.*" Make two distinct sounds at the beginning of the word: *s–t–op.* (Neither sound should be voiced. See page 97.) "What word is that?" Don't be surprised if the children have difficulty identifying it. Simply repeat the word faster: "*St–op.* What word is that? . . . Yes, *stop.* And I want some words that start the same way as stop: st–."

Concentrate on the beginnings *cr, br, cl, bl, fl, sl, sp, st.*

Work on alliteration should take only a few minutes a day.

Saying words fast

1. Introduce "saying it fast" as soon as children have completed Step 2 in rhyming: "Listen to this story. I'm going to say some of the words slowly. See if you can tell me what they are. I went to a store where I saw a wo– [pause] man. What did I see? . . . I saw a woman. She was carrying a basket full of pup–pies. What was she carrying? . . . Yes, puppies. One of the pup–pies was wearing a red neck–tie. What was he wearing? . . . Yes, a red necktie. I said, 'That pup–py sure looks fun–ny.' " Pause for about one second between the parts of the words.

For the introduction, keep the story line strong, so that the words are somewhat predictable.

Initially, use only words that break into two syllables. If the children have a great deal of difficulty with these, introduce longer words, with only a single break: *ham–burgers, Cad–illac, el–ephant, min–ister, mo–torboat.*

Work on "saying it fast" for four to six minutes a day.

2. After the children have demonstrated that they can handle words that break into syllables, break one-syllable words into letter sounds. Begin by separating the first sound from the remainder of the word: "I saw a man wearing a great big sh–oo. On his other foot he had a s–ock. His hat had a h–ole in it. And he was eating a piece of w–ood."

Begin to mix the unpredictable with the predictable to show the child that he can't always guess the word from the context.

3. Next, break short words in more than one place: "His c–a–t was b–i–g." If the children have trouble with this task, avoid words that begin with *b, c, d, g, k, p,* and *t.* Use only words that begin with *a, e, f, h, i, l, m, n, o, r, s, w*—with primary emphasis on *f, m, n, r, s,* and the vowels. (These are continuous-sound letters. They can be held as long as you wish. Stop sounds such as *b* cannot be held. See page 97.) "At one e–n–d of the r–a–t w–u–z a big r–e–d n–o–s–e."

Have the children identify each word before proceeding to the next. Then summarize the statement up to that point. For example, if the children have completed the word *was,* summarize and continue, "At one end of the rat was a big r–e–d . . . What's that? . . . Yes, a big red n–o–s–e. . . . A big red what? . . . A big red nose."

After the children have learned to handle the initial set of letters, introduce words that begin with stop sounds (*b, c, d, g, k, p,* and *t*). Work extensively on words that start with these letters. The child's success in reading depends on his ability to blend these sounds. "So h–e said . . . Who said it? . . . 'Let's play b–a–ll.' Let's do what? Play . . . But he forgot his c–a–p. What did he forget? . . ."

Remember—*c, k, p,* and *t* are not voiced. They are produced by letting air escape from the mouth.

4. After the children become familiar with say-it-fast, drop the story line and work only from words.

Present a series of three-sound words in which the first and the last sound remain the same while the vowel changes. "Listen to these words and tell me what they are: *c–a–t, c–u–t, k–i–t.*" Do not always vary the vowel changes in the same order. "Here are some other words: *g–e–t, g–o–t, g–u–t, g–a–t.*"

Never work for more than a minute or two a day on these series. The children will forget how to process the sounds after a short period of time. The best practice is to present one series of words, such as *m–a–n, m–oo–n, m–a–ne, m–ea–n,* at the beginning of the period, changing the order of the words each time a series is presented. Repeat it in the middle of the period and review it at the end of the period. At the end of the period also introduce a series the children have worked on before.

Verbal blending tasks

1. Give the children a sound or syllable that they are to link with another sound or syllable that you give, the combination forming a word.

Start with relatively easy units, such as *on, un, at, in, ar:* "O.K., John, say *at.* When I tap you like this, say *at.* Don't worry about what I say; you're going to say—what? . . . Yes, *at.*" Say *mmmm* (one long humming sound) and tap the child. "Let's do it again and see what word we have: *mmmm–at.* Say it fast and you'll see what word it is: *mat.* Let's hear it again: *mmmmm–at.* O.K., let's try another one. Remember, John, you're going to say *at.* Here we go: *ffff–*[tap]*at.* What word is that? . . . Listen again: *fff–at.* Say it fast, everybody: *fat.*"

Introduce various examples. For the first sound of these words, use the sounds of the letters *n, l, f, s, m.*

2. Present the task of adding a single-sound ending: "This is tough. Everybody say *nnn*. Come on, get it going so I can hear it. *NNNNN*. That's good. Now when I clap, you say *nnn*. O.K., here we go: *o*–[clap]*nn*. What word is that? Listen again: *o–nn* . . . *o–n*. Say it fast: *on*. Let's try another. Remember—you say *nnn*. O.K.: *i*–[clap]*nn*. Again: *i*–[clap]*nn*. Faster: *i*–[clap]*n*. What word is that? *In*." Introduce exercises in which the children are asked to produce the *i* sound, the *r* sound (*ear*), and the *m* sound (*me*) on signal.

3. Introduce exercises in which the children are required to produce a vowel sound on signal: "O.K. When I clap, you say *ee*. Come on, open up: *ee*. Here we go: *m*–[clap]*ee*. Say it fast: *me*."

Introduce exercises in which the children produce the sounds *oo* (as in *moo*), all the short vowel sounds, and the long sounds *a, e, i, o*.

Work on blending tasks until the children master them. The more thoroughly they learn to handle these tasks, the better prepared they will be to read.

Saying words slowly

After the children have completed Step 3 in saying words fast, they can start saying words slowly. This set of tasks makes the child aware that any spoken word can be broken into parts, and familiarizes him with the procedure.

Keep one point prominently in mind when presenting these tasks. The letter-by-letter breakdown with which you are familiar is arbitrary. We consider, for example, that the word *I* has only one sound. The child, however, may contend that it has two sounds: *ah–y*. If a child says this, he is thinking. He is simply not looking at sounds in the conventional way. On the other side of the coin are words which we consider to have more sounds than may be apparent to the child. The word *were*, for example, he may judge to have only two sounds: *w–r*. The instruction in say-it-slow should concentrate on vowels and word endings, because these are more difficult for children to handle.

1. Begin by telling the children, "I'm going to say a word. See if you can say it slowly: *hamburger*. Say it slow: *hammm–burrgerr*. Your turn: *hamburger*. Say it slow." Introduce three or four relatively easy words (*elephant, bicycle, hot dog, celery*). If the children break down these words into at least two parts, accept their response.

2. Move directly from the introduction to more difficult words. The children should have an idea of what is expected. "Listen to this

93

word and see if you can say it slowly: *man*. Say it with me. . . . Now see if you can say it slowly. . . ." Have the children hold each sound and produce the next sound without pausing: *mmmmaaannn*. At first, introduce words that begin with the continuous (nonstop) sounds, especially *f, m, n, r,* and *s*. Introduce both one- and two-syllable words —*farm, fan, fish, fishing, mop, mother, meet, red, reading, running, sit, sitting*. (Remember that *f* and *s* are not voiced sounds.)

3. After the child has mastered continuous-sound beginnings, introduce words that begin with stop sounds. Initially, present words that have two sounds and begin with a single consonant, such as *b–ee, p–ie, k–ey, d–o, t–oo, b–y, d–ie, t–ie, t–ea, g–o, g–uy*. Have the child produce two distinct sounds with a pause. This may be a little difficult for him at first. Go over the troublesome words until he can manage them.

4. After the child has mastered two-sound words, present three-sound words that begin with a stop sound. Have him produce at least three sounds for each word. Work in series of words, such as *b–i–te, k–i–te, t–igh–t*. Add continuous-sound words to the series: *r–igh–t, m–igh–t, s–igh–t, f–igh–t*. (First have him say each continuous-sound word slowly, with no breaks between the sounds. Then have him pause between sounds. If he is unable to pause, show him how: "*B–i–te*. Say that: *b–i–te*. . . . Good. What word is that? *Bite*."

Present the following groups of words. Work on one or two groups during each session.

> gum, come, dumb, some, hum
> big, dig, rig, gig
> tag, gag, sag, nag
> top, bop, cop, hop
> but, gut, nut, cut

5. Introduce *word endings* after the children have become reasonably proficient at handling the tasks in Step 3 above. Endings begin with vowels; initially they may give some trouble.

Use the same basic instructions as those for the tasks above. *Point out, however, that these are "funny words":* "I'm going to say a funny word. Listen: *ot*. I don't know what it means, but I can say it. How would I say it slowly? *O–t*. How would I say this one: *īt*." (Pronounce as in *fight*.) "Listen again: *īt*. Say it slowly: *ī–t*."

Begin with two-sound "words" formed by linking a vowel with a consonant (either stop or continuous-sound). Make a series of similar words by changing the initial vowel sound and holding the consonant constant. Begin with the series *at, et, ot, it, ut, oot, ite, eet, ote, ate*. Have the children pause between the sounds.

Follow the initial series with these: *an, en, in, on, un, oon, ine, een, own, ad, ed, id, od, ud, aid, ide, ood, eed, ode, am, em, im, om, um, ame, eme, ime, af, ef, if, uf, afe, efe, oof, ash, esh, osh, ush, oosh*. Mix the order in which you present these "words" so that the children will pay attention to the word, not to the order.

6. After the children have learned how to say these "words" slowly with fair consistency, introduce three-letter endings.

Have the children produce three sounds for each of these: *ant, ent, int, ont, unt, aint, ast, est, ist, ost, ust, east, ost, asp, esp, isp, osp, amp, emp, imp, omp, ump*.

Expect the children to learn the three-sound endings only after considerable exposure. The sound combinations are new, and the children may have trouble holding on to the component sounds in isolation—especially the short *e* sound (*end*), the short *a* sound (*and*), and the short *i* sound (*in*).

When the children have mastered the verbal sound drills outlined in this section, they will have demonstrated that they possess the skills necessary to hold groups of sounds constant (such as the group *ent*) while they fit the appropriate beginning sound to it to form a word (*sent*). They will understand that the word *sent* should rhyme with the group *ent*. And they will understand that words are composed of sound units which can be heard in the word and can be separated with a pause. If the children fail to read, it won't be because they lack the necessary verbal skills.

Letter Identification

Work on letters should begin on the first day of reading instruction.

The approach to teaching letters is based on the idea that letters have sounds. Initially, rigid rules are presented: a particular letter has a particular sound, and no other letter has that sound. The letter *a* always has the sound short *a* (as in *and*); the letter *l* always has the sound *l* (as in *low*). Many children fail to learn to read because they are not taught that each letter in a word has a function, and that ideally a sound value is attached to each letter. If the child fails to learn this rule, he is obviously not in a good position to find parts of words (see the *and* in *sand*), because he does not know that the letters *and* always have the sounds *a–n–d*.

To dramatize the way in which letters function, the teacher must present the general rule before presenting exceptions. This means that in early reading instruction each letter symbol is identified with one and only one sound and that all the sounds are then telescoped to produce a word. Initially, the word *to* is not pronounced *too;* it is pronounced *to* (as in *top*). Once the child has learned the universal rule that words are produced by identifying each symbol with a particular sound, he can be taught irregular words relatively easily. If he has not been taught the basic regularity of the code, however, he may never see the relation between the word and the sounds of which it is composed. Most irregular words are irregular only in the sense that the vowels do not add up. If the child has a set of rules by which to compare the behavior of vowels in various words, he is in a much stronger position than he would be if he had no idea how vowels functioned, or that they were supposed to have a function. The most efficient approach is to program a set of basic rules that allows the child to "read" words and then, as he becomes facile with the reading operation, to introduce irregularities (an irregular word being any word that deviates from the rules the child has already learned). In this way irregularities are understandable. They have been related to something the child already knows.

The program starts with the sounds of the letters—not the names. The teacher must be familiar with each sound. Unless she is, she will mislead the children.

1. Program the initial set of letters. Present no more than two letters at a time. When the children have mastered them, introduce two more. Do not drill for more than five minutes a day on letter identification. Do not rush the children. When they have learned all the sounds in the initial set, introduce reading tasks. Note that the children are not required to master all the letter sounds they will encounter before they start reading. Slow-learning children become extremely confused if they are required to learn letter sounds too rapidly. As a rule, they cannot be expected to learn more than two new sounds a week; they will need the greatest amount of practice on the vowels; they will tend to confuse letters that are presented at the same time, regardless of how different in configuration these letters may be.

96

Here are the letter sounds in the initial set:

a, ē, i, o, m, r, f, s

Note that these are continuous-sound letters. A continuous sound is one that can be held indefinitely. The first sound in the word *fan* (*fff*) can be held as long as you wish. (A noncontinuous sound, or stop sound, cannot be held. The first sound in the word *ball* must be produced very quickly; it cannot be held until the next sound is produced. Therefore there will be pauses in the word as the children sound it out. The pauses make the similarity between the sounded-out word and the say-it-fast word less obvious.) The advantage of introducing continuous sounds first is that they allow the construction of words that are easy for the children to read. The children read these words by holding a sound until they produce the next sound. *They do not pause between sounds.* Therefore, when they sound out a word, they are actually just saying the word slowly. They have already been taught the relation between words that are said slowly and the same words spoken at a normal rate. By saying the word quickly after first sounding it out, they can identify the word. The key to solving the blending problem is to start with the continuous-sound letter.

The "name" of each letter is given below. Note that these are the only names to be used in referring to the symbol. These names are the sounds the symbols make.

a   voiced sound as in *and* (represented in the dialogues of this book as *aaa*)

ē   voiced sound as in *eat* (represented as *ēēē*)

i   voiced sound as in *it* (represented as *iii*)

o   voiced sound as in *on* (represented as *ooo*)

m   voiced sound as in *mat* (represented as *mmm*)

r   voiced sound as in *ran* (represented as *rrr*)

f   unvoiced sound as in *fan* (represented as *fff*)

s   unvoiced sound as in *sand* (represented as *sss*)

A voiced sound is one in which there is a vocal effort. An unvoiced sound is produced simply by moving air; no vocalization is involved. You can feel the difference between voiced and unvoiced sounds by placing your hand on your throat and saying the word *fan* very slowly. Notice that you feel no vocal vibrations from your throat until you produce the *a* sound. The vibrations continue as you produce the *n* sound. Now say the word *fat* very slowly. You feel no vibrations for the *f* sound. You do feel them for the *a* sound. You do not feel

97

them for the *t* sound. The *f* sound and the *t* sound are unvoiced. The *a* sound is voiced.

Be very careful about accurately producing the letter sounds in the basic set. The *f* sound (*fff*) is not pronounced *fffuu*, with a voiced ending. It is produced as a single sound that does not change—*fffff*. There is no voice behind the sound, and it is possible to hold the sound until you run out of breath. The sound *ē*, on the other hand, is a voiced sound. It, too, can be held until you run out of breath. In fact, all the sounds in the basic set can be held in this way. Practice holding each of these sounds for at least five seconds. Refer to the guide word above for the correct pronunciation, and familiarize yourself with the sounds thoroughly before trying to teach them. Concentrate especially on the vowel sounds. There are many different sounds for the letter *a*. Unless you know that you are going to use only one of them—the sound that is in the word *at*—you may find yourself pronouncing *al* like *awl* rather than like the *al* in *Alfred*.

2. After the children have mastered the initial set and have begun to read words formed with these letters, continue to present new sounds at the rate of about one new sound a week. Increase this rate only if the children are thoroughly solid on the sounds that have been introduced and seem to be able to proceed more rapidly. Do not increase the rate of presentation unless every child in the group has mastered the letters that have been presented. Teach each child individually. Do not judge the performance of individual children on how well the *group* responds in unison to questions about letter identification. The group may give the impression of being very solid, but individual children in the group may not know some of the sounds.

Introduce new sounds in this order:

l voiced sound as in *lap* (represented in the dialogues of this book as *lll*)

d voiced stop sound as in *did* (represented as *d*)

n voiced sound as in *nap* (represented as *nnn*)

ā voiced sound as in *ate* (represented as *āāā*)

t unvoiced stop sound as in *tap* (represented as *t*)

u voiced sound as in *up* (represented as *uuu*)

c unvoiced stop sound as in *cap* (represented as *c*)

h unvoiced stop sound as in *had* (represented as *h*)

w voiced sound as in *will* (represented as *www*)

g voiced stop sound as in *gas* (represented as *g*)

b   voiced stop sound as in *bill* (represented as *b*)

k   unvoiced stop sound as in *kite* (represented as *k*)

e   voiced sound as in *egg* (represented as *eee*)

p   unvoiced stop sound as in *pin* (represented as *p*)

ō   voiced sound as in *open* (represented as *ōōō*)

j   voiced sound as in *jump* (represented as *jjj*)

y   voiced sound as in *yes* (represented as *yyy*)

ī   voiced sound as in *ice* (represented as *īīī*)

z   voiced sound as in *zoo* (represented as *zzz*)

x   complex unvoiced sound as in *fox* (represented as *ks*)

qu complex voiced sound as in *quick* (represented as *qqww*)

The *h* sound is particularly difficult to pronounce. It is almost a panting sound, with no voice—*hhhh*. Work on this sound.

Stop sounds are introduced as word endings rather than as word beginnings. A stop sound at the beginning of a word interrupts the flow of the sounding-out procedure, and words beginning with stop sounds should not be introduced until the children have mastered words beginning with continuous sounds.

Note that the two often-used sounds *d* and *b* are widely separated in the order of introduction. This is necessary because the letters representing these sounds appear to the child as the same object viewed from different sides. In the everyday world of the child, objects retain their identity regardless of position (a chair is a chair whether it is right side up or upside down). *D* is taught early because of its usefulness as an ending sound, whereas *b* is delayed until the children are ready to attack words beginning with stop sounds. Once both letters are introduced, the child begins to learn a new rule: Letters are named according to their position. This rule will apply also to the letters *p* and *q*.

Note that there is a long and a short variation of each vowel except *u*. The long variation is the letter name (as in the alphabet). It has a diacritical mark over it. The short sound does not have a diacritical mark. One advantage of using the diacritical mark for long vowels is that it allows you to present a number of words without misspelling them. The word *he* is presented as "hē." The child reads the word simply by combining the sounds. After he has been exposed to this word several hundred times, you can remove the diacritical mark and he will still read the word as "he." Another advantage of this use of the diacritical mark is that it introduces the child to the "double

99

take" so often required in reading new material. For example: A relatively advanced reader may identify the word *delicate* as "*dee*licate." In order to arrive at the proper pronunciation, he must "double take" and give the vowel *e* a short sound. The present program gives the children a great deal of experience in identifying the same configuration (*e*) as both *eee* (as in *egg*) and *ēēē* (as in *eat*). The program therefore prepares the child for situations in which he will have to experiment with vowel sounds.

Rules for presenting letter sounds

1. Some of the children may already have learned to identify letters by alphabet name. If they have, tell them that the letters have sounds: "Yes, this is ef. And it has the sound *fff*." Use the question form: "What sound does this have?" This should not be confusing to them. Say, "Don't tell me that it's the letter *f;* tell me what sound it has."

2. In working with children who are weak on identifying letters, spend no more than several minutes on letter identification during a session.

Don't try to explain the configuration of the letters (or at least don't rely on such descriptions to teach the children).

Give the children daily practice in writing two different letters, saying the sound of the letter as they write it.

Present plenty of examples of letters when teaching the sounds.

Present examples on the chalkboard.

Demonstrate that a given letter can be made in various sizes and colors, using various thicknesses of chalk.

From time to time, present letters on cards to demonstrate that letters can also appear on various background materials, and can be surrounded by shapes such as the rectangular outline of a card.

3. The ideal presentation is one in which the teacher works fast, asking the children to find a particular letter, identify a particular letter, find examples that are not a particular letter, and answer the yes-no questions about these.

Write five *a*'s on the board and three letters that are not similar in configuration to *a*—for example *i, r,* and *f.*

Identify one of the *a*'s: "This is the sound *a*." Then ask one of the children to find other *a*'s: "John, find another *a*. . . . Good. Tell me what it is and you can erase it." Don't require full statements, just the appropriate sound. "Good, *a*. Find another *a*. . . . And another. . . . Good. Erase them. Mary, find a great big *a*. . . . Erase it. George, find a little bitty *a*. . . . Tell me about it. . . . This *a* is little."

Next, ask the children to "find a sound that is not *a*." After a child finds an appropriate sound, ask, "Is this an *a*? . . . That's right. It is not an *a*. Erase it."

Introduce a fooler game after identifying the *a*'s and not-*a*'s: "I'm going to touch all the *a*'s. Tell me if I do it." Touch two or three *a*'s before touching a letter that is not an *a*. If the children do not respond, act amused: "Oh boy! I fooled you. This is not an *a*, and nobody caught me." If some of the children catch the mistake, praise them (or present a tangible reinforcer): "Good thinking. I couldn't fool you, could I?"

After the fooler game, move on to another task, preferably a verbal task, and return to the identification at the end of the period. Write the letter *a* on the board and ask the children, "What sound is this?" If they do not remember, remind them, and then assign the task of writing *a*'s on a sheet of lined paper. As they write, ask each child questions from time to time: "What sound is that? Is that an *m*? Is it an *a*? . . . Good." Remind them to talk to themselves: "Say the sound as you write it."

Remind the children of the letter sound they are studying as they leave the reading study group. Saying the name of the letter sound should be the last thing the children do before leaving the instructional group: "And what sounds are these on your paper, John? . . . Good boy! Mary, what are these? . . ."

Continue to work on letter identification for two to four minutes a day until the children have learned to identify the letter sounds *a*, *i*, *o*, *m*, *r*, *ʃ*, *s*, *ē*. Remember—don't spend more than a total of about four minutes a day on letter sounds.

Reading Words Formed with Continuous Letters

1. Introduce word reading after the children have mastered the initial set of sounds and after they have mastered say-it-fast, say-it-slow, and rhyming tasks.

Draw an arrow on the board from left to right. Explain, "I'm going to make letter sounds. When I point to them, you say them. Watch me." Make an *a* on the arrow shaft and produce the *a* sound: *aaa*. Point to the *a* and keep holding the sound, as one holds a note in music. While holding the *a* and pointing to it, make an *m* to the right

101

of the *a*. Point to the *m* and—*without pausing*—start making the *m* sound: *mmm*. "What word is that? Say it fast: *am*. Now you do it. Let's follow the arrow and say the sounds. Here we go: *aaaaammm*. Say it fast: *am*."

2. Erase the word and introduce the next "word": *ro* (as in *rot*). Before writing, remind the children, "When I point to it, you say it." Write the letter *r* and point to it. "Come on, keep it going. . . ." Write the letter *o* but keep pointing to the letter *r* for a moment, so that the children can formulate the sound they will produce when you move your finger. Then move it, and immediately—*without pausing*—start to produce the sound for *o* (as in *on*): *rrrooo*. "What word is it? *Ro*. That's a funny word. I don't know what it means, but I can say it."

3. Erase *ro* and present *am* again, a letter at a time, pointing to the first letter and then the second. The children will probably need some training in holding the first sound until they produce the second. Do not stress the idea that you are following the arrow. Make it a game of following your finger, which always moves from left to right and always follows the arrow. This type of demonstration is more effective in inducing the appropriate behavior. The children must know how to proceed from left to right, not merely how to describe the operation in words.

4. After working on five or six two-sound "words" (*me, if, fa, sa*, for example), introduce a three-sound word. This should be introduced very early in the reading instruction so that the child learns that "reading" applies not only to two-letter combinations but to other combinations as well. Present the word *seem* a letter at a time on the arrow shaft, holding the children on a letter until the next has been on the board for about a second. Introduce such three-sound "words" as *ram, Sam, fōm, sōl, fēl, mēl, sēl, rēl, fil, rim*.

5. Review all the examples presented two or three times. Try to make the children aware, through demonstrations, that the point of the game is to translate the sounds on the board into sounds that are sequenced in time and can be telescoped to form a word. If the game is handled properly, the children should start to see the relation between the present exercise and those involving saying words fast.

6. Present alliteration series after the children have become firm on two-sound words.

Begin by making a column of *ē*'s on the board, with each *ē* on an arrow shaft:

102

ē ⟶

ē ⟶

ē ⟶

ē ⟶

ē ⟶

Have the children identify the $\bar{e}$'s. Then return to the top line: "What sound is this? Keep it going. . . ."

Make an r after the $\bar{e}$, and after a moment's pause point to it. "$\bar{e}\bar{e}rr$. What word is this? Say it fast: *ear*. This is how we write the word *ear*."

Move to the second arrow. Point to the $\bar{e}$. What sound is this? Get it going. . . ." Add an f: "$\bar{e}\bar{e}ff$. What word is that? $\bar{e}f$. I don't know what it means, but I can say it: $\bar{e}f$." Point to the top example. "This word is $\bar{e}\bar{e}rr$, *ear*. And this word is $\bar{e}\bar{e}ff$, $\bar{e}f$."

Use the same procedure to complete the remaining "words": $\bar{e}s$, $\bar{e}m$, and $\bar{e}l$.

After the children have completed the series, play a game with them in which you supply the first sound and, when you point, they provide the second. Then they tell what "word" it is. "O.K., follow my point: $\bar{e}\bar{e}$——. Good, $\bar{e}m$. What about this one: $\bar{e}\bar{e}r$——. What word is that? $E\bar{e}\bar{e}rr$ . . . *ear*." Spend about five minutes a day on similar exercises, using the vowels i, o, and a. The tasks in which the children complete the words are very important. They are similar to the verbal exercises in which you provide one part of a word and the children complete the word by adding another part, except that the added part is no longer given, as it was in the verbal exercise (page 93). Now the children must *identify the sound*, hold it constant, and add it to the sound that you assigned. *The paradox of reading instruction becomes apparent with this type of exercise.* The most difficult verbal exercises are those in which the child must work with individual sounds such as a and r. Yet the easiest type of *reading* task is that in which there are the fewest elements, which means that the easiest reading tasks involve the most difficult verbal skills. It would be much easier for the child to read if we could start by giving him units such as *hamburger* to work with, but unless he knows how the sounds in the word *hamburger* derive from the letter arrangement, he cannot work from such units. He must work from smaller units in

103

which the verbal components of the task are more difficult. For this reason, many disadvantaged children fail to master early reading tasks. Skills in rhyming, alliterating, and saying words fast come into play in the simplest reading exercises.

7. Present consonant-first series as part of the work on alliteration.

Introduce at least one consonant-first series a day, using the consonants *m, r, f, s:*

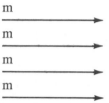

Follow each *m* with one of the vowels—*a, ē, i,* or *o* (but not always in that order). Have the children read each word as you point: "O.K., what word is this? Let's go with the arrow and find out: *mmm.*" Point to *o.* "*Mmmoo.* Say it fast: *mo.*" (Pronounce as in *mop.*)

After the children have read all the words, play the rhyming game in which you say the first sound and they supply the second on signal and then identify the word (page 88).

Repeat the same basic procedure, starting with one of the other continuous-sound consonants. Don't expect the low-performing children to become good at the convergent task immediately. They have a great deal to keep in mind at one time, and they will probably need considerable practice. The higher-performing nonreaders will probably move ahead with great speed, about as rapidly as the teacher can present new tasks.

8. Introduce a variation of the convergent game after the children have become reasonably solid on at least one consonant-first series and one vowel-first series. Have half the children in the group say the first sound: "O.K., John and Mary, you give this sound. Then, when I clap, Harold and Denise, you give the next sound. Here we go. . . ."

This game can be a great deal of fun and can be effective in changing the pace of the session. Make sure, however, that the children are reasonably familiar with the sounds that are presented. If they aren't, the game may flop.

After the children have worked on the two-sound games for several days, present a finding task. After completing a series such as

104

mē, mo, ma, mi, ash, say, "Who can find the word *ma?*" (Pronounce as in *mat.*) "Before you start looking, say *ma* slowly, so you'll know what to look for. Everybody: *ma.* Say it slow. Yes, *mmm–aaa.* That's what the word has to say: *mmm–aaa.*" If the children are having trouble, point to each of the words and ask, "Does this word say *mmm–aaa?* Read it. . . . No, this word says *mi.* Does this word say *ma? . . .*"

Present this task in connection with different series until all the children can say the word slowly and find on the board the word that has the same sounds.

9. After the children have played the two-sound games two or three times, present three-sound word games.

Present these two-letter "words" on the board:

la   (as in *lap*)
——————————→

la
——————————→

la
——————————→

la
——————————→

Make the arrow function explicit: "I follow the arrow, so I start here [below the *l*] and I go this way [moving right]. O.K., let's see what word this is. I point; you give me the sound: *lllaaa.* What is it? Say it fast: *la.* O.K., let's read the next word: *llllaaa.* And the next word. . . ."

After the children have read all the words, make sure that they can quickly identify each of the words (that is, identify them without sounding them out): "John, do you remember what word this is?" If the child doesn't remember, have him read it, a sound at a time, and blend the sounds. Then point to another word. "Who remembers what this word is? . . . Good. And this one?" Summarize: "Sure. Every word here goes *lllaaa . . . la.*" Point to each word, running your finger under the letters from left to right: "*la, la, la, la.*"

Return to the first word and ask, "What's this word?" As the children say *la,* tell them to "keep it going." As they hold the *a* sound, add the letter *m* to the word. Separate *m* from the other letters with a space:

la m
——————————→

Say both parts as you point to them: "*La–mmm.* What word? Say it fast: *lam.* See if you can do it. What's this part here?" (Point to *la.*)

105

"Say it loud. Say it again. . . ." As soon as they have produced it solidly, point to the *m*. "*La–mmm*. What word? *Lam*."

Move to the second *la*. Use the procedure outlined above and complete the word with an *s:*

la   s
———————————→

"*Lllaaasss*. What word? Say it fast: *las*."

Complete the other words in the series with *f* and *n*.

If the children confuse a word such as *lan* with *land*, point out the difference. Exaggerate the pronunciation of *land:* "No, Henry, you're thinking of *land*. This word is *lan*. I don't know what that is, but I can write it."

After the children have gone through the words in the series twice, see if they can identify words that you point to: "Let's find the word *las*. Say it slowly: *lllaaasss*. Now look at the top word, here. Does it say *las*? . . . What about this word? . . ."

10. Introduce a series of three-letter word buildups, starting with these two-letter combinations: *fa, si, li, no*. For example:

fa
———————————→
fa
———————————→
fa
———————————→
fa
———————————→

Have the children identify each word. Call on individual children to read the series of words (pointing as they read).

Have the children read each word, holding the *a* sound: "Keep it going: *fffaaaaa* . . ." As they hold the sound, complete the word by adding a familiar consonant and pointing to it: "*Fffaaaaammm*. Let's read it again: *fffaaammm*. Say it fast: *fam*."

After the children have read the entire series of words twice, call on individual children to read a word. Point to any word in the series and call on a child to read it: "John, let's hear you read this word. . . . Good: *fas*."

Plan to spend five to eight minutes a session on three-sound tasks until the children have become proficient at attacking the words.

11. Introduce buildups, starting with one letter and then adding two or three more. This exercise can be initiated as soon as the children have played the two-letter consonant-first games several times (Step 7 above).

Write the letter *f* over the arrow and have the children identify it:

f
———————————————→

Add the letter *i* and point to it:

fi
———————————————→

Then add the letters *ll* and point to them:

fill
———————————————→

Ask, "What word is this?" If the children cannot identify it, return to the beginning of the word and point: "Let's go fast: *fffiiilll*." Discourage the children from pausing between the letter sounds: "Listen to me: *fffiiilll*. Your turn. . . ."

Initially, build up three or four three-letter words a session. Don't be afraid to repeat words. After the procedure becomes easier for the children, increase the number of words to about ten.

Words containing stop sounds

Introduce stop-sound letters *at the end of words*, using the build-up procedure. As noted on page 99, stop sounds are introduced at the end of words because they do not present any particular problem there. The child will stop naturally at the end of a word. After stop sounds have been introduced as word endings, they can be taught as word beginnings.

1. First introduce the stop sound *t* as a final word sound. Present the word *fa* on the arrow. Have the children read it. Then add the letter *m* and point to it: "*Fffaaammm*. What word? Say it fast: *fam*." Erase the *m* and replace it with an *l*: "What word? *Fffaaalll* . . . *fal*. Say it fast: *fal*." (As in *fallacy*.) Erase the *l* and replace it with an *n*: "What word? *Fan*." Erase the *n* and replace it with an *s*: "What word? *Fas*." Erase the *s* and write a *t*.

Point to the *t* and ask, "What are we going to say when we get here? . . . Yes, *t*. Remember that. O.K., here we go. What's this first part? *Faaa*– Keep it going: *fffaaaa*–[point]*t*. Again: *fffaaat*. What word? Say it fast: *fat*."

2. Quickly change the first letter in the word *fat* from *f* to *m*. "Let's read it now. Careful. I point, you say: *mmmaaa*– Yes, *maaa*– Keep it going: *maaaaa*–*t*. Again: *mmmaaat*. What word? *Mat*."

Quickly change the first letter in the word to *l*. "I point, you say it: *lllllaaa*– Keep it going: *laaat*. Again: *lllaaat*. What word? *Lat*." In working on these words, summarize the first two letters for the children, placing the emphasis on the last sound: "Yes, *lllaaaa–*"

Change the beginning of the word to *n* and then to *s*, repeating the procedure outlined for the other letters. Move fast, so that the children can see what is constant about the words—the ending, which is always *at*.

3. After giving the children practice with *t* until they are firm, introduce other stop sounds in this order: *c* (unvoiced crackling sound), *g* (voiced guttural sound), *d* (voiced), and *p* (unvoiced). Use the procedure outlined for presenting *t*.

Do not introduce more than one new sound during a lesson period, and do not work on words containing that sound for more than about five minutes.

If the children are progressing reasonably well, you can introduce new letter sounds in words, without first presenting them in isolation. The value of this procedure is that it teaches children that they cannot read a word unless they know all the sounds. For example, present the word *rap*. Point to the *p*. "I can't read the word unless I know this sound. It's *p*. Let's all say that." Try to make the identification interesting: "Oh, that's hard to say: *p, p, p, p*. Like a little motor-boat. Who can do that? . . . Sure. And every time you come to this sound with the line sticking way down, you're going to go like a little motorboat: *p*. Let's read the word *rrraaap*. Say it fast: *rap*."

Demonstrate by changing the beginning sound of the word that the *p* sound is constant, that it is a functioning unit, and that it always retains its identity: "Now it says *mmmaaap*. Say it fast. . . . Yes, that's how we spell *map*."

Review the letters that have been mastered every day until the children become solid. Move slowly.

Assign the children writing tasks in which they are to make the new letters and identify them as they write: "Watch me make a *p* on the board. Then you make a bunch of them on your paper. Remember to say '*p*' as you write."

4. After the stop sounds *t, c, g* have been introduced as endings, present stop sounds as the beginnings of two-sound words. This set of exercises is critical, because it demonstrates to the child how to blend stop sounds.

Present a series of five *a*'s on the board with an arrow below each. Start each arrow one letter space to the left of the *a*.

a

———————————————▶

108

Have the children identify each *a*. Return to the top *a:* "This says *aaa*." Make an *n* in front of it:

na

"Now it doesn't say *a*. It says *nnnaaa*." Move your finger in the direction of the arrow below the letters as they are sounded. Erase the *n*. "What does it say now? . . . *a*." Replace the *n*. "What does it say now?" Make the motion of your finger very strong. If you don't, they may try to read the words backward. "Going with the arrow, it says *nnnaaa*." Erase the *n*, ask what it says, and make an *f* in front of the *a*.

For series demonstrations of this sort, it is important to move very quickly or the children will miss the point. Slow down only in spots where they are likely to become confused. For example, pause as they try to read a newly created word, so that they can orient themselves to the idea that they are moving from left to right. As soon as they finish an example, however, replace it quickly with the next, so that they will be more likely to remember what they have just read—what sound they have produced.

Proceed to the next step in the demonstration: quickly put consonants in front of the *a*'s in the series. The last word should be *ta* (pronounced as in *tack*). Put continuous-sound consonants in front of all the other *a*'s:

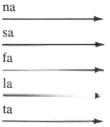

na

sa

fa

la

ta

Have the children read the first four words as you point to the sounds. Then review the words by pointing to the last letter in each word and saying, "This is *a*, so the word is *na*. See? *Nnnaaa*." Move to the other words: "This is *a*, so the word is *sa*. . . . This is *a*, so the word is *fa*. . . . This is *a*, so the word is *la*." Go through this procedure two or three times if necessary. Then, when the children have demonstrated that they can handle the pattern, move to the last word in the list. Point to the *a*. "This is *a*, so the word is . . ." If the preceding demonstration has been adequate, the children will say "*ta*."

(NOTE: The approach outlined above is designed for the most

severely confused nonreaders. You may be able to use an abbreviated version. However, before having the children attempt *ta* you should be sure that they have a firm understanding of the other "words.")

5. Repeat the same basic demonstration, using final vowels *i* and *o* and introducing the consonants *c* and *g* as beginnings.

Always precede the introduction of a new stop-sound consonant with at least two examples of continuous-sound beginnings. For example, in the series *fi, si, gi, ti,* point first to the *i* in *fi:* "This says *i,* so the word is *fi.* . . . Again, this says *i,* so the word is *fi.*" Next word: "This says *i,* so the word is *si.*" Next word: "This says *i,* so the word is *gi.*" (Pronounce as in *gift,* not as in *ginger.*) The continuous-sound words help the child to hold on to the analogy and also make it easier for you to correct mistakes. If the child has forgotten how to blend a word, you are in a position to review the procedure on the first two words. If you start with the stop-sound word, however, you put yourself in the position of not being able to relate the word to the rules the child has already learned.

Throughout these exercises, make the left-right progression of reading obvious. Always underscore the words with hand motions that indicate the direction in which you are reading.

6. As soon as the children have begun to master the two-letter stop-sound buildups, introduce three-letter buildups.

Put a series of endings on the board:

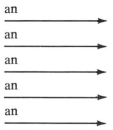

Have the children read the endings. Point to each and ask, "What word is this?"

Return to the first *an* and again establish its identity: "What word is this? . . . O.K., remember that. When we get to it, you're going to say *an.* Now it says *an.*" Put an *f* in front of *an.* "Now it says *fff–*" Erase the *f* and again say, "Now it says *an.*" Write the *f* again. "Now it says . . ."

Complete the series, leaving a slight space between the two parts of the words:

110

f an
———————————→

l an
———————————→

t an
———————————→

p an
———————————→

c an
———————————→

Point first to the end of each word, reminding the children of what it is: "This part says *an*." Then move to the first letter and indicate the direction in which they are to proceed: "So the word says *fffan*." Next word: "This part says *an*, so the word says *lan*." Next word: "This part says *an*, so the words says *tan*." And so forth.

7. Follow the demonstration with other words in which two-letter endings are held constant. For endings, use *an, in, at, ut, on,* and *ot*. Do not treat this exercise as a primary one. Work only two to three minutes a day on it, presenting one series a day.

8. Present stop-sound-first series as soon as the child has mastered the two-letter stop-sound exercises (see Steps 5 and 6 above). The purpose of this exercise is to demonstrate to the child that the procedure for handling the initial stop sound is the same regardless of the vowel that follows it.

Write the words *ti, ta,* and *to* on the board, with arrows:

ti
———————————→

ta
———————————→

to
———————————→

Point to the *i* in the first word. "What sound is this? . . . So the word is . . ." Point first under the *t* and indicate the direction in which the children are to read. If they have trouble, show them how to read the word: "This is *i*, so the word is *ti*." (As in *tip*.)

Move to the second word, again pointing first to the vowel. "This is *a*, so the word is . . ." Point to the first letter and indicate the direction in which the children are to read. "*Ta*." (As in *tap*.)

Move to the third word, pointing first to the vowel. "This is *o*." (As in *on*.) "So the word is . . ."

Repeat the exercise, using *c, g, p,* and *d* as the first letter of each word in the series. Introduce one series a day, such as *ca, co, ci,* and work on it for no more than two minutes. Repeat series that prove to be difficult. If the children have trouble with a series, introduce similar series with continuous-sound consonants and then, after they have become more firm in their operations, return to the stop-sound series. Be careful to indicate the direction in which the words are to be read. *Always begin pointing before they start reading.*

Double-consonant endings

This set of exercises is designed to help children handle words, such as *sand*, that have two consonant sounds at the end.

1. Write the letter *f* on the board, with an arrow below. "Now it says *fff* . . ." Add the letter *o:*

fo
———————————————→

"Now it says *fffooo* . . . *fo.*" Add the letter *n:*

fon
———————————————→

"Now it says *fffooonnn.* What does it say?" Have the children read the word several times. "Remember that. It says *fon.* It says what?" Add the letter *d:*

fond
———————————————→

"And now it says *fon–*" Point to the *d.* "Yes, *fond.*"

2. Demonstrate the reverse procedure: "It says *fond.* What does it say?" Erase the *d.* "Does it say *fond* now?" Answer quickly, "No, it says *ffoon.* It says *fon,* not *fond.* It says *fon.* Say it." Erase the *n.* "Does it say *fon* now? . . . No, it says . . ." Erase the *o.* "Does it say *fo* now? . . . No, it says *fff.*" Erase the *f.* "Does it say *f* now? . . . No, it says—nothing. No word."

3. Introduce variations with such four-sound words as *land, sand, cant, mint, milk, silt, film, fond, pond.* All these words have two-consonant endings, which disadvantaged children often have trouble hearing and handling. The reverse breakdown nicely demonstrates how the two-consonant endings are formed, both in speech and with letters. The children may have some trouble saying such endings as *nd* (as in *sand*). If they do, change the first letter of the word (*fand, gand, mand, land*). Also change the vowel (*lond, gond*). Most of the words presented should have continuous-sound beginnings.

Double-consonant beginnings

Start work on this task as soon as the children have mastered a few two-consonant endings. Plan to work on double-consonant beginnings over a long period of time, devoting not more than two or three minutes a day to them. Start with relatively easy two-consonant beginnings and work up to combinations that give the children a great deal of difficulty, such as *spl, shr, spl, str.*

1. Write a *p* above the arrow:

p ————————→

Have the children identify the sound. "Now it says *p*, and now . . ." Write an *a* in front of the *p:*

ap ————————→

"Now it says . . ." Write an *l* in front of *ap:*

lap ————————→

"Now it says . . ." If the children tend to read backward, say the sound of the letter you are writing and then indicate by pointing that they are to produce the remaining sounds. "Now it is *lllll* . . ." This method makes the task easier, because you have indicated the ordering of the sound elements. As the children become more familiar with this kind of buildup, you can systematically phase out this cue, so that the children are following only your pointing, not your vocalization.

Write *c* in front of *lap:*

clap ————————→

"Now it says *lap*, and now . . ." The children will probably say "*cap*." If they do, tell them, "You forgot the *l*." Cover the *c* and demonstrate. "Now it says *lap*, and now it says *clllap*. Say it: *clap*. Look at it: *cllaaap* . . . *clap*." The better rehearsed the children have been on saying words fast and saying them slowly, the better they will do on this task, although perfect performance on the verbal exercises will not assure perfect performance on the present task.

Break the word down a letter at a time: "Now it says *clap*." Erase the *c*. "And now it says . . . Now it says *lap*." Erase the *l*. "And now it says *ap*." Erase the *a*. "Now it says *p*." Erase the *p*. "And now it says nothing."

2. On the following day, present the word *lap* and have the children sound it out. "Yes, this word is *lap*. Now it says . . . what? *Lap*."

Write the letter *s* in front of the word. "And now it says—not *sap*. We still have to say *lap* . . . *lap*. Say it. . . . And this tells us to start out with *sss*. I'll say *sss*, and you say *lap*. Here we go: *sss–lap* . . . *slap*. What does this word say? *Slap*." Erase the *s*. "What does it say now? *Lap*. Remember this part says *lap*. When

113

you get to it, you're going to say *lap*."

Write a *c* in front of the word. "I'll say this (*c*); you say this (*lap*) . . . *c–lap*. Again: *c–lap* . . . *clap*. What does it say? *Clap*." Erase the *c*. "Now it says *lap*." Put an *f* in front of the word. "Now it says *fff–*" Change the word from *lap* to *clap*, to *lap* to *slap*, to *lap* to *flap*.

3. Introduce other double-consonant beginnings. Work on the words *stop, stif, grand, grip, cram, plop, plan, spit, spot, slit*. Concentrate on the last two moves of the buildups. "Now it says *pot*. . . . Now it says *sss* . . . Say it: *spot*."

$$\begin{array}{c} \text{pot} \\ \hline \longrightarrow \\ \text{spot} \\ \hline \longrightarrow \end{array}$$

After the children have mastered these, introduce the particularly troublesome words *string* and *street*. The critical part of the demonstration begins with the second consonant in the word. In the word *slit*, for example, the critical part begins with the word *lit*. The children will probably say "*sit*" when the *s* is added. It is probably a good idea to demonstrate the buildup; return to the word *lit* and then hold the children responsible for the production of the word *slit*.

Writing Words

Writing words gives the children needed practice in applying the word rules they have learned. If a child understands how to build words, he will understand how sounds work in words.

1. Lead into writing by introducing a word-completion task.

Write the word *fa* on the board. Have the children read it. "Yes, *fa*." Then introduce the construction problem: "I want to change *fa* into *fan*. How do I do that?" The children may not see the point. If they don't, remind them to say the word *fan* slowly, to see what sounds must be in it: "*Fffaaannn.* Now look at this word. Does it say *ffaann?*" Point to each of the letters as you repeat the sounds for the word *fan:* "*fffaaa–*" Now point to the space after the *a*. "*Nnnnn.* There's no *n* here. I need a *nnnn*." Write it in.

Erase the *n* and repeat the same procedure: "What's this word? . . . Yes, *fa*. I want to change it into the word *fat*. Say it slow. . . . Let's see what I'd have to do. It has to say *fffaaa–t*." Have the children repeat the "spelling" of *fat* several times. Then point to the letters in the word as you repeat the sequence: "*Fffaaa–*" Point to the space next to the *a*. "What do we need here?" Write *t*.

Erase the entire word and replace it with *mi*. Have the children read it and go through the same general procedure: "I want to change this word into *mis*. Say it slowly. . . . O.K., let's see what we need." Point to the letters *mmmiii–*. Point to the space and ask the children what is missing. . . . Write *s*.

Erase the letter *s* and present other examples, following the same format and changing the word *mi* into *mit, mig, mic, mif*.

2. Give the children sheets of paper with words to complete according to your instructions.

On the first sheet, present four examples of the "word" *ma* with arrows:

ma
———————————————▶

Allow plenty of space between the words.

Have the children read all the words on the page. Then refer to the first word and say, "I want this word to say *mat . . . mat*. Say it slowly with me." After they have said the word several times, have them point to the letters in the first word as you sound out *mat:* "You point; I'll spell *mat*. See what we have to do: *mmm–aaa–ttt*. What do we need? . . . Put it in." After they have written in the letter, have them read the word. "Yes, now it says *mat*."

Use the same procedure for writing the remaining words—*map, mas,* and *man*. You spell and the children point, identifying which letter is missing and then supplying it.

On subsequent sheets, make the children increasingly responsible for handling the steps in the operation. Have them say the word slowly; then instruct them to point to the word on the sheet while spelling the word they want: "Give the sounds for *fat*, and see what you need." If the children have trouble, go back to the procedure outlined for the first sheet.

Present these words on subsequent sheets: *sa* (changed to *sap, sad, sal, sam*); *fi* (changed to *fit, fil, fin*); *li* (changed to *lip, lit, lid*); *si* (changed to *sip, sit, sin*); *co* (changed to *cop, con, cod*); *no* (changed to *not, nod, non*); *fa* (changed to *fat, fan, fab*); *ca* (changed to *cap, cat, can*); *ga* (changed to *gas, gap, gal*).

After the first two sheets, introduce two different root words on the same sheet, perhaps *li* and *ca*. Repeat the examples that give the children trouble.

3. After the children have completed the set of words above, present a variation of the task in which they are responsible for spelling more of the word. Repeat the series presented in Step 2 above, this time requiring the children to write two of the three letters in the words.

The first sheet should contain four *m*'s on arrows. Read the letters. Then refer to the top *m* and explain the tasks: "This is tough. I want to say *man*. What do I want it to say? . . . Say it slow. . . . O.K., now point and see if this says *man: mmmmm–aaa–nn*. Again: *mmm–aa–nn*. Look, we need *aaa–nnn*. Let's write it." After they have finished, have them read the word. Ask, "Does it say *man* now? . . . Yes, *mm–aa–nn*."

Complete the words *mat, mas, map* in the same manner. If the children have difficulty, have them point while you spell the word. Then have them spell with you and point. Finally, have them write the missing letters.

Introduce similar sheets with the letters *f, l, s, c, n, g,* and have the children supply the two letters necessary to complete the words you specify (*fan, fat, fac,* etc.).

4. Go through the series again after the children have completed the tasks in Step 3 above, this time having them spell and write the entire word.

Give them blank sheets on which four arrows appear. Refer to the top arrow and say, "I want it to say *map* on this arrow . . . *map*. Spell it with me. . . . O.K., now point on the arrow—starting here—and spell *map*. What sound comes first? *Mmm*. So we have a *mmm* here. Spell *map: mmm–aaa* [moving the children's fingers to the next space] . . . Spell *map* again and point to where the sounds go: *mmm–aa–p*. Again . . ." After the children have caught on to pointing to a spot for each sound (which is not an easily learned notion), have them write the word.

Have them then write the words *mas, man, mad* in the remaining spaces.

On subsequent sheets, have them work on words beginning with *f, l, s, c, n, g.*

(NOTE: Don't be picayune over mechanical mistakes in the children's writing. The writing tasks are introduced so that the children can use the rules of spelling they have learned. The primary emphasis should be on the rules of construction, not on penmanship. A child

116

may be put off completely if the teacher does not make it clear—through her behavior—what the point of writing is all about. To write a word is to solve a problem, and in solving a problem the problem-solving steps are of primary importance, not the style with which these steps are executed.)

Plan to spend no more than eight minutes a day on writing. Some of the introductory lessons may take more time than this, but the others should generally take far less if you work on no more than two new things at once. If you find yourself presenting tasks that involve a great deal of new learning (if the child is expected to work on more than two new modules at once), the demands are too great.

Spell three to five words a day on the chalkboard. Stress words containing new letter sounds. For example: "I want to write the word *egg*." Touch the two spots on the chalkboard as you sound out the word: "*Eg*." Refer to the first touch mark. "So what do I have to put here? . . . *E* . . . Do you know how to write that sound? Watch . . ."

If the children have trouble isolating a sound such as the *e* sound in *egg*, demonstrate that the sound occurs in a number of words with which they are familiar: "Let's spell *mess*. Your mother says, 'This is a *mess.*' *Mess.*" Touch the board, leaving a little finger mark for each sound that is to be written: *mmm–eee–sss*. Write the first letter and then point to the next mark: "What goes here?" The children may say *a*, since the distinction between *e* and *a* is difficult, especially for the nonreader. "It's not *mass*, it's *mess*. So what goes here? *E*. How do I write the sound *e*? Like this . . ." Write the *e* and continue with the third letter.

Present a series of similar words that contain the *e* sound, either at the beginning or in the second-letter position: *let, pet, det, met, net, pen, men, den, leg, end, sell, tell, fell, sent, dent, lent.*

Difficult Sounds

1. Work on *h* words. The *h* sound is difficult because, although it is continuous, the quality of the sound produced is determined by the vowel that follows the *h*. The variations in the *h*'s that are produced can be demonstrated by producing the first unvoiced sound in the words *hit* and *hut*. The *h* sound in *hit* is very high; the *h* sound in *hut* is very low. Since *h* has this characteristic, it is best treated as a stop sound.

117

Present the word *hat* on the board. Point to the *a:* "This sound is . . . Yes, *aaa.* So it goes *ha.* Keep it going: *haaa . . . hat.*" Point to the *t.* Introduce various three-letter and four-letter examples: *hip, hop, ham, hit, hand, help, hot,* and so on. On every word, point first to the vowel and have the children identify it. Then return to the *h,* producing the combination consonant-vowel sound *ha, he, hi,* or *ho.*

2. Work on words beginning with *r.* The *r* sound sometimes gives trouble because the children want to pronounce it *ur,* which is natural, but which causes confusion in reading. When introducing the sound, insist that the children begin with a clean *rrrr,* allowing no vowel sound to precede it: "Be like a robot: *rrr.* Your turn." Present a variety of *r* words: *rat, ran, rack, run, rut, rip,* and so on.

3. Program words so that the children do not confuse *b* and *d.*

Present a great many words with *ad, id,* and *ed* endings. Repeat words such as *mad, sad,* and *dad* until the children recognize them as sight words.

Introduce the *b* in the word *bad.* Present it as the fourth word in an *ad* series: *sad, mad, dad, bad.* The word *dad* appears right above the word *bad* in anticipation of the mistake the children may make in identifying *b* as *d.* "No, it's not a *d.* Look at *dad.* This sound is *d.*" Point to *b.* "This sound is not *d;* it's facing the wrong way. It's facing this way . . . it's facing the way we move when we read." Additional mnemonics sometimes help, such as "It's got a belly sticking out this way . . ." Repeat the series until the child can discriminate between *bad* and *dad.*

Program a variety of words that begin with *b.* Do not present words that have *b* as an ending sound, but continue to introduce words that have *ad, ed,* and *id* endings. During this period the children will learn that *d* is principally an ending sound and *b* a beginning sound. Repeat words so that they learn to identify the *d* ending words automatically.

Next, introduce a series of paired words. For example:

ban	big	bug
dan	dig	dug

Do not labor over the identification of *b* and *d.* Program the endings, correct mistakes that arise, and be patient. The children will learn them about as quickly with an occasional reminder as they will if they receive extensive daily drill. Extended drill simply reinforces mistake patterns that can be avoided through proper programing.

Long and Short Vowel Discriminations

After the children have been introduced to the short-sound variations of the vowels (*a, e, i, o,* and *u*) and the long-sound variations (*ā, ē, ī, ō*), introduce discrimination exercises.

1. Present the following words on the board:

    met   bet   set   pet

Have the children read each word. Then refer to the word *met*. Point to the *e* and have the children indicate the sound it makes. "Watch this trick." Draw a line over the *e:*

    mēt

"Now it doesn't say *met;* it says *meet.* Say that with me. . . . This line over *met* turns it into *meet.* Let's read. . . ." Erase the diacritical mark and say, "Now it says *met,* and now"—replace the mark—"it says *meet.*"

Repeat the demonstration several times before moving to the second word: *bet.* Have the children read it. Put a diacritical mark over the *e,* reminding them of the sound it makes. Have them read the word *beet;* then erase the mark and summarize: "Now it says *bet* and now"—replace the mark—"it says *beet.*"

Handle the other words in the same way, always summarizing to show how the diacritical mark has changed the word—from *met* to *meet,* from *bet* to *beet,* and so on. Repeat the series (presenting the words in different sequences) until the children become adept at changing the vowel sound.

Introduce a variation of the task in which the words are presented with diacritical marks, which are then erased.

    bēt   mōt   rōd   sēd

2. In connection with the chalkboard drill, introduce long-*ē* words in sentences that the children are to read. Concentrate on the words *he, me, we,* and *be.* For example:

    wē have fun.
    give mē a hamburger.
    wē pet a cat.
    hē is not a bēt.
    hē will bē a man.

3. Concentrate on the long-*ō* sound next. Use a procedure similar to the one for *e* and *ē.* Start with simple words having an *ot* ending:

    not   got   rot   cot   bot

Have the children read the words, reminding them of the sound the *o*

119

makes without the diacritical mark; then add the mark to the word *not* and say, "It doesn't say *not;* now it says *note.*" Erase the diacritical mark and replace it, each time asking the children what the word is.

Add diacritical marks to the remaining words. Then go through all the words, first indicating what the word is without the mark and then asking the children to read it with the mark: "Now it is *not,* and now . . . it is *note.*" Run through the pattern very quickly so that the children can learn to hear the difference between the *o* and the *ō* sound.

Present similar series of such words as *sod, nod, lod.*

Present the words *no, go, so, ho, or, for* in sentences for the children to read:

> sō the man laft. hō, hō, hō.
>
> hē went.
>
> hē will gō fōr mōr.
>
> give mē that ōr dad will get mad.

4. After the children have mastered *e* and *o*, present the discriminations for the vowels *a* and *i.*

Present these words:

> mat   bat   fat   hat   rat

Introduce the long *ā* sound (as in *āte*) with the diacritical mark, and have the children read the resulting words:

> māt   bāt   fāt   hāt   rāt

Also begin to use the expression "make it long": "These marks make the *a* long: *aaa* turns into *āāā.*" Demonstrate what this means by erasing the diacritical marks and then saying about each word, "Now it says *mat* and now"—add the diacritical mark—"it says *mate.*" Work on the pattern until the children have mastered it. Also introduce *ad* words: *mad, lad, fad,* and so on.

5. For long- and short-*i* discrimination, begin with these words:

> bit   sit   mit   lit   fit

"Now it says *lit*"—put in the diacritical mark—"and now it says *light.* Now it says *fit* . . . and now it says *fight.*"

6. After the children have been introduced to the long sounds for *e, o, a,* and *i,* play a verbal game with them. This game is relatively difficult and is best handled in very small doses.

Take the pattern of long sounds that is the most familiar to the children, long *ē.* Present words in the short-vowel form and see if the children can "make them long": "Here's the game. Listen to this word: *et*. Say it slow. . . . O.K., now make the *eee* long: *eat*. Here's another one: *met*. Say it slow. What comes after the *mmm?* . . . Yes, *eee*. O.K., make the *eee* long: *meeeet*."

Play the game for about a minute a day—no more—until the children have mastered the long sounds verbally. Do not introduce long *u* either with the diacritical mark or verbally. The examples of long *u* are few and can easily be avoided in beginning reading material. Devote most of the time to working with long *e*, long *o*, and long *a*.

7. After the children have mastered the verbal game with long *e* and long *o* and after they are familiar with such words as *go* and *he*, drop the diacritical marks from the written exercises:

> he will go if we go.

The children may read the words *he* and *go* without any prompting. If they require prompting, tell the children to make the *e* (as in *egg*) long, or make the *o* (as in *on*) long. This cue will probably work (if the children have learned the verbal patterns in Step 6). If the cue fails, however, draw an imaginary line over the *e* with your finger, repeating the instruction "Make it long." If this cue also fails, make the long mark with chalk and repeat the instruction "Make it long." Then erase the word and tell the children, "This is a funny word. It looks like *he* (as in *help*), but we say *hee*."

Reading Statements

Statement reading should become a part of the daily session as soon as the children have learned to identify at least fifteen letters. Remember that you are limited in composing statements to words with regular sounds.

Spell words phonetically. However, if a word ends in an *e* (*give, have, save*), spell the word as it is normally spelled, making the final *e* very small:

give

have

As the children become familiar with these words, make the final *e* larger. The children will continue to read the words correctly.

Introduce the words *a* and *is* early in the statement-reading instruction. Both of these words are exceptions. We don't say "isss"

121

for the word *is*, and we usually don't say "ay" for the word *a*. We say "iz" and "uh."

1. First introduce statements that contain neither *a* nor *is*. Draw a rectangle between the words in the statement. Do not capitalize the first letter of the statement:

> let ▢ him ▢ in.

"See these boxes? They tell you that you have finished a word. Here's a word"—point to *let*—"here's a word"—point to *him*—"and here's a word"—point to *in*. "Before we read these words, let's pretend that John is outside and he knocks on the door. These words tell us what to do. Let's read: Yes, we should *let him in*."

2. Erase the statement and write another statement:

> give ▢ him ▢ a ▢ pill.

"This is what the doctor tells Henry's mother when Henry is sick. Let's see what he tells Henry's mother to do." Read to the word *a*. "Oh, oh! Here's a funny word. What sound does it make? *Aaa* [as in *apple*]. That's right. But when *a* is a word, we say 'uh.' Give him UH . . . what? Read this last word."

3. Introduce various sentences containing the word *a*. Present no more than three statements a day. If difficult words are encountered, repeat them in subsequent exercises.

> a ▢ man ▢ lafs.
> hand ▢ him ▢ a ▢ pan.
> get ▢ a ▢ rug.
> give ▢ us ▢ a ▢ pot.
> let ▢ us ▢ have ▢ a ▢ nut.
> wut ▢ a ▢ mess.

Tell the children a story, and make the sentence the punch line of the story. To find out the punch line, the child must read the statement. For example: "One day Mary and Jean were trying to lift a great big rock. They couldn't do it. They saw John and Henry walking down the street, and this is what they said: 'Give—us—a—hand.'"

4. Introduce statements containing *is* after the children have become reasonably adept at handling the word *a* as an exception. (NOTE: After the introduction of the word *a*, the children may identify the *a* sound that appears in words as "uh." Instead of *c–aaa–p*, they may say *c–uuu–p*. To correct this tendency, say, "This *a* [as in *cap*] is not a word. When it's a word, we call it *uh*. That's kind of funny, isn't it? Here it's *a*.")

122

Introduce the statement "a ☐ man ☐ is ☐ not ☐ a ☐ mat." Tell this story: "One day Henry said the wrong word when he was reading. This doesn't happen very often, but he did it. He said he thought that the word *man* was *mat*. So here's what his teacher told him: 'Let's read.'" Read the word *is*, which the children will probably read as "iss." "Oh, oh! This is one of those funny words. It tells us to say 'iss,' but this word is *is*. It's a funny word. Not 'iss' but 'izz'—*zzzz* like a saw going back and forth. Say that: *zzzzzz*. I know what we can do. We can make a little saw over the *s* so that we will remember to go *zzzzz*."

is

"Those are the teeth on the saw: *zzzzz*. So what's this word? *Izzz*."

Introduce a variety of statements containing *a* and *is*. Concentrate primarily on the statement form: a ——— is (not) a ——— (a ham is not a hat; a hot dog is red).

Introduce questions containing *is*. Do not capitalize the first letter, but put a question mark at the end:

is ☐ a ☐ man ☐ a ☐ bat ☐ ?

When the children read the statement and come to the question mark, explain its function: "We don't say it this way: is a man a bat. We say it this way: is a man a *bat?* This funny-looking thing tells us to talk that way."

Introduce a variety of questions:

is a pan a pill?

is a bat a fat man?

is a fan a pan?

The following basic story line can be used with these: "Tommy's teacher told him to get a *fan*. He came back with a *pan*—you know, a frying pan. His teacher looked at him and asked him this (read it): 'Is a fan a pan?'"

Pass out individual sheets, perhaps every other lesson, on which appear two questions and two statements. These should be printed on arrows, with boxes, periods, and question marks. For example:

is ☐ a ☐ lap ☐ a ☐ clap ☐ ?

a ☐ cat ☐ is ☐ fast.

a ☐ cat ☐ is ☐ not ☐ a ☐ dog.

is ☐ an ☐ ant ☐ a ☐ man ☐ ?

Have the children read each line. Reread each statement several times. Then call on individual children to read a statement or a question.

5. Introduce the conventions for punctuating a complete statement. The statement form "———— is ————." serves as a model for a complete statement. The exercises in punctuation should not be introduced until the children have worked with at least twenty statements of the form "———— is ————."

Present the sentence fragment *dan*, followed by a period:

    dan.

"Can I put this period after *dan?*" Some of the children may say yes. "No, because it doesn't tell me *what Dan is*. Dan is *what?* Is he a goat? Is he an alligator? It doesn't tell me what he is." Erase the period, write the word *is*, and put the period after it. "Can I put the period here?"

    dan is.

"No, because it still doesn't tell me what Dan is."

Write the word *a* and follow it with a period. "Can I put the period there?"

    dan is a.

"No, because it still hasn't told me what Dan is. Dan is a *what?*" Complete the statement.

    dan is a man.

"Can I put the period there? Do I know what Dan is? Does it tell me? Yes, it tells me that Dan is what? Dan is a man. I know what Dan is, so I can put a period there."

Introduce a statement containing an adjective:

    dan is a fat man.

Build up the statement in the manner described above. After the word *fat*, the children may indicate that you can put a period there. "No, Dan is a fat what? I still don't know. Is he a fat house? Is he a fat girl? It has to tell me."

Present other statements such as these:

    a dog is not a cat.
    red is not black.
    mike is not red.
    a can is tin.
    a rat is bad.
    a run is fun.

Work on these and similar statements until the children can handle them consistently.

6. Introduce an exercise in which the child indicates whether a question is complete, after he has been exposed to at least twenty examples of the question form "Is this . . . ?"

Write this question fragment:

is a man

Have the children read it. Then ask, "Can I put one of these things here?" Make a question mark. Some of the children may say yes. "No, I can't, because it doesn't ask me anything. Is a man *what?* It has to tell me what. *Is a man.* That doesn't ask me anything. It's silly talk." Act amused.

Add the word *a:*

is a man a

"Can I put one of these marks there now? No, because it still doesn't ask me anything. Is a man a—a what? It doesn't ask me."

Add the word *dog:*

is a man a dog?

"Can I put one of these marks up there now? Does it ask me what? Is a man a *what?* Is a man a *dog?* Yes, I can put one of those marks up there now."

The verbal explanation will probably have much less to do with the children's understanding than repeated exposure to questions of a particular form. Do not eliminate the verbal explanation, however. Use it every time you present the task. After it has been repeated several times, the children will probably state the objection themselves: "It doesn't ask us *what.*" Program some questions in which more than one word follows the subject:

is a man a hot dog?

The children will probably want to put the question mark after the word *hot.* Ask them, "A hot what? A hot tamale, a hot foot? It doesn't ask us what."

Programing Longer Words

The problem with English spelling is that it is virtually impossible to write the simplest sentence without writing words that are irregular. For example, "He went to the store," or "I have a red ball." Each sentence contains at least two irregular words. In teaching children to read, therefore, one must begin to program sight words. The way they are usually programed is not desirable, at least for the disadvantaged child, because the process may seem completely arbitrary, so arbitrary in fact that he may not see why the word *you* shouldn't be pronounced *ship* instead of *you*. He'll take your word for it, but when he does, he is relying on you, not on his own understanding.

Probably the best way to program sight words is to present the kind of word that can be related to the rules the child has learned. The first step is to encourage children to remember words.

1. Introduce the word *little*, spelled properly.

Write this sentence on the board: *An ant is little*. Point to the last word and say, "I know this word: *little*. I can just look at it and say 'little.' See? *Little*. I can say it every time I see it. See if you can remember it." Read the sentence up to the word *little*, then jump ahead of the children, point to the word *little* and say, "*Little*. I remembered it. I'm pretty good, huh?" The children will probably contend that they remembered it too. "All right, we'll see. Maybe tomorrow I'll just write on the board like this"—write the word *little* —"and I'll just see who really remembers it."

At the end of the period, write the word on the board. The children (or at least one of them) will probably remember it. Act surprised, as if the child has done something that is very important: "You remembered it! I didn't think you'd be able to." Then sound out the word with them: "Well, let's all spell this word." Proceed through the first three letters, *l, i, t*, then summarize: *"Lit–"*—point to the next three letters—*"tul . . . lit–tul . . . little."*

Present the word the next day, preceding the presentation with a buildup: "Now here's a word you said you'd remember. Let's see if you can." Write the word *little* on the board. Present it from time to time throughout the period until the children are very solid with it. Also present it in statements:

> a rat is little.
>
> a little cat is not fat.

2. Present other long but fairly regular words in the same manner. Spring them on the children in a sentence, but don't always identify them immediately. If you do, the children may get the idea that the way to recognize long words is to take a quick stab at them. Once in a while the technique of identifying the word in advance is good, especially as an introduction to the notion that the children are

126

expected to identify certain words (which is not implied by the process of building up words atomically). The technique of identifying the word in advance demonstrates rather dramatically to the child that the teacher *knows* the word. The rule should be to identify a word and then sound it out.

Present the statement *An alligator is mad*. The word *alligator* is too long for the children to read, so lead them through it: "I know this word: *alligator*. Let's spell it: *al–li–ga–tor* . . . *alligator*. I'll bet I can remember this word." At least once more during the session and once in each of the sessions that follows, present the word *alligator*. At first, preface the presentation with a warning: "Here's a word I remember. I wonder if you remember it." After the children become reasonably solid, drop the cuing.

3. After *little* and *alligator* have been mastered, present regular sight words as in these sentences:

>animal: a cat is an animal.
>insect: an insect is a bug.
>finger: a finger is on a hand.
>turtle: a turtle is an animal.
>flower: is a cat a flower?

After all these words have been programed, write them on the board and see if the children can remember them. Don't be surprised if they have some difficulty. It's easy for them to remember one sight word—*little*—by remembering that this is an "important" word. But when they have several words to remember, they must learn how to find clues in the words themselves. Demonstrate that any of the words can be spelled. Lead the children. As you spell, they will probably remember the word before you have finished. When you have finished testing them on every word, demonstrate that you can remember all of them: "*Animal, insect, little, finger, turtle, flower*. How's that?" It might be a good idea to pretend that you can't remember one of the words and show the children how you go about figuring it out: "*Fl—flow—flower*. I remember it now: *flower*."

Present the sight words from time to time. Don't become irritated if the children can't remember some of them. When they forget a word, tell them what it is and then help them "spell" it (sound it out).

Th

When the children have learned two or three longer sight words, introduce *th* (written *th* and voiced, as in *this, that, the*.)

127

1. Teach the symbol *th* as other symbols were taught. Write it on the board and show the children how to pronounce it. Exaggerate the pronunciation by sticking your tongue out and making a loud voiced sound (not the hissing sound heard in *thing*).

2. Demonstrate how the sound works by writing these words on the board:

at   em   is   an

Have the children read each of the words. Then refer to the first one and say, "Now it says *at*, and now"—put the *th* symbol in front of it —"it says *that*." If the children have trouble, erase the *th* and ask, "What does it say now? . . . Yes, now it says *at*, and now"—write *th* in front of the *at*—"it says *that*."

Refer to the second word. Have the children read it, and repeat the procedure used to form *that*. "Now it says *em*, and now . . . it says *them*. What does it say now?"

Handle the remaining words in the list the same way.

Er

Introduce *er* after the children have mastered *th*. Present these words on the board:

red   fat   hog   big   fast

Have the children read them. Then refer to *red:* "Now it says *red*, and now"—add the *er* ending, forming the word *reder*—"it says *reder*. Let's spell the word: *red–eee–r*. It should say *redaire*, but we don't say *redaire*—we say *redder*. Now it says *redder*, and now"—erase the *er* ending—"it says *red*." Add the ending and remove it until the children see that the *er* functions as a unit. Proceed to the second word, using the same procedure.

After proceeding through all the words in the list, have the children read them with the *er* endings attached. Underline the *er* ending of each word and call the children's attention to it: "Now remember—when you get to this part, you're going to say *errr*."

After the children have mastered these words, working on them about two minutes a day, introduce the word *other* on the board.

Other

Read the word with the children. It is slightly irregular. Point this out to the children: "It should say *ooother*"—as in *bother*—"but it's a funny word. We don't say *other*, we say *uther*." The children will remember the funny nature of the word if you act amused over its

128

pronunciation and will know that *other* is essentially regular.

Present the beginnings *m*, *br*, and *an* forming the words *mother, brother,* and *another.* Go fast. Begin with *other:* "Now it says *other,* and now"—add the letter *r*—"it says *rother.* . . . What does it say now? *Rother.* Now it says *rother,* and now"—add the *b*—"it says *brother.*" (The children will probably have trouble with the pronunciation.) Erase the *b* and ask them what the word is. Then erase the *r,* again asking them what the word is. Build the word back up again—*other, rother, brother.*

Erase the *br* and ask the children to identify the word again: "Now it says *other,* and now"—add the letter *m*—"it says *mother.*"

Finally, introduce the beginning *an,* building it up in two stages: "Now it says *other,* and now . . . it says *n–other.* Now it says *nother,* and now . . . it says *an–other.*" The children may have some trouble with *another* because it contains more syllables than *mother* or *brother.*

Go over these words until the children are relatively familiar with them. The buildup exercises do several things. They acquaint the children with two- and three-syllable words. They present words in which the *th* sound is in the middle of the word. And they acquaint the children with words that are slightly irregular.

Treat all irregulars as funny words: "It should say *o–ther*"—as in *bother*—"but it's a funny word. We don't say *other,* we say *uther.*" This presentation is extremely important. The child must understand that the word he hears and pronounces as *uther* is always spelled *other.* Ultimately he will generalize, from many experiences with irregular words, that spelling, while arbitrary from one point of view, does not vary from one time to another. The irregular word *other* is always spelled *other,* and always pronounced *uther.*

1. After the children have mastered *other, mother, brother,* and *another,* have them read sentences such as these:

> a moth<u>er</u> is not a man.
> is a broth<u>er</u> little?
> help moth<u>er</u> pick flowers.
> anoth<u>er</u> bug bit him.
> hand us anoth<u>er</u> cup.

2. Introduce other words with *er* endings in sentences. When you add the *er* ending to a word, call the children's attention to it.

129

Underline the ending and ask, "Who remembers what this thing says?" Spell the word correctly. The double consonants should not trouble the children if the *er* ending is underlined:

a man got fatt<u>er</u> than his broth<u>er</u>.

hand him a bigg<u>er</u> flow<u>er</u>.

hand him a hott<u>er</u> cup.

his hand got redd<u>er</u>.

As the children become familiar with *er* words, stop underlining the ending.

Ing

Use the basic procedure for introducing *er* to introduce *ing*.

1. Present a series of action words on the board:

run　　　stop　　　get　　　fan　　　sit

2. Have the children read all the words. Then add the *ing* ending to each one. Try to get the children to recognize the ending. When *ing* is sounded out, it doesn't sound the same as it does when we actually pronounce it in a word. Treat the ending as a unit, but demonstrate that it can be sounded out: "Now it says *run*, and now . . . *run–i–ng* . . . *running* . . . *ing*. This part says *ing*. Say it: *ing*. You'll see that on a lot of words, so try to remember it." The children may have trouble with words having *ing* endings. Give them plenty of practice.

3. After introducing the words in the list above, use them in stories. Underline the *ing*. Call the children's attention to the ending and try to treat it as something they should look for and remember. For example, in the sentence *Dan is sitt*ing point to the *ing* ending and say something like "Oh, oh! I remember this thing. It goes . . ."

Sh

Introduce *sh* (as in *shoe*) as a joined symbol:

sh

As the children become familiar with the unit, separate the letters.

1. Present a series of *sh*'s on the board:

sh

sh

sh

Have the children identify each unit: "Come on, keep it going: *shshshshsh*."

Return to the first *sh* and have the children hold the sound as you add the letter *ē:*

shē

"Say it fast: *she*. This is how we spell *she*."

Complete the second word with the sound *ō*. "What word is this? *Show*." Complete the remaining words with the sounds *ī* and *ā*. Repeat the demonstration several times.

2. Introduce the *sh* sound as a word ending. Present these words:

    mat   mad   mash

Introduce similar series, such as *fit, fin, fish* and *mash, sash, lash.*

3. Present similar exercises for a few days. Then begin to use *sh* words in the sentences the children are to read. Concentrate on the words *she, ship, fish*. Work on these words until the children can identify them without spelling them.

Ch

1. Initially, join the letters in *ch* to demonstrate that it is a unit:

ch

After the children have learned to handle *ch* as a unit, separate the letters. Introduce *ch* first as a beginning. Write five *ch*'s on the board:

    ch
    ch
    ch
    ch
    ch

Tell the children the sound the symbol makes, which is an unvoiced *ch* —not a voiced *chu*. Since the *ch* is a stop-sound consonant, teach it by referring to the vowel that follows. Put the letter *a* after the first *ch*. Have the children identify the *a* and summarize: "This is *aaa;* so the word is . . . *cha*."

2. Complete the remaining *ch*'s to form the words *che* (as in *checker*), *chi* (as in *children*), *cho* (as in *chop*), *chu* (as in *chug*). The children will probably find it difficult to say some of these words. After they have mastered them, present real words beginning with *ch*. Some of these can be longer words: *chop, chip, chill, children, church* (with both *ch*'s underlined).

131

3. Use these words in sentences until the children begin to recognize them. Don't be surprised if the children confuse *chop* with *chip* and *chill*. When they make mistakes, first acknowledge that their attempt to say the word quickly is commendable, but then have them look more carefully at the word: "That's pretty good, John. You're trying to remember these words, but you didn't get this one right. Let's spell it together. . . ."

Wh

Perhaps the most difficult combination for the disadvantaged child to learn is *wh*. One of the principal reasons is that *wh* usually appears in words that are hopelessly irregular—*where, what, who, why*. Since these words are so bizarre, the disadvantaged child often fails to learn how these words work. He cannot classify them as unusual or irregular words, because he often fails to learn enough about what is regular. As a result, he may learn simply to take a wild guess at any word that begins with *wh*.

1. Present the word *other*. Have the children read it. Then erase the first letter and replace it with an *e*. "Now it doesn't say *other*, it says *eee–ther* . . . *ether*. Say it with me." Next precede the word with the symbol for *wh*, which is joined:

wh

"This says *www* just like this." Write the letter *w* above the *wh*. "So now this word says . . ." Cover up the *wh*. "Now it says *eee–ther*, and now it says *www–ether* . . . *whether*. I don't know *whether* I'll give you this chalk, John. *Whether*."

2. Present the "words" *en* and *am*. Put the *wh* beginning on each. "Now it says *en*, and now it says *when*. Now it says *am*, and now it says *wham*."

Discrimination exercises

Give the children practice in completing words that begin with *th, sh, ch,* and *wh*.

1. Present each child with a sheet on which these letter combinations are written:

th

sh

ch

wh

Have the children read each of the sounds. Then have them refer to the first sound: "This says *th*, but I want it to say *them*. Say it slow with me. I'll point: *th–e–m*. Again. . . . What sounds do we need? Listen: *th–ee–mmm*. Write them. Put in the sounds that are missing."

Have the children complete the remaining words as follows: *ship, chop,* and *when.*

2. Introduce similar writing drills until the children can form the words *this, that, them, then, ship, she, shall, shop, chip, chill, chop, chant, when, wham,* and *whether.* Expect the children to have trouble with some of these. Repeat the words that present problems.

3. Present the task in which the children must write the entire word, not merely the ending: "Listen big. Write the word *wham.* Who remembers how to do that?" If a child writes *wam* instead of *wham,* tell him that his attempt is good: "That's right, JC. You write *wham,* but there's another way you can write *www.* Do you remember that? Let me show you. . . . This is the *www* we use when we write *wham.* That's sort of funny, isn't it? But that's what we do."

4. Have the children read sentences that contain the words *this, that, them,* and *when.* These are extremely important words. After they have been introduced, the teacher has a much greater latitude in the kind of sentences she can present for reading.

> this bug is red.
> hand them a fan.
> is that man big?
> when did dan get that?
> this flower is not red.

Weave a story line to go with each of the sentences:

"Mary's mother told her to pick a nice red flower. So Mary went out and came back with a blue flower. Her mother looked at her and said (read it), 'This flower is not red.' "

5. Give the children at least four sentences a day—more, if they can handle sentences with reasonable fluency. Repeat sentences that give trouble. Vary them if they are to be presented more than twice.

(NOTE: At this stage of instruction the child should spend as much of his time as possible reading sentences.)

Eliminating the word spacers

After the children have become reasonably facile at reading sentences, eliminate the rectangles between words, but leave a large space so that the words appear as individual units.

1. Write the first word of a sentence. Then say, "I'm not going to make a box after this word. I'm just going to leave a big space, like this. . . ." After completing the sentence, have the children identify the individual words by counting them. "How many words are there? Let's count them and see. Here's one. Here's another. Here's another, and . . ." Pretend that you are unable to find the last word. The children will probably help you out. "Thank you. Here's another word. Right. Let's count them. One, two, three, four. How many words? Four words."

2. *Precede the reading of all sentences with word counting until you feel certain that the children can identify words in a one-line sentence.* Always count words from left to right. Then make the spaces between the words smaller until they are only slightly larger than normal. Retain this word spacing throughout the remainder of the elementary reading instruction.

Two-Line Sentences

1. To acquaint the children with the method for reading from line to line, present a two-line sentence with an arrow under each line:

when a man fell in the pond
———————————————→

a man got wet.
———————————→

Read the first line and then point out the difficulty: "I still have to keep on reading, but where do we go from here? How do I get to this line down here?" Some of the children may suggest going down the right side and then reading backward. "Oh, but I have to follow the arrow down here on the second line. So if I come down here, I won't read anything." Perhaps the children will solve the problem. If not, lead them to a solution: "If I come down here, before the word *a*, I can follow the arrow and read all the words."

Draw a dotted arrow to show them what to do at the end of the first line:

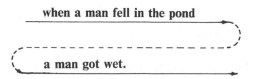

Read the statement with the children several times. When you have read to the end of the top line, ask one of the children to show you where to go.

2. After the introduction, write all sentences in two or more lines. Draw a box around the area in which you plan to write. This outline corresponds to the page of a book. Indicate the movement from line to line with broken arrows:

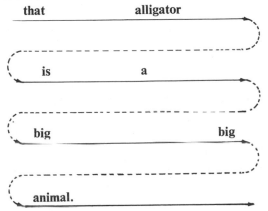

After the children have worked on about fifteen such sentences, *eliminate both the solid arrows and the dotted arrows.* The children should have no trouble without the arrows. "Look—no arrows. Who remembers which way we're supposed to go? . . . And what do we do when we come to the end of this line? . . . And what do we do when we come to the end of this line? . . . O.K., let's read. Where do we start?" If the children are still uncertain, introduce three-line sentences in which the solid arrow appears only under the first line, with one dotted arrow indicating how to proceed to the next line. Refer any children with problems to the first line. Drop the arrows when they no longer need to refer to the top line.

Stories

From this point on, the children should do almost all their reading exercises either in short stories or in writing. The stories should carry the bulk of the instruction. Any new rule or new sound combination should be introduced in stories, as should sight words. A full complement of stories cannot be outlined here, but here are rules for constructing them:

135

1. *Work on no more than two skills at a time in a story.* One should be the primary skill and the other a secondary or review skill. There should be at least eight examples of the primary skill in the story, and at least four examples of the secondary skill. For example, if the new skill is the *ooo* sound (as in *moon*), have at least eight different examples of *ooo* words, preferably more. If the skill that the children are reviewing is that of handling the *oy* words (*boy, joy, toy*), there should be at least four examples of these words in the story.

2. *The ratio of familiar to unfamiliar words should be about five to one.* When the percentage of unfamiliar words increases, the children tend to read atomically, often failing to recognize words that are familiar to them.

3. *Underline all irregular or "funny" words until the children have mastered them.* The purpose of the underlining is to call attention to the fact that the word does not follow strict rules of pronunciation.

(NOTE: Perhaps the most difficult exercise in learning to read is to try out one vowel sound, and if it doesn't produce a familiar word, try another vowel sound. The vowels are usually what make words irregular, which means that a particular vowel sound may not work in every word. Other sounds must be tried. The good reader knows this and does it unconsciously. The culturally disadvantaged child does not know it and must be taught, very carefully. Until now, he has not encountered many "funny" words. The simplified code was necessary to teach him how reading is supposed to work, to teach him the "ideal" reading process. Unless the presentation of the ideal is quite articulate, the child may never fully understand what is expected of him. But when he reaches the point in instruction where he understands what words are and how to attack regular words [and when he has learned that the object of reading is not only to sound out words, but also to remember them], he is ready to take the next, and perhaps the most difficult, step in instruction—learning to handle irregulars. This means that he must be shown—very carefully—how words are irregular. They are not totally irregular. The word *heat* is not pronounced *yellow*. The irregularity occurs in the vowels of the word. Unless this point is made quite clear, the child may lose a great deal of what has been carefully programed. He may assume that there is nothing stable in reading and that perhaps the best way to figure out a word is to take a wild guess. If this kind of mistake is to be avoided, the child must be shown something about the range of variations in

136

words that result when a vowel takes on an irregular sound.)

4. *Words that are being integrated into the children's sight vocabulary should be repeated at least three times in every story until they are mastered.* If the children develop a chronic mistake pattern, drop the word for about a week and then go back to it.

5. *Begin a story with variations of stock sentences.* The children will learn these quickly and get in the habit of reading quickly instead of stumbling through the story a letter at a time. A good basic opening is "This is a story about . . ."

6. *Keep the themes interesting.* Don't be afraid of exaggeration. Children like to read about dogs as big as houses, hot dogs as big as boys, a man who wears his shoes backward, and so on.

7. *When a theme works* (that is, when the children enjoy it), *use it again.* When a theme doesn't go over very well, drop it.

8. *When children have trouble with particular words, construct a story that will give them practice handling these words.*

The best procedure is to introduce a series of analogous words into the next stories. For instance, if the children have trouble with the word *bar*, pronouncing it *bear*, construct a story that contains several words ending with *ar:*

> this is a story about a car that went far. the car tried hard, but it did not go fast. it went past a big red barn, but it did not go fast. it went past a farm, but it did not go fast. it went over a jar, but it did not go fast. it went over a bar of soap, but it did not go fast. the car did not go fast, but the car tried hard. so the car got home at last.

In this story there are examples of *ast* words (*fast, past, last*) and of *ar* words (*car, hard, barn, jar, bar*). There are also groups of words that are repeated (*but it did not go fast*). These groups encourage the children to read words as words, rather than as the sum of atoms. There is also a variation of the word group to keep the children alert (*The car did not go fast*). The ratio of familiar to unfamiliar words is reasonable. Stories such as these are not constructed in a minute or two, but with practice a teacher can become expert at constructing them. The secret is to watch for errors in the present story. At this point in instruction, the children should be sophisticated enough to focus on new words. So if the teacher finds it difficult to say something she wants to say without using the word *before*, for example, she should introduce the word in the story and repeat it several times.

9. *Introduce sight words and groups of words in this approximate order:*

- *Said.* This word is very useful. It allows the teacher to write out a story line that has already been presented verbally. It allows her to use verbs in the present tense, which otherwise would have to be in the past tense:

John's mother sent him home. She said, "John, get me a red pot." John got her a black pot. His mother said, "John, this pot is not red. This pot is black."

Teach *said* as a funny word: "It looks like *sa–id*, but we don't say *sa–id*, we say *sed*. This is a funny word, isn't it?" Use *said* often in stories. Underline it to call attention to the fact that it is a funny word.

- *You, to, do.* These words are basic. They should be introduced after the *oo* words. Begin by constructing stories in which many *oo* words appear, always underlined:

> when the moon got big, the baboon went oo. a man said, "that baboon is a fool. he is cool and he is going oo. soon I will get mad. I will lock him in a coop. then he will not go oo at the moon."

Treat these words as funny words. Point to the double *o*'s and say, "When you see two *o*'s together like this, they go *ooo*."

After the words *moon, soon,* and *fool* have been repeated in other stories and the children can attack them as sight words, introduce the word *to:* "It looks like *to* (as in *tot*), but we say *too*. It's a funny word." Show them on the board what the word *to* should look like (*too*); then erase one of the *o*'s. "We still call it *to*."

Have the children write sentences that incorporate the word *to*. Use it liberally in all stories after the introduction. Underline it until the children become reasonably solid. Then drop the underline. Warn the children: "I didn't underline, but it's still a funny word."

After the children have mastered *to*, introduce *do*. Use the procedure outlined for presenting *to*. Explain that the word looks like *do* (as in *doll*), but we say *doo*. Use it liberally in stories, underlined until the children can read it as a sight word.

- *Out* words. Introduce the words *out* and *loud* in the introductory story, with the *ou* underlined in each word. Also underline the *ou* in the word *about* (programed as a sight word): "This is a story about a dog with a big loud bark. His bark is so loud that he has to sit out in the yard. Tom said, 'He is so loud we had to get him out in the yard.' " In subsequent stories, introduce the words *shout, round, around, found, ouch.*

(NOTE: Words with *ow*, such as *cow, how,* and *now,* present no real problem, because they are not irregular. They should be programed together: "This is the story about a cow. This cow did not *know* how to get to the barn." The word *know* is presented as a funny word. Point out that both ends of the word are silent—the *k* and the *w* are not pronounced.)

After the children have learned the various *ou* words, present the primary exception, *you:* "This is a funny word. It looks like *yow*, but we don't say *yow;* we say *you.*" Present *you* often. Expect the children to have some difficulty with it.

• Words that end in *y.* These words fall into two basic groups—those that have the long-*i* sound, and those that have the long-*e* sound.

Present the long-*i* group first. Initially introduce two of the following words: *try, my, why, by, fry, dry.* Then add to the list. Repeat troublesome words until the children have learned them. The potentially most troublesome word is *why*, because it is easily confused with the array of irregular words that begin with *wh.* The most important words in the list (that is, those that occur most frequently) are *my, why,* and *by.* Concentrate on these. The children will confuse *me* with *my* and *be* with *by* unless they become thoroughly familiar with *by* and *my.* The reason is that some words ending in *y* are pronounced as if they ended in long *e.* The child may therefore say *me* instead of *my.*

Introduce the long-*e y* ending after the children have mastered *my* and *by.* Introduce the words *many, very,* and *happy.* Call attention to the *y* ending on the word *story.* (This is a story about . . .) Other words, such as *sleepy, grouchy,* and *sticky,* can be introduced after the basic set has been mastered.

• *Or* and *for.* Initially present these words with the long-vowel mark over the *o* (*ōr, fōr*). After *or* and *for* have been mastered, drop the diacritical mark. This will probably take the children at least forty days. Next introduce *forget, form, orange* (which is irregular because of the soft *g*), *torn, born, horn,* and so on. Initially present the words *sore* and *more* with the final *e* very small. Make it larger as the children become familiar with the words.

• *Of.* This is a very strange word and is often confused with *for. Of* is completely irregular. It should be spelled *uv.* "This is really a funny

139

word. It looks like *off*, but we say *uv*." The stories in which *of* appears should also contain the word *for* (at least three times in each story).

After *of* has been mastered and can be distinguished from *for*, introduce the word *off*. Both *of* and *for* should appear in the initial stories, so that you can refer to an example of the word the children will most likely confuse: "No, this word is not *of*. Look up here: this word is *of;* and we say *uv*. This word down here has another *f: ooff–ff* . . . *off*." If the children become confused, delay the introduction of *off* for a month or more. During that month give the children plenty of exposure to *of* and *for*.

- *Oy* words. Although these words can usually be sounded out, they are learned more readily if they are grouped together, so that the children can learn some kind of analogy rule for handling them. Construct a story that contains at least three examples of these *oy* words: *boy, toy, joy*. In subsequent stories concentrate on the words *boy* and *toy*.

- Long-vowel sound words ending in *e*. The rule that is usually presented, that the final *e* makes the vowel long, can be supplanted by a series of demonstrations that give the child some kind of operational knowledge of the rule rather than mere verbal knowledge.

As noted earlier, the first step is to place a diacritical mark over the long vowel and make the final *e* very small:

I līke to go hōme.

I tāke a nōte hōme.

I līke to tāke a nōte.

After a word has been presented often enough for the children to read it as a sight word, make the final *e* normal size. When the children try to sound out the final *e*, remind them, "You never say the *e* at the end of the word. It's not *hom–e*, it's *home*. It's not *not–e;* it's *note*." Point out other words that end in *e*: "We don't say *littl–e*. We say *little*. We don't say *hav–e;* we say *have*. When you see an *e* at the end of a long word, don't say it." Include the words *he, me, we, be,* and *see* in stories having words with silent final *e*. Don't make a production out of trying to explain the rule. Simply demonstrate through reading that the *e* ending on the short words is pronounced, but on the longer words it is not pronounced.

140

Work on the words *lake, take, rake, snake, bake, cake, save, gave, like, bike, ripe, drive, live, dive, hope, note, smoke, hole, stove.*

After the children have become familiar with all the above words, drop the diacritical marks. Present them as funny words.

When the children are unable to produce the appropriate vowel sound for a word such as *save*, remind them, "This is a funny word. Make the *a* long." If the children don't respond readily to this instruction, give them additional cues and spend a few minutes in each session reviewing the verbal game in which they are to make words long. (See Long and Short Vowel Discriminations. p. 119.)

If the children try to sound out the final *e*, remind them of the rule—in an amused way: "Oh, oh! you forgot the rule. You never say the *e* at the end of a long word." Through much repetition of the instructions "Make it long" and "You don't say the *e* at the end of a long word," the children will learn a pattern. In order to facilitate this learning, they must be exposed to enough words that follow this pattern every time they read—until the procedure becomes natural. Each story should contain at least ten examples of long-vowel words ending in *e*. And after the selection has been read, the long-vowel words should be reviewed. Place the emphasis on quick recognition: "Let's go over all the funny words. Here's a funny word. Who remembers what it is? . . . Well, I remember. It's *like*. It looks like *lick–e*, but we say *like*. Here's another funny word. . . ." Through this presentation the children learn the pattern: when the word looks as if it should be pronounced with a short vowel and an *e* ending, it is pronounced with a long vowel and no ending. The rule is not easily induced and depends upon the programing of many examples.

The words *those* and *these* follow the long-vowel rule. They should be introduced after the initial set of long-vowel-silent-*e* words have been programed. Present them first with the diacritical mark and a small final *e*. Make the *e* larger as the children become familiar with the words. Then drop the diacritical mark.

• *Come, some, have, live,* and *give*. These words should be avoided as much as possible while the children are working on long-vowel-si-lent-*e* words. After the latter have been mastered, *some, come, have, live,* and *give* can be programed systematically. (NOTE: The word *have* can be introduced early in reading instructions. With the final *e* made small, it presents no particular problems. However, when the children are concentrating on long-vowel-silent-*e* words, they may become

141

confused by *have*.) The best strategy for handling these words is simply to point out that the final *e* is not pronounced. "This word looks like *hav–e*, but we don't say *hav-e;* we say *have*. That's a hard one to remember. I bet I'll fool you on that later."

Teach one or two of the words at a time and balance the story with words that follow the long-vowel-silent-*e* rule.

• *Where, what, who*. These are perhaps the most troublesome words the children will encounter if they are introduced prematurely. If in her presentation the teacher is not careful to preserve the rules that have been taught, the children may forget a great deal of what they have learned about attacking regular words.

Introduce the word *where* first. Use it in a story that contains the word *here* (which is a long-vowel-silent-*e* word). Point out that when the *w* is removed from the word *where*, the word *here* remains. Later show them that when *t* substituted for *w*, the word *there* is formed: "Boy! This is a funny word isn't it? *There, where*. Say them with me: *there, where*." In this context the word *where* is not merely a strange isolated entity. In working with *w* words, it is important to tie them to other words, especially those that do not follow the rules.

Use the word *where* frequently in stories. Let the children overlearn it before proceeding to the next word—*what*. Present *what* as a funny word: "It looks like *what*"—rhymes with *fat*—"but we say *wut*"—rhymes with *but*. "That's one you'll just have to remember. If you see a word that's spelled *what*, you say *wut*." Use the word liberally in stories: "And *what* do you think they found? He opened the box and said, '*What* is it?' "

The word *who* is perhaps the most difficult of all. To give it a personality, treat it as a fun word: "Listen to what this word says: *hooooo hoooo*. It looks like it should say *wwwooo*, but it doesn't. It says *HOOOOOOO*. Say it with me." Whenever the word is encountered in reading, make a joke about it: "Yes, *hooo* found the box? What a silly word."

After *where, what,* and *who* have been programed, use the words in stories for some time. Expect the children to forget how to attack these words and to make mistakes. Be patient. The best way to help a child who forgets one of these words is to say, "I know that word: *where*. Let's spell it." This approach is far more productive than requiring the child to sound out the word and then take a stab at identifying it.

142

• *All* words. Introduce the word *all* as a funny word: "It looks like *al*, but we say *awl*." Point out that the double letters are pronounced as one. Use *all* liberally in stories until the children can read the word at sight. Then begin programing *all* words: *fall, tall, call, ball, small, hall*. Underline *all* in each of these words. If the children have trouble, cover the first letter of the word and show them that the word *all* remains. "Now it says *all*, and now . . . it says . . ." After the children have learned to read most of the basic *all* words at sight, introduce the words *also, always, although*. To help cue them, underline the *al* in each word. As they become more familiar with the words, drop the underline.

• *Ur* words. These should not be introduced in any systematic fashion until the children have become reasonably proficient with long-vowel words. Words that have the *ur* sound—*dirt, burn, first*—represent a threat to what the child has learned about vowel sounds. If the child has not been firmly grounded in vowel sounds, he may conclude that what he has learned about vowels doesn't actually hold, and may start pronouncing all vowels *uh*. Introduce the words *hurt, burn*, and *turn* first. These words are regular; the children should have no trouble with them. After they have been mastered, introduce the words *dirt, first*, and *shirt*. Underline the *ir* in each word, and point out that these letters make the sound *ur*. Drop the underline after the children have learned to read the words quickly in stories. Use the words in stories until the children have overlearned them.

• Soft *c* and soft *g*. These sounds should be avoided until the children have become reasonably stable with a sight vocabulary of several hundred words. (If necessary for the construction of a story, words with soft *c* or *g* can be introduced, but they should generally be avoided.) Introduce soft-*c* words as they happen to come up. Do not try to establish the basis for any general rule; do not try to demonstrate through the presentation of analogous words that *c* and *g* are generally soft when followed by *e* or *i*. Repeat any soft-*c* and soft-*g* words that have been introduced, treating them as funny words. As the child builds up a sight vocabulary of such words as *city, cents, face, strange, change, huge*, begin to put them together in stories, but don't try to point out a general rule. The child will need many examples before he is in a position to appreciate the rule. One of the reasons is that many of these words are irregular in ways other than having a soft sound. *Change*, for example, has a long *a* in addition to a soft *g*.

• *Oi* words. These can be introduced relatively early in the story series. Introduce the word *oil* first. Underline the *oi* and point out that these letters go together to make the sound *oi:* "They always go together. Whenever you see them, you say *oi;* say that with me: *oi.*" After the children have learned to read *oil* at sight, introduce the words *boil* and *soil.* Be sure that the word *oil* appears in the same story with the other *oi* words. "This is a story about a man that liked to boil oil." In these stories, avoid such words as *toy* and *boy.* Show the children that when the first letter in the words *boil* and *soil* is removed, the word *oil* remains: "Look. Now it says *oil*, and now . . ." It is very important to make it clear that analogous constructions are usually sounded out analogously.

After *boil, soil,* and *oil* have been mastered, introduce the words *point* and *joint.* Use these words liberally in stories until the children have learned them reasonably well. Then present *oy* and *oi* words in the same stories.

How to present stories to the children

1. Try to establish momentum in the first sentence. Do not let children start out a sound at a time. If they start atomically, they will probably continue atomically. "Everybody, let's read this first sentence. Let's see what it says." Have the children reread the first sentence if they lack momentum: "Oh, come on! We can do it better than that. Get speedy. Here we go." The first sentence should be in a relatively familiar form, so that the children will be reading new words in a context they are used to: "This is a story about a man and a big, big hot dog." "This is not a story about a dog." "This is a story about a frog that looks like a dog." "Is this another story about Tom and his little tiger? Yes, this is another story about Tom and his little tiger." After the children get the set of reading in the first sentence, they can often maintain their momentum.

Expect the children to recognize words that they may have trouble sounding out. If a child persistently reads words rapidly but cannot handle them more slowly, have him spell the word after he has identified it: "Yes, *always.* Let's hear you spell it. Make all the sounds." Make the child conscious of the spelling, but do not require him to go slowly unless he makes mistakes. If he does and the mistakes are reasonable, don't lecture him. If he reads *little* instead of *letter*, tell him, "That's a good try. But it's not *little*. Let's spell it: *llleeet–terr* . . . *letter.* Take a good look at it, so you'll remember it next time."

144

Another mistake that children make when they try to read fast is calling a word by a synonym. Some children remember the word but can't produce the right sounds. If the word is *children*, they may say "kids"; if the word is *people,* they may say "persons." The best way to handle this mistake is to give the child credit for having remembered the concept but to help him figure out how to produce the correct word: "That's pretty good, JC. You've got the right idea, but the word is not *kids*. Let's spell it and see what it is." Usually the child will identify the word correctly before he spells more than a few letters.

Another reading difficulty to be on the lookout for is the "fourth-time" mistake. What happens is that a child will read a familiar word in a story three times without hesitation and then, with almost uncanny regularity, treat the word on the fourth trial as if he had never seen it before. This kind of mistake should be expected. Why it happens is not always clear. Sometimes the word is preceded by a difficult word, and in sounding out the difficult word, the child loses the set of reading words. He therefore attacks it as an unfamiliar group of letters. At other times the word just looks different to the child. Perhaps it is preceded by a quotation mark or followed by a question mark. Perhaps it appears at the beginning of a line. In any case, the fourth-time mistake is as natural for a child as falling down when he is learning to walk. Don't make him feel like a failure if he falters on familiar words. Sometimes it helps to point out that he read the word right in a previous sentence: "Hey, look up here. What's this word? . . . O.K., now look at this word again." Sometimes this approach does not jar his memory. If it does not, don't make an issue out of sounding out the word, especially if it is a "funny word." Tell him what it is, remind him that you'll test him on the word later, and proceed: "This word is *water*. See? It looks like *water*"— rhymes with *later*—"but we say *waw–ter*. Take a good look at it. I'll see if I can fool you on it later."

Still another common mistake is the reversal, which for some reason has been treated as a symptom of severe reading difficulties. Every child reverses elements when he learns to read, whether his IQ is 90 or 150. When he reaches the point of sounding out entire words at once, he is playing a rather difficult game, much like the game in which one is asked to pick up a series of objects as quickly as he can and arrange them in a certain order. If the player is supposed to arrange them from smallest to largest, he may arrange them in the opposite order, not because he has some constitutional difficulty but because he is trying to attend to many things at once and gets confused. Sometimes the reversals the children come up with are wild: *pel* for *help*, *isth* for *this*, *tsop* for *post*. However, if you think of what the child is trying to do, most of these mistakes are explicable. Sometimes a child will get in the habit of reading words backward. *Be on guard against this kind of mistake and try to catch it early*. For the child with a tendency to read backward, too much emphasis on speed is dangerous. Have the child slow down to a more leisurely pace and point to each word, moving from left to right. If the reversing tendency is caught early enough, it can be corrected rather easily. However, if it is allowed to develop into a habit, a great deal of slowdown work may be required to correct it.

Another mistake that can be expected when children are attempting to read words rapidly is that of mistaking words that are similar in structure—mistaking *every* for *very*, *there* for *here*, *hot* for *not*, and the like. These mistakes are quite reasonable. Expect them. Correct them casually and go on.

2. Have the children read in unison as much as possible.

Pay special attention to children who are moving slowly.

Familiarize yourself with the kind of mistakes that each child is likely to make. *He will probably make the same kind of mistakes again and again*. Knowing this, you can selectively listen to each child as they read together.

Keep the units to be read relatively small. If there are about four words on a line, one child will not get too far ahead of the others, and the prompting that the children receive from each other is often quite useful in helping them figure out an individual word. Often all the children will encounter a difficult word. One child will get the first several sounds. He will repeat these but be unable to form them into a familiar word. However, his efforts will aid another child, who completes the word. Through this procedure the children will become familiar with the strategies used by other children.

Do not limit reading to unison reading. Require each child to read a few words or a line alone. The amount of time devoted to this kind of reading should be determined by how well the children are doing. If they are moving along and every child is attacking the words, don't spend a great deal of time on individual performances. Let them move along and enjoy both the story and their accomplishments.

146

However, if they are having difficulty, or if one child is lagging behind, introduce individual reading.

Don't expect all children to perform well when called upon to read individually. Some children, who read well in the group, fall apart when they must read by themselves. The best way to handle this type of child is to make him a helper: "O.K., JC, you read, and if you have any trouble Mary will help you out." In the role of helper, Mary will probably be able to read many words that she would be unable to read if she were called on to perform alone.

A variation of the helper task is to have all the children help you out as you read. Use this technique to go over material that has already been read by the class: "O.K., now I'm going to read and you help me out if I make a mistake." Have the children follow by pointing to each word as you read it. Read very slowly, a word at a time. When you encounter a funny word, make the process of reading the word explicit: "Oh, oh! This is a funny word. I remember that these letters (*oi*) go together. But what sound do they make? Let me think." The children will probably identify the combination or tell you the word. Act defensive: "You didn't give me a chance. I would have figured it out. You're just too fast for me." Misread about every fifth word. If the children don't catch you, act triumphant: "I knew I could fool you on that one. I said *look*, but it's really *looking*. Ho, ho! I'll bet I can get you on that one again later."

On some words, act as if you were having difficulty sounding out the word. Give proper sound values, but proceed hesitantly. The children will probably jump ahead and tell you the word. "Gee, you guys are just too fast for me."

For another variation on the helper game, have the children read every other word: "I'll read this word. Then you read the next. O.K., here we go." What will actually happen is that the children will read all the words, and they will probably be able to read more rapidly than they would if they were required to read every word. It is sometimes surprising how rapidly the children can read when they play this game.

For still another variation of the helper game, read three or four words slowly; then stop and let the children read the next word or words. A good procedure is to read the first words in a sentence and let the children complete it.

3. Do not give the children advance warning that a new word or set of words is to appear in the story. Instead, treat the new word or

147

set of words as an obstacle—a problem to be solved. For example, if the focus of the story is on *all* words, read to the first *all* word and then point out the rule: "This is the story about a *small* . . . Oh, oh! This is a funny word. Do you want to know how to read it? Look." Cover the letters *sm.* "Who remembers this word? . . . It looks like *al*, but we say *awll* . . . *all.* Now it says *all*, and now it says—this is tough —*small.* See the word *all* in *small?* O.K. Well, maybe you'll be able to find *all* in other words. Let's see."

At this point you may want to have the children scan the page to see if they can find other words containing *all.* If they are unable to find any, suggest that you can. When you find a word, act triumphant: "I found one. Look here—*all.* Now it says *all*, and now . . . it says *fall.*"

After finding other examples, continue to read. Don't be surprised if the children fail to identify *all* words when they come to them in the story. Be patient. If they have a great deal of difficulty with the new words, take a few moments from the reading and review them on the chalkboard. Don't expect a quick demonstration to make up for inadequate exposure to the word. If the children need only a quick review, the chalkboard demonstration will suffice. However, if they need practice in seeing the word *all*, they will not receive the needed practice in a few minutes, and it is a mistake to try to cram. Go over the *all* words lightly, and plan to introduce stories that contain many examples of words containing *all.*

4. After the children have read the entire story, take a few minutes to review words that presented problems and words that are covered by the rule being emphasized in the story. Do not point only to difficult words. For every difficult or new word, point to *two* words the children have mastered. The purpose of this convention is to encourage the children to read words at sight. The two familiar words will establish the set of "reading" words, which may carry over to the more difficult words.

(NOTE: *Children almost always read isolated words with greater facility than they do the same words when embedded in sentences.* Don't be surprised if the children, when reading stories, have trouble with words that present no problem in isolation.)

The review should be presented as a kind of game: "O.K., now we'll see just how good you are. I'm going to point to some words— move in so you can see my story—I point, and you say them. O.K., here's a hard word." Point to an easy one and act surprised when they recognize it: "Pretty good. Here's a harder word." If the children have trouble with a word, tell them what it is—spell it if necessary—then return to it after pointing to three or four other words. Always warn them about words that are chronically troublesome: "Here's that word again. I wonder who remembers it. It's tough."

Introduce a variation of the game if one or two of the children in the group are identifying words too quickly for the others: "O.K., don't say the word until I clap my hands. Take a good look. . . ." Some of the children may not be able to play this game because they will be unable to talk to themselves and figure out what the word is without producing the sounds verbally. Tell these children that they should talk very softly. As they learn to do this, tell them to whisper, and demonstrate how to do this: "Watch me whispering: *fffiiishsh*. I've got it: *fish*." After the children have mastered this step (which may take some time), go on to the next step; moving the lips without saying the word audibly. If at first they have trouble sounding out words to themselves, do not play the game for more than about a minute a session, but play the game every day until the children can sound out words inaudibly.

5. Repeat stories no less than two weeks after they have first been introduced. Plan to repeat all stories once. Do not repeat the stories more than once unless a number of the children are absent when the story is repeated or unless no new stories are on hand. Keep copies of all stories in a "library." Allow the children to read these stories during free time. Expect them to perform considerably better on a repeated story than on a story of equal difficulty presented for the first time. Watch out for context reading, that is, for the tendency to express the idea of a sentence without using the words that actually appear in the story. The children will probably remember a story very well, even after a month or more.

6. Allow the children to take copies of a story home with them after it has been read in class. Remind each child, "I want you to read this story to your mother. I want you to show her what a good reader you are." At the beginning of each session, ask the children if they read their stories: "Who did you read your story to, John? Did you read it at home? O.K., I'll be able to tell. When you work hard at home, you read better, so I'll be able to tell." The home-rehearsal effect is probably the most noticeable when stories are repeated. The

children who actually save their books and read them will be able to read the stories much better than the children who do not.

Capital Letters

Introduce capital letters casually.

1. Begin with letters that look like their lowercase counterparts —*C, J, K, O, P, S, U, V, W,* and *Z.* Present these letters at the beginning of sentences the children are to read:

> See the big dog.
> We will go in the pond.
> Can you eat a hot dog?

If the children ask about their size, say that they are capital letters or big letters. "We always start the sentence with a capital letter."

2. After the children have been exposed to capital letters in sentences for perhaps a month, introduce the set of capital letters on a large chart. Identify each letter *by the sound it makes.* Point to the various letters and ask, "What sound is this?" The answer is "capital *mmm*" or "capital *aaa.*"

Present three or four letters on the board every day. Have the children identify them by their sound.

3. Next teach the letter names. Do this by telling the children that each of the sounds has a name.

Point to each of the capital letters in alphabetical order and give the name, "*A, B, C, D* . . ." The children may already know the letter names.

Present the lowercase letters in alphabetical order and have the children identify them by their names. Point out that you are not discarding what the children have learned about sounds: "When we read we call it *mmmm*, but the name of the letter is *em.*"

4. After the children can identify the letters by name, introduce the task of reciting the alphabet without looking at the letters: "I can name all the letters without even looking at them. Here I go . . ." Recite the alphabet with the group at the beginning of each reading session. From time to time, call on individual children to recite it. Before long, the children will have mastered it.

To help them remember the order, introduce the alphabet song. The melody will help the children keep the parts in proper sequence.

150

Reading in Basal Readers

After the words and the attack skills outlined in this chapter have been programed, the children should be ready to read from basal readers. Don't push them into basal readers until they have mastered all the skills specified in this chapter. Begin with second-grade material even though you may feel that they can handle third-grade material. When the child moves into readers, he is quickly going to move away from the kind of careful programing you have given him. There is usually repetition in these readers, but it is often the wrong kind of repetition. Structurally similar words may be repeated, but usually not nearly often enough to teach the child, merely to remind him. For this reason, it is probably a good idea to work with the lower-level books first and make sure that the child manages to consolidate the skills he has acquired. If he moves into a book that is too difficult, he may find himself not reading, but attacking the material a sound at a time, or he may try to read in larger units and develop bad habits of guessing and paying insufficient attention to the details that make one word different from another.

If, in reading basal readers, the children have trouble with new words, give them chalkboard practice. Also, after reading a selection, point to the words that give trouble and have the children identify them. If the children don't learn new words adequately from the book presentation, present the more difficult words on the chalkboard from time to time as words the children should remember. Don't expect them to remember these words unless they are presented frequently: "Here's a word we had the other day when we were reading about little Quacky, the duck. Let's see who remembers it."

5   Reading and Language
for the More Advanced Child

The child who has learned how to decode words has overcome the major obstacle to reading. There is, however, more to reading than being able to translate printed symbols into words; the child is expected to understand the message the printed page conveys. He may fail to understand this message not because he has a reading deficit, but because he has a verbal-language deficit. In other words, if the message were spoken he still would not understand it. The remedy for such a deficit is not reading, but verbal-language training. Reading practice alone may simply reinforce the child's tendency to overlook segments of what he reads—to skim from one point of understanding to another without being concerned about what lies between. This tendency is dangerous. One who does not understand every word in a sentence may easily misinterpret it. *The child should be taught a reading strategy based on attention to the meaning of every word.*

The child can be taught the intent of communication by being shown, in detail, how words and sentences function in solving communication problems. The first step is to show him that instructions give specific directions and that each word used carries a part of the meaning. He must be shown that instructions do more than give the reader a cue. They tell the reader precisely what to do. The next step is to show that instructions apply to many kinds of problems—including those in which the reader must construct something that is specified in the instructions. The next step is to demonstrate that descriptions and definitions are a simple extension of instructions. Descriptions tell what something is in such a way that it will not be confused with the other things in a group. Definitions tell what a group of things is in such a way that the group will not be confused with other groups. The final step is to give the child practice in using language skills to form complex analogies.

This chapter outlines the steps, starting with simple instructions and working into the more complex language-reading operations.

Many of the reading and language tasks presented in this section might seem too advanced for children in the primary grades. The tasks are not difficult, however, if they are programed properly—that is, presented so that each of the subskills involved in the task is *taught*.

Try to follow the format outlined in this chapter closely. If children have trouble with a particular task, try to figure out what their difficulty is and give them practice in the skills they have not learned. Proceed through the tasks as rapidly as possible. Do not spend more than about fifteen minutes a day on the kind of exercises outlined in this chapter. The remainder of the reading period should be spent on reading. Children become proficient readers only if they practice every day. It is probably a good idea to spend at least fifteen minutes a day working on oral reading in small groups. During seatwork periods, the children can read to themselves. When children are engaged in silent reading, ask them questions about what they are reading. Ask them to show you which words indicate that someone is doing something or that something is going on.

Following Written Instructions

The best way to show the child the importance of careful reading is to construct tasks that illustrate what happens if instructions are not read carefully. The objective is to show dramatically that a discrepancy results if the instructions are not carried out exactly, and that the discrepancy can be explained by reference to the specific *words* in the instructions that do not correspond to the action carried out.

Simple imperatives

1. As an introductory exercise, give each child a sheet of paper with four instructions:

    1. Put a stick on the floor.
    2. Put a stick in your hand.
    3. Put a stick on the teacher's desk.
    4. Put a stick under your chair.

Give the children the material they need to carry out the instructions (four ice-cream sticks or toothpicks).

Tell the class, "See where it says number one. Point to the one. O.K., point to the two . . . point to the three . . . point to the four. . . .

O.K., point to one. Now read what it says after number one. Read it to yourself."

After they have read the instruction, tell them, "I'm going to do what this sentence tells me to do." Take an *eraser* and put it on the floor. "There. Did I do what it told me to do?" The children may object. Act puzzled. "But why not? Didn't I put it on the floor?" The children will probably agree. "Well, what's wrong then? I did just what it said."

Try to get them to pinpoint the discrepancy: "Well, what word tells me that I made a mistake? Find that word. It says *put*. I put. It says *on the floor*. I put it on the floor. So show me the word that tells me I made a mistake."

The children may indicate a word other than *stick*. If they do, point out that you did what the word told you to do. For example, if they point to the word *put*, say, "I put it. I didn't eat it, did I?" After the children have located the word *stick*, commend them: "You're right. It doesn't say 'Put the *eraser* on the floor.' It says 'Put the *stick* on the floor.' The word *stick* tells me that I made a mistake, because this isn't a stick."

Have the children read the third instruction next. (Do not present the items in numerical order.) "Find the three. Put your finger on it. Now read what it tells me to do." After they have read the sentence, tell them, "O.K., now I'm going to do what it says. Watch me." Take a stick and place it under your desk. "There. I did it."

If the children object, have them find the word that indicates you did not carry out the instructions: "What word tells me that I made a mistake?" Try to defend what you did: "I used a stick, didn't I?" Confirm that the word that indicates the discrepancy is the word *on:* "On. I didn't put it *on* the desk. I put it *under* the desk."

(NOTE: When working on the kind of exercises outlined in this section, teachers sometimes get carried away. They savor the role of one who poses questions that children may have trouble answering. They should keep in mind that their role is not that of a gadfly but that of a teacher. The exercises are designed to point out the function of key words, the necessity of understanding every word in the instructions, and the necessity of comparing the written instructions with the reality that is created when the instructions are carried out. The questions are designed to point out that each word has a function, that to understand a set of instructions is to understand what is called

154

for, what is not called for, and why. The present exercise, for example, is designed to show the children that if they describe what the teacher has done in precise language [she put a stick under the teacher's desk] and then compare this description with the operation called for in the instructions [put a stick on the teacher's desk], there is a discrepancy. When the children point out the word that identifies the discrepancy, the teacher should not continue to ask questions, but should confirm their observation and let them know that they are on the right track.)

Refer next to the second instruction (put a stick in your hand): "Find number two. Read what it says and watch me. I'll do what it tells me to do." Take the stick and place it in the hand of one of the children. "There. I did it."

Describing the discrepancy in this statement is difficult, and the children may not be able to do it. They may be able to identify the word *your* as the seat of discrepancy, but they may not be able to tell why. Have all the children show what they should do after reading the instruction. Do not attempt a long verbal description of the relative nature of *your*. Simply say, "*Your* means the person who is reading the instructions. When you read the instructions, it means *your* hand. When I read the instructions, it means *my* hand."

Refer to Item 4. Again tell the children that after they read it, you will carry out the instruction. First put the stick under one of the children's chairs. The discrepancy in this presentation has to do with the word *your*, as it did in the preceding exercise. Repeat the explanation of *your* after the children have identified the word. Then move the stick so that it is on your chair. Now the discrepant word is *on*. Lead the children to it by acting as if you have satisfied the requirements of the instruction: "I'm reading. It says *your* chair. So that's *this* chair, right?" After the children have identified the word *on*, substitute an eraser for the stick and put it under your chair. "O.K., it's under my chair, isn't it? Well, what word tells me that I made a mistake?"

The tasks presented for Item 4 represent a summary of what has been demonstrated in the preceding items. The instruction calls for a specific action. It is possible to select the wrong object to work with, or to do the wrong thing with the right object. In Item 4 each violation is related to a particular word in the instruction.

2. Introduce similar tasks until the children have become relatively proficient at handling them. Vary the tasks by asking the children to

155

carry out some of the instructions. Do not assign an instruction until the children have read the instructions to themselves. They will read the instructions more carefully if they do not know ahead of time who will carry them out. They will be especially careful if they know they will be required to catch you in a mistake.

Present four instructions on individual sheets. Vary the objects and the preposition, but keep the verb constant—*put*. Try to use the word *your* in at least one of the tasks. For example:

1. Put an eraser on John's desk.
2. Put an eraser next to Mary's desk.
3. Put an eraser under Tony's desk.
4. Put an eraser between your desk and the teacher's desk.

After a child (or the teacher) has carried out an instruction, ask the class if it has been done correctly: "Did he do it?" If the children answer yes, ask them, "Well, how do you know?" Demonstrate the rule for checking the correctness of the action: *a statement of what the child did corresponds to the written instruction.* Lead them to awareness in two steps:

a. "Well, what did it tell you to do in number three, JC? Read what it tells you to do. . . . Yes, put an eraser under Tony's desk."

b. "And what did Mary do? . . . Yes, she put an eraser under Tony's desk. It says put an eraser under Tony's desk, and she put an eraser under Tony's desk. She did what it told her to do."

Use the two steps to evaluate the execution of every instruction. Have the child read what the instruction tells them to do; then compare the instruction with a statement of what the person who carried out the action actually did. If there is a precise correspondence, the requirements of the instruction have been satisfied.

If the children agree that a child has satisfied the requirements of the instruction, suggest alternative interpretations and ask them to specify the word in the instruction that has been violated. For example, after the child has placed the eraser under Tony's desk, substitute a stick for the eraser and ask, "What if Mary did this? Would this be O.K.? . . . Why not? Find the word that tells you this is wrong." After they have identified the word *eraser*, place the eraser on Tony's desk. Ask, "What if Mary had done this? . . . Find the word that tells you this is wrong." After the children have found the word, compare the instruction with a statement of what has been done: "Yes, it said to put an eraser *under* Tony's desk. I put an eraser *on* Tony's desk."

156

3. After the children have learned to handle the object and preposition discrepancies in the exercise outlined above, introduce a variation in which the children must identify which of a set of instructions has been carried out.

Give each child a sheet on which these instructions appear:

1. Put the eraser on the teacher's desk.
2. Put the eraser on John's desk.
3. Put a stick on the floor.
4. Put a stick on John's desk.

Say, "Read instructions one, two, three, and four." The children may need further direction, but keep your explanation brief. "Listen carefully: read all the instructions. Read one; read two; read three; and read four." After the children have read all the instructions, present the rules of the game. "I'm going to do something, and you have to tell me if I did number one, number two, number three, or number four. Watch carefully." Place a stick on the floor. The children may volunteer that you put a stick on the floor. "Yes, but you have to tell me what number that is."

If the children are confused, go through each instruction and have them indicate whether it corresponds to what you did: "Did I do number one? Read number one, Mary. . . . O.K., did I do that? . . . No. . . . Did I do number two? . . . No. . . . John, read number two. . . ." After they have identified instruction three as the one that was carried out, ask, "And what number is this instruction? . . . Yes, number three. So which number did I do? . . . Number three."

Next carry out instruction number two. "Watch what I do and tell me what number it is." Some of the children may indicate that you carried out instruction four. If they do, have them (1) read instruction four; (2) describe what you did; (3) note whether there is a discrepancy between the description and the instruction; and (4) indicate the discrepant word.

After going through the remaining instructions (one and four) and having the children identify each action by giving the corresponding number, let members of the class take turns carrying out an instruction while the class identifies it by giving the corresponding number: "O.K., JC, I want you to do what one of these instructions tells you to do. Choose any instruction you wish. Maybe three, maybe four, maybe two, maybe one. It's up to you. You do it, and then we'll see if we can tell which number you did. Go."

Tell the other children to raise their hands when they know which instruction he did. The hand-raising technique, although generally not advisable, is quite useful in a situation where the children are required to carry out an operation that cannot be observed on the behavioral level. If the child is to read instructions to himself and compare them with an action that has been carried out, the behavior (the act of comparing) is not obvious. The child can best indicate that he has completed the operation by raising his hand.

Wait until all the children have raised their hands or until it becomes obvious that some cannot handle the task. Call on one of the children who have raised their hands: "O.K., Tony, give me the number."

If the children have trouble with the task of referring to an action by the corresponding number, cover the instructions on the child's sheet with another sheet of paper so that only the numbers of the items are visible. "O.K., all I can see is the numbers. You've got to tell me which number to uncover. Choose a number. If you tell me number one, I'll uncover this number and read what it says. . . ." By using this variation, you can make the point that each number refers to a specific item.

4. Introduce similar tasks until the children have become proficient in referring to an action by the corresponding number. Increase the difficulty by constructing pairs of items that are similar. For example:

1. Put a stick on the teacher's desk.
2. Put an eraser under the teacher's desk.
3. Put a stick under the teacher's desk.
4. Put an eraser on the teacher's desk.
   or
1. Put your stick on the teacher's desk.
2. Put the teacher's stick under your desk.
3. Put your stick under the teacher's desk.
4. Put the teacher's stick on your desk.

In this exercise, have the children carry out all the actions. If you carry out any of them, confusion will result.

5. Introduce variations of the tasks in which (*a*) the numbers on the pages are out of order; (*b*) each item is preceded by a letter rather than a number; (*c*) some items are preceded by numbers, others by letters. These variations should be introduced relatively early if the children are confused about referring to items by their numbers. For example:

    a. Put a stick on an eraser.
    b. Put an eraser next to a stick.
    c. Put a stick next to an eraser.
    d. Put an eraser on a stick.

(NOTE: The "next to" task in this case may be difficult for the children. They may not see that the thing that is to be put is the thing that must be operated on and brought next to the other—if the eraser is to be put next to the stick, the eraser must be moved, not the stick. If children have trouble with these tasks, introduce variations until they have learned the convention: "It says 'put an eraser,' so I have put an eraser. Where? Next to a stick.")

6. As the children become familiar with the tasks, carry out actions that are not specified by any of the instructions on the child's sheet. For example, the child's instructions might be as follows:

    b. Put your stick on your head.
    a. Put your head on the teacher's stick.
    2. Put the teacher's stick on your stick.
    4. Put your stick on the teacher's head.

"O.K., I'm going to do one of these and you are going to tell me which one I do. Give me the letter or the number. Here I go." Put your stick on a child's head. "Which instruction did I do?" If the children indicate that you carried out *b* or *2*, have them compare what was done with the instruction. Have them find the discrepant words. Then say, "I really fooled you on that one."

If the children have trouble grasping the idea that not all possible actions are included on the sheet of instructions, introduce a more obvious violation: "O.K., watch me and tell me which instruction I do." Put a chair on your desk. "O.K., which one did I do?" Perform several other acts that are not specified by the instructions, and then one that is—put your stick on your head. "Which one did I do?"

As the children become familiar with this fooler game, encourage them to introduce foolers of their own. But remind them, "If we catch you, you have to follow one of the instructions on the sheet." When a child purposely violates a set of instructions, he has grasped an idea that the slow-learning child sometimes finds difficult.

7. Introduce sets of instructions in which the verbs are varied. In all the preceding exercises the same verb (*put*) was used. The following exercises, however, show the child that the verb represents another part of the instruction that can be violated.

Present the following instructions:

  a. Touch the chalkboard.
  b. Slap the chalkboard.
  c. Print your name on the back of this paper.
  d. Draw a picture of a house on the back of this paper.

Tell the children that you will do *a.* Then slap the chalkboard. "Did I do *a?* . . . What does *a* tell me to do? . . . And what did I do? . . . So what word tells me that I made a mistake? . . . Yes, *touch.* I didn't touch. I slapped."

Next tell the children, "O.K., I'll do it right this time. Watch." Print your name on the chalkboard. "Did I do it right? . . . Why not? What word tells me that I made a mistake?"

Now tell the children that you will try again. This time, draw a simple picture of a house on the chalkboard. Work fast to keep the children from becoming frustrated waiting for you to finish so that they can tell you that you made a mistake. "What did I do? . . . What was I supposed to do? . . . What word tells me that I made a mistake?" Gently touch the chalkboard. "What did I do? . . ."

Through this demonstration you have introduced the actions that are contained in Instructions *a, b, c, d.* The stage is set for the children to carry out the instructions. "Everybody, read *c* to yourself. Raise your hand when you've read it. . . . O.K., do it." If a child has trouble, have him read the instruction aloud. (NOTE: If a child finds a word in the instructions that he cannot read, repeat the word in other instructions on subsequent sheets until he learns it: "O.K., that's what it tells you to do. Do it.")

After the children have carried out *b, c,* and *d,* introduce the exercise in which you carry out one of the actions and they identify it by the corresponding letter. Also, have children carry out an action which is to be identified by other children. Compliment them for being good foolers: "That was a good one, John." But after each fooler, make the child follow one of the instructions on the sheet.

Introduce a variety of verbs on subsequent sheets. For example:

  34. Stand on your chair.
  32. Sit on the floor next to your chair.
  6. Turn your paper upside down.
  7. Throw your stick into the wastebasket.

Have the children provide missing verbs. Present sheets in which the verb is missing and must be filled in before the instructions can be carried out:

1. _____ on your chair.
2. _____ on your chair.
3. _____ on your chair.
4. _____ on your chair.

"What can you do on your chair? . . . Yes, sit. Let's write *sit* in number one. What else can you do on a chair?" If the children have trouble, demonstrate some of the actions that are possible. Kneel on the chair. Jump up and down on the chair. Put your feet on the chair. Put a piece of paper on the chair. Write with chalk on the chair. Encourage the children to find other ways to complete the sentence. Have them exchange sheets and carry out one of the instructions. Ask the other children to identify the action. Compare their observations with the verb on the sheet.

Present similar exercises until the children have learned how to describe various actions.

8. Introduce compound violations of an instruction—that is, violations that relate not to a single word but to several words or a phrase. For example, present this set of instructions:

1. Draw a line on the chalkboard.
2. Draw a circle on the floor.
3. Crawl on the floor.
4. Sit on your desk.

Tell the children that you will do instruction number one. Draw a circle on a sheet of paper. "O.K., what did I do wrong? What tells me that I did something wrong?" If the children indicate that you did not draw a *line*, draw a line on your sheet of paper. "There. Did I do it right this time? I changed the word you told me to change." After the children point out that the word *chalkboard* has also been violated, return to the instruction and show them that two words were violated.

Violate instruction number two by drawing a line on the chalkboard. If the children identify only one violation, ask, "Are there any other words that tell me I made a mistake?" If they cannot identify the other word, have them give the instruction you followed (draw a line on the chalkboard) and compare it with instruction number two (draw a circle on the floor): "The word *circle* tells me that I made a mistake, and the word *floor* tells me that I made a mistake."

161

Introduce compound violations as part of the daily sessions. After the children have worked out the instructions presented on a sheet, select an instruction and violate it twice. For example, violate the instruction "put the paper on your desk" by putting an eraser under your desk. Jump over the wastebasket instead of standing on a chair. Throw the eraser onto a desk instead of putting it on a chair.

Imperatives involving "and"

1. Introduce instructions using the word *and:*
   a. Put a stick and a pencil on the floor.
   b. Stand up and put this piece of paper on your head.
   c. Draw a circle and a line and a triangle on the back of this paper.
   d. Put this paper on your head and stand up.

In these exercises the two major types of *and* relationships are presented: grouping and narration. The grouping *and* does not imply a particular order of events. In Item *a*, for example, the instruction is satisfied if stick and pencil are placed on the floor simultaneously, if the pencil is placed on the floor first, or if the stick is placed on the floor first. The narrative *and*, however, does imply a particular order of events. Item *b* is not satisfied unless the child first stands up and then places the piece of paper on his head.

To demonstrate the distinction between the two *and*'s, refer to Item *a*. Ask, "What am I supposed to put on the floor?" As the objects are named, show that they form a group and that you can treat them as if they were one. "These. I'm supposed to put these on the floor. Here I go." Put them down simultaneously. "Did I do it? Did I put these on the floor?" Pick them up and repeat the operation, this time placing the pencil on the floor first. "Did I do it? Sure. I put these on the floor." Pick them up again and this time, put the stick on the floor first. "Did I put these on the floor? Are they on the floor? Did I put them there? Yes, so I did what it told me to do." This basic demonstration may have to be repeated several times.

Refer next to Item *b*. Have the children read it. Then say, "I'm going to do what it tells me to do. What does it tell me to do first? *Stand up.* Here I go. . . . O.K., what does it tell me to do next? *Put the paper on my head.* . . ." Repeat the demonstration, this time reversing the order of the actions. Put the paper on your head and then stand up. "I didn't do what it told me to do. It told me to stand up, but I put this paper on my head. . . ."

162

Have the children carry out Instructions c and d.

If the children have difficulty distinguishing between the two uses of *and*, introduce imperatives of this kind: "Put a stick and a piece of paper on your head and bend over as far as you can." If both objects are on the child's head, the grouping *and* has been satisfied, but it is virtually impossible to carry out the two actions in this order. What results if the child bends over first and then puts the objects on the back of his head is not the same as what results if the child puts the objects on his head and then bends over.

Present a simple instruction such as "stand up"; carry out the instruction by standing up and then clapping. The purpose of this task is to familiarize the children with the use of *and* to describe what happened. "What did it tell me to do? . . . Well, didn't I do that?" The answer is "Yes, but you did more." "What else did I do? . . . O.K., who can tell me what I did? I stood up *and* I clapped.

After the children have caught on to the idea of how the word *and* works, lead them to increasingly elaborate uses. For example, present the instruction "walk to the wastebasket." Carry out the instruction by walking to the wastebasket, picking it up, carrying it to a child's desk, and placing it on the desk. "Did I do what it told me to do? . . . Well, what did I do?" Have the children reconstruct the events in the order they occurred: "And what else did I do? I walked to John's desk. And then what?" After they have identified all the major actions involved, present your performance as a statement with the moves connected by *and*'s: "I walked to the wastebasket, and I picked it up, and I walked to John's desk, and I put the wastebasket on John's desk."

Provide a few ruled lines at the bottom of an instruction sheet. After the children have worked the instructions presented for the day, perform a series of three simple actions (stand up from your chair, turn all the way around, and sit down). Have the children use the ruled lines at the bottom of the page to describe what you did, using the word *and*.

Introduce *and* to relate instructions on the sheet. For example:

1. Do what it tells you to do in Number 2 and Number 3 and Number 4.
2. Stand up.
3. Clap three times.
4. Bend over and touch your toes.

Introduce variations. Change the position of the instruction that refers to the other items. Introduce more complicated examples after the children have caught on to the basic scheme. For example:

1, Walk to the chalkboard and draw a circle on the chalk- board.
2. Do what it tells you to do in Number 3 and Number 4.
3. Do what it tells you to do in Number 1.
4. Erase the circle and hand the teacher a stick and an eraser and a piece of chalk.

Instruct the children, "Do what number two tells you to do." This task requires the child to use everything he has learned to date. He must know how to refer to items by their numbers; he must know how to follow the instructions precisely; he must know how to create outcomes by using different verbs, prepositions, and the word *and*.

For more advanced children, the teacher should proceed to these tasks as quickly as possible. In fact, starting with these tasks provides a good test of what the children must work on.

2. Introduce the concept *not*. Provide each child with a stick, a pencil, and an index card. Identify the index card as a card. Pass out sheets containing these instructions:

1. Hold up the things that are not a pencil.
2. Hold up the things that are not a stick.
3. Hold up the things that are not a card.
4. Hold up the thing that is not a pencil and not a card.
5. Hold up the thing that is not a card and not a stick.
6. Hold up the thing that is not a pencil and not a stick.

Have the children read the items in order and do what each tells them to do. Some children may have trouble with plurals. Demonstrate the difference between *thing* and *things* by holding up a single object and saying "thing." Add another object and say "things," emphasizing the *z* ending. Add another object and say "things." Repeat this procedure until you have assembled about six objects. Then hold up the objects one at a time and say "thing" each time.

Make the point that the words contained in the statement function as specific guides to the operation called for. For example, after the children have worked Item 1, use the words *not a pencil* as your criterion: "Look, it says 'not a pencil.' So I look at this"—the card—"and I say 'Not a pencil,' I look at this"—the stick—"and say 'Not a pencil.'" Point to each of the objects. "Not a pencil. Not a pencil. These are the ones I hold up?" Now refer to the pencil: "Should I hold this one up? No, because I can't look at it and say 'Not a pencil.' "

Go through the remaining exercises in the manner outlined above. First have the children read an item to themselves and carry out the operation. Then analyze the statement: "It says to hold up the things that are not a card. Not a card. . . ." Point to the objects that are not a card. "So I say, 'Not a card. Not a card.' These are the things I should hold up. I can't hold this other thing up because I can't look at it and say, 'Not a card.' It *is* a card."

After the introduction to *not* statements, use *not* to refer to items on the sheet:

    a. Do Item *c.*

    b. Do an item that is not Item *d.*

    c. Write the names of three things that are not in this room.

    d. Do an item that is not Item *b.*

Item *a* introduces the word *item*. The children should have no trouble seeing what is meant by the word. If they do, give a quick explanation: "Find *d.* See what it tells you to do there? That's Item *d.* Find *b.* See what it tells you to do there? That's Item *b.* Where's Item *a?* . . . And Item *c?* . . ."

The children will probably have fun with this kind of exercise. If they become confused, however, repeat it until their understanding of the concepts involved—primarily *not*—has become more stabilized.

After the children work Item *a,* stress the function of the words in Statement *b*: "It tells me to do an item that is not Item *d.* Not Item *d.* Find the items that are not Item *d.* . . . That's it. You've got to be able to point to them and say, 'You're not Item *d.*' " The children may point out that Item *b* is not Item *d.* Agree, but point out the problem: "I can't do this item, because it tells me to do another item; I don't do anything in this item." After the children agree that the two possibilities remaining are Items *a* and *c*, say, "O.K., Mary, you do Item *a;* and Tony, you do Item *c.* Go." Both children should write the names of three things that are not in the room.

Refer to Item *d.* Use the criterion "not Item *b*" to identify *a* and *c.* Have one child work *a* and another work *c.* After they have finished, assign each child one of the items on the paper: "Tony, you do *a.* Mary, you do *b.* . . ." All should do the action specified in *c.*

Construct similar examples, using the same format.

Imperatives involving numbers

1. Introduce examples that contain numbers:

1. Do Items 2 and 3 and 4 in order.
2. Put three sticks on the chair.
3. Take two sticks from the chair and put them on the floor.
4. Take one stick from the floor and put it on the chair.

Instruct the children to do the first item (which instructs them to do the remaining items). When they have finished Item 4, there should be two sticks on the chair and one on the floor.

2. Use variations of the task to express simple addition and subtraction operations:

1. Put five sticks on your desk.
2. Take three of the sticks and put them on the floor.
3. Tell the teacher how many sticks are on the floor and how many are on the desk.
4. Tell the teacher how many sticks you would have to move to have five sticks on the floor.

Introduce the following number tasks on the children's worksheets:

Put _____ sticks in a particular place.

Do the item that comes after Item _____.

Do the item that comes before Item _____.

Do the items that come after Item _____.

Do the items that come before Item _____.

Write down how may sticks you would have to add to have _____ in a particular place.

Write down how many sticks you would have to get rid of to have _____ in a particular place.

Concentrate on the items that give trouble. In working on these, stress the function of the words in the sentence: "I've got to know how many I'd have to move. Let's see how many I'd have to move. . . . Three. I'd have to move three. That's how many. What do I do now? It tells me to write down how many. I know how many. Three. So I write down *three*." The procedure is very logical. The words in the sentence dictate the action. *But you must show the children how you are operating from these words*. It's not easy to do. In fact, it's quite easy to become involved in long, fruitless explanations. However, if you focus your explanation on the words in the sentence and treat

166

them as guides, you can demonstrate how to construct the answer: "Write down how many. How many? I have to know how many. . . . How do I find that out? I count. . . ."

Instructions involving "all"

The concept "all" has been demonstrated in a number of preceding exercises. (Do the items that come before Item _____.) *All* is very simply introduced by adding the word *all* to the familiar instruction: Do all the items that come before Item _____.

Pass out five sticks to each child.

1. Put all your sticks on the floor and stand on them.
2. Put one stick on your desk and all the other sticks on your chair.
3. Take all the sticks from your chair and put them on the floor.
4. Take all the sticks from your desk and put them on your chair.
5. Take all the sticks from your chair and put them on your desk.

(Note that the instructions are getting longer and that the number of instructions is increasing. The number of items included on the sheet should depend upon the rate at which the children can work. At this point, they should be able to handle five items in a ten-minute session.)

Use the exercise to demonstrate that *all* can refer to one object or no objects. Have the children first carry out Item 1. Then have them do Items 2 and 3. They should not encounter any serious difficulties. When they move to Item 4, they encounter something that might be new. In this item, *all* refers to only one object. The children will be ready for this move if you introduce 1 and 3 by saying "It says to take *all* of them, so I have to take all. I take this one and this one and this one and this one. There, I've taken all." Use the same demonstration for Item 4: "It says to take all of them, so I take this one . . . and . . . that's *all* there is. Just one."

After the children have completed Item 5, present the tasks in a different order. Leave the sticks as they are at the completion of Item 5 (four sticks on the floor and one on the desk), and have the children work Item 2 (Put one stick on your desk and all the other sticks on your chair). The children may object that there is already one stick on the desk. Point out that the item specifies what you must *do:* "It tells you that you have to put one stick on your desk. So do it. It doesn't matter how many sticks are already on your desk; you have to *put one on the desk.*"

Next present Items 3, 4, and 5. Each item now refers to a different number of objects than it did when the items were worked previously. After completing Item 5 on the second round, return to Item 2. Now there are three sticks on the floor and two on the desk. Again go through Items 2, 3, 4, and 5. Now there are two on the floor and three on the desk. When the series 2, 3, 4, and 5 is repeated twice more, the children can see the properties of the word *all:* "Item 3 tells me to take all of them from my chair and put them on the floor. All of them. . . . How many is that? . . . None. So that's what I do. I take none, like this"—pick up a handful of air from the chair—"and put them on the floor. . . . There." Used to describe an operation, *all* can refer to several, one, or none.

Repeat the exercises during the next session if the children have trouble following the instructions. The double-sentence item (2) may give them a little trouble. If the exercise is repeated, use a different number of sticks, so that the children learn that *all* refers not to a particular number but to all the objects that satisfy a certain criterion of selection, whether there are no members that satisfy the criterion or a thousand. When repeating the exercise, give each of the children *six* sticks and have them go through the items in the regular order first. Then have them do 2, 3, 4, 5, 2, 3, 4, 5, 2, 3, 4, 5, and so on.

After the children have mastered the operations called for in the introductory exercise, introduce variations.

1. Present each child with four long sticks and two or three short sticks. Have the children carry out these instructions:

1. Put all the long sticks on the floor.
2. Put all the short sticks and one long stick on the chair.
3. Put all the long sticks that are on the chair on your desk.
4. Put all the short sticks that are on the floor on your desk.
5. Put all the short sticks that are on your desk on the floor.
6. Put all the short sticks that are on your chair on the floor.

In presenting these exercises, begin with the sticks on the child's desk. Skip around, for example, starting with Item 5 and then going to 2, to 1, 3, 5, and so on. Repeat exercises similar to the ones above until the children can work them quickly.

168

2. After the children have mastered the exercise above, introduce the notion of "all but one" and "all but two":

1. Put all the sticks on your desk.
2. Put all but one of the long sticks on the chair.
3. Put all but two of the short sticks on the floor.
4. Put all the sticks that are on the floor on your desk.
5. Put all the sticks that are on your chair on your desk.
6. Put all but one of the sticks that are on the floor on your desk.
7. Put all but one of the long sticks that are on your desk on your chair.

3. Introduce a variation in which half of the long sticks and half of the short sticks are black. The other sticks are white. In these exercises the child must use a compound criterion.

1. Put all the sticks that are short and black on the floor.
2. Put all the sticks that are long and black on your chair.
3. Put all the sticks that are black on your desk.
4. Put all the sticks that are white on the floor.
5. Put all the sticks that are long and white on your chair.

Throughout these exercises, stress the criterion of selection that is specified in the instructions: "What kind of sticks are we talking about? Sticks that are short and black. How many of them are we talking about? All of them. And what do we do with them? Put them on the chair."

4. Introduce examples in which the child must use compound criteria of selection and "all but one" or "all but two":

1. Put all but one of the sticks that are short and black on your chair.
2. Put all the sticks that are on the chair on the floor.
3. Put all the sticks that are short and white on the floor.
4. Put all but two of the sticks that are on the floor on your desk.
5. Put all but one of the sticks that are long and white on your desk.
6. Put all the sticks on your chair.

If the children begin to become confused with the long selection criteria presented in 1 and 4, present 6 and 2 and then return to 1. Show how the words in the statement function to tell what kind of sticks we're talking about, then how many, then what to do with them:

"What kind of sticks are we talking about? . . . Sticks that are short and black. . . . Show me where it says that. . . . Yes. That's the kind of sticks we're talking about. How many of them are we talking about? . . . All but one—this many. One stick stays here. . . . And what do we do with the all-but-one of them? . . . We put them on the chair." When the sentences are broken down in this manner, the children learn both how to handle them and what kind of questions one asks himself when decoding the instructions.

Instructions involving "some"

1. To introduce the concept "some," present each child with ten sticks, half of them short, some of them black. Then give them this instruction sheet:

1. Put some of the sticks on the floor.
2. Put some of the sticks on the chair.
3. Put some of the sticks that are on the floor on your chair.
4. Put all the sticks that are on your desk on your chair.
5. Put some of the sticks that are on the floor on your desk.
6. Put some of the long sticks that are on the floor on your desk.

After the children have read Item 1, explain, "What kind of sticks are we talking about? Just sticks. How many? Some." Demonstrate by picking up two sticks. "Here are some of the sticks." Add another stick and hold up all three. "Here are some of the sticks." Add another stick. "Here are some of the sticks." Add another. "Here are some of the sticks." Repeat until you come to the last stick. When you pick it up, say, "Do I have some of the sticks? No, this is *all* the sticks."

Repeat the demonstration quickly; then return to the item. "We're talking about some of the sticks, and what are we going to do with them? . . . Put them on the floor. . . . Do it." Have the children work the other problems on their own. They shouldn't have much trouble. Repeat any items they find difficult.

2. In subsequent exercises, introduce compound criteria (put some of the sticks that are long and black on your chair), *not* criteria (put some of the sticks that are not long on the floor), *and–not* criteria (the sticks that are not long and white).

In working some of these items the children may be confronted with a situation where there is *one stick* or *no sticks* with which to satisfy the requirements of the item. There is no problem when there

170

are no sticks, because there are no sticks to move. When there is one stick, however, there is a problem. To move some of the sticks, the children must move all of them. In the initial demonstration of *some*, you showed them that *to move all was not to move some*. The rule should hold in this case too. If the children cannot take some without taking all, they cannot move. "Oh, oh! You can't take some of the sticks that are long and white without taking all of them." If there is more than one stick and the child chooses to move one of them, this move is allowable. Some of them can be one of them. We normally use *some* to refer to more than one (and you should point this out to the child), but in the game he can move one stick.

If a child continually moves the same number of sticks (always moving one stick, for example), be suspicious that he doesn't understand what *some* means. Ask him questions. Pick up a few sticks and ask, "Is this some of the sticks?" Add another stick or take one away and repeat the question.

Instructions involving "or"

There are two uses of *or* with which the child should become familiar. The first functions to demonstrate how objects or events are to be treated in the same way and classified together: "You win if you roll a seven or an eleven." Rolling the seven and rolling the eleven both lead to winning. "The fly is not in the bedroom or the kitchen." The bedroom and the kitchen are alike in the sense that the fly is not in either room. We can demonstrate this similarity:

> The fly is not in the kitchen.
> The fly is not in the bedroom.

The other use of *or* excludes something from a class or shows how one object or action is different from another: "Take a red one or a white one." The action of taking a red one excludes the action of taking a white one. This use of *or* is the most common. The following exercises program the various uses of *or*.

1. Present the following introductory sheet.
    1. Put a long stick or a short stick on the floor.
    2. Put a black stick or a white stick on the floor.
    3. Put a stick that is black or a stick that is white on the floor.
    4. Put a stick that is short on the chair or on the floor.
    5. Put a stick that is short on your head or on the floor or in your shoe.

171

Have the children read Item 1 and carry it out. Most of the children will probably put a long stick on the floor; however, some of them will put a short stick on the floor. Call their attention to the fact that not everybody did it the same way: "Look, Tony put a short stick on the floor. Mary put a long stick on the floor." Point out the choices that are open to the reader: "Let's see how this works. I read the sentence. Then can I do this?" Put the long stick on the floor. "O.K., let's try it another way. I read the sentence. Then can I do this?" Pick up a short stick and put it on the floor. "Yes, I can do this." Put a long stick on the floor. "Or I can do this." Put a short stick on the floor. "What can I do, Tony?" Have the child demonstrate.

If the children have trouble with the idea of more than one possibility, refer to Item 5. "O.K., I read the sentence. Now who can show me what I can do with the short stick? Can I do this?" Put the stick in your shoe. "Show me where it says I can do this. . . . O.K., I can put it in my shoe *or* what else?" If the children mention one of the other possibilities contained in the sentence, have them show you where it says that you can do that. Then summarize: "O.K., I can do this." Put the stick in your shoe. "Or I can do this." Put the stick on your head. "Or I can do this." Put the stick on the floor. Introduce a possibility that is not given in the instructions. Put the stick on your desk. "Can I do this? . . . No, it doesn't tell me that I can do this." Put the stick on your chair. "Can I do this? . . . No, it doesn't tell me that I can put it on my chair. Can I do this? Put it in *your* shoe?" After the children can answer the questions, have each of them show the possibilities that are specified by the sentence. If they become confused, refer them to the sentence: "Look at the sentence, Tony. It tells you what you can do with the stick. . . ." After they have demonstrated that they understand the choices that are open to them, indicate the idea of choice by saying, "So I read the item and I know that I can put the stick in my shoe, or on my head, or on the floor. Then I ask myself, What do I want to do? Do I want to put the stick on my head? No. Do I want to put it in my shoe? No. Do I want to put it on the floor? Yes. I think that's what I'll do. Maybe you don't want to do that, but I do."

Have the children read the other instructions on the sheet and carry them out. If they get into trouble, have them show what choices are open to them: "Well, what kind of stick is it talking about? A stick that is short or maybe a stick that is long. So you could do it with this stick—a stick that is short—or maybe you want to do it with that stick. Show me how you'd do it with this stick. . . . Now with that stick. . . . O.K., which one do you want to do it with?"

Give the children similar exercises until they are solid on the basic usage of *or*.

2. Present exercises in which the criterion of selection involves the word *not*. Give each child four sticks. Have him put one on the floor, one on his desk, one on his chair, and one on the chalkboard tray (or in another convenient place).

1. Pick up the stick that is not on the floor or on your desk or on the chalk tray.
2. Pick up a stick that is not on the floor or on your desk.
3. Pick up a stick that is not on your chair or on your desk.
4. Pick up a stick that is not on the chalk tray.
5. Pick up a stick that is not on the chalk tray or on your desk.
6. Pick up the stick that is not on your desk or on the chalk tray or on the chair.

Present Item 1 first and show how the words in the sentence tell you what to do: ". . . not on the floor or on your desk or on the chalk tray." Pick up the stick that is on the floor. "Can I do this? . . . Where does it tell me that I can't? . . . O.K., to pick one up I have to be able to look at the stick and say, 'You're not on the floor.' So it's not this one. What about this one? . . . What about this one? . . ." Summarize: "It can't be this one *or* this one *or* this one. So which one is it?"

Proceed to Item 2. There are two possible sticks that can be picked up. Point out that the child can pick up only one stick: "It says to pick up a stick. One stick. Where is that stick? Well, it's not on the floor, so it can't be this one. And it's not on your desk, so it can't be this one. What does that leave? This one . . . or this one."

Present instructions containing *not* and *or* until the children have mastered the procedure. Then introduce a variation in which the child operates on more than one stick. Put five sticks in each of four different locations:

1. Pick up a stick that is not on the floor or on your desk.
2. Pick up all but one of the sticks that are not on the floor or on your desk.
3. Pick up all the sticks that are not on the chair or on your desk.

    4. Pick up a stick that is not on your chair, or on your desk, or on the floor, or on the teacher's desk.

    5. Pick up all but two of the sticks that are not on your desk or on the floor.

    6. Pick up all the sticks that are not on the floor or on your desk.

3. Introduce another variation in which a choice of action is given. Pass out ten sticks, some long, some short, some black, some white, to each child.

    1. Pick up all the white sticks, or pick up one stick that is short and black.

    2. Pick up a stick that is not long, or pick up some of the sticks that are white.

    3. Pick up all the sticks that are long and white, or pick up all the sticks that are short and black.

    4. Pick up some of the sticks that are not white, or pick up some of the sticks that are not long.

    5. Put some of the sticks that are not long on the floor, or put all the sticks that are white on your chair.

    6. Put all the sticks on the floor, or put one of the sticks on your head.

In these sentences, *or* is used to link two complete instructions. Although this concept is new (and should be repeated in subsequent exercises), the children should not have any trouble with it. "What does the sentence tell you you can do? Well, it tells you to do this . . . or this." Have the children first point out the possibilities that are presented in each item. Then have them take one of the possibilities and carry it out.

4. After the children understand the uses of *or*, present instructions including items that refer to other items. With the following set of instructions, give each child ten sticks of different sizes and colors.

    1. Put all the sticks on the floor, or do Item 2.

    2. Put all the sticks on the floor.

    3. Put all the long sticks on the floor, or do Items 4 and 5.

    4. Put some of the sticks that are not short on the floor.

    5. Take all the long sticks that are on your desk and put them on the floor.

    6. Put some of the sticks that are long on the floor, or do Item 4.

Show the children that the instructions are playing games: "This item says 'not short.' This items says 'long.' That's the same thing. Both items are talking about the same sticks. Somebody's trying to be funny." Children have a lot of fun with instructions of this sort.

Instructions involving "if–then"

1. Present the following introductory sheet:

1. If the teacher claps, stand up.
2. If the teacher smiles, clap.
3. If the teacher puts her hands on her head, put your hands on your knees.
4. If the teacher puts her hands on her knees, put your hands on your head.
5. If the teacher puts her hands over her ears, put your hands over your ears, or put your hands over your eyes.
6. If the teacher stamps her feet, stand up or put your hands over your ears.

Have the children read the first sentence. Then say, "Watch me." Perform various actions, such as turning around, touching your head, blinking your eyes, stamping your feet. If the children object that you are not clapping, explain, "I don't have to clap. Just watch me. *If* I clap, you're supposed to do something; but it doesn't say that I'll ever clap. I might just keep on doing this kind of stuff all day."

Stand up as one of the extraneous actions. If the children clap, correct them: "It doesn't tell *you* to clap. It tells you that maybe *I'll* clap. And if I do, what are you supposed to do? . . . That's right—stand up." After performing various actions that are not called for, clap your hands. Do it casually and proceed to another action. If the children do not respond, remind them of what they are supposed to do: "It says, if I clap you're supposed to stand up. I clapped, so you have to stand up. You have to remember what to look out for and what to do if you see it."

Go through the other exercises in a similar manner. Ask the children to analyze them. Take it in steps:

a. "Does it say that I will smile? . . . No."
b. "But if I do smile, are you supposed to do something?"
c. "What?"

2. Follow with similar exercises. When the children have mastered the basic tasks, introduce *and, not,* and *or,* and begin to use numbers.

1. If the teacher smiles or claps, stand up.
2. If the teacher stamps her foot, pick up a stick or slap your desk.
3. If the teacher picks up a book or picks up two sticks, hold up something that is not a pencil.
4. If the teacher picks up a book, stand up and turn around and sit down.

After the children have learned to handle this kind of task, introduce exercises in which *if* and *or* lead to other items:

1. If you are told to do this item, do Item 4 or Item 6.
2. If you are told to do this item, do an item that is not Item 1 or Item 4 or Item 3 or Item 6.
3. If the teacher claps, put three sticks on the floor and do Item 5.
4. Put three sticks on your chair.
5. Take all the sticks that are on your desk and put them on the floor or the teacher's desk.
6. If you are told to do this item, do Item 1.

Study these items before presenting them so that you will be familiar with the various moves the children can make. Nothing really new is introduced, but some of the items involve quite a few steps. Tell the children which item they are to do. For example, tell them to do Item 6. The instructions will lead them to Item 4.

3. Present games using the *if–then* construction. Place several cards in a box, each card displaying a number from one to four. Give each of the children this set of game rules:

The first person to do what the rules say to do, wins a stick.

1. If the number is 4, clap.
2. If the number is 3, write your name on the back of this sheet.
3. If the number is 1, stand up on your chair.
4. If the number is 2, put this sheet on your head and slap your desk.

Draw cards from the box one at a time and show them to the class. Continue the game for about five minutes. If some of the children lag behind, play several rounds from which the other children are excluded: "This game is just between John and JC."

Introduce different rules for the game. Make one item involved, so that the children might miss it if they don't read it carefully.

176

The children may have some difficulty with the game, because the items, which refer to a set of numbers, are themselves numbered with another set of numbers. If you hold up a four, their first impulse may be to read Item 4. If they become too confused, use letters to identify the items. Return to number designation after they have learned to disregard the symbols preceding the items.

Introduce a more sophisticated variation of the game, in which the children respond to a number drawn from the box by saying another number. Put a quantity of cards in a box, each card displaying a number from one to ten. Present these rules:

    a. If the number is 1, say "three."

    b. If the number is 2 or 3 or 4 or 5, say "six."

    c. If the number is 7 or 10, say "eight."

    d. If the number is 6 or 8 or 9, do what the rules tell you to do for a number 3.

Draw enough numbers so that the children will get used to the game. Do not hurry. If the game proves to be too complicated, go back to simpler versions and return to it later.

In some of the games, use the word *when* instead of *if.*

Instructions involving "only"

The final structural word the children should learn is *only.*

1. Pass out ten sticks for the introduction:

    a. Pick up the white sticks and the black sticks.

    b. Pick up only the white sticks.

    c. Pick up only the black sticks.

    d. Pick up the long sticks and the short sticks.

    e. Pick up only the short sticks.

    f. Pick up only the long sticks.

As implied in the exercise, *only* means that something has been eliminated or excluded. Instead of picking up the white sticks *and* the black sticks, the child is instructed to pick up only the white sticks. The black sticks have been excluded.

The children should have no trouble with the introduction. Present questions so that the children can see how the word *only* functions: "Should you pick up the long sticks and the short sticks? No, it says to pick up only the long sticks."

2. Next introduce instructions in which *only* designates a unique object. Present the children with four sticks, one of which is short and black and another long and white.

1. Pick up the only stick that is short and black.
2. Pick up the only stick that is long and white.
3. If the teacher claps, pick up all the black sticks.
4. If the teacher stands up and smiles, pick up all the long sticks.
5. If the teacher says, "Pick up all the black sticks," pick up the only stick that is long and white.
6. If the teacher says, "Pick up all the long sticks," pick up only one long stick.

3. Introduce variations such as these:
   1. Put four sticks on the floor.
   2. Pick up only two sticks from the floor and put them on your desk.
   3. Pick up only the long sticks and put them on the floor.
   4. Pick up some of the sticks from the floor and put them on your desk.

New words and new concepts

The child who completes the preceding program will understand the function of the various structural words used in instructions—*and, not, or, all, some, if,* and *only.* He will also have learned that it is possible to convey the same instructions by using different words. He will have learned that the same instructions may be used to refer to various groups of objects. Perhaps the most important lesson he will have learned, however, is that he must understand every word in the instructions in order to know exactly what to do.

1. At this point the child is ready for the next part of the program for learning to follow instructions, that of working with unfamiliar words. The following exercises are designed to demonstrate that new words are introduced to achieve economy in the number of words used.

1. If the teacher holds up an object, draw a circle on the back of this paper.
2. If the teacher holds up a pencil, draw a circle on the back of this paper.
3. If the teacher holds up a piece of chalk, draw a circle on the back of this paper.
4. If the teacher holds up a piece of paper, draw a circle on the back of this paper.
5. If the teacher draws a rectangle on the board, stand up and say "rectangle."

There are two words in these instructions with which the children may not be familiar—*object* and *rectangle*. Have them read the first item. By now they may have learned enough about following instructions to know that they have to find out what a word means if they don't understand it. If they don't ask about the word *object*, however, say, "What's an object, JC?" If the child does not know, or if he offers an explanation that is inadequate, help him out: "An object is a thing." Point to various things in the room, including the children. "This is an object; this is an object; here's another object. . . ." Have the children read the item again, and then hold up various objects. The children are to draw a circle on the back of their paper every time you hold up an object. After holding up about ten objects, ask, "I wonder how many objects I've held up so far?" If they don't know how to figure out the answer, say, "Well, every time I hold up an object, you made a circle on the back of your paper. So you should have a circle for every object. Count the circles. . . ."

After the children have counted the objects, present Items 1, 2, 3, and 4 again. Then point out the advantage of Item 1: "I don't need these other items for the game if I have Item 1, because Item 1 talks about *all objects*—pencils, pieces of chalk, pieces of paper, elephants, buildings, anything. I would need a lot of items like these others to say what Item 1 says."

2. Follow the introduction with similar exercises. In each exercise, have at least two review items that use words presented in previous exercises:

> *a.* If the teacher holds up a picture of a truck, draw a rectangle on the back of this paper.
> *b.* If the teacher holds up a picture of a train, draw a rectangle on the back of this paper.
> *c.* If the teacher holds up a picture of a rectangle, say "rectangle."
> *d.* If the teacher holds up a picture of a vehicle, draw a rectangle on the back of this paper.
> *e.* If the teacher holds up a picture of a car, draw a rectangle on the back of this paper.
> *f.* If the teacher holds up a picture of a bus, draw a rectangle on the back of this paper.

Go through the items in order. The children may not know what a vehicle is. Explain, "A truck is a vehicle, a car is a vehicle, a train is a vehicle. Here's the rule: If it's something that is made to take you places, it's a vehicle. Listen to the rule again, and then say it with me."

After the children have worked the exercises, tell them, "Look at Items *a*, *b*, *d*, *e*, and *f*. Let's say we could keep only one of these items. Which one would you keep? Why?" The answer, of course, is *d*, because it uses the class name *vehicle:* "Item *d* talks about all vehicles —trucks, cars, buses, trains. So if we could keep only one item, we would want to keep this one. It says what all the others say."

Next introduce new class names, using a similar format:

1. If the teacher holds up a picture of a chair, draw a horizontal line on this paper.
2. If the teacher holds up a picture of a table, draw a horizontal line on this paper.
3. If the teacher holds up a picture of a piece of furniture, draw a horizontal line on this paper.
4. If the teacher holds up a picture of a vehicle, draw a rectangle on this paper.
5. If the teacher holds up a picture of an animal, draw a circle on this paper.
6. If the teacher hold up a picture of a bed, draw a horizontal line on this paper.

Before instructing the children to read Item 1, say, "Remember that you have to know what every word means. If you don't know what a word means, find out. Don't guess." Show pictures of animals, vehicles, and pieces of furniture. Present them slowly enough so that the children can play the game. After the game, ask questions about the most important item: "Say that we could keep only one of these items—1, 2, 3, or 6. Which one would you keep? Why?" After the children have selected Item 3, remind them of its value: "It says what all the other items say, because it talks about all pieces of furniture."

In subsequent games, introduce such class designations as vegetables, articles of clothing, and things to read. Also introduce the term *vertical line*.

1. If the teacher holds up a picture of clothing, draw a vertical line on this paper.
2. If the teacher holds up a picture of a shoe, draw a vertical line on this paper.
3. If the teacher holds up a picture of a shirt, draw a vertical line on this paper.

    4. If the teacher holds up a picture of a plant, draw a horizontal line on this paper.

    5. If the teacher holds up a picture of a piece of furniture, draw a cross on this paper.

    6. If the teacher holds up a picture of a coat, draw a vertical line on this paper.

Have the children read all the items. Go through Items 1, 2, 3, and 6 before playing the game. Play a few rounds of the game, and then ask if it is possible to simplify the instructions: "We still want to play the game, but we can do without all these instructions. I think we can cross out three of them and still play the game. Let's see if you can find those three. Which three could we cross out and still play the game?" Through this exercise the children are introduced to the rationale behind class designations such as *vehicle* and *articles of clothing*. A class designation allows one to talk about a large group of objects. The class designation sometimes represents a great economy of effort.

Introduce other variations of the crossing-out exercise. Suggest that the children can cross out unneeded rules before the game starts: "O.K., read these instructions carefully and see if we can play the game with fewer rules. See which rules you can cross out."

3. Introduce a variation of the game in which the children must write a rule. To introduce this variation, present the following set of instructions:

    1. _____

      _____

    2. If the teacher holds up a picture of an animal, draw a vertical line on this paper.

    3. If the teacher holds up a picture of a car, draw a rectangle on this paper.

    4. If the teacher holds up a picture of a truck, draw a rectangle on this paper.

    5. If the teacher holds up a picture of a train, draw a rectangle on this paper.

Explain, "Read all these rules. Then see if you can make up a new rule that will take the place of three of these rules."

Introduce variations of the make-up-the-rule game, using the format above; however, do not always arrange the items in the same order (that is, do not always have the last three items the ones that are to be replaced). The children may have some trouble making up rules at first. Help them: "I look at this one [Item 3], this one [Item 4], and this one [5], and I see that they all tell me to draw a rectangle. Why do they all tell me to do the same thing? They must be talking about the same kind of objects. A car, a truck, and a train. What kind of objects are they? Vehicles. These items all talk about vehicles. Let's make an item using the word *vehicle* to take the place of these items."

If the children have not caught on to the procedure after working on the rule-finding task for three days, return to the preceding task (that of crossing out the unnecessary rules) and emphasize why the remaining rule is important: "All these objects are animals. So the rule that tells me about animals is the most important one."

After the children have worked on these tasks for several days, introduce the rule-writing task again. Make the tasks increasingly difficult, until they can construct more than one general item at a time.

1. If the teacher holds up a picture of a hat, draw a horizontal line on this sheet of paper.
2. If the teacher holds up a picture of a truck, draw a rectangle on this paper.
3. If the teacher holds up a picture of a tree, draw a vertical line on this paper.
4. If the teacher holds up a picture of a tomato, draw a vertical line on this paper.
5. If the teacher holds up a picture of a dress, draw a horizontal line on this paper.
6. If the teacher holds up a picture of a car, draw a rectangle on this paper.
7. If the teacher holds up a picture of a coat, draw a horizontal line on this paper.
8. If the teacher holds up a picture of a tractor, draw a rectangle on this paper.
9. If the teacher holds up a picture of a flower, draw a vertical line on this paper.

a. _____

_____

b. _____

_____

c. _____

_____

Have the children read the items. Then explain, "We've got to find a way to write the rules so that it will be easier to play the game. I'll bet we can write three rules that will do what all these rules do." Continue with variations of this rule-writing exercise until the children can handle it.

Introduce multiple-choice test items.

Draw a circle around the correct answer:

a. If something is made to take you places, it is

an animal	a tool	a vehicle	a plant

b. If something grows in the ground, it is

an animal	a horse	a vehicle	a plant

c. If something is alive and moves around after food, it is

an animal	a tree	an article of clothing	something to read

d. If something is made for a person to wear, it is

an animal	a tree	an article of clothing	something to read

e. If something is made to help you do work, it is

an animal	a tool	a vehicle	an article of clothing

f. If it is a car, it is

an animal	a tool	a vehicle	an article of clothing

In subsequent exercises, introduce more items similar to f. (If it is a hammer, it is . . . If it is a tomato, it is . . . If it is a hat, it is . . .)

Through these exercises the children will not only become acquainted with a new item form. They will also learn how to express relationships between a class and a member of that class.

The children may have trouble at first with the multiple-choice format. Use the concept of *or* to explain how the items work. Have the children read the first item. Then refer to the choices and say, "Look,

183

these are the things I can say. I can say an animal, or I can say a tool, or I can say a vehicle, or I can say a plant. But I want to say the one that is right. Let's see which one is right. First, I'll say this one." Point to an animal. "If something is made to take you places, it is an animal. Is that right? No. Well then, I don't want to say that. Let's try another one. JC, you read it and say this one." Point to *a tool*. Go through the choices in this manner until you have identified the one that is correct. "I know which one is right. But what do I do about it? Does it tell me what to do? . . ." If the children do not find the instructions at the top of the page, refer to them: "Look at this. It says, 'Draw a circle around the correct answer.'"

In subsequent exercises, use different instructions at the top of the page, such as these:

Draw a horizontal line under the correct answer.

Draw a horizontal line over the correct answer.

Draw a rectangle around the correct answer.

Write the letter of the correct answer in the blank space.

For the last direction, set up the items this way:

1. If it is a bus, it is _____A_____.

A. a vehicle   B. a building   C. a tool   D. clothing

Now the children must treat the items according to their code symbol. If they have trouble with these exercises, review some of the code-symbol exercises. (See pages 157-158.)

Introduce another variation in which the child must complete the statements:

Complete the following statements so that they are correct.

a. If it is a screwdriver, it is _____.

b. If it is a saw, it is _____.

c. If it is a hat, it is_____.

d. If it is a tree, it is _____.

e. If it is a tiger, it is _____.

f. If it is a bed, it is_____.

Again, point out the rules of the game in terms of choices: "Look, I can say whatever I want to say. I might say, 'If it is a screwdriver, it is an elephant.' I might say, 'If it is a screwdriver, it is a hat.' But I've got to do what the instructions say. I've got to make a correct statement. Tony, what does that mean—a correct statement? . . . O.K., so I've got to say the right thing. What do I say? . . . Yes, a tool. So I write down the word *tool*."

184

Children often fail to learn how to handle multiple-choice and statement-completion exercises because they don't completely understand that the point is to make correct statements. The notion of the correct statement is best expressed in terms of choice. The child can say this or this or this. But only one of these statements is correct. That's the one he must use.

Continue giving practice on statement-completion items until the children can handle them.

Creating figures from instructions

At this point in the program on following instructions, the children are ready to learn how to create figures from verbal descriptions. Some of the words they will need have already been programed —*rectangle, circle, horizontal line, vertical line.*

1. Begin by giving instructions that can be carried out by performing various actions.

Give each child a sheet of paper on which to draw and a sheet of instructions.

> *a.* Draw a horizontal line on your paper.
> Intersect the horizontal line with a vertical line.
> *b.* Draw a horizontal line on your paper.
> Draw a circle so that the bottom of the circle is resting on the horizontal line.
> *c.* Draw a horizontal line on your paper.
> Draw a vertical line that meets the horizontal line but does not go past the horizontal line.

Instruct the children to do Item *a*. They will not know the word *intersect* and it is hoped they will ask what it means. If they do, commend them. If they don't, remind them: "You've got to know what every word means. If you don't know, find out—ask. . . . The word *intersect* means 'to cross.' In this case the vertical line crosses the horizontal line." After the children have made their drawings for Item *a*, make the observation that there is more than one correct drawing. "Look at all the different pictures we can draw by following the instructions."

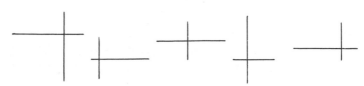

Point out that each drawing satisfies the requirements of the instruction. Then draw some figures that do not satisfy the requirements of the instructions—figures with curved lines, slanted lines, irregular lines.

Have the children carry out the instructions for *b* and *c*. After they have finished each item, point out that a number of drawings would satisfy the instructions—long lines with small circles, short lines with large circles, lines with the circle positioned near the end of the line or in the middle.

2. Follow the introductory exercise with several similar exercises:

    a. Draw a vertical line on your paper.

    Intersect the vertical line with a horizontal line.

    b. Draw a circle.

    Intersect the circle with a vertical line.

    c. Draw a circle.

    Intersect the circle with a horizontal line.

The children may have some trouble with the problems that call for the intersection of a circle. Point out, "That means that the line crosses the circle—goes through it." After the children have worked each item, demonstrate that a number of drawings would satisfy the requirements of the instruction.

3. Introduce instructions in which the children become acquainted with the terms *end, middle,* and *left*:

    1. Draw a horizontal line on your paper. Put the letter *a* in the middle of the line. Put the letter *b* at one end of the line. Put the letter *c* at the other end of the line.

    2. Draw a vertical line on your paper. Put the number 2 at one end of the line. Put the number 4 in the middle of the line. Put the number 7 at the other end of the line.

    3. Draw a slanting line on your paper. Put the letter *r* in the middle of the line. Put the number 2 at one end of the line. Draw a triangle at the other end of the line.

    4. Draw a curved line on your paper. Put a triangle in the middle of the line. Put a circle at one end of the line. Put a + sign at the other end of the line.

After the children have worked these problems (perhaps asking help for the meaning of the words *middle, end,* and *slanted*), point out that there is more than one acceptable diagram for each of the problems. The letter *b* in Item 1, for example, may be on the left end of the line or on the right end. The number 7 in Item 2 may be at the top of the vertical line or at the bottom. Draw figures that are consistent with each instruction.

Refer to the acceptable figures for Item 1:

"This figure or this figure is right. But what if I wanted to tell you to draw this figure [left] and not this other one? How would I do that?" The answer is to provide a more detailed set of instructions: "I would have to tell you more about what you should draw. I would have to tell you how to draw this figure. I would have to tell you to put the *b* at this end of the line and not at this end. But what can I call this end of the line?" If the children do not know the concept *left*, introduce the term: "This is the left end of the line. Which end is it? . . . The left. That's the end we start at when we read." Draw various horizontal lines on the board and have the children locate the left end of each. After each successful trial, point to the other end of the line and ask, "Is this the left end of the line? No, this is not the left end of the line." Do not introduce the term *right* until the children have learned how to identify *left*. Relate *left* to reading: "This is where we start when we read."

Write adequate instructions for the left figure.

Draw a horizontal line on your paper. Put the letter *a* in the middle of the line. Put the letter *b* at the left end of the line. Put the letter *c* at the other end of the line.

"Now I get the picture I want."

Refer next to the acceptable figures for Item 2:

2|

4|

7|

7|

4|

2|

Pose this problem: "What if I wanted the instructions to tell me to make this figure [left] and not this other one? How would I do that? How would I say that the two has to be up here and not down here?" The children probably understand the concepts "top" and "bottom."

187

Rework the instructions after they have pointed out (or after you have told them) that the 2 must be at the top of the vertical line. Rewrite the instructions:

> Draw a vertical line on your paper. Put the number 2 at the top of the line. Put the number 4 in the middle of the line. Put the number 7 at the bottom of the line.

After making up the new instructions, test them: "O.K., let's see if these instructions work. Let's see if I can use them to make this other figure (the one with the seven at the top). The instructions tell me to put a number two at the top of the line. That means the number two would have to go here. I can't have the seven at the top."

4. Introduce exercises in which the children are required to construct simple figures using the concepts of left, top, and bottom:

1. Draw a horizontal line on your paper. Put a circle at the left end of the horizontal line. Put a letter *t* at the other end of the horizontal line.

2. Draw a long horizontal line on your paper. Write the word *cat* in the middle of the line. Write the word *left* at the left end of the line. Write the word *right* at the other end of the line.

3. Draw a vertical line on your paper. In the middle of the line, put a 1. At the top of the line, put a 3. At the bottom of the line, put a 5.

4. Draw a large *T* on your paper. At the left end of the horizontal line, put the letter *r*. At the bottom of the vertical line, put the letter *s*.

5. Draw a large *T* on your paper. At the middle of the vertical line, put the letter *e*. In the middle of the horizontal line, put the letter *w*.

6. Draw a large *T* upside down. At the left end of the horizontal line, write the word *left*. At the other end of the horizontal line, write the word *right*.

Note that a new kind of sentence is introduced in these instructions. Instead of saying "Put the letter *e* at the middle of the vertical line," the instructions say "At the middle of the vertical line, put the letter *e*." This new sentence form may slow down the children momentarily, but it should not present any serious stumbling block. Read the sentence with them and show them that it means the same as the familiar regular-order sentence.

188

After the children have carried out each of the instructions, ask them if it is possible to make a different kind of diagram. Play devil's advocate by suggesting figures that are not acceptable. For example, in working on Item 1, ask the children why this figure is not acceptable:

T _____ O

Make them refer to the words in the instructions that tell why it is not acceptable: "Yes, it says to put a circle at the left end of the line. JC, show me the left end of the line. What do the instructions say I should have there? . . . Yes, a circle. And do I? No, so this figure does not do what the instructions say."

Present exercises involving horizontal lines, vertical lines, and the *T* (upside down, tipped to the left, tipped to the right) until the children are relatively solid on *left* and *not left*. Also use squares, with corners labeled.

5. Introduce the concept "right":

1. Draw a horizontal line. Put a *T* at the left end of the line. Put an *E* at the right end of the line.
2. Draw a *T* tipped all the way over with the top on the left side. Write the word *cat* at the top of the vertical line. Write the word *dog* at the bottom of the vertical line.
3. Draw a *T* tipped all the way over with the top on the right side. Draw an *O* at the middle of the vertical line.
4. Draw a *T* upside down. At the top of the vertical line, draw a picture of a man. At the right end of the horizontal line, put the letter *R*. At the left end of the horizontal line, write the letter *L*.
5. Draw a square. At the top left corner, write the letters *TL*. At the top right corner, write the letters *TR*. At the bottom left corner, write the letters *BL*. At the bottom right corner, write the letters *BR*.
6. Draw a square. At the middle of the top horizontal line, write the letter *N*. At the middle of the bottom horizontal line, write the letter *S*. At the middle of the left vertical line, write the letter *W*. At the middle of the right vertical line, write the letter *E*.

Some of these exercises may take more than ten minutes. Do not hurry the children. If they use what they have learned and follow the

189

instructions one step at a time, they will be able to handle them. They will become more skillful in time. But at first, make sure that they are reading, are comprehending what they read, and are paying attention to the details in the instructions. They may ask what the word *right* means in Item 1. Tell them simply: "It's not left. It's the other one. That's right." They will have written the word and will be partially prepared for the new learning. If they have trouble with the tipped *T*, join two pencils to form a *T*. Tip the *T* to the left and then to the right. Draw the two tipped *T*'s on the board. "If I get stuck, I draw it both ways and then I look at what it says in the sentence. It says that the top should be on the left side. Which one has the top on the left?"

Show the children how to figure out in advance which way to tip the *T*. "I know what a *T* looks like when it's standing up. I say to myself, 'I want the top on the left side! Where is that? Over here.'" Point to the left of the imaginary *T*. "So I have to tip it this way."

Point out that in Item 5, *TL* stands for top left, *TR* stands for top right, *BL* stands for bottom left, and *BR* stands for bottom right.

Point out that if the children follow the instructions for Item 6 properly, they will make a map with *N* (north) at the top, *S* (south) at the bottom, and east and west on the sides. "All maps work this way. North is always at the top and south at the bottom."

Repeat the tasks in this series, especially 5 and 6.

Demonstrating the need for precise language

The way to show children the need for precise language is to demonstrate that vague and general instructions lead to a host of interpretations. The more precise the instructions, the greater the number of possibilities that are ruled out. Very precise instructions lead to only one interpretation.

1. Give the children the following sheet:

1. Write a number on this paper.
2. Write a number that comes after 1 and comes before 11.
3. Write a number that comes after 1 and comes before 11 and is made with a curving line.
4. Write a number that comes after 1 and before 11 and is made with a curving line, and is not 2, 3, 5, 6, 8, or 10.

190

Have the children work these items in turn. After each task has been carried out, point out the number of possibilities that satisfy the requirements of the instruction.

After Item 1, point out, "I could write any number. I could write this number." Write a small number on the board. "Or this number." Write a very large number on the board, such as 133456200147.

Have each child write down five numbers that would satisfy the requirements of the instruction. Refer to each child's numbers and indicate that each is acceptable: "Yes, you could write this, or this, or this . . ." Have each child write five things that would not be acceptable: "Write down some things that the instruction tells you are not correct." The children may require some prompting. Write the letter *T* on the board. "Well, here's something that is not a number. Could I write this? JC, why isn't this correct? Find the words in the instructions that tell you why. . . . Yes, it has to be a *number*."

Refer to Item 2 and have the children do what the instruction tells them to do. After they have written down their numbers, have them see if they can identify all the numbers that are possible according to the instruction: "Let's see if we can figure out all the numbers that I could write down. Read the item carefully. . . . O.K. Now can I use this number?" Write 11 on the board. "Why not?"

"Can I use this number?" Write 1 on the board. "Why not?"

"Well, what numbers can I use?"

As the children mention the numbers, list them in order:

2 3 4 5 6 7 8 9 10

Summarize, pointing to each number in turn: "I could write down this number, or this number, or this number . . ." Have several children say which of the numbers are acceptable, using the word *or*.

Refer next to Item 3. Have the children carry out the instruction. If they have difficulty, tell them to refer to the numbers on the board and note which numbers meet the requirements of the instruction. Another procedure is to have them write the numbers on their paper and then cross out the ones that do not satisfy the requirements. If they cannot work the problem on their own, show them how to do it: "The instruction tells me the number comes after one and before eleven. That means it's one of these numbers here. Which one? Well, the instruction tells me that it is made with a curving line. So I look at each of these numbers and ask myself if it's made with a curving line. Is the first one made with a curving line? Yes. So I can write that number. What about the next number—three? Does it have a curving line? Yes, so I can keep it. What about the next number—four? Does it have a curving line? No. So I can't use four." Cross out the 4. Continue in this manner, crossing out all numbers that are not made with curving lines. When you have finished, these numbers remain:

2   3   4̸   5   6   7̸   8   9   10

"Any of these numbers is right. If it has a curved line, we can use it. If it doesn't have a curved line, we can't use it." Write down various numbers and have the children indicate whether or not they meet the requirements. Write numbers that are unacceptable because they are not between 1 and 11; write others that are not acceptable because they do not comply with the curved-line requirement; write others that are not acceptable for both reasons. As in all previous exercises, have the children back up any objection to a number by referring to the words in the instruction that denote a discrepancy: "Show me in the instruction where it says that this number is wrong. Find the words."

Next have the children read Item 4. If the children have trouble with the task, point out that you can cross out any number that will not satisfy the instructions: "If it tells you that it is not a three, cross the three out. If it tells you that it is not a six, cross the six out. . . ." After the children have worked the problem (hopefully writing the number 9 on their papers), ask if any other numbers would be acceptable. "Why can't I write down this number?" Write a 4 on the board. "What about this number?" Write an 8 on the board. Continue in this manner, always requiring the children to refer to the instructions when specifying why a particular number is not acceptable.

2. For subsequent exercises, follow the general format of the introductory sheet. Describe a particular object, starting with the description of a class in which the object is included. Narrow the number of possibilities in each of the following items until, in the last item, there is only one possible object that satisfies the instructions.

Select for the object a particular number, a particular letter, a particular window in the room, any object that is a member of a set. Describe the object using *not* statements and statements that set the object apart from other objects. For example:

1. Write a capital letter on your paper.
2. Write a capital letter that comes after *c* and before *s*.
3. Write a capital letter that comes after *c* and before *s*, and is not *g, h, i, j,* or *k*.

4. Write a capital letter that comes after *c* and before *s*, and is not *g, h, i, j,* or *k,* and is made with curved lines.

5. Write a capital letter that comes after *c* and before *s,* and is not *g, h, i, j,* or *k,* and is made with curved lines, and comes after *o.*

6. Write a capital letter that comes after *c* and before *s,* and is not *g, h, i, j,* or *k,* and is made with curved lines, and comes after *o,* and has a tail.

Have the children list all the letters that are possible in Item 1 and then cross out those that are ruled out by each of the other items: 2, 3, 4, 5, and 6.

Another example:

Give the children a sheet on which appear the following figures:

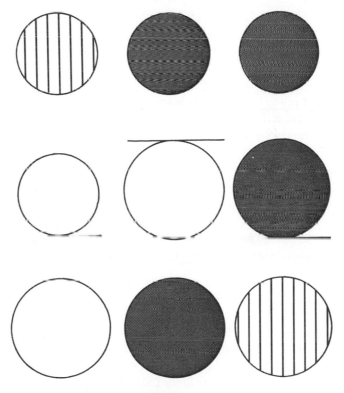

a.
1. Touch a circle on this sheet.
2. Touch a circle that does not have a horizontal line at the bottom.

   3. Touch a circle that does not have a horizontal line at the bottom and is not striped.

   4. Touch a circle that does not have a horizontal line at the bottom, and is not striped, and is black.

   5. Touch a circle that does not have a horizontal line at the bottom, and is not striped, and is black, and has no horizontal line at the top.

   6. Touch a circle that does not have a horizontal line at the bottom, and is not striped, and is black, and has no horizontal line at the top, and is big.

b.
   1. Touch a circle on this sheet.

   2. Touch a circle that is not big.

   3. Touch a circle that is not big, and is striped.

3. After the children have worked on these examples and learned how to follow the instructions a step at a time, introduce a variation in which they are asked to identify the appropriate object *in the fewest possible steps.*

Present the arrangement of circles above and point to the large circle in the middle of the sheet. Explain, "I want to write instructions that will tell somebody to point to this circle, but I want to do it as quickly as I can. I don't want to write and write. I want to make it easy on myself. How could I do that? I have to start out saying 'Touch the circle that . . . ,' and now I've got to let them know that this is the circle I want."

There are a number of quick solutions, such as these:

Touch the circle that is in the middle.

Touch the circle that is between a little circle and a big circle.

Touch the circle that is big and white and has a line touching it on top.

Help the children reach these solutions. Acknowledge good thinking: "Good boy, John. It's a big circle and it's in the middle of the sheet, and it's white."

4. Present similar exercises. After the children have worked on the instructions that are presented on the sheet, have them see if they can condense the instructions. This is an exercise in classifying objects economically so that each descriptive word or phrase rules out the maximum number of objects. Practice in economical classification is important in the tasks to come.

194

Present each child with a set of cutout geometric figures:

Have the children sit so that they cannot watch each other. Assign each child the task of describing one of the figures. The seating arrangement and the use of cutouts will eliminate the possibility of describing the objects in terms of spatial arrangement—"the second from the right."

After each child has written his description, hand the description to another child and see if he can identify the correct object. If a description is inadequate, go through the steps of item construction with him.

1. First have the child name the object that he is trying to identify. He may have omitted the name of the object. In some cases this will result in ambiguity. Show the children that unless the object is named, the other child may not know whether he should select a square, a triangle, or a circle: "The first rule about writing instructions is that you have to tell what kind of object you're talking about. Are you talking about a man, an airplane, or a triangle? If you're talking about a square, start out by saying 'Pick up a square.'" Repeat this rule often.

2. After the child has named the object, have him describe it. Point to the square he is writing about and say, "Tell me about this square. Tell me about it so that I know it is not this square, or this square, or this square." Each square must be described in terms of color and size.

Other examples that can be used include figures on lines:

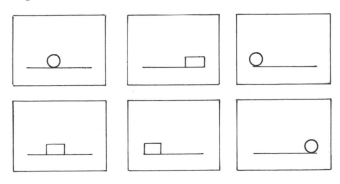

Triangular figures can make an interesting exercise. Remind the child to start by naming the figure.

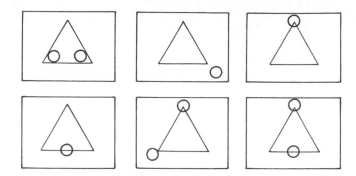

Make sure that the children arrange the cards so that the top of the figure is up. Mark the top of the cards with a line or an *x*. Tell the children to lay out the cards with the mark at the top.

Work on these construction tasks until the children are very solid at classifying the object they are discussing (stating whether there are two circles or one circle on the card, whether the object is a circle or a square) and at using the word *that* to introduce the clause describing the properties of the triangle in question: "Pick up a card that . . ."

Do not devote the entire fifteen-minute segment of the period to construction tasks. Rather, assign the children two construction tasks (which should take about four minutes each) and then spend some time on related instructions. For this part of the session, present a sheet that gives instructions about particular objects. For example:

1. Pick up a card that has two circles on a triangle. The circles are in the lower left corner and the lower right corner of the triangle.
2. Pick up a card that has a triangle and one circle. The circle is at the top of the triangle.
3. Pick up a card that has a triangle and two circles. One circle is at the top of the triangle. The other circle is at the middle of the bottom line.
4. Turn over a card that has a triangle and one circle. The circle is in the middle of the bottom line.
5. Turn over a card that has a triangle and two circles. One circle is at the top. The other circle is at the lower left corner of the triangle.

196

Extraneous Elements in a Statement

Before the children move on to descriptions and definitions of objects, they must learn to recognize parts of statements that give no additional information. They must understand that these extraneous parts are not desirable, since they do not help in the process of selecting an object from a group.

1. To introduce the idea of extraneous matter in instructions, start with simple examples. Pass out four cards to each child:

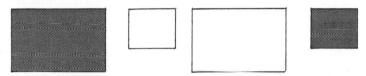

Arrange the cards in this order. Give each child a sheet with the following items:

1. Pick up a square that is white, that is not black, and that is big.
2. Pick up a square that is little, that is black, and that is not big.
3. Pick up the square that is third from the left, that is white, and that is little.
4. Pick up the square that is big, that is black, and that is on the right.
5. Pick up the square that is a rectangle, that is on your desk, that is not blue, and that is big and white.
6. Pick up the object that is not an elephant, not a tiger, not a horse, not a tree, not a house, not a circle, not a triangle, and that is a square on the left of the others.

Explain, "We're going to play a game. These instructions have words that we don't need. We're going to read them carefully, find the right object, and then see how many words we can cross out of the instructions and still find the right object. Remember that we have to cross out only the words we don't need."

Refer to the first item. Have the children read it and carry out the instructions. Then ask them if there is anything that can be eliminated from the instructions. "I don't need all these words. Let's see which ones." You are demonstrating the rule that words which don't tell you anything new are not necessary. Analyze the instructions a step at a time: "O.K., it tells me to pick up a square that is white.

197

Which squares are we talking about? . . . Yes, we know it has to be either this square or this square. Now let's go back to the instructions and read on. It says that the square is not black. O.K., which ones are we talking about? . . . Yes, the same squares. Did the instructions tell us anything new when they said that the square is not black? No, we're still talking about the same two squares. So we can cross out the words *that is not black*. Cross them out. Now let's go on. It says that the square is big. It's white and big. Show me which squares we're talking about. . . . Yes, just that one. Now the instructions tell us only something new."

Don't labor over the explanation if the children seem a little hazy. Proceed to Item 6, in which the rule is made quite obvious: "It says to pick up the object that is not an elephant. Which object is that? . . . Yes, this one, or this one, or this one, or this one. Now let's read on and see if the instructions tell us how to get rid of some of these objects. It says that the object is not a tiger. Which object is that? . . . Yes, we're still talking about the same objects. The instructions haven't done anything for us. So we cross out these words and go on. It says that this object is not a horse. Which object is that?"

After working Item 6, return to Item 1 and proceed through the others in order: Emphasize that the instructions have to help us rule out some of the possibilities. If a part of the explanation does not do this, we can cross it out.

2. Give the children exercises similar to the introductory one. If they are unsure of how the extraneous elements fail to function, set up the items so that a bit of valuable information is followed by a phrase that does not rule out any of the candidates. For example, give the children four squares:

1. Turn over a square that is not a circle, that is big, that is not little, that is black, that is not white.
2. Hold up a square that is second from the left, that is not first from the left.
3. Turn over a square that is not little, that is big, that is white, that is not black.
4. Turn over a square that is fourth from the left, that is not first from the right, that is not big, that is little, that is not white, that is black.
5. Turn over a square that is not first from the left, that is not second from the left, that is not third from the left.

198

The last item may be a little tricky, but if the children work it a step at a time, they will see that each part of the statement functions to rule out one of the squares. Therefore each part of the instructions is needed. However, acknowledge that there might be a better way to write the instructions.

Work on extraneous-element exercises until the children can find the extraneous elements quickly. Stress the procedure: "Test it out. See if it lets you rule out some of the objects." Use examples that involve letters, numbers, figures. Use plenty of *not* statements in which *not* is used to rule out one of the members. For example, in connection with the series of letters

$$s \qquad d \qquad f \qquad g \qquad u \qquad r$$

Pick up a letter that is not *s*, that is not *f*, that is not *r*, that is not *u*, that is not *g*.

Introduce larger sets so that the children become familiar with the limitations of *not* when it is used in this way. For example, present this set of numbers:

$$1\ 2\ 3\ 4\ 5\ 6\ 7\ 8\ 9\ 10\ 11\ 12\ 13\ 14\ 15\ 16\ 17\ 18\ 19\ 20$$
$$21\ 22\ 23\ 24\ 25\ 26\ 27\ 28$$

"Let's give instructions for the number two by telling what number it is not. We'll say, touch the number that is not one, that is not three, that is not four, that is not five . . ." After proceeding through three or four more numbers, point out that this is a poor way to isolate a member of a set if the set is large: "Boy, this is going to take us forever, isn't it? And just think of the problems we'd have if we had two hundred numbers instead of twenty-eight. We'd be writing all day."

From time to time present similar examples, always emphasizing the lack of economy of the approach: "There's got to be a better way to do it."

Drawing a Route

The first step in teaching children how to construct representations of a route from one point to another is to introduce the task of constructing simple designs from instructions. This is an extension of tasks that the children have already worked on.

1. Give each child four index cards, each marked to indicate the top of the card. Provide each child with a sheet containing these instructions:

1. Put a dot in the middle of the top edge of the card. Put a dot in the middle of the card. Put a dot in the middle of the bottom edge of the card. Draw straight lines to connect the dots.
2. Put a dot in the middle of the top edge of the card. Put a dot in the middle of the bottom edge of the card. Put a dot in the middle of the left edge of the card. Put a dot in the middle of the right edge of the card. Draw straight lines to connect the dots.
3. Put a dot in the middle of the card. Put a dot in the top right corner of the card. Put a dot in the bottom left corner of the card. Draw straight lines to connect the dots.
4. Put a dot in the middle of the card. Put a dot in the top left corner of the card. Put a dot in the bottom left corner of the card. Draw straight lines to connect the dots.

2. Work on similar problems during every session until the children can easily construct the designs described. Make the explanations more complicated as the children begin to master the basic ones. (If the children have no trouble with the basic problems, proceed directly to the more complicated ones.) For example:

1. Put a dot in the middle of the top edge of the card. Put a dot between this dot and the top left corner of the card. Draw a line from this dot to the lower right corner of the card.
2. Put a dot in the middle of the card. Put a dot in the middle of the bottom edge of the card. Put a dot between these dots. Draw a line from this dot to the top left corner of the card.
3. Put a dot in the middle of the card. Put a dot in the middle of the top edge of the card. Put a dot in the middle of the bottom edge of the card. Put a dot in the middle of the left edge of the card. Put a dot in the middle of the right edge of the card. Draw straight lines connecting all the dots.
4. Put a dot in the top left corner of the card. Put a dot in the top right corner of the card. Put a dot in the bottom left corner of the card. Put a dot in the middle of the bottom edge of the card. Draw straight lines connecting all the dots.

Making up instructions for designs

Give the children practice in constructing instructions for dot-line arrangements. Present a drawing of a simple design on the board and instruct them to make up the instructions so that someone could construct the design.

1. Start with this design:

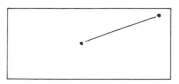

Tell the children to watch you as you construct it: "Watch, so you'll know what to say." Make the dots first, calling attention to what you are doing: "See where I'm making this dot. . . . And this one." Then draw a line connecting the dots. "O.K. Write the instructions."

2. Progressively increase the difficulty of the designs. At first, concentrate on the corners and the middle of the card. As the children become familiar with how to write the instructions for these, introduce examples that involve the middle of the top, the middle of the bottom, and the middle of the sides—in that order. Do not introduce more than one construction task during a session.

If the children have difficulty, have them make up statements about what you are doing as you construct the diagram. For example:

"O.K., what did I do? . . . Yes, I put a dot in the middle. But the middle of what? The middle of the street? . . . O.K., say the whole thing. I put a dot in the middle of the card."

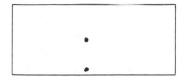

"What did I do now? . . . Yes, I put a dot in the middle of the edge. Which edge? The right edge? The top edge? . . . The bottom edge."

"What did I do now? . . . Yes, I put a dot in the left corner. But which left corner? . . . This one down here? This is a left corner. . . . Yes, in the top left corner." Finally, draw lines to connect the dots.

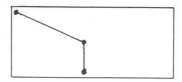

"What did I do now? . . . Yes, I made lines. But where? . . . I made lines that connected the dots. I connected the dots with lines. What kind of lines? I connected the dots with straight lines. Say that with me."

If the children have difficulty expressing the idea of connecting dots with straight lines, connect the dots with wavy lines. Now the importance of specifying the type of line becomes obvious. After the children have mastered the expressions used in these problems, assign each child a different simple design and have him make up the instructions for the construction of that design. Give each child's instructions to another child and let that child construct the design on the board, following the instructions. These exercises are extremely valuable, because they underscore the need for clarity. Although the child making up the problem may understand how to solve it, he may have difficulty placing himself in the role of the reader who knows nothing. The attempt of another child to carry out his instructions helps him learn about the problems of the reader. Assuming the role of the reader is essential to the task of writing for one who does not share your information, and it points up the fact that written material must be constructed so that it delivers a precise message to the reader.

When assigning the child a design, take him off by himself and construct the design for him. Ask him to tell you what you are doing at each step. Then have him return to his seat and write instructions. After he has finished, give his instructions to another child. Have the child attempt to draw the appropriate design on the board. Then hold up the card with the original design on it and compare it with the design drawn by the other child. If they do not correspond, ask the class to find out why. Perhaps the child working from the instructions did not follow them correctly. Perhaps the child who wrote them was not precise. "All right. This is the card John worked from. Now look at it carefully and then let's read what he wrote and see if it's right. . . ."

If a child working from inadequate instructions happens to reproduce the appropriate design, point out that it is possible to draw another design from the same instructions: "Look, JC says to put a dot in the top corner. That means you can put a dot here, or here. If you put it here, your design will look different. It will look like this. . . ."

Instructions for routes

As the children become proficient at handling the design-construction problems, introduce the task of following routes. In the route problems, actions must be performed in a certain order, whereas it is possible to change the order of actions in a design-construction problem.

1. Start by giving the children the following written instructions

1. Go to the teacher's desk, pick up a piece of chalk from the desk, walk to the chalkboard, and draw a rectangle on the chalkboard.

2. Go to the front window of the room, take a piece of red chalk from the windowsill, and draw a circle inside the rectangle on the chalkboard.

3. Go to the teacher's desk, take a piece of yellow chalk from the desk, go to the chalkboard, and draw a triangle inside the circle.

4. Go to the back window of the room, take a piece of white chalk from the windowsill, go to the chalkboard, and draw a circle around the rectangle.

After the children have worked on similar examples in several sessions, ask them to describe in writing a sequence of actions that *you* perform. Walk to the door, open it, close it, walk back to your desk, and sit down. Repeat the sequence, calling the children's attention to each new action: "Watch this. . . . Now I'm going to do something else. . . ."

After the children have written out instructions for the sequence, tell them to exchange instructions. "Do exactly what the instructions tell you to do." If the child happens to perform the sequence correctly from inadequate instructions, point out the inadequacy.

Play a game in which one of the children steps out of the room while an action sequence is demonstrated to the other children. Have the children describe the sequence. Then have the child come back into the room, hand him one of the instructions, and see if he can duplicate the original action sequence. Keep the sequence of events relatively simple for this exercise.

2. After every child has had at least one turn at reconstructing a sequence from instructions, introduce a variation. Have each child write a set of instructions and exchange with another child. Before any child carries out the instructions he has been assigned, send him out of the room while the child who wrote the instructions shows what he wants the other child to do. He must show, not tell.

3. Introduce exercises in which the child must draw a route that is described in written instructions. The child must know how to read a map to complete these tasks.

Introduce the concept of a map by drawing a rectangle on the board and writing *north, south, east,* and *west* in the appropriate places:

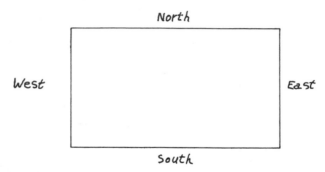

Show the children how to determine the direction in which something is moving: "Ask yourself which side it's going toward. Watch this line. . . ." Slowly draw a line from the middle of the map toward the east edge. As you draw, ask, "Which side am I going toward? . . . This one. This is the east side." Erase the line and start another line from the middle to the north edge of the map. "Which side am I going toward? The north side." Draw other lines until the children have caught on to the procedure. Draw them slowly and don't hurry the children. If they encounter difficulties, have them touch the side of the map toward which you are going: "Touch it, John. Show me the side I'm going toward. . . . O.K., and which side is that? . . . Yes, the west. So I'm going west."

Next introduce written exercises. Draw a diagram similar to the one below with the names of children in the class near boxes representing houses.

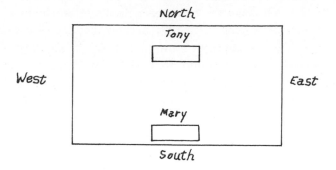

Pass out a sheet containing these instructions:

1. Go north from Mary's house until you reach Tony's house. Go inside Tony's house.
2. Go south from Tony's house until you reach Mary's house. Go inside.
3. Go east from Mary's house until you come to the east edge of the map. Go north to the northeast corner of the map. Go west along the north edge of the map until you come to Tony's house. Then go south and go inside the house.
4. Go south from Tony's house until you come to Mary's house. Do not go inside. Go around to the east side of the house, circle the house, and go back to Tony's house.
5. Go south from Tony's house until you come to Mary's house. Do not go inside Mary's house. Go around to the west side of Mary's house, circle the house, and go north to Tony's house.

Have the children work problems as a group. Have them read each item carefully and raise their hands when they know what kind of route to draw. Wait until most or all of the children have raised their hands. Then call on one of the children. After he has drawn the route, ask, "Is that right?" Ask each child if he agrees with the drawing: "What about it, John? Did he do what the instructions told him to do?" If one of the children disagrees, have him show how the route should go and then find the words in the instructions that tell him his route is correct: "Where does it say to go around the house that way? Show me in the instructions."

If the children have difficulty working the problems in this manner, give them each a drawing that corresponds to the one on the board. This will make the task easier, because the children can take the instructions in steps. After they have worked a problem on paper, have one child reproduce his route on the board: "Get a good picture of it so you'll know how to do it on the board. Watch the way it goes around Mary's house and then up to Tony's house. O.K., don't look at your drawing anymore, and see if you can draw it on the board."

As the children work on problems presented on the board, encourage them to trace imaginary routes in the air with their fingers: "It says go south from Tony's house, so I point to Tony's house and I go south. It says to go south until I reach Mary's house. . . ."

After the children have learned how to handle the problems in which the objects on the board are labeled with children's names, introduce tasks in which the objects are not labeled. For example:

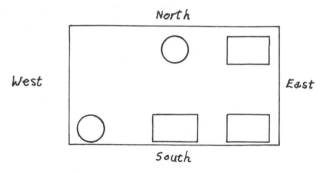

1. Find the circle in the lower left corner of the map (the southwest corner). Go east from this circle until you come to a rectangle. Go to the center of the rectangle. Then go north until you come to a circle.

2. Find the rectangle in the lower right corner of the map (the southeast corner). Go to the center of this rectangle. Then go north until you come to another rectangle. Go to the center of this rectangle. Then go west until you come to a circle.

3. Find the rectangle in the upper right corner of the map (the northeast corner). Go west from the center of this rectangle until you come to a circle. Go south from the circle until you come to a rectangle. Go to the center of this rectangle. Then go east until you come to the center of another rectangle. Go north from this rectangle until you come to the center of another rectangle.

4. Find the circle that is in the middle of the north side of the map. Go south from the center of this circle until you come to a rectangle. Go west from the center of this rectangle until you come to a circle. Go north from the center of this circle until you are west of a circle. Go east to the center of that circle.

The children may find several parts of Item 4 difficult. Some of the instructions are split into two sentences. For example, the second sentence tells the child to go south from the center of the circle in the middle of the north side of the map until he comes to a rectangle. There is no note about going to the center of this rectangle. The next sentence, however, tells him to go west from the center of this rectangle. If the children have trouble with these instructions, refer to the third sentence and point out that you somehow had to get to the middle of the rectangle: "This is tricky. It says 'Go south from the *center of this rectangle.*' We can't go south from the center unless we're at the center. We've got to go to the center before we can go south from the center."

Another part of the instructions may present problems—the part that directs one to go north until he is "west of a circle." If the children have trouble, draw a point that is west of the upper circle and ask, "How would you get to this point from the center of this circle? Which way would you have to go? . . . Yes, you'd have to go west. So this point is west of the center of the circle."

When explaining why a point is west of another point, keep your explanation clear. It is west because you have to go west to reach that point.

The exercises above set the stage for the introduction of such designations as *northeast* and *southeast*. In the exercises above, the children do not have to rely on these designations, because the instructions include equivalent expressions (upper right corner, lower right corner). The children may wonder about the parentheses in Items 1 to 3 above. Point out that the words in the parentheses say something that has already been said: "Look, it says upper right corner. Then it says northeast corner. That's the same place. Northeast is just another way of saying upper right." Have the children locate the upper right corner. Then have them find the north side of the map and the east side of the map. Have them put a finger on each side, then move the fingers together until they meet. "This is the north and east corner. The northeast corner." When the children are given the presentation suggested above, they usually have little difficulty learning such designations as *northeast* and *southwest*.

After the children have worked on three or four sets of instructions in which the terms *northeast, northwest*, and so on, are included in parentheses, introduce examples in which these are the primary terms.

The next step is to introduce tasks that require moving in one of the diagonal directions. For example: "Find the triangle that is in the southwest corner of the map. Go northeast from the top of this triangle until you come to a circle."

Describing alternative routes

When the children are well grounded in the preceding tasks, introduce exercises in which they are required to make up instructions about how to get to a point on the map. Begin with simple examples:

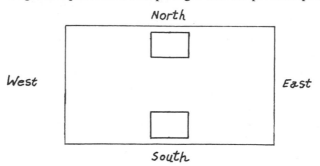

Explain, "I want you to tell me how you would go from this rectangle"—point to the top rectangle—"to this rectangle." Point to the bottom rectangle. Have the children give their instructions verbally. Help them with the steps:

1. "Tell me where I start. *Describe* the rectangle."
2. "Tell me where I go from that rectangle. *Describe* the path I take."
3. "Tell me where I stop. *Describe* how I know when to stop."

Accept any description that unambiguously describes what is called for. For instance, a child may refer to the rectangle from which you start as the "top rectangle." This response is acceptable. If it is given, however, ask if there is another way of describing the top rectangle. The route can be described as "going down," but again ask if there is another way of describing it (going south). The terminal rectangle can be described as the "bottom rectangle." When a child offers a description, ask one of these questions: "Does that tell me which rectangle?" "Does that tell me which way to go?" Take the words that the child uses and see if it is possible to identify more than one rectangle or more than one route. If an alternative is possible, the description is unacceptable. If only one route or object is possible, the description is acceptable.

After the children have worked the first problem, have them describe how one goes from the bottom rectangle to the top rectangle. Follow with similar examples:

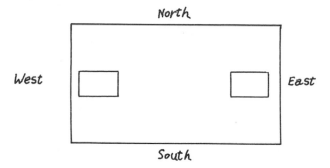

Ask the children to describe how to go from the east rectangle to the west rectangle and from the west rectangle to the east rectangle.

Next, present this map on the board:

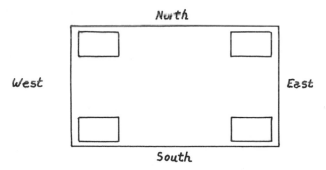

Explain, "I want you to tell me how to get from this rectangle"—point to the northeast rectangle—"to this rectangle." Point to the southwest rectangle. "There is more than one way to get there. Let's see how many ways you can figure out."

Have each child who has a route to suggest trace it on the board before giving his directions. Then have him give the directions as you follow his instructions exactly. *If his instructions are ambiguous, take the wrong route.* The children can have a great deal of fun with these exercises, because there are a number of ways of getting from the northeast to the southwest rectangle. A straight diagonal route is possible. An L route is possible. Variations of an N route are possible.

Present one alternative-route problem every day until the children can give a variety of accurate directions. Present problems in which the children must go from the southeast rectangle to the southwest rectangle, from the northeast rectangle to the northwest rectangle, and so on. When working on these verbal tasks, make sure that all the children are learning. Call on the children who don't volunteer answers: "O.K., JC, show me another way to get from this southeast rectangle to this southwest rectangle."

When the children have learned to give accurate descriptions, have them write out three alternative routes for getting from one rectangle to another. Spend about fifteen minutes on this exercise.

1. Specify the starting and terminating rectangles.

2. Have the children write out three alternative routes for getting to the goal rectangle.

3. Have each child read aloud each of his instructions after he traces the route on the board.

4. Follow the route he outlines when he reads his instructions. Take the wrong course if his instructions are not sufficiently clear.

5. Have *him* specify what his instructions should have said. If he is unable to do so, ask the other members of the class what he should have said.

6. Praise the children for "creative" routes, especially those in which one must proceed until he is west or east of another rectangle and then go the rectangle: "Oh, that's hard to explain, and Mary did a good job."

Descriptions

Descriptions are similar to instructions. The difference is that an instruction tells you to do something, whereas a description tells you to *picture something.* The test of a good description is similar to the test of a good set of instructions. A set of instructions is good if it unambiguously specifies the appropriate set of moves; a description is good if it unambiguously specifies the desired picture. One should ask himself, Would I be able to identify what is described in any group of things presented?

1. Demonstrate to the children that a description must allow one to identify the object referred to.

Present the following sheet:

> Descriptions: They tell you what kind of picture you should form in your mind. (Explain that all the descriptions refer to the same object.)

> 1. He looked through the window and saw something that looked like a triangle.
> 2. He looked through the window and saw something that looked like a wavy triangle.
> 3. He looked through the window and saw something that looked like a wavy triangle that was standing on two posts.
> 4. He looked through the window and saw something that looked like a small, black, wavy triangle that was standing on two short posts.

Have the children read all four of the descriptions. After they have read them, call on individual children to read each of the descriptions. Ask them what *wavy* and *posts* are. Then ask which of the descriptions is the best: "Which one gives you the best picture of what he saw when he looked through the window?" Have the children defend their choices.

Then put each description to a test: "Let's see which one is best. Let's see what kind of picture each of these descriptions gives us." Read the first description and ask, "What kind of picture does that give you?" Refer to each of the triangles at the top of the page. "Could the person looking through the window have seen something that looked like this? . . . Could he have seen something that looked like this? . . . like this? . . . like this? . . . like this? . . . I don't really know what kind of triangle he saw. All I know is that he saw something that looked like a triangle. Maybe he saw something that looked like this? . . ." Draw an upside down triangle. "Or like this? . . ." Draw a long, narrow triangle on its side.

Encourage the children to give other examples of what the person might have seen.

Refer to the second description and go through the same procedure. Cross out the triangles that have been eliminated by the description. Ask the children to give other examples of what the person might have seen.

Go through the third and fourth descriptions in the same manner, concluding that the fourth description is the best because it gives the most precise description of what the person saw through the window: "This description lets me form the best picture in my mind, so I can pick out the right picture."

Point out that the description is still not perfect. Have the children read the fourth description again; then ask them if the person could have been something that is different from the drawing on the page: "Can you get a picture of a different kind of triangle?"

The children may be unable to formulate an alternative. After they have thought about the problem for about fifteen seconds, draw an alternative on the board:

Show that this figure is consistent with the descriptions: "Is it small? Is it black? Is it wavy? Is it a triangle? Is it standing on two short posts?" Conclude, "Then maybe he saw something that looked like this." Help them make the instructions more precise by adding the word *upright*— ". . . standing upright on two short posts." Demonstrate that upright means that the base is at the bottom. "Otherwise it would fall over."

2. Introduce the following sheet:

Which description is the best? Remember that they all describe the same door.

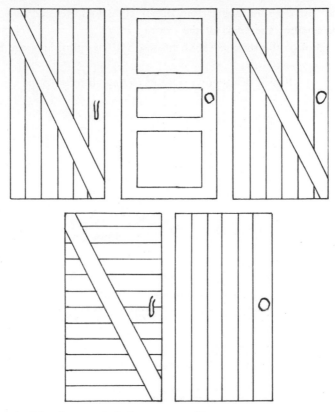

1. The door to their house was old.
2. The door to their house was old. It was made with vertical boards and a diagonal board.
3. The door to their house was old. It had no window. It was made of vertical boards.
4. The door to their house was old. It had no window. It was made of vertical boards and a diagonal board with a piece of rope for a door knob.
5. The door to their house was old. It was made of boards.

Use the approach outlined for the introductory task. Have the children read the five descriptions and choose the one they think is best. (They may need help with the word *diagonal*.) Have them defend their choice. Then apply each of the descriptions to the illustrations, concluding that the fourth description is the best because it gives the clearest picture of the door being described and can apply to only one of the drawings. Ask for alternative pictures of the door (with the diagonal going from upper right to lower left and with the rope on the other side of the door).

3. For the third exercise in descriptions, introduce the following sheet:

Which description is best? (They all refer to the same coin.)

1. In the sand, he found a strange gold coin. It was almost square. All around the outside of the coin was funny writing, and in the middle was the head of a bird, facing right.
2. In the sand, he found a strange gold coin.
3. In the sand, he found a strange gold coin, with a bird on it.
4. In the sand, he found a strange gold coin. It was almost square, with a bird on it.
5. In the sand, he found a strange gold coin. There was funny writing all around the outside of the coin.

Have the children read the five items, choose the one they think is best, and defend their choice. Ask them which description is the worst, and why. Test the various descriptions, concluding that the first is the best. Ask if it is possible to form another picture of the coin from the first description.

4. Introduce exercises in which the children are to help construct pictures from descriptions. The preceding exercises acquainted them with the "test" of a description: allowing one to identify one object in a larger set. The present exercises go a step further and acquaint the children with the procedures for constructing a picture.

1. The slices of bread he used for his sandwich were so hard that the ends curled out. Inside the sandwich was a large pickle and a thick layer of peanut butter.

2. The road was straight, but the car started to skid. First it went off the right side of the road; then it came back, went across the center line and off the left side of the road. It swerved back onto the road and stopped, having made a giant S.

Have the children read the descriptions carefully. The children may not know what some of the words in the instructions mean. Remind them, "If you don't know what the words mean, find out." After they have read the instructions, explain, "Now we're going to see if we can make pictures from these descriptions."

Have one of the children read the first description aloud. Ask the children about the bread: "What does it mean to say that the ends curled out?" The answer is that they curve away from the center of the sandwich. Make a simple drawing:

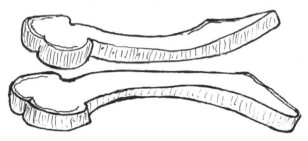

"That's curling out. How would they look if they were curling in?"

Next have the children specify what is inside the sandwich. If they say a pickle, draw a very small pickle and ask, "Is that right?" If they say peanut butter, draw a very thin layer of peanut butter and ask, "Is that right?" The final drawing should look something like this:

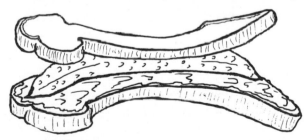

For the second description first draw the road on the board. Represent it with two vertical lines. Ask the children to find the words in the description that tell why the road would look like this. (The road was straight.)

"Read the description and see if it tells you anything else about the road." Help them out if they do not find the reference to the center line. Draw it in. Then start to draw in the path the car took when it skidded. Start at the bottom of the road and move up. (If you start at the top, the children may become confused with left and right, which will be the opposite from what they are if the car is going up the road.)

Draw a backward S:

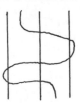

Ask the children if this picture is correct. Have them find the words that would indicate that it is not.

Change the drawing:

Ask them if this picture is correct.

5. Present two descriptions during every session until the children have become proficient at translating the descriptions into pictures. Plan to devote about ten minutes of the session to descriptions. Here are some descriptions from which chalkboard drawings can be made:

> Rex lived in a fancy doghouse. Unlike most doghouses, it was made of brick. It had a brick chimney and a large front porch. The roof of the house went over the porch. The house had a large window on each side.

216

The end of his bat broke off, so he rounded off the broken end. His bat was shorter than most bats and it looked funny because the tape went almost to the end of the bat.

Mr. Smith's face was long and thin. His eyes were so close together that they seemed to be growing out of the sides of his nose. And his nose was so big it almost covered his mouth. His head was bald, but he had a strange little beard growing like an arrow out of his chin.

To chop trees in thick forests, you need a special kind of ax. It should have a short, thick handle so that you can get a good grip and twist the handle to knock out big chips of wood. The head of the ax should be heavy and the cutting blade should be large.

Waldo looked funny. He had a huge body, but his head looked as if it hadn't grown from the time he was a child. Some of the guys used to call him pinhead. To make his head look bigger, Waldo let his hair grow very long over the ears, and he combed it so that it stuck out. Sometimes he wore a big cowboy hat, but this just made him look even funnier.

His shoes were old. They came up to his ankles and they didn't have holes for shoelaces; they had little hooks. The heels were almost worn down flat, and the soles were loose. When he walked, the soles would flap open and shut in front like the mouth of a smiling fish.

The blacksmith took the red-hot bar from the fire and held it with a tool that looked like a pair of pliers with long, long handles. He hit the bar with a hammer a few times and put the bar back in the fire. Then he hit it again and again. When he was done, the bar had been changed into a flat U-shaped piece of metal about the size of your hand. I asked him what it was and he told me.

She was tired. Her glasses had slipped down to the end of her nose and her eyes were almost closed. A strand of hair hung down the middle of her forehead and her mouth was half open.

217

Although the pickup truck was old, it looked good with its fresh red paint job. The back fenders were badly dented and the right front tire was flat, but the old truck looked pretty good. Hank put a sign in the window across from the driver's side: "For sale $75."

He got the watch on his twenty-first birthday. That was fifty years ago, but the watch was still in perfect shape. It was a big watch, about as big as the palm of your hand. On top, it had a big winder circled by a large gold ring. A big gold chain hung from the ring. To open the lid that covered the face of the watch, you would press a button at the bottom of the watch. The numbers on the face of the watch were large and clear. The hands were thick and black, shaped like arrows.

She had rings on every finger of her right hand. The ring on her index finger was the most amazing. The center stone was a diamond as big as the end of your little finger, and around the center stone were five grass-green emeralds, each a perfect cube. Around the emeralds was a sparkling ring of diamond chips. Someone said that the ring was worth twenty thousand dollars.

The desk belonged to Tom's brother before he went to college. Before Tom's brother got it, the desk belonged to an uncle. There were initials carved in the top of the desk, but Tom didn't know who made some of them. There was a large "J.B." in the middle of the top, and a heart to the right of these initials. Inside the heart was "J.B. loves N.R." The initials "B.L." were on the left side of the desk. Right above the center drawer was carved "Jack M." The desk had three drawers, one in the center and the other two on the left side. The right side of the desk was supported by two sturdy legs.

The children will probably find descriptions such as these interesting, but difficult. The best procedure is to have them read the descriptions several times and ask about words that they cannot pronounce or do not understand. Then have them suggest how to draw a picture of what is described. When a suggestion is given, ask, "What

218

words tell you that I should do it that way?" With some descriptions, more than one drawing is possible. For example, in the description of the blacksmith making a horseshoe, there is a reference to tongs. In the description of the elaborate ring, there is reference to the fact that the woman had rings on every finger of her right hand.

There will be parts of each description that remain unspecified (for instance the rings on the woman's other fingers, and the features of the tired woman's face). Point out that the description does not tell everything: "I don't know what this woman looks like. I just know that her glasses are on her nose, and her hair is hanging down, and her eyes are almost closed, and her mouth is half open. I don't know whether she's young or old. I don't know whether she's fat or skinny. I don't know a lot of things about her."

If the children have particular difficulty with some of the descriptions, alter some of the details and present them again. Also, if the children have trouble with some of the concepts introduced (perfect cube, half open, across from the driver's side, and the like), present these concepts in other examples or alter the descriptions and present them again.

The concepts in these descriptions are not programed the way concepts were programed in previous exercises. In previous exercises, a given concept was taught before it was presented. These descriptions, however, contain concepts that have not been previously taught. The children are faced with the kind of problem that will confront them throughout their academic careers. In order to understand what is being presented, they must seek information about the concepts they do not understand. Before they can formulate a clear picture of what is being described, they must seek information. Then they must use the information to construct the appropriate mental picture.

Further examples of descriptions can be found in storybooks for children from nine to fourteen years of age, especially books about dogs and horses. Since each description will be analyzed intensively, do not reject those that contain words that are not familiar to the children. Also do not reject poor descriptions—those that don't give a very clear picture. The children can learn a great deal from working on such descriptions. It's a good idea to make the point repeatedly that descriptions are made up by people and sometimes a person doesn't do a good job: "The person who wrote this description didn't tell us very much about what his house looked like." Also comment on good descriptions: "The person who wrote this description sure made a good picture." Soon the children will make similar comments, which is very desirable. They should think of a description in terms of constructing, or formulating, a word picture of something seen, a job that can be done well or poorly.

To make this point, have the children add details to descriptions that are not clear. For example, first present a general description of a ranch house. Then show a picture of a ranch house. Have the children study the picture, then add details to the description until it conforms more closely to the picture: "We don't want to talk about just any old ranch house. We want to talk about *this* ranch house. Study it and tell me what I should write down."

Writing descriptions

Introduce writing tasks after the children have worked at least four of the descriptions presented in Step 5 above.

1. Present an object to the children—a ball, a desk, one of the children's shirts. Have them examine the object carefully and then describe it in detail: "Remember—we don't want a description of just any shirt. We want a description of *this* shirt. We want a word picture of it."

2. Give the children about ten minutes to examine the object presented and write their descriptions. Help them find the details that make this particular object different from others in its class: "What makes this shirt different from all other shirts? Look, this button is cracked. Who can find something else?"

3. After they have finished, have each child read his description. Take what the children agree are the best details from the various descriptions and write a description on the board: "Mary mentioned this little brown mark on the left shoulder. Let's put that in our description."

4. Present one object-describing exercise during a session.

Identifying what is being described

After the children have written descriptions of familiar objects every day for about a week, present tasks in which the children are to identify objects and events that are described *but not named*. These exercises are good because they give the child practice in trying out various "names" and testing them against the description.

220

1. Introduce the task with this sheet:

Write the name of what is described.

1. There are 11 players on each team. At each end of the field (which is 100 yards long) are a goal line and a set of goal posts. The ball used in the game is not round. It is shaped something like a watermelon. The idea is to carry the ball over the other team's goal line. The game is _____.

2. It has a long handle, and a steel scoop at the other end. You force the scoop into the ground, pull back on the handle, and lift a scoop full of dirt from the ground. The tool is _____.

3. This article of clothing is worn by men. It goes around the back of the neck under the shirt collar. It is tied in the front of the neck and hangs down in two long strips from the knot. This article of clothing is _____.

4. This vehicle is used by children. It looks like an open box resting on four wheels. A long handle is attached to the front wheels and can be used to steer the vehicle. You can move the vehicle by pushing, by pulling, or by scooting. This vehicle is _____.

2. Have the children write their answers in the spaces provided. Remind them to ask questions if they don't understand a word or a sentence. After they have finished writing their answers, have a child read an item, give his answer, and defend it by referring to the details provided in the description. When answers are correct, let the children know immediately. Then ask them how they know that the description does not refer to something else. For example, if the child suggests that the answer to Item 1 is football, say, "You're right. But how do you know it's not baseball? Find the words that tell you it can't be baseball." If a child notes that the article of clothing in Item 3 is a necktie, acknowledge his answer: "That good figuring out." Then ask him, "How do you know it's not a shoelace? . . . What about a belt?" Require the children to find the appropriate words.

3. Present a sheet containing three or four descriptions during each session until the children can correctly identify the objects described and successfully defend their answers. Here are some descriptions that can be presented:

It is a brown coin with a picture of Abraham Lincoln on it. Five of these coins are worth a nickel. The coin is _____.

You take a long, thin stick with a point on one end and feathers on the other. You hold the feather end of the stick against a string and pull the string back. The string bends a curved, springy piece of wood. You hold this curved piece with your other hand. You let go of the string and it shoots forward, sending the stick through the air with great speed. This weapon is _____.

This animal has stripes, heavy claws, and a long tail. He is strong enough to kill a full-grown water buffalo. This animal is _____.

This writing instrument has a piece of "lead" running down its center, from one end to the other. Around the lead is wood. At one end of the instrument is an eraser. You write by pressing the lead against a piece of paper. This writing instrument is _____.

This vehicle is very popular with young people, because the top of the vehicle is made of a soft material. It can be folded down when the weather is nice; it can be raised when the weather is not nice. In the summer you often see young people riding with the top down. This vehicle is _____.

These things come filled with beans, with soup, with dog food, with corn, with peas, with spinach, with apples, with motor oil, with paint, or with orange soda. These things are made of very thin metal, in the shape of a cylinder. You open them by punching a hole in the top or by cutting the top off. These things are _____.

It has a broad flat head and a short shaft coming from the center of the head. The other end of the shaft comes to a sharp point. You press your thumb against the head of this thing and push hard. The shaft will go through cardboard or even wood. You have to watch out for this thing when it is on the floor. It is small and it will stick in your shoe (or your foot). This thing is _____.

This article of clothing is worn by women and girls. The top fits around the waist, and the bottom is in the shape of a circle that hangs loosely around the knees. This article of clothing is usually made of wool, cotton, or a man-made fiber. This article of clothing is _____.

This instrument gives you a picture and sound. This instrument has a selector that lets you choose different channels. It also has controls for making the sound louder and for making the picture sharper. People usually have this instrument in their living rooms. This instrument is _____.

A kind of food that is popular as a dessert is made of layers of sweetened, breadlike material that is usually covered with a candylike material called frosting. This food is _____.

This game is played with a ball that is about as big as a man's fist and a piece of wood that is fat at one end and thin at the other. The player using the piece of wood holds it with both hands around the thin end. Another player throws the ball, and the first player tries to hit it with the piece of wood. If he hits the ball on the field, he runs along a path. There are three plates on this path, in addition to the plate he stands in front of when swinging the piece of wood. There are nine men on each team. This game is _____.

This thing is shaped like a small shoe box. It usually has three holes running through it from top to bottom. This thing is used to build buildings. It is made of a hard, stonelike material. This thing is held in place with a kind of cement. The cement goes into the holes of this thing and when the cement hardens, this thing is held tightly in place. To build a house, you would need hundreds of these things. This thing is _____.

These things grow on trees. They usually turn red when they are ripe. They have a hard, smooth skin and a core in the middle. They are sweet and people eat them raw. There is an old saying that if you eat one of these things a day, you will keep the doctor away. These things are _____.

This thing has a head and a shaft. The shaft is sometimes made of wood and sometimes of cardboard. The head of this thing is made of a material that bursts into flame when it is rubbed against a scratchy surface. This thing usually comes in a pack, with a strip of the scratchy surface attached to the pack. This thing is _____.

(NOTE: These descriptions contain new words, some of which are repeated. The idea "made of" or "material" is repeated often. If the children have trouble with the concept, take time out to explain what it means. Go over the common materials—glass, wood, brick, concrete, cloth, and so forth—and have them name things that are made of these materials: "O.K., who can name some things that are made of leather?")

When working on these descriptions, have the children account for every part of the description. Children sometimes name an object or event on the basis of a single word or phrase. If a child does this, have him read the description aloud and *indicate whether every part of the description fits the object or event he suggested:* "John says that this thing is a tomato. Let's have him read the description and see if we can say 'Yes, this is a tomato' about every part he reads." If any part of the description does not apply to the object the child has named, he will not be able to defend his choice.

Using made-up words in descriptions

One particularly severe deficiency of the slow-learning child is his inability to substitute one word for another. The following set of exercises (which should be introduced only after the child has mastered the preceding language tasks) is designed to acquaint him with word substitution.

1. Present exercises in which a made-up word is used in place of a familiar one. The children are to figure out what the key word is, cross out the made-up word, and write in the familiar word.

Present the following introductory sheet:

1. A glam is used to cut things. It has a handle and a blade. Some glams are made so that the blade folds into the handle.
2. A gleek is a piece of furniture. A gleek is found in the bedroom. A gleek has drawers and a flat top. Sometimes a mirror is attached to a gleek.

3. A flem is a bird. Flems go north in the spring of the year and go south before winter. Flems have orange breasts.

4. A dink is something you use to write with. A dink usually has an eraser at one end. The shaft of a dink is made of wood. You sharpen it in a dink sharpener.

Call on children to read the items aloud. Make sure that every child in the group can read each item.

Then refer to the first item. If the children do not agree on the word that should be substituted for *glam*, suggest a word that will not work: "I'll bet I know what a glam is. A glam is a scissors. Let's read Item 1, and wherever it says *glam*, we will say *scissors*. . . . A scissors is used to cut things. It has a handle and a blade. Some scissors are made so that the blade folds into the handle." Have the children point out specifically why the word *scissors* will not work.

Suggest another substitution word, perhaps *saw*. "That means that wherever Item 1 says *glam*, we will say *saw*." Have one of the children read the item, substituting *saw* for *glam*. Don't be surprised if he has some trouble. This kind of operation is often difficult for slow-learning children. Again have the children find the words that indicate why a glam cannot be a saw.

After the children have agreed that a glam is a knife, write the words *knife* and *knives* on the board. Tell the children to cross out *glam(s)* and insert the correct words. Have the children read their correct items.

2. Present other problems with made-up words.

a. Make sure that every child can read the item.

b. Ask the children what they think the strange word stands for.

c. Suggest alternatives that won't work.

d. Require the children to specify why they won't work.

e. Have the children put in the correct word.

f. Call on children to read their corrected items.

Present four or five tasks a day with made-up words, until the children have learned that the idea is to find a word that satisfies the requirements of the description. Here are some items that can be presented:

A het is a vehicle. A het has two wheels and a seat. To operate a het, you start the motor and steer using the handlebars.

A chit is a vehicle. A chit has two wheels and a seat. To operate a chit, you push on the pedals and steer using the handlebars.

A freet is a part of a house. When you walk up the front walk of a house, you come to the front freet. A freet has hinges so that it can open and close. To open a freet, you turn the freet knob.

A reeg is a part of a room. A reeg is sometimes covered with a rug. Sometimes reegs are made of wood. Sometimes reegs are covered with tile. A reeg is the part of a room that you stand on.

A glom is a plant. Some gloms are large, so large that children like to climb them and build glom houses in them. The parts of a glom are branches, leaves, trunk, and roots.

A greel is a plant. People like to have greels in their garden, because greels are very pretty when they are in bloom. Some greels are red, some greels are blue. Some greels are white. Some of the nicest greels are tulips, petunias, roses.

The shane is something you see in the sky. The shane comes up in the east and sets in the west. The shane gives off heat. When the shane is out, everything is bright.

The bane is something you see in the sky. The bane comes up in the east and sets in the west. Every month the bane changes from a full bane to a half bane, to no bane at all.

A glop is a vehicle. A glop has a motor and wheels. A glop also has a tail. The glop can go very fast and very high. Some glops fly more than a thousand miles an hour.

A greem is an animal. A greem has long ears and a funny little tail. Greems hop. Greems can go very fast, too. Dogs like to chase greems, but they don't often catch them.

A slem is an animal. A slem is cold-blooded. A slem has no legs and no arms. Slems move by wiggling along. Fish like to eat slems, and fishermen sometimes put slems on hooks to catch fish.

Having the children use made-up words

Tell the children that you want them to describe something called a glam. Don't be surprised if they have some trouble with the task. They are not used to substituting *glam* for a known word.

1. Instruct them to write three or four sentences about a chair. "Tell about a chair so that everybody knows what you're talking about." After they have finished, call on individual children to read what they have written. Ask the others in the group if they would know, from the statements, that the object being described is a chair. Put it to a test. Have the author cross out the word *chair* wherever it appears in his statements and substitute the word *glam*. Now have him read the statements. "Would we know that a glam is really a chair?" The children will probably be able to make suggestions about how to make the description more accurate.

2. Have the children write about bicycles, roller skates, and shoes. Use a procedure similar to that outlined for *chair*. Have them first write three or four sentences describing the object. Call on different children to read what they have written. Then have them substitute the word *glam* for the key word in the description and have them reread the description. Ask the other children whether the description is clear.

Acknowledge good writing—that is, writing that clearly describes the object in question. Do not become too excited over grammatical errors. These are minor compared with conceptual errors.

Praise children for noting that a description is ambiguous. Such comments as "He could be talking about boots, or slippers, or anything" deserve special commendation. The child who makes such observations is aware that more detail must be added to the description if it is to apply to only one object.

Question the children to determine whether a description is adequate: "Do we know that he's talking about a shoe? Or could he by talking about something else, too? . . . What else?" The more possibilities that can be offered, the poorer the description.

Try to work as much as possible from what the children say. Use their suggestions to revise the original description. Encourage them to discuss the problems associated with a description. However, don't let the discussions get out of hand. Try to resolve them by putting the burden on the child who says a description is inadequate: "O.K., John. You say he could be talking about a bicycle or a tricycle. So what would he have to say to let us know that he is talking about a bicycle and not a tricycle?"

3. Assign each child a different object to write about. Introduce a different set of ground rules. Whisper the assignment to each child or pass out slips of paper with the name of the object written on it. Some good objects are monkey, dog, zebra, ice cream, toothbrush, chair, ladder, shirt, hat, coat, snowball, apple, hamburger, hammer.

Tell each child to write about his object, calling it a glam: "You can't tell us what it is. Whenever you talk about that thing, you have to call it a glam."

Allow the children no more than twelve minutes to finish their assigned writing (three or four sentences).

Call on children to read their descriptions. Have the others in the class see if they can identify what object is being referred to.

If the other children in the class do not know what the description refers to, have them list the possible things a glam could be.

After various interpretations have been offered (if there are any), have the author tell what he attempted to describe.

If any description is criticized as vague, ask the author if he knows how to change the description so that the ambiguity will be eliminated: "Glen pointed out that you might be writing about a motorcycle. How could you change what you have written so that we wouldn't think that a glam is a motorcycle?" If the author has trouble, ask other members of the class for suggestions.

After the corrections have been made, write the corrected version on the board and have various children read it before proceeding to the next child's description.

Work on made-up word descriptions for two to three weeks. The children must develop the ability to see that a word is only a symbol. A word is not a concrete thing. We can introduce made-up words that serve the same purpose as the accepted word. *What is real is not the word but the idea behind the word.*

4. Have the children describe whatever they wish, referring to it as a glam.

Tell the children, "Pick anything you want to describe and write about it." If some of the children have trouble deciding on an object, tell them to look around the room and name some of the objects they see: "You could write about any one of those things. Just pick one and start writing." Allow no more than twelve minutes for writing.

When they have finished, call on individual children to read their descriptions. Ask others in the class to identify the object being described. If a description is ambiguous, list the various things it may be describing.

Have the author tell what object he tried to describe. If the description is ambiguous, ask him how he plans to reduce the ambiguity and make his description clear.

Write the corrected description on the board, and call on three or four children to read it.

Encourage the children to describe interesting objects, events, and actions. Work on this exercise for at least a week; then present similar tasks from time to time throughout the school year. The children enjoy this task after they have mastered the technique of substituting made-up words for known words.

Definitions

The preceding exercises have brought the children very close to the concept of a definition. In contrast to a description, freely written, the definition is more formal. One must first place the object to be defined in a class; one must then tell enough about the object to distinguish it from all other members of the class. Distinguishing the object being defined from all others in the same class is the difficult part of the definition. When a child is told that his definition of an alligator could also apply to a snake, he may try to amend the definition *by talking about snakes*. The criterion of a good definition is the same as that used for descriptions in the preceding section. Could a reader who has never seen an alligator use the definition to identify an alligator, and only an alligator, in a group of animals? If he would choose only the alligator, the definition is adequate. If he would choose other animals also, the definition is not adequate.

Note that the requirements of the definition vary with the range of animals under consideration. If one is asked to define an alligator in such a way as to distinguish it from a crocodile, a highly technical definition is required. If one is asked to define an alligator to distinguish it from a few other common reptiles, a far less detailed definition is required. The adequacy of the definition in each case is determined by whether it succeeds in distinguishing between an alligator and the objects from which it must be distinguished.

229

The exercises in this section do not call for the construction of highly technical definitions. Their purpose is to show the children how to distinguish one member of a class from a small group of representative members.

1. Present definitions as problems. Tell the children that they are going to work on definitions. Do not try to explain what definitions are. Simply indicate that you will show them how to define *eagle*.

Put *eagle* in an appropriate class of objects: "What is an eagle? Is it a building? Is it a piece of furniture?"

After the children have agreed that an eagle is a bird, write on the board *An eagle is a bird* and ask, "Now do I know what an eagle is?" The children may say yes.

Present pictures of three or four birds—perhaps a robin, a chicken, an ostrich, and an eagle. Point to each picture and say, "This is an eagle." Counter the children's objections by pointing out that you are simply using the definition they offered: "Look at what you told me. An eagle is a bird. These are birds, aren't they? So they must be eagles."

Pose a solution to the problem: "Your definition doesn't tell me enough about eagles to keep me from getting mixed up. You've got to tell me more about eagles."

To help the children see the problem, construct a large circle and divide it into eight parts:

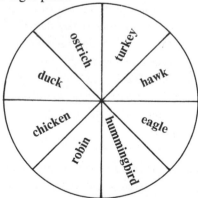

Present pictures of each bird for the children to study. "These are all birds. So if your definition of *eagle* only tells me that an eagle is a bird, I might think that any one of these birds is an eagle. Tell me more about an eagle. What can you say about an eagle that you can't say about a duck or a turkey?

230

The children may attempt to tell you something about ducks: "Ducks swim in the water." Respond by saying, "Yes, that's true. But you've got to tell me about eagles, not ducks. What does an eagle have that ducks don't have? What does an eagle do that ducks don't do?"

The children may observe that an eagle has claws (talons). Write the addition to the definition: An eagle is a bird with claws.

"O.K., let's see who we can cross out." Refer to each of the birds and ask, "Does this bird have claws?" If not, cross it out.

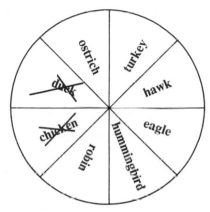

Point out the need for more detail: "If I used this definition, I still might think that an eagle is a robin or a hummingbird."

Accept all suggestions about what an eagle is or what it does. *A suggestion is not useful if it does not allow you to cross out at least one of the candidates.* For example, a child may observe that an eagle has a curved beak. Write his addition to the definition:

An eagle is a bird with claws and a curved beak.

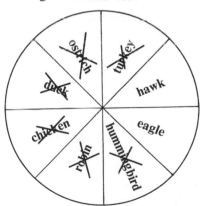

231

Now only one candidate remains to be eliminated—the hawk. "Tell me about an eagle so that I know an eagle is not a hawk. What can you say about an eagle that you can't say about a hawk?"

"An eagle is big."

Change the definition:

An eagle is a big bird with claws and a curved beak.

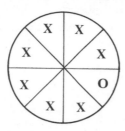

Call on children to read the completed definition.

Some readers may not accept this definition. They may want more details about the kind of claws an eagle has; to note that an eagle is a bird of prey; and to specify its size more precisely. While all these requirements are valid, it should be remembered that the task must not be made so difficult that the children cannot handle it.

2. Work one or two definitions with the class every day until the children have become proficient at placing the object to be defined in an appropriate class and then contrasting the object with other members of the class.

Have the children define words denoting actions as well as words denoting objects: "Let's define the word *running*. What class is *running* in? The class of actions. So we make a circle."

Actions

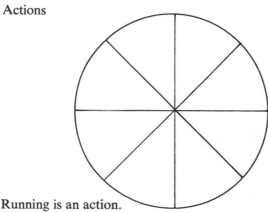

Running is an action.

"Is running the only action? . . . No. What are some of the others?" Fill in the cells of the circles as the children make acceptable suggestions.

Actions

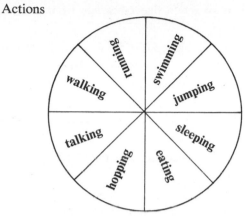

"All I know at this time is that running is an action. It could be any one of these actions. I might think that running is sleeping, or that running is eating. You've got to tell me more about running so that I know it is not sleeping."

If the children have trouble, point to the word *sleeping* and ask, "Is running the same as sleeping? How is running different? Tell me about sleeping." The children may point out that when you run, you move. Begin to write the definition and cross out the actions that have been excluded:

Actions

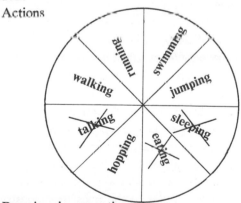

Running is an action
that takes you from
place to place.

Now focus on the remaining actions: "How do I know that running is not swimming? What can you say about running that you can't say about swimming?"

> Running is an action that takes you from place to place on land.

"Now, how does running differ from walking? When you run, both feet are off the ground at the same time. How does running differ from jumping and hopping? When you run, you alternate legs."

The final definition might read something like this:

> Running is an action that takes you from place to place on land. When you run, you put your feet down one after the other, and both feet are sometimes off the ground at the same time.

Some good words for the children to define are:

> hand, shoe, coat, eye, chair, bed, table, washing machine, bicycle, airplane, hammer, paintbrush, quarter, dime, dollar, moon, sun, tree, tiger, snake, book, ceiling, window, jumping, eating, sleeping, thinking.

Dictionary Work

By the time the children have worked on most of the above words, they will be ready for dictionary work, because they will have a clear understanding of the purpose of a dictionary definition. They will understand the problem facing a definer, that of putting the word to be defined in an appropriate class and then telling enough about the word to distinguish it from all members of its class.

Use the dictionary only for words denoting objects such as *canoe, cat, cape,* and *plate.* Look up words before assigning them. Use poorly written definitions (there are a good many) as well as good ones. Encourage the children to tell why a definition is poor (it does not eliminate all the members of a class except the one being defined). If the children are to use the elementary edition of *Webster's New World Dictionary*, have them look up some of the words they have already defined, such as *eagle,* and comment on the dictionary definitions (which will often be quite similar to the ones they constructed).

Children often have trouble looking up words in the dictionary because they are not familiar with alphabetical order. Here is a good procedure to prepare them for dictionary work:

1. Introduce "what comes after" tasks. Present about eight or ten tasks a day. Repeat examples that present particular difficulty.

"O.K., I'm going to say a letter, and you have to tell me what letter comes after it. *R*. What comes after *r?* . . ." If the children have trouble, recite the letters from the beginning of the alphabet until you reach *r*. They will be able to tell you the next letter.

As the children become increasingly skillful, begin reciting five or six letters before the letter in question: "What comes after *k?* Let's see —*g, h, i, j, k*. . ." Slowly decrease the number of letters until the children are able to operate from a one- or two-letter prompt: "What comes after *k? j, k* . . ."

Allow the children several weeks to become reasonably skillful. Do not try to cram all their learning into a few sessions.

2. Teach them to recite the alphabet backward. Spend no more than two minutes a day working on the task.

3. Introduce "what comes before" tasks. Initially, the children may become confused. They may want to tell you the letter that comes after when you ask for the letter that comes before.

If the children have difficulty with a problem such as "What comes before *m?*" have them recite the alphabet backward until they reach *m*. As they become more familiar with the procedure, cut down on the prompts. "What comes before *m?* Let's see: *o, n, m* . . ."

Present eight to ten examples every day, until the children become reasonably good at the tasks. Then begin mixing "what comes after" and "what comes before" tasks in the same session. Make your instructions quite clear: "Now you have to listen to what I say. What comes before *r?* . . . What comes after *r?*"

4. The final step in predictionary training is to present pairs of words on the board and have the children indicate which word comes before the other in the dictionary.

Begin with words that start with different letters. Write one word immediately below the other, and draw a line connecting the first letters of the words:

cat
|
dog

"*Cat* starts with *c*, and *dog* starts with *d*. Which letter comes after the other? *D* comes after *c*. So which word will come after the other in the dictionary? *Dog* will come after *cat*."

Continue with similar word pairs until the children can quickly indicate their order in the dictionary.

Introduce words that begin with the same letter but have a different second letter:

cow
|
cat

"They begin with the same letter, so we don't know which word comes after the other one. How can we find out? Go to the next letter."

Draw a line connecting the second letters of the words:

cow
|
cat

"Which letter comes after the other? *O* comes after *a*. So which word comes after the other? *Cow* comes after *cat*."

Present three to five examples a day. Mix pairs with the same initial letter and pairs with different initial letters.

Don't always pair words of the same length:

| go | helper | mother | tiger | if |
| grass | hop | me | tree | inside |

5. Introduce word pairs with the first two letters the same.

tree

trip

Refer to the first letter of each word. "Which letter comes after the other? They're both the same so we don't know which word comes after the other one. How do we find out? Look at the next letter. Oh, oh! They're both *r*. So we still don't know which word comes after the other one. How can we find out? Look at the next letter." Draw a line connecting the *e* and *i:*

tree
trip

"O.K., which letter comes after the other? *I* comes after *e*. So which word comes after the other in the dictionary? *Trip* comes after *tree*. Why? Because *i* comes after *e*."

236

Present such word pairs as these:

run	got	take	sun	read	and	of
rut	go	table	supper	red	ant	often

Word pairs such as *go–got* may cause a little trouble. There is a convention associated with such pairs. The third letter of the shorter word is nothing, which is assumed to come before *a* in the alphabet.

got
||||
go

"Which comes first, *t* or nothing? Nothing does. It comes before *a*."

The children should not have much trouble with this convention. It is sometimes assumed that they should learn it without being told or shown. When one thinks about it, however, it is a rather strange idea.

Present four to six pairs of words in which the first two letters are the same every day for about a week.

6. Present words in which the first three letters are the same. Include some words that have only three letters:

from	for	treat	clap	ear	car	the	swim
front	forget	tree	clam	earth	cart	then	swish

Have the children attack these words in the same way. First, compare the first letters. Then compare the second letters—then the third. Finally the fourth.

"Which letter comes after the other, *a* or *e*? *E* comes after *a*. So which word comes after the other? *Tree* comes after *treat*."

7. After the children have mastered the word pairs (working on them for perhaps a month), introduce the task of looking up words in the dictionary.

First write on the board the word to be looked up (*ax*, for example). Open the dictionary to a page near the word. Find the first word and the last word on that page and write them on the board under the key word:

ax

and
ant

Ask which comes after which. Conclude, "O.K., *ax* comes after both of these words, so we have to keep going in the dictionary."

Repeat the procedure for every page considered (although it is permissible to skip around). Do not hurry the children. It is important that they understand what they are supposed to do; otherwise they will just scurry frantically through the dictionary without a clear idea of how to find words.

(NOTE: The children may have trouble with the last part of the conclusion. "*Ax* comes after these words, so we keep going." They may not realize that the letters that appear last in the alphabet are on the last pages of the dictionary. To make this point, remind them that *z* is at the end of the dictionary: "We want to go toward *z*.")

Analogies

In the preceding sections the child was shown how to follow instructions, how to describe objects and events, and finally how to define words and treat them as symbols for something observable in the world (something that can be expressed with made-up labels). He has been equipped with valuable tools of thought. He needs one more tool —the analogy. For the middle-class child, analogical thinking is usually intuitive. He perceives the relation between two situations, seeing the way in which they are the same. The disadvantaged child often lacks this insight and must be taught. The programing of skills on which analogical thinking is based is well worth the effort, although it may never be reflected in achievement test scores. It will be reflected in the child's increased ability to handle ideas.

Analogy is difficult to teach, because the teacher perceives analogical relations intuitively. Before she can teach it precisely, she must learn a precise set of operations.

Let's take a simple analogy: *A* is to *B* as 1 is to _____.

The answer is obviously 2. But why? What is so compelling about the answer 2 and how do we defend it? How do we show the child it has to be 2?

1. The first step is to show the relation between the *first statement and the second statement*. It is only from this relation that an answer can be derived. *A* and 1 are the same in one way—they are both the first in a series.

The first
| *A* | is to *B* |
| 1 | is to _____. |

238

2. We now make up a similar statement that relates A and B. How are A and B the same? How are they different? B is another letter. It is the second letter in the alphabet. The rule must be that the first is followed by the second in a series:

The first is to the second—

$$\text{as}\begin{vmatrix} A \\ 1 \end{vmatrix}\text{is to}\begin{vmatrix} B \\ 2. \end{vmatrix}$$

Higher-order statements

Handling analogies involves formulating higher-order statements, such as "The first is to the second." These statements group the first terms of each statement and the second terms.

1. Present the following problem to the children:

2 is to 3

as 9 is to _____.

Some of the children may give the answer, but they may have arrived at the answer by a guess, not by considering all the elements.

First have them classify the first terms in the analogy: "What do we know about two and nine? How are they the same? They're both the same because they're both numbers. Nine, you are a number, and two, you are a number. You're both numbers."

Above the first terms of the analogy write

A number

2 is to 3

as 9 is to _____.

Now refer to 3. "We called two a number. What can we call three?" Some of the children may suggest calling it a number also. "We could do that, but I don't think that will give us an answer. How is three different from two?" Lead the children to the notion that three comes right after two and that the rule for the analogy is:

A number is to the next number—

2 is to 3

as 9 is to 10.

Show that the rule holds for both statements. Refer to the first statement of the analogy. "Two is a number and three is the next number." Refer to the second statement. "Nine is a number and what is the next number? Ten. So we have to put a ten here."

2. Present three or four similar examples every day:

c is to d	8 is to 7	r is to q
as p is to _____.	as 13 is to _____.	as c is to _____.

239

Have the children *write the rule* for each analogy above it. The form for all the rules will be similar.

Work on examples similar to those above until the children have a relatively solid understanding of the rule-making procedure.

Use a step-by-step procedure to help children if they get in trouble:

> 7 is to 6
> as 10 is to _____.

1. "What can we call seven and ten? Numbers. So we write . . ."
   A number—

> 7 is to 6
> as 10 is to _____.

2. "Now what can we call six? How does it differ from seven? It is the number that comes before seven when you count."
   A number is to the number before—

> 7 is to 6
> as 10 is to _____.

3. "What comes before ten? Nine. So that must be the answer."

> 7 is to 6
> as 10 is to 9.

3. Introduce number and letter examples that involve more complicated rules:

> 6 is to 8   3 is to 1   *b* is to *d*
> as 10 is to _____. as 7 is to _____. as *k* is to _____.

The children will probably have some difficulty expressing the rule. Let them work on it for a few minutes. Then work with the group:

> 6 is to 8
> as 10 is to _____.

"Now what are we going to call eight? It is not the next number, is it? And it is not the number that comes before six. What is it? It is the second number after six."
   A number is to the second number after it—

> 6 is to 8
> as 10 is to _____.

"So what's the second number after ten? Twelve. That's the answer."
   Similarly, for the analogy

> *c* is to *a*
> as *r* is to _____.

The rule is this: A letter is to the second letter before it—

Introduce three or four of these problems every day until the children become expert at expressing the rule. Many of them will be able to work the problems without expressing the rule, but it is important for them to learn how to verbalize the procedure.

4. Introduce mixed examples. These require a more sophisticated rule.

>3 is to 4
>
>as *r* is to _____.

The children will probably have little difficulty giving the correct answer. But one of the purposes of the present exercises is to acquaint them with the procedures for writing the rule. No longer can the first term be referred to as *number* or *letter*. "What can we call three and *r?* . . . They are symbols. We could call them things, but let's call them symbols."

Completing the rule should present no problem for the children:

>A symbol is to the symbol that comes next—
>
>3 is to 4
>
>as *r* is to *s*.

Present a series of similar examples such as these:

3 is to 2	*u* is to *w*	6 is to 4
as *j* is to _____.	as 4 is to _____.	as *d* is to _____.

3 is to 6	*j* is to *m*	*l* is to *i*
as *e* is to _____.	as *l* is to	as 4 is to _____.

Present four or five examples a day. Place primary emphasis on writing the rule.

5. Present the rule and let the children make up the analogy. Select any of the rules that have been used in the preceding exercises:

A number is to the next number—

A number is to the second number after it—

A number is to the number that comes before it—

A number is to the second number before it—

A letter is to the letter that comes before it—

A symbol is to the next symbol—

A symbol is to the second symbol after it—

Write this rule on the board: "A number is to the next number —" Tell the children, "Here's the rule. I want you to make up an analogy that fits the rule." If the children have trouble, take the procedure in steps. Refer to the rule. "It says a number. That means that both statements have to start out with a number. Tell me a number. Any number. . . . O.K., give me another number."

4

7

"Go back to the rule. It says, 'A number is to the next number—' We've got some numbers. Now all we have to do is put down the next numbers. What's the next number after four? Five."

4 is to 5

7

"What's the next number after seven? Eight."

4 is to 5

as 7 is to 8.

During the introductory session, work four or five examples with the children. Then present sheets with instructions. For example:

1. Write one analogy for this rule: A letter is to the next letter—
2. Write three analogies for this rule: A number is to the number that comes before it—
3. Write two analogies for this rule: A number is to the second number after it—

Present similar daily sheets until the children are proficient at writing examples for all of the rules that have been introduced.

6. Introduce analogies involving material. Present the following analogy to the group:

A tire is to rubber

as a window is to _____.

Let the children attempt to write the rule before giving them help: "Don't fill in the blank. Just write the rule."

Have the children read the rules they have written. Then go through the rule, formulating procedure with them. Refer to the first term in each analogy. "What are tires and windows? They are objects or things. So we write the first part of the rule."

An object—

A tire is to rubber

as a window is to _____.

Now refer to the second term of the statement about a tire: "What does rubber have to do with a tire? . . . Yes, a tire is made out of rubber. So we write the second part of the rule."

242

An object is to what it is made of—
A tire is to rubber
as a window is to _____.

"A window is an object. The rule says: An object is to what it is made of. What's a window made out of? Glass. So that's the answer."

Let the children work on other analogies involving material until they are able to write the rules without much difficulty:

A can is to metal
as a towel is to (cloth).

A coat is to fur
as a magazine is to (paper).

A floor is to wood
as a cloud is to (water).

A knife is to metal
as an ocean is to (water).

A ladder is to wood
as a light bulb is to (glass).

A football helmet is to plastic
as a shoe is to (leather).

A belt is to leather
as a doorknob is to (metal).

A tire is to rubber
as a bumper is to (metal).

A shirt is to cloth
as a log is to (wood).

A bubble is to air
as a mountain is to (rock).

7. Introduce analogies involving whole-part relationships.

Present this example to the group:

A handle is to a hammer
as a sole is to a _____.

Refer to the first terms. "What can we call handles and soles? They are parts of something. We can write the first part of the rule."

A part—
A handle is to a hammer
as a sole is to a _____.

Next refer to the first statement in the analogy. "If a handle is a part, what is a hammer? . . . The whole thing. So we can write the rest of the rule."

A part is to the whole thing—
A handle is to a hammer
as a sole is to a _____.

"A sole is a part of what whole thing? It's part of a shoe."

Give the children three or four part-whole problems a day. Present other analogy forms on each sheet (members of a series and materials):

A fender is to a car
as a collar is to a _____.

A motor is to a car
as pedals are to a _____.

A cap is to a bottle
as a roof is to a _____.

A heel is to a shoe
as a wheel is to a _____.

A fingernail is to a finger
as a buckle is to a _____.

A finger is to a hand
as a toe is to a _____.

A beak is to a bird
as a nose is to a _____.

A wing is to a bird
as an arm is to a _____.

Legs are to a man
as wheels are to a _____.

A ceiling is to a room
as a drawer is to a _____.

Hands are to people
as paws are to _____.

Doorknobs are to doors
as handles are to _____.

A neck is to a bottle
as a stem is to a _____.

A petal is to a flower
as a root is to a _____.

Some of these analogies admit of more than one answer. For example:

A fender is to a car
as a collar is to a _____.

This analogy can be completed with the words *coat, shirt, jacket,* and the like.

Some of the analogies involve more than part-whole relationships. They involve part-whole relationships in which the parts have a similar function. Although the analogies are set up in such a way that the child will not have to take the analogous function into account, the rules should be written so that they account for the coordination of part to whole. For example, take this analogy:

Hands are to people
as paws are to _____.

The rule should be analyzed in the following manner: "What are hands and paws? They are parts. But what kind of parts are they? They are the parts you find at the end of the 'arm.' "

The part at the end of the arm is to the living thing—
Hands are to people
as paws are to (dogs, wolves, cats, and so on).

8. Present part-whole analogies in which the similar function of parts or similar location must be taken into account:

People are to hands
as dogs are to (paws).

A snail is to a shell
as a camel is to a (hump).

A pencil is to lead
as an apple is to a (core).

A table is to a top
as a house is to a (roof).

A bottle is to a cap
as a can is to a (lid).

A bird is to a wing
as a boy is to (an arm).

A banana is to a peel
as an egg is to a (shell).

A book is to a cover
as a sandwich is to a (slice of bread).

A tree is to roots
as a man is to (feet).

A cigarette is to a filter
as a pipe is to a (stem, mouthpiece).

A man is to his arms
as a tree is to its (branches).

A picture is to a frame
as a yard is to a (fence).

Make the rules for these analogies specific. The functional (or spatial) relationship of the parts must be expressed, as well as the part-whole relationship:

A bottle is to a cap

as a can is to _____.

"What can we call a bottle and a can? Either objects or containers. Let's call them containers."

A container—

A bottle is to a cap

as a can is to _____.

"If a bottle is a container, what is a cap? A part of a container. What part? The top part."

A container is to a top part of a container—

A bottle is to a cap

as a can is to a lid.

Another example:

A picture is to a frame

as a yard is to a _____.

"What are pictures and yards? They are objects—whole objects."

A whole object—

A picture is to a frame

as a yard is to a _____.

"If a picture is a whole object, what is a frame? It is a part. What part? The part that circles the outside of the picture."

245

A whole object is to the part that circles the outside—
A picture is to a frame
as a yard is to a fence.

9. After the children have mastered part-whole analogies, present analogies involving action:

A dog is to running
as a fish is to _____.

"What can we call a dog and a fish? Animals."

An animal—
A dog is to running
as a fish is to _____.

"If a dog is an animal, what is running? Running is a way this animal moves from place to place."

An animal is to how it moves—
A dog is to running
as a fish is to _____.

"A fish is an animal. How does it move from place to place?"

An animal is to how it moves—
A dog is to running
as a fish is to swimming.

Present three or four examples a day, emphasizing the rules:

A baby is to diapers
as a boy is to (pants).

A colt is to milk
as a horse is to (grass, hay).

A man is to a house
as a dog is to a (doghouse).

A dog is to a collar
as a woman is to a (necklace).

A baby is to a crib
as a boy is to a (bed).

A man is to talking
as a dog is to (barking).

A man is to a house
as a bird is to a (nest or tree).

A bird is to a nest
as a dog is to a (doghouse).

A dog is to dog food
as a fish is to (fish food).

A pilot is to an airplane
as a jockey is to a (horse).

Write the rules so that an action is expressed:

An animal is to where it lives—
A man is to a house
as a bird is to _____.

"Where does a bird live? In a nest. In a tree."

246

10. Present rules for various action analogies and have the children make up analogies that fit the rule. Begin with this rule: An animal is to how it moves—

Demonstrate how to use the rule: "The first part of the rule tells us that we have to talk about animals." Have the children name some animals. Take the first two animals suggested. For example:

> a worm
>
> a cat

Next, refer to the second part of the rule: "The rule tells us that we have to say how each of these animals moves."

> A worm is to crawling
>
> as a cat is to (walking, running, leaping).

Accept any true statement about how each of the animals moves. Some of the analogies may have identical second terms:

> A cat is to running
>
> as a dog is to running.

Have the children write four other analogies that satisfy the rule. Encourage creative examples. Encourage the children to think of animals that move in different ways: "Think of all of the animals you know."

If the children are not familiar with many animals, introduce pictures of about fifteen animals engaged in their typical mode of locomotion (snail, worm, fish, bird, mole, frog, rabbit, turtle, deer, and so on). After briefly naming the animals, place the pictures in view of the children. Require them to make up analogies using each of the animals pictured. Repeat the exercise until they have become reasonably familiar with these animals.

Next, present action rules and have the children make up at least three analogies for each rule. Present only one rule a day and spend no more than ten minutes on the task.

For example, present this rule:

> An animal is to what it eats—

"O.K., the first part of the rule tells us that we're talking about animals. Name some animals." Require specific animals, not merely 'birds' or 'fish.' "

> a horse
>
> a tiger

"The second part of the rule tells us that we've got to say what these animals eat."

A horse is to (grass, hay)
as a tiger is to meat.

"Now you make up three analogies of your own. I'll put some pictures up here. If you have any questions, raise your hand. You've got ten minutes. Go."

Here are several rules that could be presented:

An animal is to the kind of noise it makes— (A lion is to roaring as a mouse is to squealing.)

An animal is to where it lives— (A camel is to the desert as a whale is to the ocean.)

An animal is to how it fights— (A deer is to antlers as a man is to fists.)

A person is to what he wears— (A cowboy is to boots as an Indian is to moccasins.)

A driver is to what he drives— (An engineer is to a train as a milkman is to a milk truck.)

An animal is to where it sleeps— (A man is to a bed as a squirrel is to a tree.)

An animal is to the kind of baby it has— (A horse is to a colt as a sheep is to a lamb.)

11. Introduce analogies based on locations.

Begin with this analogy:

Tractors are to the country
as buses are to ____.

"What are tractors and buses? Vehicles." Refer to the first statement in the analogy. "If a tractor is a vehicle, how is it related to the country? You find a tractor in the country. So here's the rule."

A vehicle is to where you find it—
A tractor is to the country
as a bus is to ____.

"Where do you find a bus? In the city."

A vehicle is to where you find it—
A tractor is to the country
as a bus is to the city.

Have the children work on four or five analogies of this type each day. Here are some to work from:

A toothbrush is to the bathroom
as a frying pan is to ____.

A typewriter is to an office
as a stove is to ____.

A bathtub is to the bathroom
as a stove is to _____.

A wristwatch is to the wrist
as a hat is to _____.

A bed is to the bedroom
as a couch is to _____.

A shoe is to the foot
as a glove is to _____.

A monkey is to a cage
as a pig is to _____.

A shirt is to the chest
as a sock is to _____.

A Hawaiian is to Hawaii
as an Eskimo is to _____.

A belt is to the waist
as a scarf is to _____.

A bubble is to water
as a cloud is to _____.

Glasses are to the eyes
as earmuffs are to _____.

Boats are to lakes
as cars are to _____.

Clothes are to a dresser
as ice cream is to _____.

Submarines are to water
as airplanes are to _____.

A handkerchief is to a pocket
as goldfish are to _____.

A sixgun is to a holster
as dollar bills are to _____.

Bullets are to a gun
as gasoline is to _____.

After the children have worked these and perhaps other go-together analogies, present the rules and have them make up three analogies. For example, present this rule:

> An object is to its container— (Money is to wallet, violin is to violin case, book is to bookcase, bread is to breadbox, and so on.)

Give the children ten minutes to work the assignment.

12. Present mixed sets of analogies and have the children both write the appropriate rule and complete the analogy.

Lemon is to yellow
as grass is to _____.
(*Rule:* An object is to its color—)

Spring is to rain
as winter is to _____.
(*Rule:* A season is to the weather in that season—)

Milk is to drinking
as hamburgers are to _____.
(*Rule:* Food is to what you do with it—)

A tiger is to stripes
as a leopard is to _____.
(*Rule:* An animal is to its markings—)

An apple is to red
as an elephant is to _____.
(*Rule:* An object is to its color—)

A book is to reading
as a shovel is to _____.
(*Rule:* An object is to what you do with it—)

An umbrella is to rain
as suntan lotion is to _____.
(*Rule:* An object is to the weather conditions—)

George Washington is to dollars
as John F. Kennedy is to _____.
(*Rule:* A president is to the kind of money on which you find his picture—)

Roller skates are to having fun
as shovels are to _____.
(*Rule:* An object is to the kind of activity in which you use it—)

A desk is to a rectangle
as a plate is to _____.
(*Rule:* An object is to its shape—)

A boy is to his father
as a girl is to her _____.
(*Rule:* A child is to the parent of the same sex—)

A boy is to a girl
as a man is to a _____.
(*Rule:* A male is to a female of the same age—)

Uncle is to male
as aunt is to _____.
(*Rule:* A relative is to the sex of that relative—)

Mix these analogies with some that the children have already worked.

250

Conclusion

Reading is many things. It is a vehicle that transports the reader to strange places and involves him in exciting adventures. Reading is a guide that tells the reader how to assemble his mail-order bookcase. It is a source of information about events and a course of instruction. All reading is based on the assumption that the reader will comprehend the word picture that is being drawn for him. But comprehension is sometimes conceived of in broad terms. This is not the case in this book. Comprehension depends on specific understanding. The goal of the two reading chapters has been to program such specific understanding. Before a child can comprehend, he must understand the code by which the spoken word is represented on the page. The first chapter concentrated on code-cracking skills. After these were programed, comprehension skills were taught—beginning with how to follow simple instructions. The children were shown that the words in ideal instructions function to specify a particular course of action. Instructions that are less than ideal may have words that don't function and may include words that are not specific enough.

Next the various concept words that are used in precise instructions were programed—such words as *all, if, only.* The child was shown that instructions are closely related to descriptions and that descriptions are closely related to definitions. An instruction tells you what to do. A description tells you what to think about. It tells you what kind of picture to formulate. Definitions tell you what kind of picture to formulate about a class of things, rather than an individual object. Finally, the child was shown how to construct analogies.

The program is certainly not comprehensive, but it is critically important. It provides a foundation on which vocabulary and an expanded knowledge of grammar and syntax can be built. It teaches the child the core language principle: words are chosen to do a particular job. To know whether or not the words are wisely chosen, one must understand what the particular job is.

6 Arithmetic for the Beginning Child

If the child who is failing in school is to catch up with the average child in arithmetic performance, the teacher cannot adhere to the grade-level achievement norms established for middle-class children. The disadvantaged child will proceed more slowly than the middle-class child. If the same program that is given to the average child is given to the slow-learning child, he will fall further and further behind. This is especially true in arithmetic, where the middle-class child is expected to memorize hundreds of arithmetic facts. The slow-learning child should not be required to learn these facts. The time normally devoted to fact learning should be used for teaching the slow-learning child the structure of arithmetic, what the statements mean, and why the general rules for solving arithmetic problems must be followed. Fact learning can be distributed throughout the program, rather than lumped into large segments.

The program outlined on the following pages bears only a slight resemblance to the new math, especially with respect to the teaching techniques. While the new math has sound objectives, the discovery techniques advocated by most new-math programs have no place in an elementary teaching program. Children cannot discover rules until (*a*) they understand the structure of rules in general, and (*b*) they have had enough experience with rules to see that they provide a means of attacking a great range of problems.

The program outlined here is a catch-up program. It proceeds as rapidly as possible in programing new operations. In fact, the child who is taught according to this program very shortly masters operations that are considered beyond his grade level. At the same time, the work on facts (which cannot be appreciably accelerated through careful programing) lags behind the grade level, at least for several years. After the child has become firmly grounded in the operations and strategies of basic arithmetic, greater emphasis can be placed on facts, because at this point the child has worked with the various operations enough to see the relationships between facts. He now has a framework for his factual knowledge, a basis for seeing arithmetic as meaningful.

Some teachers have a strong aversion to arithmetic because they don't understand it very well. This is probably a function of the arithmetic instruction they received. There is nothing particularly difficult about arithmetic, which is basically statements, similar to statements in everyday language. Just as some statements in everyday language are false, some arithmetic statements are false: $3 + 4 = 1$. Just as there are questions in everyday language, there are questions in arithmetic: $2 + 6 = a$ (two plus six equals how many?). Another kind of question is $4 + a = 7$. Four plus *how many* equals seven? Substitute a number for the words *how many* and you will answer the statement. Your answer will be either true or false. $4 + 1 = 7$. Is that statement true? No. $4 + 2 = 7$. Is that true? No. $4 + 3 = 7$. Is that true? Yes. Then that's the true answer to the question $4 + a = 7$.

Arithmetic lessons are to be handled the same way as reading lessons. Work in small groups with the children for about twenty to thirty minutes a day. Work on a variety of tasks during this period, devoting perhaps five minutes to a counting operation, five minutes to the introduction of a new operation, five minutes to work on a more familiar operation, and ten minutes on worksheet problems. As soon as the children have mastered a new operation, move on to the next task outlined in the chapter. Be careful not to move on before they have achieved mastery.

This chapter outlines procedures for teaching the basic arithmetic operations—addition, subtraction, and multiplication. These operations are presented so that the child can see how they are related to counting. The program is based on the assumption that the child can count. Specifically, this means that he can (a) count ten objects that are placed in a row, starting at either end, and answer the question "How many are there?"; (b) count to a given number, and count out a specified number of objects from a group of ten objects; (c) indicate the number that comes after any number in the 1–10 series; (d) predict the number of objects that will be in a group when one is added.

If the child does not meet these criteria, work on basic counting tasks. Suggestions are provided in *Teaching Disadvantaged Children in the Preschool*, by Carl Bereiter and Siegfried Engelmann.

Basic Addition Concepts

Children who have not been exposed to arithmetic concepts through a variety of experiences at home may have difficulty repeating and understanding arithmetic statements. Furthermore, they may be unable to handle arithmetic problems that are presented verbally. The first set of exercises is designed to establish "verbal awareness" in these children. Devote four to six minutes a day to these tasks until the children have mastered them.

Teaching zero

Establish the meaning of zero. Place a raisin in the child's hand and ask, "How many raisins in your hand?" After the child responds, tell him, "Eat it." Then ask, "How many raisins did you eat?" "One." Give the other children in the group similar tasks, handing them one, two, or three raisins, asking them how many they have, telling them to eat the raisins, and then asking them how many they ate.

Next, pretend to put a raisin in the hand of one of the children. "How many raisins do you have?" The child will probably say "None," or "I ain't got none." Say, "That's right. Do you know how many you have? Zero." Ask the other children in the group, "How many raisins does he have? Zero. Say it with me: 'Zero.' " Instruct the child with zero raisins, "Eat your raisins." If he balks, say, "I'll eat them." Pretend to take them from the child's hand and eat them. "How many raisins did I eat? Zero. I ate zero raisins." Act amused.

Repeat the exercise several times every day until the children have an understanding of zero. If a child says "none" or "no" for zero, tell them that he is correct. Then say, "And we call that zero. How many do you have? Zero." After the children understand zero in this context, introduce a variation of the task. Put two raisins in a child's hand and ask him how many he has. Take one away and repeat the question. Take the remaining raisin away and repeat the question. "How many do you have now? . . . That's right. Zero raisins."

Present a variation of the task with lines on the chalkboard. Draw two lines on the board. Ask the children how many lines there are on the board. Erase one line. Repeat the question. Erase the remaining line, and repeat the question.

Ask questions about children and objects in the room: "How many boys are there in this room? Count them. . . . Four. How many girls are there in this room? . . . Three. How many fish in this room? Count them. . . . Zero."

254

Have the children make a specified number of lines on the chalk-board: "John, make three lines on the board." You may have to remind the children to count as they make the lines. If they don't count, they often forget how many they have made and how many they are supposed to make. Structure the situation for these children: "How many are you going to make on the board? . . . Yes, three. Now count big. What are you going to count to? . . . Three." If the children have trouble with the task, have them tell how many lines you are making on the board: "I'll do it, John, and you count as I make lines. One . . . two . . . three. How many, John? . . . Three." From time to time, tell one of the children to make zero lines on the board. If he has trouble, demonstrate how to do it. Make the procedure seem like a great deal of fun: "Oh boy! I get to make zero lines. Here I go." Wave the chalk around with a flourish, making no lines on the board. "There. How many lines did I make on the board? . . . Zero."

Adding as counting

1. Teach the children to predict how many objects there will be if you add one (or a few) more. Do not spend more than two or three minutes a day on this exercise (which can be introduced concurrently with the first task). (NOTE: At this point, introduce the term *plussing*. In this way the children will be introduced to the meaning of the symbol +.)

Erase the chalkboard. Then ask, "How many lines are there on the chalkboard? . . . Zero. And if I plus one line, how many lines will there be on the chalkboard?" If the children do not answer, tell them how many there will be and *then make a line* on the chalkboard. "See. If I start out with zero lines and plus one, I'll have one."

Before plussing another line, say, "There is one line, and if I plus one line there will be . . . Yes, there will be two." Always make the statement before drawing the line on the board. "If I have one line and plus one line, I'll have two lines." Again, tell the children how many lines there are on the board before asking the next question. "There are two lines on the board. Two, and if I plus one . . . Yes, three." Draw another line. "If I have two and plus one, I'll have three. There are three lines on the board. Three, and if I plus one . . ."

When you get up to the larger numbers, the children may have trouble. To help them over the rough spots, summarize in this manner before presenting the question: "There are four lines. Four, one-two-three-four. And if I plus one . . ." Say "if I plus one" very rapidly, so that the children will hear the counting numbers one-two-three-four with a minimum of interference. As they become more proficient in the task, say "if I plus one" more slowly, until you are saying it at a normal speaking rate. As they become still more proficient, drop the counting introduction.

Continue the series up through nine: "I have nine—one-two-three-four-five-six-seven-eight-nine—and if I plus one . . . Yes, ten." Draw in the final line. "How many lines are up there? Ten."

After the children have become reasonably skillful at working the basic game, introduce a variation in which you challenge their conclusions. For example, "O.K., there are seven lines on the board—one-two-three-four-five-six-seven—and if I plus one . . . Eight. . . . Wait a minute! You think that if I plus one line, I'll have eight? That doesn't sound right to me. Let's see. I've got seven. Now I'll plus one." Draw in another line. "Now you think I've got eight. It doesn't look like eight lines to me. I'll tell you how we can find out. Let's count them." After counting them, act disappointed. "You were right and I was wrong." To make the game interesting, pass out raisins to the children who predicted correctly. "Three raisins for you, and for you—and do you know how many I get? Zero. I was wrong."

The purpose of this game is to dramatize the fact that if one understands the counting numbers, he can predict results without seeing a physical presentation. This ability is extremely important. The children should be rewarded for predicting correctly.

From time to time, introduce examples in which you plus either zero or two. Do not require correct answers with the plus-two problems. Do not expect the children to handle the plus-zero problems immediately. They will probably give the answer that was acceptable for the plus-one problems. For that reason it is a good idea to introduce this task as early as possible. Present one or two plus-zero problems every day, perhaps starting with the first day of instruction, or as soon as the children have learned to listen to your instructions. Tell them, "Now you have to listen big. You have three raisins. Three. And if I plus zero raisins . . ." To plus zero raisins, pretend to put a raisin in your hand. The children may not understand what you are doing when you plus zero raisins. To clarify the operation, have the child count the raisins in his hand. "O.K., you've got three." Have him hold out his other hand. "Now in this hand, I'm going to plus *zero* raisins. . . . There. How many did I give you in this hand? . . . Zero. O.K., put the zero raisins with the others. You had three raisins before. How many do you have now? . . . Still three. If you have three and I plus zero, you still have three." (Note the wording of this routine. It is possible to get into a number of binds if you violate it too drastically.)

Now show the difference between plussing zero and plussing one: "You've got three raisins. Three. And I plus one. . . ." Have the child hold out his other hand. "How many am I going to put in this hand? . . . One." Drop one. "O.K., put this raisin with the others. You had three, and then you plussed one. How many do you have now?"

Work on exercises in which you plus zero, one, or two, increasing the pace as the children become more familiar with the plus-one series. These exercises will ensure that the children will learn that "plussing" doesn't always mean "getting one more."

In presenting the plus-two concept, warn the children not to draw hasty conclusions. Have the child hold out his other hand. "You've got three. Three. And I'm going to plus two. How many am I going to put in this hand? . . . Two. . . . There. O.K., you've got three in your other hand. Three." Transfer one of the raisins to the hand with three raisins. "Now you've got . . . Yes, four. And now . . ." Transfer the second raisin. "If you have three and I plus two, you'll have five."

Work on the basic plus-two procedure until the children have learned to listen for the words *plus one*, *plus two*, and *plus zero*. Then introduce a variation of the task in which the *child* transfers the raisins from one hand to the other. Before he does, however, remind him how many there are in his receiving hand: "You've got four. Four. One-two-three-four"—have the child count as he adds each of the raisins—"five-six. . . . Four, and I plus two—six."

2. Introduce a variation in which the child cannot see the raisins in his hand. This is an important transition task. The child will see the raisins going into his closed fist, but he will not be able to see how many there are. If he has any doubt about the total, however, you can always have him open his hand and count the raisins. He will not have to rely on your judgment; the evidence will be right there.

Have the child hold his fist in the position used to pound the table. Have the child open his fist slightly to make an opening at the top. Drop the raisins in the opening, one at a time, as you count. Drop four raisins in his hand. "How many are in your hand? Four. You have to remember that—four." Have the child hold his hand still. "And I'm going to plus this many." Present two raisins in your open hand.

"You've got four and I'm going to plus two. Here we go. . . . How many in your hand? . . . Four"—drop a raisin in the opening—"five"—drop another—"six. Now how many do you have in your hand? . . . Six." Have the child open his hand and count the raisins. "Yes, if you have four raisins and get two more, you end up with . . ."

After working on similar tasks (with the fist containing four, five, or six raisins and plussing one, two, or three raisins), introduce a set of exercises that encourages the child to rely on what he *knows*, not on what he *sees*. Put three raisins in the child's closed fist. Then plus three, using the procedure described above. Make sure that the child holds his fist out and tells you how many are in it before you add any raisins. "Tell me. How many are in there? . . . Yes, three. Now you've got three and now"—drop a raisin—"you've got four"—drop another raisin—"five"—another—"six." Now challenge the child: "Do you think there are six raisins in there? I don't." Ask the other children, "Who thinks there are six raisins in John's hand?"

Have the child who worked the problem open his hand and count the raisins. "Oh, I was wrong. There *are* six raisins in his hand." Award raisins to every child who said there were six raisins in the hand: "John gets some raisins. He was thinking. He didn't see the raisins, but he knew how many were in his hand. But Henry doesn't get any raisins. Neither do I. We weren't thinking. We'll do better next time."

Before very long, all the children will be able to handle the task and receive the raisin payoff. In the process they will learn that they can rely on what they know, not merely on what is immediately before their eyes.

3. Lead the children to take the next step by having them work with raisins while using their fingers as counters. This task should be introduced only after they have mastered the preceding tasks, working plus-one, plus-two, and plus-three problems.

Have each child hold up a closed fist. "You've got to pretend. Pretend that you have three raisins in your hand. How many? . . . Three. This is silly, isn't it? We don't really have any raisins; we're just pretending." Hold up two fingers on your other hand and have the children do the same. "Pretend that these are two raisins. How many raisins? . . . Two. How many are in your other hand? . . . Three. You've got three and you're going to plus two. Here goes." At this point it is extremely important for each child to hold out his fist and say how many raisins are in it. This step is important because the children must

258

learn that when they add the first "raisin" they will have more than three. This point is made more easily if the children follow the procedure of saying how many "raisins" are in their hand before they start adding more.

"Three." Now stick your fingers in the opening at the top of the fist, one at a time. "Four, five. We end up with five." If the children have trouble with this operation, demonstrate it with several different problems and then come back to the original example, $3 + 2 = 5$. After they have worked the problems, have them repeat the statement several times. "I can say it. Three plus two equals five. That's hard to say, but I can do it. Who thinks he can do it?" If the task seems like something that is difficult to do and yet is a sign of smartness, the children will try very hard to repeat the statement. In repeating it, they will become familiar with the form of arithmetic statements.

Introduce a variety of "pretend" problems—plus-one, plus-two, plus-three, plus-four, and plus-five problems. Have the children work six to eight of them during a session, and try to work in unison as much as possible. If a child lags or seems to be faking it, call on him individually, and plan to call on him again for a few days. But do not waste too much time calling on individual children.

4. Present problems that involve thinking or figuring out what the answer must be without referring to physical objects. This step is often a very big one for the slow learner.

Begin by presenting the verbal problem, "If you have three raisins and you get one more, how many will you have?" The children, especially the slower ones, may give bizarre answers. Act amused. Tell them, "You're guessing," and then show them how to figure out the answers. "Listen—if you have three raisins . . . how many? . . . Three. So how many are in my fist? . . . Three." Have the children hold up their fists. "How many do you have in there? . . . Three. O.K., you have three raisins and plus one more. How many more are you going to plus? . . . One more. So how many fingers are you going to hold up on your other hand? . . . One. Get it up there." Refer again to the closed fist. "If you have three raisins and you get one more, you'll have . . . " If the children can't handle the problem, prompt them. Refer to the closed fist. "How many are in here? . . . Three. One, two, three . . ." Now guide the child's finger toward the opening. "Yes, four."

Present similar problems, involving plus one and plus two. Let the children's fingers stand for raisins, horses, cars, sheep, apples, pennies, and so on. Always present the problem verbally first and encourage the children to think and figure out how to answer the question. "If you have four cars and you get one more, how many will you have?" Repeat the problem several times and then instruct the children to figure it out. After they have worked out the correct answer, repeat the original problem. "If you have four cars and get one more, how many will you have?" Do not be concerned if they cannot give the correct answer without working out the problem on their fingers. It may be some time before they are able to work with abstractions.

Number symbols

1. Introduce the number symbols 1, 2, 3, 4. Do not spend more than two or three minutes a session on number identification. The children will learn as rapidly from a two- or three-minute presentation, if handled properly, as they will from a twenty-minute drill. Probably the best procedure for motivating the children is to introduce a payoff game in which a child erases all the numbers he can identify. If he can identify all the numbers on the board, he receives a reward, perhaps a few raisins. He also receives praise from the teacher. To play this game, first convince the children that they are going to have a real opportunity. Write five or six numbers on the board—not in counting order. "John, you lucky guy, I'm going to let you erase these numbers. But you have to tell me what each number is before you can erase it." Point to a number. "What is it?" If the child identifies it correctly, say, "O.K., erase it." As the child erases the number, say, "Goodbye three," or "Goodbye two."

After the child successfully erases all the numbers on the board, applaud him: "John did a good job. He got to erase all the numbers. Wow! Let's clap for him." If a child misses a number, do not allow him to proceed. Have him sit down. If the child calls a 4 "three," write several 4s and several 3s on the board. Have the child identify them from his seat. Then let him return to the board and try to erase the remaining numbers: "Let's give Willy another chance. I'll bet he can erase the rest of the numbers without making a mistake."

2. There are several good techniques for demonstrating to the child the importance of knowing number names.

Laugh when he makes a mistake. Talk to the other children in the group: "He called that a four. Oh, that is funny, isn't it?" After a few exposures, the other children in the class will laugh when one of the members makes a mistake in number identification. While this type of response can get out of hand, especially when one member of the group tends to make a large number of errors and is laughed at by his peers continuously, the approach can—if kept within bounds—be used to demonstrate to the child that correct identification responses are important. When it appears that the children in the class are exerting too much pressure, stick up for the child who made the mistake: "Wait a minute. Willy is trying hard and he's going to get it. I don't want you to laugh at him. You'll see, pretty soon he'll be able to name these numbers every time."

Call the offender by another name, preferably the name belonging to someone from the opposite sex in the group. For example, if a boy continually makes mistakes, say, "Come on, Tina, you can do better than that." The child will probably object. Now make the point: "You don't like it when I call you Tina. But you call that four 'three.' That's just as silly."

These techniques are designed to demonstrate to the children that it is important to identify numbers by their correct names. These techniques are not intended as punitive devices. A teacher should not allow the children in the class to keep on laughing at a particular child and make a scapegoat out of him. She should not make a habit of referring to a child by another name, entertaining the other members of the class and punishing the offender. She should use these techniques to make the point she wishes to make, and then she should abandon them.

3. Introduce new numbers at a relatively slow rate, making sure that the children have mastered one number before introducing the next. Children often confuse letters and numbers that were learned at the same time. For this reason it is probably a good idea to introduce new numbers one at a time. Have the children write each new number and indicate, as they write, the name of the number they are writing: "John, what number are you writing? . . . Six. Good."

4. After the children have mastered numbers up to four, the learning of new numbers can be introduced in a more casual (and somewhat more rapid) manner. Stage a race with the children.

Draw a box on the board:

Y	
M	

"The M is me. Here's where I put my points." Run your finger along the bottom box. "The other row is you. Here's where I put your points. Every time you beat me, I put a point here."

Write a 2 on the board. Pause about one second before identifying the number. If the children have not already identified it, act delighted: "I beat you. I won that round." Make a tally mark in your score box. Present other familiar numbers, remembering not to rush the children. The game may backfire if you force them to go too rapidly. They may become more intent on saying something than on identifying the number.

From time to time, try to distract the children: "Hey, look at the bus over there!" As the children turn to look, write a number on the board and identify it. After you have tricked the children in this manner several times, they will become extremely attentive. They will not be distracted. Always act delighted when you manage to distract them, and act disappointed when they don't bite.

Introduce new numbers one at a time. At first, concentrate on the numbers one through ten. When they are mastered, introduce eleven through twenty. Present larger numbers in this order: sixties, seventies, eighties, nineties, forties, twenties, thirties, fifties.

When the children fail to identify a number, say, "I know how to fool you every time. All I need to do is write a six up here. I'm going to win the game now." Present the new number frequently (preferably on every other round). Before long, the children will identify it.

Rig the game so that the children always win. Act disappointed: "I'll get you guys tomorrow. You were just lucky today."

Operational statements

An addition problem is an operational statement in which every part of the written problem plays a role. Just as one must read every part of every statement in a story to be sure of understanding it, so one must know how to treat every part of the arithmetic statement as a signal for doing something. Only in this way can one understand the relation of the statement to the real, physical world.

1. Present the statement $4 + 2 = a$. Say, "Let's read it." Read the statement slowly enough so that the children are actually reading and not merely trying to imitate what you say. Identify the symbols $+$ and $=$ as *plus* and *equals*. "Four . . . plus . . . two . . . equals . . . *a*." Draw a thick vertical line below the equals sign of the problem. "Look, I'm drawing a line under the . . . What is this? . . . Equals. I'm drawing a line under the equals."

Point to the 4. "What number is this? . . . Yes, four. So how many lines does it tell me to make? . . . Yes, four. Who can do that?" As the

262

child approaches the board, ask him again how many lines he is going to make. "O.K., do it."

$$4 + 2 = a$$

|||| **|**

Point to the plus sign. "What's this? . . . Plus. The plus tells me to plus. . . ." Move to the 2. "What's this number? . . . Two. So how many lines does it tell me to plus? . . . Two. Who can do that? Who can plus two more lines?" Call on a child.

$$4 + 2 = a$$

|||| || **|**

Now refer to the a. "What's this? . . . a. How many lines does a tell me to make? I don't know." If the children have trouble with this conclusion, refer to the four and the two, asking about each. "What's this? . . . And so how many lines does it tell me to make?" Then return to the a. "What's this? . . . So how many lines does it tell me to make? It doesn't tell me anything. It doesn't tell me to make two; it doesn't tell me to make four. It doesn't tell me to make seven."

If one of the children insists that it tells you to make a lines, give the child a piece of chalk and tell him to make a lines. After the child finishes making lines, count the lines and inform him that he didn't make a lines: "John, how many lines are here? . . . Five. You didn't make a lines; you made five lines."

2. Next, introduce the rule about equations. Tap on the left side of the line that extends below the equals sign. "See how many there are on this side of the equals sign." Point to the right side (below the a). "That's how many we have to have on this side of the equals sign." Point to the left side. "If we have seven on this side"—point to the right side—"we have to have seven on this side." Present a series of similar statements, having the children complete them.

"If we have six on this side . . . we have to have . . . yes, six on this side."

"If we have four on this side . . . we have to have . . ."

After presenting six to eight examples, introduce a restatement of the conclusion: "If we have seven on this side . . . we have to have seven on this side. Because what does seven equal? . . . Seven."

Slap the left side of the equation. "Six equals . . ." Slap the right side of the equation.

Repeat the procedure four or five more times. "Eight equals eight . . . Nine equals . . . Four equals . . ."

If the children have trouble completing these statements, ask, "Well, what's the same as six? . . . *Six* is the same as six. Is five the same as six? That's silly. What is the same as six? . . . Yes, six equals . . ."

Before proceeding with the problem, present the rule again: "We have to have just as many on this side of the equals sign (pointing to the right) as we have on this side of the equals sign (pointing to the left)."

Point to the left side. "How many lines do we have on this side of the equals sign? Count them and find out." The children may have some trouble counting all the lines on the left of the equals sign.

$$4 + 2 = a$$

They may count the group under a number and then stop. They may count the group under the 4 and then start counting the group under the 2, beginning with one. To help them perceive that you are now regrouping the two groups into one group, press your finger against the chalkboard immediately to the left of the line under the equals sign and move left, leaving a mark through all the tallies on the left of the equal sign:

$$4 + 2 = a$$

After a child counts the lines on the left side, ask, "How many lines are on this side? . . . Yes, six. Six on this side, so we have to have how many on the other side? . . . Six. Six on this side [left], so we have to have six on this side [right]." Call on a child to make six marks on the right side of the equals sign. "How many lines are you going to make? . . . Six. O.K., count out loud so that we can hear you. Count six lines."

Point to the *a*. "Do we know how many we have on this side of the equals sign? Sure. How many do we have? . . . Six. So I know what number goes here where the *a* is. The number six." Erase the *a* and replace it with a six.

3. Read the statement with the children. "Let's read it." Do not rush the children. Plan to read the statement four or five times, starting very slowly and then increasing the speed slightly. Then say, "I can

264

say it. Four plus two equals six. Listen to how well I can say it. Four plus two equals six." Repeat the statement two or three times, rhythmically, perhaps clapping three times between each repetition. "Say it with me, everybody: 'Four plus two equals six.' " Repeat the statement with the group three or four times. Then ask, "Who thinks he can say it all by himself?" Do not be surprised if the children cannot repeat the statement. Some children require many, many trials with various addition statements before they can finally say them. Here are some typical mistakes that they make initially:

Four plus equals six.

Two plus equals six.

Two three four equals six.

These children can't be expected to learn addition facts. They are not ready because they cannot appreciate the difference between one statement and another. *They need a great deal of work in repeating statements.*

Present two or three addition problems a day until the children are reasonably proficient at handling them. Use the basic procedure outlined above. *At first, do not introduce problems in which the first number is smaller than the second.* Also, do not introduce problems in which both of the numbers to be added are the same (such as $2 + 2 = m$).

As the children become proficient, drop out the cues you had used on earlier problems.

• Ask them what the group of numbers on the left side of the equals sign equals: "How many do I have on this side of the equals sign?"

$$4 + 2 = a$$

"There are six on this side of the equals sign. And what does six equal? . . . So how many do we have to have on the other side of the equals sign? . . . Six. We want them to be equal, don't we?"

• Fade out the finger-tracing procedure. Replace it first with a pass over the lines on the left side of the equals sign (without leaving a mark on the board). Then drop the cue completely.

• Encourage the children to specify the number that should be written on the right side of the equals sign. At first refer to the *a* and ask, "Do we know how many four plus two equals? Sure we do." Point to the lines below the *a*. "How many? . . . Six. So tell me what to do." Later, simply point to the *a* and ask, "Do we know how many four plus two equals? . . . So what should I do?" (Erase the *a* and write 6.)

4. Ask questions after the children have worked the problem. Point to the 4. "Does four equal six? . . . No. What does four equal? . . . Four. And what does six equal? . . . Six." Point to the 2. "Does two equal six? . . . No. What does two equal? . . . Two. And what does six equal? . . . Six. Does four plus two equal six? . . . Yes. Four plus two is the same as six. Four plus two equals six." Show the children: "See, here's four . . . and here's two more. Four plus two. That's the same as six. Watch." Count the lines.

Verbal problems

The following tasks require the children to work from abstract verbal presentations rather than with concrete things such as fingers and lines on the chalkboard.

1. Present the plus-one series verbally.

Begin with zero and proceed in the counting order: "Zero plus one. One. One plus one. Two. Two plus one. Three. . . ." To help the children see the relation between the plus-one series and counting, say the first number very loudly and hold it for perhaps two seconds: "Threeeee . . ." Then very quickly say "plus one" in a relatively soft voice. The idea is to interrupt the child's fix on *three* as little as possible. Finally, say "four" very loudly and quickly.

As the children catch on to the idea that they should listen to the first number presented and then say the number that comes next when one counts, start making the *plus one* part of the statement more pronounced. And start including the word *equals*. Make a slight pause between the first number and *plus one:* "Four . . . plus one equals five. Five . . . plus one equals six. Six plus one equals . . ."

Have the children repeat the statement after they have given the correct answer: "Yes, four plus one equals five. I can say it. Four plus one equals *five*. Who can say it with me? . . . Again . . ." Encourage the children to speak loudly.

Before proceeding to the next statement in the series, summarize the statement in a way that will prompt the children: "Yes, four . . . plus one equals five. And five . . . plus one equals . . . Let's all say it. Five-plus-one-equals six. . . ."

The final step is to present plus-one problems out of the counting order. Use verbal prompts initially: "You have to listen big or I'll catch you on this. What does seven plus one equal? Don't guess." If the children balk, say, "Listen—seven (one-two-three-four-five-six-seven) plus one . . ." Present three or four of these problems during a session. Follow the problems with a review of the plus-one series presented verbally (zero plus one . . . one plus one . . . and so on).

2. After the children have learned to diagram addition problems on the board by putting lines under the numbers and have learned to use their fingers as counters, present simple story problems: "Here's a story about John. John starts out with four marbles and gets two more. How many does he end up with?" Have the children work the problem with a finger operation first. "Listen again. John starts out with four." Hold up your left hand, clenched into a fist. "How many are there in here? . . . Four. And then he gets two more—he plusses two. How many does he plus? . . . Two. So get two ready to plus two." Hold up two fingers on the other hand. Refer to the fist. "How many are in this hand? . . . Four. Four"—stick a finger into the opening—"five"—and another—"six. He ends up with six. Four plus two equals six."

As the children become more proficient with problems of this kind, eliminate the cues. When you present the problem, have the children get their hands ready for addition: "Here's a story about Mary. Mary starts out with seven teeth. . . . Let's see your fists. How many are in there? . . . O.K., and then Mary grows two more teeth. Let's see them. . . . Come on, get your fingers up. How many fingers are you getting up? . . . Two." Later you should be able to pause after giving the information and the children should be able to translate the story into the appropriate finger operation.

After each problem has been worked with the fingers, present the same problem on the board. Encourage the children to tell you what to write. "Listen. John starts out with four and gets more—he gets two more. Help me write it. What do I put down first? . . . Four. And then John gets more. He plusses. How do I write that?"

$$4 +$$

"How many did he plus? He plussed two.

$$4 + 2$$

"If we don't know how many he ended up with, what do we write?

$$4 + 2 = n$$

"That says we end up with how many? Do we know how many? . . . No. That's what we have to figure out."

Work the problem with tally lines. When the children have completed the problem, make the point: "We end up with six. When we work this problem with our fingers, we end up with six. When we work it on the board, we end up with six."

3. Begin to fade out the remaining cues when children can work addition problems on the board without any assistance.

Do not draw lines on the right side of the equals sign. During the early phases of work with addition problems on the board, the children may need practice in making a specified number of lines. The addition problems give them practice in making lines, in reading from left to right, and in identifying symbols. The task, in other words, is justified in terms of the practice it gives children in basic skills. In the more advanced stages, they do not need the practice in these skills.

When you drop the lines from the right side of the equals sign, indicate to the children that they are not necessary.

$$4 + 2 = a$$

$$\text{IIII} \quad \text{II} \quad \textbf{I}$$

"There are six on this side of the equals sign, so I know how many lines I have to have on the other side of the equals sign. I don't have to draw them. I know. Who else knows? . . . Yes, six. There will be six lines over here. And so what number do we write up here where the a is?"

In later problems, drop the heavy line beneath the equals sign. "I don't need that line. I can see how many are on this side of the equals sign. I'm smart. I can do it without the line." The children will probably indicate that they are smart and they don't need the line either. "Let's see. Let's take it out and see who can work the problem. . . ."

Later still, drop the lines under the first number in the problem.

$$4 + \underset{\text{II}}{2} = r$$

"I don't have to make lines under the four. I know how many will be there. Who else knows? . . . Yes, four. So when I want to count the lines on this side of the equals, I just look at the four and say 'four' and then I keep counting—five, six."

4. Give the children practice in working problems individually. Present three or four problems on a sheet:

268

$$7 + 3 = \square \qquad\qquad 6 + 2 = \square$$
$$5 + 4 = \square \qquad\qquad 8 + 1 = \square$$

Allow about four minutes for working the problems (perhaps more time during the first session). Include at least one plus-one problem in each problem set.

(NOTE: When the children work the problems individually, substitute boxes that can be filled in for the letters at the end of the problems. Although boxes don't demonstrate clearly to the children that they are substituting a numerical value for the question-asking element in the problem, they are preferable to letters that have to be crossed out.)

Introduce problems involving numbers larger than ten after these numbers have been taught in the number-identification segment of the lessons:

$$14 + 1 = \square \qquad\qquad 17 + 2 = \square$$
$$6 + 9 = \square \qquad\qquad 10 + 9 = \square$$

Introduce problems in which the first number is smaller than the second. Problems of this kind were not introduced earlier because the children typically confuse statements of arithmetic with counting. The confusion is encouraged if they encounter problems in which the first number is smaller than the second. If a teacher introduces a problem such as $1 + 2 = 3$, she may later discover that the children cannot repeat addition statements without first arranging the terms in the counting order. When asked to repeat the statement "Four plus two equals six," for example, they may say "Four plus five equals six." The kind of confusion implied by a mistake of this sort can be crippling.

When the children have mastered the various steps outlined in the preceding sections, they should have no trouble handling a series of problems in which the second number is larger than the first (although it is probably a good idea to avoid such sums as $5 + 6$ and $8 + 9$ with the slower children). The best procedure is to include several problems of the new form on a sheet with several problems of the old form:

$$8 + 2 = \square \qquad\qquad 1 + 9 = \square$$
$$6 + 3 = \square \qquad\qquad 9 + 1 = \square$$
$$2 + 8 = \square$$

By pairing problems in which the first and second terms are reversed ($1 + 9 = \square$ and $9 + 1 = \square$), you can casually demonstrate that the order of these terms does not matter in addition. Do not labor the explanation. Let the children discover that they can fool you on some of these problems: "Oh, look at what John did! He didn't even work his last problem. He just looked at the one above it and he knew he'd end up with the same number. I thought I could fool him and make him work that problem out, but I couldn't."

After a while the children will scan the sheet for problems that have the same answer (such as 8 + 2 and 2 + 8). They will take pride in not being fooled.

Algebra as an extension of counting

1. The first step in presenting algebra problems is to make the children aware that some numbers are bigger than others. The children will have encountered this idea in the races that you have staged. Provide a further demonstration (if necessary) with lines on the board.

Ask, "Which is more—nine or two?" If the children answer incorrectly, try to relate the question to their experiences: "Oh, come on! Which would you rather have—two pennies or nine pennies? Which is more—nine pennies or two pennies?"

Demonstrate why nine is more than two: "I'll show you that nine is more than two." Draw two lines on the board. Below the two lines, draw nine lines:

"See how much bigger nine is."

Erase the line that is farthest right in the group of nine. "Now there are eight down here. Which is more—eight or two?" Erase the next line and repeat the question. "Now there are seven. Which is more—two or seven?" Erase another line. "Six. Which is more—six or two?" Continue erasing the lines from the bottom row until only two remain. "Which is more—two or two? . . . They are the same. They are equal. What does two equal? . . . Two." Erase another line from the bottom row. "Now how many are down here? Which is bigger—two or one?" Erase the remaining line from the bottom row. "Which is bigger—two or zero?"

Repeat the exercise with different numbers. "Which is more—four or seven? . . . Which is more—ten or three?"

Initially, make sure that the top row is smaller than the bottom row, and make sure that you alternate the questions you ask so that the children can't answer your questions without listening to them. For example, don't always phrase the questions this way: "Which is more —x or two?" The children can learn to answer "x" for every question. Turn the question around from time to time: "Which is more—two or x?" Now the children must listen carefully to every question.

Present two "Which is more?" exercises a day until the children are relatively solid.

2. Then introduce this question: "How much more?" Begin with the verbal question "Which is more—five or three?" Diagram the problem after the children have answered the question correctly:

"There are five lines down here and three lines up here. Which is more —five or three? . . . Yes, five. How many more is five than three? Let's see." Draw a thick vertical line after the third tally in each row (preferably with colored chalk):

Refer to the lines in the bottom row that are to the left of the colored line. "How many lines are here? . . . Yes, three." Refer to the lines in the top row that are to the left of the colored line. "How many lines are here? . . . Yes, three. Three up here, and three down here. Which is more—three or three? . . . They are the same—they are equal." Touch the colored line. "This line shows where they are equal. But look. There are some more lines in the bottom row. Let's count them: one-two. This row is how many more than the top row? This row is *two* more than the top row. There are five in this row, and three in the other row. So five is how many more than three? . . . Five is *two* more than three. Say it with me: 'Five is two more than three.' Five is how many more than three? Let's hear it. . . ."

Erase the line that is farthest right in the bottom row:

"How many are in this row now? . . . Four. Is four more than three? . . . Yes, it is. How many more than three? . . . One more than three."

Erase another line from the bottom row:

271

"There are three in the top row and three in the bottom row. Which is bigger—three or three? . . . They are the same—they are equal."

Present two problems every day involving "How many more?" Use examples in which one of the rows is substantially more than the other, such as 8 and 3, 2 and 10, 1 and 7. Have the children indicate where the "equals line" (the colored chalk line) should be drawn. Place emphasis on the statement that describes how much more one number is than another. (Eight is five bigger than three.) Before presenting the "How many more?" question, make sure that the children understand how many lines there are in each row. Always summarize: "There are how many in this row? . . . Six. And how many in this row? . . . Two. Six is more than two. How many more?"

3. Introduce the word *less*. "Which is more—seven or one? . . . Yes, seven. *So* which is less—seven or one? . . . One. How much less? Let's see." Use the procedure outlined above for determining how much smaller one is (counting the lines to the right of the "equals line"): "One is six less than seven. That's hard to say, but I can do it. One is six less than seven. Who can say it with me? . . ."

4. Introduce problems involving changing one of the rows to make it equal to the other row. Present this problem to the children:

| | |

| | | | | | |

Have them indicate how many lines are in the top row and how many in the bottom row. Have them indicate where the "equals line" should be drawn in. Have them indicate how much more seven is than three. Then pose the question, "What would I have to do if I wanted this top row to have as many lines as the bottom row? I know what I'd have to do. I'd have to plus some more lines. How many more lines? Let's see." Draw a line in the top row for every line in the bottom row. "How many lines are there in the top row now? . . . And how many in the bottom row? This top row has as many lines as the bottom row, doesn't it? Seven up here and seven down here. But look, I had to get some more lines, didn't I? Let's see how many more lines I got." Count from the equal line. "I had to get four more lines." Erase the four lines and have one of the children work the problem. Instruct him to draw a line over every line in the bottom row. "O.K., you got some more lines, didn't you? And here they are." Indicate by passing your hand over all the lines to the right of the equals line. "Count them and tell me how many more lines you had to get."

Introduce two or three of these problems a day. As the children become proficient at working them, give them individual sheets containing five problems. Tell them to indicate how many more lines they would have to get to make the rows equal.

A typical worksheet might look like this:

1. | | | | | | | | |
   | | | _____

2. | | | | | | | | | | |
   | | | | | | | _____

3. | | | |
   | | | | | | | _____

4. | | | |
   | | | | | | _____

5. | | | | | | | | |
   | | | | | | | | _____

Have the children write their answers in the blanks that follow each problem. Ask questions about the problems they are working. Ask how many lines there are in each row, which row contains more lines, and how many more lines. Also, ask them what they had to do to make the two rows equal. (Answer: I had to get _____ more lines in this row.)

5. Introduce problems designed to relate the concept of plussing to the concept of equal. Write a problem on the board leaving large spaces between the symbols:

$$4 \quad = \quad 6$$

Ask, "Is that right? Does four equal six? Is four the same as six? What does four equal? What does six equal?" Demonstrate how to correct the statement.

First draw the appropriate number of lines under each number:

$$4 \quad = \quad 6$$
| | | | | | | | | |

"They're not the same at all, are they?" Point to the lines under the 4. "This side is not the same as that side. What would we have to do on this side to make it the same as that side?" After the children have offered suggestions, say, "Let's see. We have four on this side. But how many are on that side? . . . Six. We've got four but we want to end up with six. So what do we have to do? Do we have to get some more lines or get rid of some of these lines? . . . Yes, we have to get more. How many more? We've got four. One-two-three-four." Draw in another line, shorter than the others:

$$4 \quad = \quad 6$$
||||ı ||||||

"Now we've got five." Draw in another shorter line:

$$4 \quad = \quad 6$$
|||||ıı ||||||

"Now we've got six." Refer to the short lines. "We had to get these short lines. How many did we have to get? Count them. . . . We had to plus two lines. How many lines did we have to plus? . . . Two."

Refer to the equation $4 = 6$. "Let's write what we did. What did we do? . . . We plussed two. So that's what I write."

$$4 + 2 = 6$$
|||||ıı ||||||

Ask a series of questions about the equation: "Does four equal six? What does four equal? What does six equal? Does two equal six? What does two equal? What does six equal? Does four plus two equal six? . . . Yes, four plus two equals six. Four plus two is the same as six. See the lines. Four and two more. Count them. . . . Six."

Give the children four to six problems of this type every day. At first keep the differences between the numbers on either side of the equals sign great, with the number on the right always greater than the number on the left. The following problems might be introduced during an early session:

$$3 \quad = 8$$
$$2 \quad = 9$$
$$3 \quad = 7$$
$$4 \quad = 10$$

Hold the children increasingly responsible for indicating how the statement should be amended: "What should I write up here? What did we do? . . . Yes, we plussed five. So what should I write? . . . Sure. Plus five. I can do that." Later, call on children to perform the entire operation, adding the small lines until the number of lines is the same on both sides of the equals sign, then writing in the number that was added to make the sides of the equation equal.

During the later sessions, make the differences between the numbers in the equation smaller. Introduce pairs that allow the children to apply their knowledge of "plus one." Present six to eight problems (to be completed in five minutes or less). A typical series might be:

$$3 \quad = 4$$
$$7 \quad = 9$$
$$7 \quad = 8$$
$$4 \quad = 5$$
$$9 \quad = 10$$
$$1 \quad = 3$$

The children should be able to work some of these problems without drawing the lines: "Oh, I can do this problem without drawing the lines. How many more?" If they are not able to give the correct answers without drawing lines, allow them to do so.

The preceding problems acquaint the child with the function of the equals sign in equations and the meaning of something being equal to something else. We will come back to equalities later.

Algebra problems

After the children have mastered the preceding tasks, they are ready to work algebra problems (problems in which one of the terms on the left side of the equals sign is not known):

$$5 + a = 7$$

1. To demonstrate the solution of this problem, begin by drawing a heavy colored line under the equals sign. Go over the basic rule: "I have to have as many on this side of the equals sign as I have on this side of the equals sign. The sides have to be equal." Cup your hands around $5 + a$. "This side has to be the same as this side." Cup your hands around 7. Refer to the 7. "We know how many are on this side. How many? . . . Seven." Make seven lines below the 7:

$$5 + a = 7$$
$$\mathbf{|} \, ||||||$$

"So how many are we going to have on the other side? . . . Yes, seven. But it doesn't tell us to make seven lines. It tells us to make how many? . . . Five." Make five lines under the 5:

$$5 + a = 7$$

||||| ▮ |||||||

Refer to the *a*. "We've only got five lines, not seven, so it tells us to plus some lines. Plus some lines." Point to the *a*. "Does it tell us how many lines to plus? . . . No, it says plus lines until you have seven on this side of the equals sign. How many lines do we have? . . . Five. So let's plus lines until we have seven." Refer to the lines under the 5. "Five"—make a line under the *a*—"six"—another line—"seven."

$$5 + a = 7$$

||||| ||▮ |||||||

"How many did we have to plus to get seven lines? Here they are." Point to the lines under the *a*. "We had to plus two lines. I know what *a* is now; *a* equals two. So I can erase the *a* and put a two in its place." Present three to five of these problems a day (devoting about five minutes of each session to algebra problems).

2. As the children become familiar with the procedure, use a shorter explanation.

$$4 + c = 7$$

Refer to the seven. "How many are we going to have on this side of the equals sign? . . . Yes, seven. So how many are we going to have on the other side of the equals sign? . . . Seven. But it doesn't tell us to make seven lines. What does it tell us to do? . . . Yes, make four lines. Then it tells us that we have to plus some more. How many more? I don't know. But we have to end up with seven lines on this side of the equals sign."

Draw in the lines under 7 and 4. Then say, "O.K., let's see how many more we need. We've got four and we want seven. Four"—point to the four lines under four—"five, six, seven."

$$4 + c = 7$$

|||| |||▮ |||||||

"Now we've got seven lines on this side of the equals sign. We started out with four and we plussed some more. How many did we plus? How many? . . . Yes, we plussed three. So I know what number to put in place of the *c*. What number? . . ."

3. As the children become familiar with this procedure, give them sheets with four to six problems:

$$3 + \square = 5 \qquad\qquad 5 + \square = 8$$
$$2 + \square = 8 \qquad\qquad 6 + \square = 7$$

Tell the children, "Put the right number in the box. Figure it out." When they have trouble working the problems, say, "Do what it tells you to do." Have them indicate how many lines will be on either side of the equals sign (referring to the number on the right of the sign). In the first problem above, for example, there will be five lines on either side of the equals sign.

Have the children draw lines under the numbers. Refer to the left side of the equals sign and ask, "Do you have five lines on this side of the equals sign? . . . You need some more, don't you? Get the lines you need right under the box so you can see how many more you need."

After the children have worked problems of this kind for perhaps a month, show them a faster way of working them.

$$5 + \square = 7$$

Refer to the 7. "We know how many are going to be on this side of the equals sign. That's how many we have to have on the other side of the equals sign. Let's get them. Do what the problem tells you to do: Get five. Then plus some more until you have seven."

After the children have become quite familiar with problems in this form, introduce worksheets that contain both "regular" addition problems and "algebra" problems:

$$5 + 4 = \square \qquad\qquad 3 + 5 = \square$$
$$2 + \square = 5 \qquad\qquad 9 + \square = 10$$
$$6 + \square = 10 \qquad\qquad 4 + 1 = \square$$

It is important to present the two kinds of problems together before the children get the idea that problems on a sheet are always in the same form.

Expect the children to have some difficulty the first few times they encounter both kinds of problems. If they do, have them analyze the problems. Ask, "What does it tell you to do?" If they answer the question correctly, say "Do it." If they answer the question incorrectly, analyze the problem with them. For example, if a child indicates that the problem $9 + \square = 10$ tells him to get nine and then plus ten, have him point to the part of the statement that tells him to plus ten. Then point to the box following the plus sign. "It tells you to plus some, but it doesn't tell you how many. It says that when you're all done, you'll have ten on this side of the equals sign."

4. Use a finger operation to solve algebra problems. Introduce the operation as soon as the children have learned to work the board problems without a great deal of prompting and leading. The finger operation is quite simple, and similar to the operation that was used to solve regular addition problems.

Present this problem:

$$4 + a = 6$$

Point to the 4. "How many are we starting out with? . . . Four." Hold up your closed fist. "I've got them right in here. Let's see your fists. . . . How many do you have in there, John? . . . Yes, four."

Refer to the $+ a$ in the problem. "It tells us to get some more. I don't know how many more." Refer to the 6. "But I know I'm going to end up with six. So I count until I end up with six. How many are in here? . . . Four. And I want to end up with six. Four"—stick in a finger from the other hand—"five"—and another finger—"six. There. How many more did I have to get?" Hold up the two fingers that had been added to the fist. "I had to plus two."

$$4 + 2 = 6$$

Present three to five finger-operation problems a day until the children can work them rapidly and accurately. Before working a problem, have the children indicate how many are in the fist and how many they will end up with. Then hold out the fist and state how many are in it before adding any fingers. This is extremely important. If there are four fingers in the fist, the children may add a finger and say "four." For this reason, make a very firm rule that *before any fingers are added the children must hold the fist out and indicate how many are in it.*

After the children have demonstrated proficiency with the finger operation, have them work problems two ways—with lines and with fingers. Always make the point that the answer is the same both ways. A good way to make this point is to work the problems on the board first. Then tell the children, "We had to get four more. But I'll bet we won't have to get four more if we do it with our fingers. Let's see." After the children have demonstrated that you are wrong, act somewhat dejected. The children will laugh and, more important, they will remember that the answer was the same as it was on the board. After a dozen such demonstrations, the children will side against you: "You're wrong. It'll be the same. We still get seven more."

Algebraic word problems

The finger operation leads nicely into simple word problems.

Start with this kind of problem: "When John leaves home he has two shoes. When he comes back home, he has five shoes. How many more did he get?" Repeat the problem and cue the children about how to translate the problem into an operation: "John starts out with how many shoes? . . . Two. Come on, get your fists up. How many are in your fist? . . . Two. John starts out with two and then ends up with five. How many more did he get? Go ahead, end up with five and see how many more you get. How many are you going to end up with? . . . Five: two, three, four, five. How many more did he get? Count them. . . . Three more."

Summarize the statement and write it on the board:

$$2 + 3 = 5$$

Ask, "Two plus how many equals five?"

Present two to four word problems a day. Make them interesting: "John goes to bed with three teeth—just three. When he wakes up in the morning, he has seven teeth. How many more teeth did he get during the night? Listen again: he goes to bed with three and he ends up with seven in the morning. How many teeth did he get during the night?"

Basic Subtraction Concepts

Introduce subtraction problems after the children have completed regular addition problems and have begun to work on algebraic addition problems. Devote about five minutes of each session to subtraction.

Minusing

1. Demonstrate subtraction with lines.

Draw four lines on the board. Have the children count the lines. Then say, "We have four lines, and if I minus one line, how many will I have?" The children probably won't be able to answer the question. Erase one line. "There. I minused one line. How many lines do we have? . . . Three. We've got three lines, and if I minus one . . ." Hold the eraser over the line you will erase next (preferably the line on the far right). Erase the line. "Two. We've got two lines. And if I minus one, we'll have . . . Yes, one. We've got one line, and if I minus one, we'll have . . . Yes, zero."

Repeat the demonstration, using the expression *minus one line.* The children should have little difficulty in seeing what the minus operation means. When working on these tasks, try to have the children predict how many lines will be left. (Don't say "How many will be left?" however, because later you will refer to "getting less" and the children will probably confuse *left* with *less*.) If the children guess, play a game with them: "You guys can't do this, but I can. Watch me. There are four lines on the board, and if I minus one line, I'll have three." Erase one line. "See? I told you I'd have three. I'm smart, I think, and I can do this. I've got three lines, and if I minus one, I'll have two." Erase a line. "See? I'm right again."

After the children have seen you show off in this manner a few times, they will stop guessing and announce that they can work the problems too.

As the children become accurate with the four-line task (which may require daily, one-minute sessions for several weeks), introduce five-line tasks. Expect the children to have some trouble at first with the larger numbers. Demonstrate that you can work the problem. Repeat it every day until the children can handle it. Work from the five-line task to six- and seven-line tasks.

2. Demonstrate subtraction with raisins. On the same day the line tasks are introduced, present problems using raisins.

Put three raisins in your hand. Have the children count them. Then present this problem: "I've got three raisins, and if I minus one raisin, how many will I have?" The children may not give the correct answer. If they don't, point to one of the raisins and say, "I'm going to minus this raisin. I'm going to get rid of it." Move it slightly away from the others. "How many will I have?" After the children answer the question correctly, say, "Yes, if I have three and I minus one raisin —this one here—I end up with two."

Summarize the problem: "If I have three raisins and I minus one, I'll end up with two." Ask the children questions about the problem: "John, if I have three raisins and I minus one, how many will I end up with?" If the child does not answer the question correctly, put three raisins in your hand and repeat the question: "If I have three raisins— there they are—and I minus one"—remove one raisin—"how many will I end up with?"

280

Next present a minus-two problem. Put three raisins in your hand. Have the children count them. "I've got three raisins. If I minus two raisins, how many will I have? How many am I going to minus? . . . Two. How many am I going to get rid of? . . . Two. Let's let Mary do the minusing for us. Mary, minus two raisins and see how many we end up with." Conclude, "We end up with one raisin. Here it is."

Next present the problem in which you start out with five raisins and minus three raisins. Have one of the children do the minusing for you. Make this part of the task seem like a privilege: "John, you get to do the minusing."

Present four to six of these problems during each session. They will reinforce the exercises using lines on the chalkboard.

After the children have worked a problem, repeat the problem (with the raisins in view): "If I start out with six raisins and minus one raisin, I'll end up with how many? . . . Yes, five." Remove the raisins and ask the question again: "If I start out with six raisins and minus one raisin, I'll end up with how many?" Children who are able to answer the first question correctly, using raisins, may not be able to answer the second.

There has been a great deal of speculation about the specific arithmetic deficiency of the slow learner. One prevalent view is that the slow learner does not understand "number." Actually, he probably has little difficulty with number—he has trouble working from the words in arithmetic statements. He can't seem to formulate an image from the words. He may be able to answer a question when he is confronted with objects and be completely unable to answer the same question when the objects are removed. To help program the child's understanding of the "image" that is implied by statements such as "If I have four raisins and minus one," repeat the question without presenting the raisins after it has been answered correctly with the raisins in view. If the children seem to have difficulty answering the questions, confine yourself to problems that involve small numbers of raisins (problems in which you start out with four raisins or less and minus no more than two). As the children become more able to dispense with the physical presentation, begin presenting problems involving larger numbers.

Subtraction as counting backward

To help articulate the relation between counting and subtracting, teach the children to count backward.

1. Teach the "blast off" series, ending with zero. Refer to the task as counting backward: "O.K., let's count backward from ten. Here we go: ten, nine, eight, seven, six, five, four, three, two, one, zero—blast off." Present the series several times a day. Do not push too hard on it. (Typically, the children learn the last part of the series first: three, two, one, zero—blast off. It often takes them some time to learn the order of the numbers in the middle of the series.)

2. After the children have learned to count backward from ten, introduce tasks in which they have to count backward from numbers other than ten: "Listen big, or I'll catch you on this one. Let's hear you count backward from six. What are you going to count backward from? Here we go: six . . . five . . . ."

Introduce a variety of counting-backward tasks (four to six a day).

3. Do not allow the children to complete a series when they count backward. Present this task: "Let's count backward from eight. Here we go: eight . . . seven . . . six . . . five." Stop the children at this point and say, "That's good." Then present another counting-backward task: "Let's count backward from four. Here we go: four . . . three . . . two." Stop. As the children become familiar with this procedure, stop them after they have counted only one number. When stopping the children, do not make them feel that they are being penalized. Say "Good, you've got it" and proceed to the next task: "O.K., let's count backward from five. Go: five . . . four . . . O.K., that's it."

4. Next, teach them to count backward *a given number of steps.*

Introduce the task by saying, "O.K., this is tough. I want you to count backward three numbers from eight. What are we starting with? . . . Eight. And we're going to count backward how many numbers? . . . Three." Hold up three fingers on one of your hands. Have the children hold up three fingers also. "Here we go. Eight. We're starting with eight: eight . . . seven"—touch the first extended finger—"six"—touch the second finger—"five." Touch the third extended finger.

Use the same procedure with a variety of problems that involve counting backward no more than three numbers. When the children work the finger operation, *make sure that they say the number from which they are starting before they touch any fingers.* This is very important: "Tell me how many you're starting out with. . . . Six. Say it big. . . . O.K., go. . . ."

5. Introduce the term *minus* after the children have demonstrated that they can handle the tasks in Step 4 above: "Here's a hard problem, but I can do it. What's six minus two? Six minus two. I'm starting out with six. And I'm going to minus two. Minus how many?" Put two fingers from the other hand into the opening at the top of the fist. "How many are in here? . . . Six. And I'm going to minus two. Six"—remove one finger—"five"—remove the second finger—"four." Hold up the fist. "I end up with four." The essential point to understand in these problems is that when the fingers from the other hand are in the fist we have six fingers. The children may have some trouble with this point. They may want to add the two fingers as they put them in. Say, "Let's do it again. We've got six and we want to minus two. Let's get ready to minus two. . . . Put two fingers in there. . . . O.K., now we're ready to minus those two fingers. We've got six, right? O.K., here we go. How many are in there? . . . Six. Say it big. Six." Remove fingers as you count. "Five . . . four. How many are in the fist now? . . . Four."

6. Present chalkboard problems involving the finger operation.

$$7 - 3 = a$$

"It says to start out with seven and minus three. Do we know how many that equals? . . . No. Let's find out. Let's get ready to minus three. Get three fingers in there. . . . O.K., how many are we starting out with? . . . Seven. Let's go: seven . . . six . . . five . . . four." Hold up the fist. "How many do we end up with? . . . Four."

Present three to five board problems a day (minusing one, two, three, and four). Work on these until the children can operate without any prompts from you. Withdraw the prompts as early as possible. If the children have trouble, reintroduce the prompts.

Focusing on the equals sign

1. Present a line-drawing operation for subtraction problems.

Introduce the operation in connection with this problem:

$$7 - 3 = a$$

Cup your hands around $7 - 3$. "How many are on this side of the equals sign? . . . Seven minus three." Cup your hands around a. "How many are on this side of the equals sign? . . . We don't know, but we can find out." Refer to $7 - 3$. "It tells us to start out with seven." Draw seven lines under the 7:

$$7 - 3 = a$$
||||||||

Point to the minus sign. "Now it tells us to minus—to get rid of some of these lines. How many lines?" Point to the three. "It says to minus three. Let's do it." Cross out three lines by striking them with horizontal lines:

$$7 - 3 = a$$

||||卅

As you cross out each line, say, "Goodbye, one. . . . Goodbye, two. . . . Goodbye, three." (This procedure will help the children see that you are getting rid of the lines.) "How many lines do we end up with? Let's count." Count the lines that are not crossed out. "We have four lines on this side of the equals sign. So how many lines do we have on the other side of the equals sign? . . . Four." Draw four lines under the *a*. "We've got four lines on this side of the equals sign. So what number do I have up here? . . . Four." Write a 4:

$$7 - 3 = 4$$

||||卅

Read the equation with the children three or four times, very slowly at first and then speeding up slightly. After the third or fourth reading, say, "I can say it. Seven minus three equals four. Oh, that's hard to do, but I can do it. I'm the only one here that can. Listen: Seven minus three equals four." The children will probably rise to the challenge and demonstrate that they can say the statement too. If they can't repeat it individually, have them say it with you three or four times. Then move on to another problem.

Present three to five board problems a day for several days. Have the children work them both with lines on the chalkboard and with fingers. Work the problems with lines first. Then point out the answer: "We end up with five. I'll bet we won't end up with five if we work this problem with our fingers. Who thinks we'll end up with five? . . . John does; Mary does. . . . Well, you guys are wrong. You'll see. We're going to start out with eight and minus three. Get ready to minus three. . . . Here we go: eight . . . seven, six, five. See? We end up with five, but when we did the problem on the board we ended up with . . ." Point to the 5 and look sad. "Oh, John was right and Mary was right. I was wrong."

2. Present a sheet with problems for the children to work.

At first limit the problems on the sheet to minus problems:

$$9 - 1 = \square \qquad 8 - 2 = \square$$
$$5 - 3 = \square \qquad 8 - 3 = \square$$
$$8 - 1 = \square \qquad 9 - 4 = \square$$

Like the initial addition sheets, each sheet should contain at least two minus-one problems. Allow the children to work the problems any way they wish—either with lines or with fingers. If a child works all his problems with lines, have him check several of them by using the finger operation. Similarly, if a child works all his problems with fingers, have him check several of them by drawing lines. Praise children who work some of the problems with lines and others with fingers. By working the problems both ways, the children learn the relation between the finger operation and the line-drawing operation.

After the children have demonstrated that they can handle problems both ways, introduce problems in which they must pay attention to the sign in the problem. Include with the subtraction problems several regular addition problems (no algebra problems initially). Present about an equal number of addition and subtraction problems:

$$6 + 4 = \square \qquad 5 + 3 = \square$$
$$6 - 4 = \square \qquad 5 + 1 = \square$$
$$8 - 1 = \square \qquad 6 - 2 = \square$$

Before handing out the sheet, work the first two problems on the board. Do not prompt the children unless they have trouble. If they do have trouble it will probably be with the sign. Then say, "Wait a minute. This doesn't tell us to minus. It tells us to plus—to get some more. We have to do what it says. If it says plus, we have to plus."

Word problems

Present word problems involving subtraction after the children can work the sheet problems with a minimum of help: "Here's a story about Mary. Mary starts out with six teeth, and do you know what happens? One tooth falls out. How many does she end up with? Listen again: She starts out with six teeth and she loses one tooth. Does she get more teeth? No, she gets less. We've got to minus. How many teeth did she lose? . . . One. We've got to minus one." Place one finger in your fist. "Six . . ." Remove the finger and say, "Five. She ends up with five teeth."

Present similar problems until the children are able to prepare their hands as the problem is presented: "John starts out with seven buttons. Get your fists up. . . . And he loses four. Get ready to minus four." This means put four fingers in the fist. "How many are in here? . . . Seven. Let's go: seven . . ."

Introduce problems involving losing, getting rid of, selling, and consuming: "Harold has six pies, and do you know what he does? He eats four of them. He has six pies and then does he get more pies? No, he eats some. He minuses."

Present two or three story problems a day until the children can handle them without prompting. Then mix the subtraction story problems with addition story problems. Present addition problems that involve finding, making, and buying. Work on these until the children are familiar with the signals that tell him to minus and the signals that call for the plussing operation.

Algebra problems of subtraction

1. Present two rows of lines on the board, five lines in the top row and four in the bottom row:

Ask, "Are these rows equal? . . . Which row has more? . . . So which row has less?" Now refer to the top row and present the problem: "If I had this many—how many? . . . Five. If I had this many and I wanted to end up with this many"—point to the bottom row—"how many lines would I have to cross out?" If the children have trouble, draw in the equals line:

Point to the top row and repeat the question: "How many lines would I have to cross out to make this row equal to this row?" After the children have given the correct answer, cross out one line and count the lines in both the top row and the bottom row. "Four here . . . and four here. If I start out with five and I want to end up with four, I have to minus how many? . . . I have to minus one."

Present a variety of similar problems, always phrasing the question like this: "If I have this many and I want to end up with this many, what do I have to do?" Hold the children increasingly responsible for expressing the operation as minusing: "You have to minus three."

Present some problems in which you do not allow the children to count the lines in each row:

286

Make sure that the lines in the bottom row are directly below the lines in the top row so that the children can see where the rows are equal. Have them draw in the equals line and then tell what they would have to do to make the rows equal. ("You've got to minus three lines.") Cross out three lines. "That's right. If I have this many"—point to the top row—"and I want to end up with this many"—point to the bottom row—"I have to minus three lines."

Do not set the problems up so that the top row always contains more lines than the bottom row. Make the top row bigger in one problem and the bottom row bigger in the next.

2. Present the statement for such problems on the board. Demonstrate how to work the problems with $7 - c = 2$.

Summarize the basic rule: Cup your hands around $7 - c$. "We know that this is the same as this." Cup your hands around the 2. "Seven minus c is the same as two. Seven minus c equals two."

Refer to the 2. "How many are we going to have on this side? . . . Two." Draw two lines below the 2:

$$7 - c = 2$$
$$||$$

Refer to $7 - c$. "This has to be equal to two. But it tells us to start out with seven. So we do it."

$$\overset{7}{||||||} \quad c = 2 \\ ||$$

"Now it tells us to minus some. How many? We know that we have to end up with two on this side, because we have two on the other side. So we take lines away until we end up with two. Let's draw a circle around the two we want to end up with."

$$\text{(||)}||||\quad \overset{7 - c = 2}{||}$$

"Now we have to get rid of all of the other lines. We want to end up with two. Let's see how many we have to minus." With a horizontal line, cross out each of the lines that is not circled. As you cross out each line, say "minus one, minus two, minus three . . ."

$$\text{(||)}\cancel{|||||}\quad \overset{7 - c = 2}{||}$$

"How many did we have to minus? . . . Five." Refer to the equation. "It says 'seven minus how many equals two?' We know how many. Seven minus five equals two."

Erase the c and replace it with a 5:

$$7 - 5 = 2$$

Demonstrate that the equation balances: "How many lines on this side? . . . Two. How many lines on this side? . . . Two. Two equals two. What's another way of saying two? . . . Seven minus five."

Present four to six problems of this type every day until the children can handle them without prompting. Before they work a problem, have them identify the term in the problem that is not known.

Drill them on using the appropriate language to specify what they must find out—what kind of question the problem asks. For example:

$$5 - b = 2$$

"Do we know how many we're going to start out with? . . . Yes, five. Then what does the problem tell us to do? . . . It tells us to minus. Does it tell us how many to minus?" Point to the b. "No, that's what we have to find out—how many we minus. Does the problem tell us how many we'll end up with? . . . Yes. How many? . . . Two."

Have the children draw the lines and, most important, give the answer. Do not accept one-word answers such as "three" or "two." Say, "Tell me the whole thing," which in this case is: "We have to minus three," or "We have to get rid of three." If the children are allowed to give number answers only, they may become very confused when they are required to distinguish between problems of the form $5 - b = 2$ and problems of the form $5 - 3 = b$. These problems ask different questions. The child will be in a better position to answer the question appropriately if he has been drilled on the kind of answer demanded by each problem form.

3. After the children have demonstrated that they can handle the problems on the board with a minimum of assistance, give them daily sheets with five to seven problems on each. Allow them about five minutes to work the problems. An initial sheet might look like this:

$$8 - \square = 1 \qquad\qquad 7 - \square = 2$$
$$5 - \square = 2 \qquad\qquad 7 - \square = 1$$
$$5 - \square = 1$$

The children have less difficulty trying to keep the steps of the operation straight if they are required to circle only one or two lines. With practice, they will be able to work sheets like this:

$8 - \square = 5$ $7 - \square = 2$
$6 - \square = 1$ $7 - \square = 3$
$10 - \square = 4$ $7 - \square = 4$

4. Introduce a finger operation for algebra problems.
Present this problem:

$6 - d = 4$

Explain, "We are starting out with six, but we want to end up with four. Do we know how many we want to end up with? . . . Yes. How many? . . . Four. But do we know how many we have to minus to get from six to four? . . . No. That's what we have to find out—how many we minus. We have to find out how many fingers we're going to pull out of the fist. Let's do it. Hold up your fist. There are six in here. Six. And if we pull out one finger"—hold up a finger on the other hand— "five. And if we pull out another finger"—hold up another finger on the other hand—"four." Refer to the two fingers. "Here's how many we have to pull out." Put the fingers in the fist. "Six." Pull out one of the fingers. "Five." Pull out the last finger. "Four. How many did we have to minus to end up with four? . . . We had to minus two fingers."

There is an added step in this problem. One has to figure out how many fingers he has to remove. To do this, he counts backward, holding up a finger every time he counts. The number of fingers he holds up is the number he has to remove.

Present two to four finger problems every day, in addition to the other problems being presented that day. Expect the children to have some trouble with the operation. After they have mastered the operation and are able to work the problems without much prompting, have them work problems both with the lines and with the finger operation.

5. Present the basic algebraic subtraction problem as a word problem, in this basic form: "John leaves home with five apples. When he comes back home, he has only two apples. How many apples did he eat?" Have the children indicate how the problem should be written on the board: "Tell me what to write. Listen again. John starts out with five, and he ends up with two. How many did he eat? What do I write first? . . . Five. Why? . . . Because he started out with five. What hap-

pened then? Did he get more apples or did he get rid of some? . . . He
got rid of some, so we write a minus. How many did he minus? . . . We
don't know, so we put something that says 'I don't know.' Do we know
how many he ended up with? . . . Yes, he ended up with two. So what
do I write? . . . Equals two."

$$5 - m = 2$$

After the problem has been written on the board, call on one of
the children to work it. Caution the other children, "Watch him and
tell him if he makes a mistake."

Present a variety of algebra problems involving subtraction (two
to four a session). To make up these problems, tell the children how
many the hero of the story started out with and how many he ended
up with. Ask "How many did he (sell, eat, give away, lose, etc.)?"

Consolidation

At this point in arithmetic learning the children have mastered four
basic operations—addition, subtraction, addition algebra, and subtraction algebra. They have learned to solve each of the problems with
a finger operation and with a line-drawing operation. They are ready
to work sheets on which all four types of problems appear.

Present sheets with at least eight problems (two from each of the
four categories). Keep the problems relatively simple at first. The children will probably have some trouble concentrating on the question
each problem is asking.

1. Initially, pair the problems on the sheet (two addition-algebra
problems followed perhaps by two subtraction problems, etc.)

$$2 + \square = 3 \qquad\qquad 4 + 2 = \square$$
$$7 + \square = 9 \qquad\qquad 8 + 1 = \square$$
$$8 - 1 = \square \qquad\qquad 7 - \square = 1$$
$$7 - 3 = \square \qquad\qquad 7 - \square = 2$$

Later, break up the pairs:

$$5 + 6 = \square \qquad\qquad 3 + 1 = \square$$
$$8 - \square = 2 \qquad\qquad 6 - \square = 3$$
$$6 - 4 = \square \qquad\qquad 5 - 4 = \square$$
$$5 + \square = 8 \qquad\qquad 8 + \square = 10$$

2. If children have difficulties, ask them (*a*) what the problem is asking them; (*b*) what they know: "Do you know how many you're starting out with? Do you know how many you're going to plus (or minus)? Do you know how many you're going to end up with?"

3. As the children become proficient at working these problems, allow them to use shorter methods to figure out the answer. When children work out shortcut methods, point them out to the other children: "Mary does it the fast way. Let me show you. . . ."

$$6 - \square = 2$$

"We know there will be two lines over here. But we don't have to draw them. We know we'll end up with extra lines on the other side of the equals sign." Encourage the children to use this shorter operation after they have mastered the basic one. The advantage of the basic operation is that it demonstrates to the children that the equation balances—if there are two lines on one side of the equals sign, there are two on the other. After they have learned this rule, however, they should be able to work from the symbol and they should no longer need the lines on the right side of the equals sign.

Expressing Numbers in Different Ways

A number is a unique value that can be expressed in various ways. We can express the number concept "four" by saying that it is three plus one, or two times two, or half of eight. Expressed somewhat differently, a given counting number is related to any other counting number. Four is related to eight because four equals the fraction $\frac{8}{2}$. Four is related to three because four equals three plus one.

1. After the children have mastered the four basic operations outlined in the preceding sections, present quick exercises that help clarify what a number is and how it is related (through addition and subtraction) to other numbers.

Write this series on the board:

6 = 7	6 = 7
6 = 4	6 = 2
6 = 5	6 = 1
6 = 9	

Point to the first equation and ask, "Is this right? Does six equal seven? . . . Well, what equals seven? . . . Yes, seven. And what does six equal? . . . Six." Ask the same questions about each of the statements. Then return to the first statement. "This is silly, isn't it? But let's fix it up." Draw lines under both the 6 and the 7:

$$6 = 7$$
||||||　||||||

Refer to the lines under the 7. "We've got seven lines. But we don't want seven. We want six." Count off six lines and draw a circle around them:

$$6 = 7$$
|||||| (|||||)|

"That's how many we want. So what do we have to do? We've got to get rid of one line. We've got to minus one line. Who can write that for me?" Call on one of the children.

$$6 = 7 - 1$$
|||||| (|||||)|

Cross out the line. Refer to the statement. "Now we've fixed it up. Does six equal seven? . . . No. Six equals seven minus one."

Work the other problems in a similar manner, either minusing or plussing on the right side of the equals sign to make the statement true.

The second problem requires "plussing":

$$6 = 4$$
|||||| ||||

Refer to the lines under the 4. "I have only four lines here. But I want to have six. So what do I have to do? . . . I have to plus. How many do I have to plus? Let's see. I've got four. Five . . . six."

$$6 = 4$$
|||||| |||| ||

"I had to plus two. Who can write that?"

$$6 = 4 + 2$$
|||||| |||| ||

"Does six equal four? . . . No, six equals four—plus two."

After the children have learned to work these problems on the board, present daily sheets with seven incorrect statements about a number ($4 = 6$, $4 = 2$, $4 = 9$, etc.). Ask the children questions after they have finished working the problems: "What would you say if a

292

guy came up to you and said 'Four equals six'? . . . Do you know what I'd say? I'd say 'Four equals six—MINUS TWO!' ' "

After the children have worked on various numbers, they will have a rough idea of what a number is and how it is related to other numbers.

Regrouping and making up statements

1. Present five lines on the board:

|||||

Ask the children how many lines are on the board. After they have counted them, say, "Yes, when we count all of them, we end up with five. I can write that." Write a large 5 on the board. "Now let's figure out what equals five."

$$5 = |||||$$

Draw a little arc under each of the lines:

|||||

"I can count all the lines this way. And I can write it."

$$5 = 1 + 1 + 1 + 1 + 1$$

"That's just like counting. One, and I get one more—two. And I get one more—three. And I get one more—four. And I get one more—five." Refer to the expression on the right of the equals sign. "This equals five. And I can write five another way."

Draw a horizontal line through 1 + 1. "I know what this is. One plus one equals . . ." If the children have trouble, refer to the lines below. "Look, one . . . and one more. Two." Write a 2 above the crossed-out 1 + 1. Also erase the arcs under the left two lines and replace them with a single arc:

$$5 = \overset{2}{\cancel{1+1}} + 1 + 1 + 1$$

Demonstrate that the right side of the equation adds up to five: "Look—two . . . and we plus one. Three. And we plus one. Four. And we plus one. Five. So another way of saying five is two plus one, plus one, plus one."

293

Refer to the right side of the equation. "I know what two plus one is. Three. So I can cross out the two plus one and put a three." Change the arcs beneath the equation:

$$5 = \cancel{1} + \cancel{1} + \cancel{1} + 1 + 1$$

Refer to the right side of the equation. "I know what three plus one equals. What does it equal? . . . Four. So I can cross out the three plus one and put a four."

$$5 = \cancel{1} + \cancel{1} + \cancel{1} + \cancel{1} + 1$$

"It still equals five. We've counted all the lines. Four here and one here. And look at this. I know what four plus one equals. Four plus one equals five. So I can cross out the four plus one and put a five."

$$5 = \cancel{1} + \cancel{1} + \cancel{1} + \cancel{1} + \cancel{1}$$

"And look what it says now. Five equals five. That's right."

2. Use the regrouping demonstration in connection with a variety of numbers. Concentrate on the larger numbers (five through ten). Handle each number in the manner outlined above. First have a series of plus ones on the right of the equals sign. Show the grouping that you are using with arcs under each number. Then start from the left and regroup, making the first group one larger with each regrouping. Continue until all the lines are grouped with a single arc, at which time the statement should be familiar to the child (7 = 7, 5 = 5, 9 = 9, etc.). The purpose of this exercise is to demonstrate to the children that one can write a number such as seven as a series of plus ones, and that it is possible to regroup the plus ones in different ways.

3. When the children understand the procedure, give them individual sheets, using lines and arcs to show all the possible groupings for the number five.

Instruct them to write appropriate expressions for each grouping: "Look at these little arcs. How many are in this arc? . . . One. So what number do you write up here? . . . One. And then you're going to plus some more. So what do you write? . . . A plus sign. How many do I plus? How many are in this next little arc? . . . One. So I plus one. . . ."

Have the children work on daily sheets with numbers from five through ten until they are *very solid*.

4. After the children have demonstrated a solid understanding of the regrouping operation, introduce different regrouping patterns. Write $6 = |\ |\ |\ |\ |\ |$ on the board. Have the children count the lines. "I think I'll have some fun with this. Watch how I can make six." Draw arcs as shown below.

$$6 = \underset{\smile}{||}\ \underset{\smile}{||}\ \underset{\smile}{||}$$

"I counted them all, didn't I? Who can write what I did?"

$$6 = \underset{\smile}{2} + \underset{\smile}{2} + \underset{\smile}{2}$$

"See, I have two and then I get two more: two . . . three, four. Now I've got four. And I get two more: five, six." If the children have trouble, refer to the lines below the equation.

Erase the expression to the right of the equals sign and the arcs below the lines. "I think I'll have some more fun. I can make six another way."

$$6 = \underset{\smile}{|||}\ \underset{\smile}{|}\ \underset{\smile}{||}$$

"Who can write what I did?"

After demonstrating several more groupings, call on children to group the lines in different ways and write what they did. The rules of the game are simple. Every line must be "arced," or counted. If a child does not count a line, point out that he hasn't counted all six lines.

5. Give the children lesson sheets on which they are to group lines in different ways and write an expression that tells what they have done. Concentrate on numbers from four through eight.

"See how many different ways you can group these lines. Remember, you have to count every line, because this side has to be equal to five. So you have to count all five lines."

Praise children who discover new ways of grouping. Demonstrate to the children that they can group the lines any way they wish.

Negative Numbers

At this point in the program the children are ready to learn how to handle problems involving negative numbers. Before they can be expected to understand numbers that are less than zero, they must have a firm idea of how zero is related to the counting numbers. Zero is the gateway to negative numbers, simultaneous equations, and the formal rules about statements of subtraction.

1. Present a series of subtraction problems in which the remainder is zero:

$$7 - 7 = \square \qquad\qquad 6 - 6 = \square$$
$$9 - 9 = \square \qquad\qquad 3 - 3 = \square$$
$$4 - 4 = \square$$

After the children have worked these (using the line-drawing operation), present a series of problems verbally: "If I start out with four shoes and get rid of four shoes, how many shoes will I have? . . . Yes, zero, because four minus four equals zero."

"If I start out with seven teeth and get in a big fight and have all seven teeth knocked out, how many teeth will I have? . . . Yes, zero, because seven minus seven equals zero."

As the children become familiar with the form of these problems, ask such questions as these: "Does four plus four equal zero? . . . No, four minus four equals zero. Does four minus three equal zero? . . . No, four minus how many equals zero? Four minus four equals zero."

2. Give the children problems in which they have to indicate how many one has to minus to end up with zero:

$$4 - \square = 0 \qquad\qquad 8 - \square = 0$$
$$6 - \square = 0 \qquad\qquad 9 - \square = 0$$
$$5 - \square = 0 \qquad\qquad 2 - \square = 0$$

Give the children a different slant on working these problems: "Look at the first problem. How many are you starting out with? . . . Four. And what do you want to end up with? . . . Zero. Well, if you have four and you don't want any at all, how many do you have to get rid of? . . . Four. *You have to minus as many as you start out with if you want to end up with zero.*"

Repeat this rule in connection with every problem presented. Make the children work from the rule: "Look, we're starting out with six and we want to end up with zero. To end up with zero, we have to

minus as many as we start out with. How many do we start out with?
So how many do we have to minus?"

Call attention to the zero: "Look at this third problem. What are
we ending up with? . . . Zero. That means we have to minus as many
as we start out with. How many are we starting out with? . . . Five.
So how many do we have to minus? . . . Five."

Introduce problems in which the children must use the converse
of the rule:

$$\Box - 6 = 0 \qquad\qquad \Box - 1 = 0$$
$$\Box - 8 = 0 \qquad\qquad \Box - 7 = 0$$
$$\Box - 4 = 0$$

"See the first problem? We're ending up with zero. That means that
we minus as many as we're starting out with. How many are we minusing? . . . Six. So how many do we have to start out with? . . . Six." The
children should have no trouble with these rules.

3. The preceding tasks have demonstrated to the children that if
you have a given number of objects and you want to end up with zero
objects, you have to minus all the objects you have. After learning this
relationship, the children are ready to work problems in which they
minus more than they start out with—an operation that takes them
into negative numbers.

Present these problems on the board:

$$4 - 3 = c \qquad\qquad 4 - 5 = c$$
$$4 - 4 = c \qquad\qquad 4 - 6 = c$$

Work them with lines on the board. The problem $4 - 5 = c$ introduces something new: "It tells us to start out with four. Then it tells
us to minus five. Oh boy! We don't have five to minus. Let's go."

$$4 - 5 = c$$

"Look at that funny line we end up with. Do you know what that is?
That's a negative. How many negatives do we have? . . . One. We end
up with negative one." Write the negative one as ~ 1.

$$4 - 5 = \sim 1$$

Work the problem $4 - 6 = c$ in the same way. Start out with
four and minus six:

$$4 - 6 = c$$

卄卄丿丿

"Oh, we've got some negatives again. How many negatives do we have? . . . Two. We end up with negative two (written ~2)."

4. After the introduction of negative numbers, let the children apply their rule about zero to see whether or not the number will be negative.

Present this problem:

$$5 - 5 =$$

"How many are we starting out with? . . . And how many are we minusing? Are we minusing just as many as we start out with? . . . Yes, so what are we going to end up with? . . . Zero. We're going to minus all that we have."

Change the problem:

$$5 - 4 =$$

"Are we minusing as many as we're starting out with? . . . Which is bigger—five or four? . . . Five. So we're starting out with more than we're minusing. Will we end up with zero? . . . No, we'll still have some left. We'll have one left."

Change the problem again:

$$5 - 6 =$$

"Are we minusing as many as we're starting out with? . . . No. Will we end up with zero? . . . No. Which is bigger—five or six? . . . Six. We're minusing six, but we're only starting out with five. So we're minusing more than we're starting out with. Do you know what's going to happen? We'll end up with a negative number." Work the problem and demonstrate that the answer is a negative number.

Present similar exercises until the children can judge whether or not they will end up with a negative number. Use an abbreviated presentation after they have learned the general rules: "Are we going to end up with zero? . . . No. Why? Because we are not minusing as many as we're starting out with. If we minus more, then we'll end up with a negative number. We're taking away more than we've got."

5. Introduce problems in which the children have to relate a negative number to zero. This is a key exercise. It can be introduced after the children have encountered negative numbers in several sessions.

Present the following problem on the board:

$$\sim 2 = 0$$

"Is that right? . . . No, of course not. Negative two is not the same as zero. Let's draw a picture and see how silly this statement is."

$$\sim 2 = 0$$

"There. We have zero on one side and negative two on the other." Refer to left side of the equation. "What would I have to do to this side to make the same as that side?" Some of the children may say "minus" or "get rid of the lines." Acknowledge their responses: "We want to get rid of these lines, don't we? But how do we do it? We've got to plus. We've got to cross the lines out. That means we have to plus."

If the children have trouble with this point, abandon the problem above and present this problem:

$$4 - 1 - 4 + 2 = c$$

"Let's work this problem. Let's do what it tells us to do. Start out with four. Minus one."

$$4 - 1 - 4 + 2 = c$$

"Now it tells us to minus four. Who can do that?"

$$4 - 1 - 4 + 2 = c$$

"Now it tells us to plus two. Who wants to try that?" Stress the rule that you've got to take care of the minuses before doing anything else.

$$4 - 1 - 4 + 2 = c$$

"We end up with one."

Present several similar long problems every day until the children understand the convention that minuses have to be canceled out. Present problems in which there are many minuses that must be canceled:

$$3 + 2 - 7 + 5 = c$$
$$1 - 6 - 1 + 9 = c$$
$$4 - 8 - 1 + 3 + 7 = b$$

After the children master these problems, return to this one:

$$\sim2 = 0$$

Refer to the left side of the statement. "What would we have to do to this side to make it equal to that side?" If the children have trouble, say, "Watch. Here's what I do. Plus two lines."

$$\sim2 + 2 = 0$$

Refer to the left side. "How many on this side? . . . Zero." Refer to the right side. "How many on this side? . . . Zero. Zero equals zero. We did it. Do you want to try another problem?"

$$\sim5 = 0$$

"Read it. Negative five equals zero. Is that true? . . . It sounds good to me. Draw me a picture and show me that it isn't true."

$$\sim5 = 0$$

Point to the lines under the ~5. "What do I have to do on this side to make it equal to that side? Who can do it?"

$$\sim5 = 0$$

"That's it. Now, can you write down what you did?"

$$\sim5 + 5 = 0$$

Present a number of similar problems (with the right side of the equation equal to zero). When it appears that the children can handle the problems quickly and accurately, have them solve the problems verbally.

For example, present the problem $\sim2 = 0$. Point to the left side of the equation. "What do I have to do to this side to make it the same as the other side?" If the children are unable to give the correct answer, say, "I know what I have to do. I have to plus two." Diagram the problem and demonstrate that you were right. Act somewhat amused. "These are easy, at least for me (maybe not for you). If you've got negative two and you want to get to zero, you plus two. If you've got negative five and want to get to zero, you plus five. If you've got negative seven and want to get to zero, you plus seven."

300

Present the problem $\sim3 = 0$. Refer to the negative three. "What do I have to do to this side to make it the same as that side? . . . Good. I'm at negative three, so I plus three to get to zero."

6. Present problems in which the right side of the equation is equal to one:

$$\sim4 = 1$$
$$//// = 1$$

Tell the children that you can work these problems. Talk to yourself as you pretend to be trying to work the problem: "Let's see. I've got to plus four to get rid of these four negatives. But that just brings me to zero. I'll need one more. I'll need"—point to the negative lines as you count—"one . . . two . . . three . . ." Some of the children will probably have figured out the answer by this time.

Present three or four similar problems during each session (with 0 or 1 on the right side of the equation) until the children can work them without any prompting. Continue to use the technique of trying to figure out the problem as you talk to yourself. The children will become highly motivated to beat you.

7. Introduce problems that have negative numbers on both sides of the equals sign:

$$\sim3 = \sim1$$

Don't be surprised if the children have some trouble with these initially.

Diagram the problem:

$$\underset{///}{\sim3} = \underset{/}{\sim1}$$

Refer to the lines under the ~3 and tell the children, "I want to work on this side of the equals sign and make this side look just like that side. What do I have to do?" Show the children that you have to plus two lines. "How many on this side now? . . . Negative one." (Don't accept the answer "one.") "And how many on the other side? . . . Negative one. They're equal. What did I have to do to make them equal? . . . I had to plus two."

$$\underset{\#\!/\!\!/}{\sim3} + 2 = \underset{/}{\sim1}$$

Present three or four similar problems during each session until the children become solid in the operation. Make the number on the right side of the equation either ~1 or ~2.

8. Introduce discrimination exercises. Give the children worksheets on which appear pairs of problems that are similar in all respects except the sign in front of the last number:

$$\sim4 = \sim1 \qquad\qquad \sim5 = 1$$
$$\sim4 = 1 \qquad\qquad \sim5 = \sim1$$
$$\sim3 = \sim2 \qquad\qquad \sim6 = 2$$
$$\sim3 = 2 \qquad\qquad \sim6 = \sim2$$

Present similar sheets until the children can handle these problems quickly and accurately (with no coaching). If they have trouble initially, take them through the steps involved in arriving at a solution.

9. Present word problems involving negative numbers: "A man has three pennies and he spends four pennies. How many pennies does he end up with?" Explain how someone could spend four pennies if he has only three. Act out the sequence, with one of the children playing the role of a storekeeper and you playing the role of the spendthrift.

After the children have had sufficient exposure to problems in which the man ends up owing money, present a variation: "A man owes four dollars. He gets some money, pays what he owes, and ends up with two dollars. How much money did he get?" Ask the children leading questions: "What did the man start out with? . . . Negative four. Then he got some more. Do we know how many more? . . . No, but we know that he ended up with two dollars."

$$\underset{\text{////}}{\sim4} + \Box = 2$$

"He has to plus six dollars."

$$\underset{\text{卅卅}}{\sim4} + \underset{\text{||}}{\boxed{6}} = 2$$

After working one or two problems of this type, the children usually have no trouble with them.

Addition–Subtraction Fact Learning

Fact learning should not be introduced until the children have mastered both the regular and algebraic operations outlined in the preceding sections. Fact learning should not be forced. Children will learn facts as rapidly if they work on them for several minutes a day as they will if they are drilled for protracted periods.

302

Addition facts

1. After the children have demonstrated that they can figure out (without assistance) the problems presented so far, present these number pair facts:

$$1 + 1 = \qquad\qquad 6 + 6 =$$
$$2 + 2 = \qquad\qquad 7 + 7 =$$
$$3 + 3 = \qquad\qquad 8 + 8 =$$
$$4 + 4 = \qquad\qquad 9 + 9 =$$
$$5 + 5 = \qquad\qquad 10 + 10 =$$

Spend no more than two minutes a day on fact learning. Present the series of facts in the above order. Use a rhythmical presentation, clapping three times between statements.

After the children have mastered the facts in order, begin mixing the order. Also race the children on fact answering. Initially use only three or four facts in a race. As the children master these facts, introduce additional facts two at a time.

2. Introduce a method for using known facts as a base for solving other problems.

Present this problem:

$$6 + 4 =$$

"I'll show you a new way to work this problem. I don't know what six plus four equals, but I do know what six plus zero equals. Six plus zero equals six. So six plus one equals—not six but seven. SEVEN. Six plus two equals—not seven. Eight. EIGHT. Six plus three equals—not eight. Nine. NINE. And six plus four equals ten."

After presenting the series verbally, write it on the board and have the children read it with you:

$$6 + 0 = 6$$
$$6 + 1 = 7$$
$$6 + 2 = 8$$
$$6 + 3 = 9$$
$$6 + 4 =$$

Then have them give the answers as you read the first part of each equation: "Six plus zero. . . . Six plus one. . . . Six plus two. . . ." It will take at least a week before the children can *hear* the relationship between the statements. Repeat basic series such as $5 + 0$, $6 + 0$,

$7 + 0$, $10 + 0$ until the children are solid. Place increasing emphasis on working from the verbal presentation. Always start with plus zero and work up to a given number.

At this point of instruction the children know only that they are to say the next number when you present the next equation. They are not necessarily listening to the statements that you are making. To make them more critically aware of your statements, *repeat* a statement in a verbal series before proceeding to the next statement: Five plus zero equals . . . Five plus one equals . . . Five plus one equals . . . Most of the children will say seven. Act amused: "Oh, I got you on that. You have to listen to what I say. I'll bet I can catch you."

Continue to repeat some of the statements in a sequence until it is no longer possible to catch the children. Then introduce a variation of the task in which you repeat a statement introduced earlier in the series: Five plus zero . . . Five plus one . . . Five plus two . . . Five plus one . . .

Again, some of the children will give the wrong answer, saying eight. "Oh, I got you. You have to listen. I didn't say five plus three. I said five plus one." Introduce only one of these tests in a series, putting it initially at the beginning of the series (five plus one . . . five plus zero . . .) and then placing it farther back in the series (seven plus four . . . seven plus three . . .).

Finally, introduce more than one test in a series: Six plus zero . . . Six plus one . . . Six plus two . . . Six plus one . . . Six plus two . . . Six plus three . . . Six plus four . . . Six plus three . . . Six plus four . . . Six plus five . . .

3. When the children have demonstrated that they can handle these series without making mistakes, introduce a method for using the sequence to figure out how to work a problem starting with a known fact.

Present this problem:

$$6 + 4 =$$

"I don't know what six plus *four* equals, but I do know what six plus *zero* equals. What does it equal?" Write the equation on the board above the original problem (leaving space between the two for three additional equations):

$$6 + 0 = 6$$

$$6 + 4 =$$

304

"Now we just keep going until we get to six plus four. Six plus zero equals six. Six plus one . . ." Write the equation. "Six plus two . . ." Write the equation. "Six plus three . . ." Write the equation.

$$6 + 0 = 6$$
$$6 + 1 = 7$$
$$6 + 2 = 8$$
$$6 + 3 = 9$$
$$6 + 4 =$$

"So six plus four equals ten."

Work one or two similar problems with the children every day. As they become familiar with the pattern, let them write the statements that lead to an answer of the problem. For example:

$$8 + 5 = a$$

"Eight plus five. Do you know what that equals, John? . . . No? Well, what do you know about eight? Do you know what eight plus anything is? . . . Yes, eight plus zero equals eight. Can you write that for me? . . . Good. We know that eight plus zero equals eight. So what else do we know about eight? . . . Eight plus one equals nine." Continue until the children have worked up to eight plus five.

Give the children worksheets. Draw lines above each problem—one line for each statement that precedes the statement that is given:

		8 + _____
7 + _____	5 + _____	8 + _____
7 + _____	5 + _____	8 + _____
7 + _____	5 + _____	8 + _____
$7 + 3 = \Box$	$5 + 3 = \Box$	$8 + 4 = \Box$

Let the children work on similar problems until they are solid.

4. Introduce problems in which the children use *number pairs* as the starting point for figuring out the answer to a problem.

Present this problem:

$$7 + 9 = c$$

"I don't know what seven plus nine equals, but I do know something." The children will probably say, "Seven plus zero equals seven." Acknowledge their answer. Then tell them, "But I know something that's closer to seven plus nine than seven plus zero. Nine is pretty far

305

from zero. Listen to this: seven plus seven. Seven is pretty close to nine. What does seven plus seven equal? . . . Fourteen." Write the statement on the board. "If seven plus seven equals fourteen, what does seven plus eight equal? . . . Fifteen. And seven plus nine? . . ."

$$7 + 7 = 14$$
$$7 + 8 = 15$$
$$7 + 9 = 16$$

Present similar problems, in which the children are to start with familiar number pairs. First establish that the number-pair statement is closer to the goal than a statement about zero: "Yes, but six plus zero is a long way from six plus seven. Zero is a long way from seven. What's closer to seven than zero? . . . Yes, six plus six."

If the children have difficulty seeing what you mean when you say that a number is far from zero, put the numbers on the board and demonstrate:

$$0$$
$$1$$
$$2$$
$$3$$
$$4$$
$$5$$
$$6$$
$$6 + 7 =$$

"Let's see how close to seven we can get. Do you know what six plus zero equals? . . . Yes. Do you know what six plus six equals? . . . Good. Which one is closer to six plus seven? . . . Let's use that one."

Repeat the demonstration until the children can look at the column of numbers and specify what facts they know and which fact is closest to the problem.

5. After the children have learned to handle the preceding tasks, present problems that involve counting backward from a known fact. Do not introduce backward-counting tasks prematurely. And do not push them too hard. Present one or two problems a day, and don't expect the children to learn the operation overnight. Some will pick it up very quickly. Others will require a considerable amount of work before they perform consistently. Continue to present forward-counting series while the children work on backward-counting series.

Present this problem:

0
1
2
3
6 + 4 =
5
6
7

"Let's see what we know that is close to six plus four. We know six plus zero. What else do we know? . . . Six plus six." Write it in. "If six plus six equals twelve, does six plus five equal twelve? . . ."

Some of the children will probably respond that six plus five equals thirteen. If they do, avoid lengthy explanations. Write in all the statements from six plus zero through six plus seven. Then go back to six plus six: "It equals twelve. So six plus *five* equals eleven. And six plus *four* equals ten." Read the remaining statements so that the children can see that you're counting backward.

As the children become increasingly familiar with the pattern of the presentation, drop some of the cues until they can handle the problems verbally (without having to write them on the board).

Subtraction facts

Demonstrate how to work from known statements of subtraction to unknown statements.

1. Present problems in which the children must work from zero:

6 − 4

To arrive at the answer, write in the known statement, six minus zero, and the intermediate statements:

6 − 0 = 6
6 − 1 = 5
6 − 2 = 4
6 − 3 = 3
6 − 4 = ☐

2. Then work from the other end—from statements in which one ends up with zero. To work the problem 6 − 4, one would begin with 6 − 6 and then work backward:

$$6 - 6 = 0$$
$$6 - 5 = 1$$
$$6 - 4 = \square$$

Do not rush the children through the subtraction problems. They will probably have some initial difficulty and may confuse those problems with addition. If they do, place a very light stress on subtraction problems, introducing series only about every other session. Then increase the exposure until the children are working one or two series during a session. Have them read and repeat the statements that you present in the demonstrations. Make sure that every child can produce the statements. Expect some of the children to work on this series for more than a month. Take the time that is necessary to teach the relationships between statements. It will be time well spent.

After the children have learned the number pairs and the method for working from known statements to unknown statements, introduce the various addition and subtraction facts that are required of second- and third-graders. The children are now in a position to categorize facts and order them logically, instead of trying desperately to remember isolated things that have no apparent connection. They are less likely to give bizarre answers to addition and subtraction problems (such as saying that six plus two equals three). Furthermore, if they get confused, you have a method of appealing to their common sense. If a child says that six plus seven equals eleven, you can correct him by saying, "Does that fit in with what you know? What do you know about six? . . . Yes, you know that six plus six equals twelve. So six plus seven equals what? . . . Good. Let's say it a couple of times so that you remember it. . . ."

Multiplication

The procedure for teaching multiplication is similar to that outlined for teaching addition and subtraction. First the children are introduced to the operation of multiplying. They are taught what one does when he multiplies; they are taught how to translate written symbols into the multiplication operation; and they are taught the relationships in various series of statements. Finally they are taught the facts. This procedure assures that they will learn the basic operations (which they may not do if the emphasis is on the facts) and that they will have some basis for checking whether a statement of multiplication is true or false.

Multiplication as counting

Multiplication is nothing more than counting by a given number so many times. When a person counts by ones, each group that he counts contains only one thing. When he counts by twos, each group contains two. When he counts by forty-two, each group contains forty-two.

1. The first step in teaching children to multiply is to demonstrate that it is possible to count by any given number. Demonstrate the operation by writing 1 to 5 in order on the board, with large spaces between the numbers:

1   2   3   4   5

Say to the children, "I'm going to slap the board five times. How many times? . . . Five times. Here I go." Slap the board under each number, counting with each slap (one . . . two . . . three . . . four . . . five). Ask, "How many times did I slap the board? . . . Five times." Call on individual children to slap the board five times as they count from one to five.

Slap the board three times (once under each of the first three numbers). "How many times did I slap the board?" If the children have trouble answering the question, act amused. "The numbers are right up here. Watch again. . . . And I stopped under number three. So I must have slapped the board three times. Let's see if I did. I'll slap. You count." Repeat variations of the task (slapping the board two, four, one, and five times) until the children answer correctly without hesitation.

Then announce that you are going to count by twos five times. "What am I going to do? . . . Count by twos five times. When I count by twos, I make two lines every time I count. How many lines am I going to make every time I count? . . . Two. Here goes." Quickly make two lines under the number one and say "one time." Make two lines under the number two and say "two times." Continue until you've made two lines under every number: "five times."

"I counted by two. See? Two here." Point to the lines under the one. "Two here." Point to the lines under the two. Continue until you've pointed out that there are two lines under every number. "I counted by two. Do you want to see me count by three?"

Erase the lines under the numbers. "O.K., when I count by three, how many lines do I make every time I count? . . . I make three lines every time I count." Make three lines under each number and simultaneously indicate how many times you are counting (one time, two times, three times . . . five times):

| 1 | 2 | 3 | 4 | 5 |
| ||| | ||| | ||| | ||| | ||| |

Ask the children how many lines you end up with when you count by threes five times. Some of the children may say five. "No, I counted five times, but look at all of the lines I ended up with. Let's count them and see how many." Count the lines, pausing after each group of three has been counted (one, two, three . . . four, five, six . . . seven, eight, nine . . .).

Erase the lines under the numbers and demonstrate that you can count by fours and by fives. When making a group of lines, try to make it quickly. After each set of lines is completed, have the children count them with you. "How many lines do I end up with when I count by fours five times? . . . I end up with twenty lines."

2. After you have demonstrated how to count by fives five times, erase the lines and have the children identify what number you are counting by: "O.K., watch me and see if you can tell me what number I'm counting by. If I make two lines every time I count, what am I counting by? . . . Counting by twos. If I make three lines every time I count, what am I counting by? . . . Counting by threes. O.K., watch me." Make one line under each number. "What am I counting by?" Make four lines under each number. "What am I counting by?" Make two lines under each number.

Even if the children seem to have a good understanding of the operation, briefly return to the task during at least three more sessions.

3. When the children can identify the number you are counting by, present the task without the numbers. Simply make the groups of lines on the board. First make five groups of three lines:

Ask, "What did I count by?" Then ask, "How many times did I count?" If the children have trouble with this question, put your hand over the first group of lines. "I counted one time here." Put your hand over the next group of lines. "I counted one time here." Continue in this manner until you've identified each of the times you counted.

"Let's see how many times I counted . . . one, two, three, four, five."
Erase the lines and make three groups of four lines each. Ask the ques-
tions in this order: "What did I count by? . . . How many times did
I count?"

Present similar problems until the children can answer both ques-
tions correctly. (NOTE: Present the questions in the order noted above
—"What did I count by?" followed by "How many times did I count?"
Avoid counting by threes three times, fours four times, and the like.
These tasks do not provide clean tests of whether the children under-
stand what they are supposed to do, and they may be confusing.)

4. Demonstrate that the number of lines counted can be totaled.
Put five groups of two lines on the board. Ask, "What did I count by?
. . . How many lines did I count?"

Draw a line to the right of the first group:

Put your hand over the group and ask, "How many times did I count
when I was here? . . . I counted one time. What did I count by? . . . Two.
So how many lines did I make? . . . Two." Write 2 under the lines:

2

Erase the large divider line and move it to the right of the second
group of lines. Ask, "How many times did I count when I was here? I
counted one time"—point to the first group of lines—"two times"—
point to the second group of lines. "Now listen big. How many lines
did I make when I was here? Look at all the lines I made. I made all
of these lines." Run your hand back and forth from the first group to
the dividing line. "Let's count them and see how many lines I made."

2   4

Move the divider to the right of the next group of lines. Show the
children how many times you counted when you were at the third
group (one time . . . two times . . . three times). Ask, "How many lines
did I make?" Indicate all the lines up to the divider:

2   4   6

"Yes, when you count by twos three times, how many lines do you end up with? . . . Six."

Continue moving the dividing line and counting the lines to the left of the dividing line.

After the children have counted all ten lines, erase the lines, leaving only the numbers:

2	4	6	8	10

"Look. This is counting by twos. When you count by twos one time" —point to the first number—"you have two. When you count by twos two times . . ." Point to the second number. "When you count by twos three times . . ." Point to the third number. Continue until you've pointed to all of the numbers.

Make five groups of three lines each. Have the children indicate what you counted by and how many times you counted. Then total the number of lines for each time you counted—first the total for counting two times, and so forth. When you have finished, erase the lines and indicate that the numbers tell "how many you have when you count by threes." Copy the numbers on the next line:

2	4	6	8	10
3	6	9	12	15

Repeat the demonstration with one line in each group, four lines in each group, and five lines in each group. When each demonstration is completed, copy the numbers on the matrix you are forming. When you are through, the matrix should look like this:

1	2	3	4	5
2	4	6	8	10
3	6	9	12	15
4	8	12	16	20
5	10	15	20	25

5. Demonstrate how to use the chart.

Draw a heavy line to the right of the first column of numbers:

1	2	3	4	5
2	4	6	8	10
3	6	9	12	15
4	8	12	16	20
5	10	15	20	25

Run your finger up and down to the left of the line as you talk.

"Watch how this works. If I want to count by threes, what number do I start with? . . . Yes, three. If I want to count by fours, what number do I start with? . . . Four. If I want to count by ones, what number do I start with? . . . Yes, one. So I just look over here for the number I want to count by. If I tell you to count by twos, where would you start? Show me. . . . Good. And, John, this is for you: If I tell you to count by fives, show me where you start. . . . Good. Mary, if I tell you to count by ones, where do you start? . . . Good."

Present tasks that involve counting by a given number three or four times: "Henry, show me where you'd start if you wanted to count by fives." As the child touches the 5 in the left column, tell him, "O.K., count by fives *three times*. How many times are you going to count? . . . *Three times*. O.K., count three times." The child may touch the number 10 and say "one time." If he does, stop him; put his hand on the 5 and say "one time." Move to the 10 and say "two times." Move to the 15 and say "three times." Then say, "Now you do it all by yourself: count three times." Have the child count aloud as he advances. When he has counted the third time, *hold his hand on the 15 and say*, "Look at it. How many do you end up with when you count by fives three times? . . . Read it: fifteen."

Next have someone count four times by a given number: "John, show me where you'd start if you wanted to count by twos. . . . Good. Now let's see you count by twos four times. Count four times. How many times are you going to count? . . . Four times. Go." If the child has trouble, lead him through the counting procedure; then have him repeat the operation on his own. When he has finished, hold his hand on the 8 and ask, "When you count by twos four times, how many do you end up with?" Point to the 8.

Give each child turns at counting by different numbers three or four times. Avoid counting by threes three times, fours four times, and the like. Also go light on counting by ones.

After working on two or three simple counting tasks a day for ten days, introduce tasks that involve counting one time, two times, and five times.

"Listen big, because this is tough. Who can count by threes five times? . . . Wait a minute. What are you going to count by? . . . Threes. And how many times are you going to count? . . . Five times." If the child seems confused as he approaches the matrix, ask, "What are you going to count by?" If he answers correctly, say, "So find the three." After he finds the 3 in the left column, ask, "And how many times are you going to count? . . . Yes, five times. So count five times."

Withdraw the cues as quickly as possible, until the children can handle the task when it is presented as a whole rather than as two separate operations: "O.K., John, count by fours two times. You know what you're going to do? . . . What? . . . O.K., do it."

6. Introduce graphic problems as soon as the children have begun to grasp the basic operation of counting by a number so many times (perhaps after the third day).

Draw a rectangle on the board and divide it as shown below.

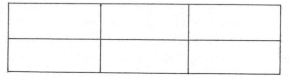

Point to the left column. "How many boxes are here? . . . Two." Point to the middle column. "How many boxes are here? . . . Two." Point to the right column. "How many boxes are here? . . . Two." If we wanted to count all of these boxes, we could count by what? . . . By twos." Point to each column and say, "Two here. . . . So we can count by twos."

Ask, "How many times would we have to count?" Put your hand on the first column of boxes, then on the second and third columns. "One time . . . two times . . . three times. We could count by twos three times. I can write that."

2 ×

"That tells me to count by twos." Erase the 2 and replace it with a 4:

4 ×

"What does that tell me to do? . . . Count by fours." Erase the 4 and write a 5:

5 ×

"What does that tell me to do? . . . Count by fives." Erase the 5 and replace it with a 2. "What does that tell me to do? . . . Good. Does it tell me how many times to count? . . . No. It says to count by twos."

Complete the statement:

$$2 \times 3 = b$$

"Now it tells me to count by twos three times. . . ." Point to the 3. "Do we know how many we'll end up with? . . . No, that's what we have to figure out."

Go over the statement several more times, until the children can indicate what the statement tells them to do. Don't have them read the statement; merely indicate that it tells them to count by twos three times. (NOTE: A number of elementary school texts interpret the statements differently, translating 2×3 into "counting two times by three." Do not use this interpretation. For the algebra problems that are to come in the following sections, the children must have a clear idea of the number they are counting by, and the traditional translation does not work well with algebra problems.)

Refer back to the boxes. "Remember, if we want to count these boxes a fast way, we can count by twos how many times? . . . Three times. Let's do it." Move to the matrix. "I'm going to count by twos, so I find the two. . . . Got it. I'm going to count by twos three times, so I count three times: one time . . . two times . . . three times. What do I end up with? . . . I end up with six." Complete the equation:

$$2 \times 3 = 6$$

Refer to the rectangle. "Hey, look at that. The chart says that there are six boxes in here. I don't think that chart is right. It doesn't look like there are six boxes to me." Some of the children may agree with you. "Let's see who thinks there are six boxes there. Raise your hand if you think there are six boxes. . . . O.K., let's see. How can we find out how many boxes are there? Count them." Call on a child to count the boxes. Conclude, "Oh, oh. The chart was right. We ended up with six boxes. Let's try another problem and see if we can fool the chart."

7. Draw a rectangle divided into three rows, each of which contains five boxes:

"I'll bet we can fool the chart with this one. Let's see what we can count by." Point to each column and ask, "How many here?" After referring to each column, conclude, "So we can count by fives. I can write that."

$$5 \times$$

"We can count by fives. I wonder how many times we count." Run your hand over each column, saying, "One time . . . two times . . . three times. We can count by five three times. I can write that."

Refer to beginning of the statement you had written on the board: "Count by fives"—write the 3—"three times."

$$5 \times 3 = c$$

"What does this tell us to do? Count by fives three times, and we don't know how many we'll end up with. Let's see what the chart says. Who can count by fives three times?"

After the child carries out the operation, say, "O.K., the chart says we end up with fifteen. Let's write that down."

$$5 \times 3 = 15$$

"Now I know we've fooled the chart. Look at those boxes. There aren't fifteen boxes there. I'll bet there aren't even ten boxes there. Who thinks the chart is right? . . . Let's see. How do we find out? . . . Count the boxes."

Count the boxes and act disappointed about being "wrong": "That chart is hard to fool, isn't it? But I haven't given up. I'll think of some way to fool it tomorrow."

8. Use the same procedure every day until the children are very firm in their understanding that the chart cannot be fooled. Introduce a variety of problems that can be worked on the matrix (1×5, 4×3, 3×5, 3×2, 5×1, etc.). Refer to multiplying as counting a fast way: "We can count the boxes one at a time, but I know a fast way. We can count this column and this column and all the other columns because each column has four boxes. We can count by fours. That's the fast way."

As the children become familiar with the operation, withdraw the cues used initially.

If they have trouble with the operation, however, structure the task so that they can ask themselves the right questions: "What are you

going to count by? . . . How many times are you going to count? . . .
What do you end up with?" The answer to the last question may give
some children trouble. If they count five times, they may say five instead of reading the number on the chart. To help them work through
the operation, tell them what they have done as soon as they have finished counting: "Good—you counted five times. What did you end
up with?" The child is less likely to answer five because you have explained how the five fits into the operation. "Look. How many do you
end up with? . . . Twenty. Good."

9. As the children become familiar with the box problems, introduce graphic problems of another kind: "Here's a story about John.
Every time John is a good boy, his mother gives him two pennies. Hey,
that sounds like fun. So one time, John is a good boy and what happens? His mother gives him two pennies." Draw two circles on the
board. "There they are. Then another time, John is a good boy and
what happens? Two pennies." Draw two more circles to the right of
the first pair. "Another time, John is a good boy and what happens?
Two more pennies. . . . And another time. . . . And another time."

"Look at all those pennies. John wants to count them. How can
he do that? Who wants to show me?" Let one of the children count the
pennies. "Yes, John has ten pennies. But you counted them the slow
way. There's a fast way to count them. Here's how." Point to each
group of pennies and ask, "How many pennies are here? . . . Two."
Then conclude, "Two here . . . two here, two here, two here, two here.
So we could count by twos. How many times would we count?" Touch
each group as you count. "One time . . . two times . . . five times. We
could count by twos five times. I can write that. What do I want to
write? Count by twos five times."

$$2 \times 5 = c$$

"Now who can work that on the chart?" Call on a child and have
him carry out the counting operation. "The chart is right. We end up
with ten."

$$2 \times 5 = 10$$

317

Introduce a variety of similar problems that can be worked on the chart. For example, one of the children in the class finds three marbles every time he goes to the playground. He goes to the playground one time, another time. How many marbles does he find? One of the children in the class gets three pennies every time he's a good boy. Another child grows two new teeth every time he goes swimming. Another child buys four candy bars every time he goes to the store. And so forth. Work each of the problems in the same way. Diagram it, using circles or rectangles to represent the objects that are being accumulated. Then have the children make a statement about how they could count all the objects a fast way. Hold the children increasingly responsible for the production of the statement. Then indicate that you can write what they have said ($5 \times 3 = a$, $2 \times 4 = a$, etc.).

After the children become familiar with the form of the multiplication statement, you may pretend to have some difficulty writing the problem and ask the children if they can help you out. Soon they will ask if they can write the problem for you. Lavishly praise the children who write the problem correctly.

10. Introduce a permanent multiplication chart after the children have worked both types of problems outlined in the preceding sections and can write the appropriate statements for a given problem. The permanent chart should be on heavy poster board, measuring about 20 inches on each side.

1	2	3	4	5	6	7	8	9	10
2	4	6	8	10	12	14	16	18	20
3	6	9	12	15	18	21	24	27	30
4	8	12	16	20	24	28	32	36	40
5	10	15	20	25	30	35	40	45	50
6	12	18	24	30	36	42	48	54	60
7	14	21	28	35	42	49	56	63	70
8	16	24	32	40	48	56	64	72	80
9	18	27	36	45	54	63	72	81	90
10	20	30	40	50	60	70	80	90	100

Also prepare a small individual chart for each child. Make these on standard $8\frac{1}{2} \times 11$ paper.

The children should have no trouble with the larger chart. The procedure for working a problem is the same as with the smaller matrix. One first finds (in the left column) the number he is going to count by.

He then moves to the right, counting as many times as the problem specifies. After he has completed the counting operation, he reads the last number counted. That number tells him how many he ends up with.

Present more elaborate problems that can be worked with the larger chart: "Look at this chart. See? It shows how to count by different numbers. But I figured out a way to fool it." Draw this figure:

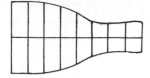

"How many are in the first column? . . . Two. In the next column? . . . Two." And so on. "So I could count by twos. Who knows how many times I would count? . . . Yes, eight times. Who can write that?"

$2 \times 8 = r$

"Now I know we can fool the chart with this one, because some of these boxes are small and some are big. Who thinks we can fool the chart now?" Perhaps none of the children will agree with you. "Let's see what the chart says. Henry, do it. . . . The chart says we end up with sixteen squares. Oh, that's silly. There aren't sixteen squares. We can see that, can't we? So why don't I just erase everything. The chart is wrong." The children will probably object that the squares should be counted. "O.K., I'll count them." Count with great confidence until you come to the last two squares. Then begin to act dejected. The children will probably be delighted that the chart is right. "I just can't seem to fool that chart. But I'll keep trying."

Introduce two problems of this type a day and two problems involving object counting (counting four pennies seven times, etc.).

From time to time, demonstrate the relation between the numbers on the chart and boxes in the figure. After the children have worked the problem on the chart, have them count the boxes.

As they count each column, put the number of the last box counted below the column: "One, two, three, four, five, six"—write 6 below the first column (do not interrupt the children's counting)—"seven, eight, nine, ten, eleven, twelve . . ." Write 12 below the second column. Continue until all the boxes have been counted.

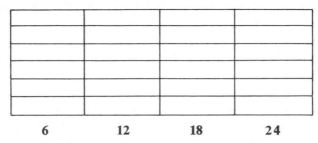

| 6 | 12 | 18 | 24 |

Compare the numbers below the boxes with those on the chart: "Look at these numbers. They are the same numbers that are on the chart." Have a child point to the numbers in the 6 row of the chart and read them. As he reads each number, point out that you have the same number below the figure.

Use the same procedure with the story problems. Write the total under each group of objects. Then point out that these numbers are the same as those on the chart:

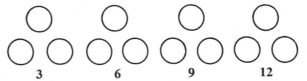

| 3 | 6 | 9 | 12 |

"John, read the numbers on the chart when you count by threes. See if we have the same numbers here."

These exercises help remind the children that the information on the chart is based on object counting.

11. Have the children read the problems before working them. After they have indicated what to write—for example, $5 \times 8 = r$—say, "Let me show you how to read this problem." Point to each symbol as you read. "Five times eight equals how many?"

After the children have worked the problem, have them read the completed statement and repeat it several times: "Five times eight equals forty."

Relate this statement to the familiar counting operation: "Yes, if you count by fives eight times, you end up with forty. Good."

320

12. Next, have the children work problems without the help of graphic representations.

Present this problem:

$$6 \times 4 = r$$

Tell the children to read it. Some of the children may start saying "Count by six four times." Correct them. "That's what *it tells you to do*. But let's *read it*. Do it with me." Point to each symbol as you read. "Six times four equals how many?" Call on several children in the group to read it. "Good reading. Now tell me. What does this problem *tell* you do do?"

Present three to five similar multiplication problems during each session. At first, have the children read the problem and then indicate what it tells them to do.

After they have become familiar with this sequence, begin reversing the order. Put a problem on the board and ask, "What does it tell me to do?" After the children answer this question, have them read it, then work it. The purpose of these exercises is to demonstrate that the written problem is both a statement that can be read (or treated as a fact) and a directive that tells you what to do. The children must become thoroughly familiar with both functions of the written statement.

13. Teach the children to count by various numbers. Do not devote more than about two minutes of each session to rote counting.

Teach them to count by fives first. Some may already know how to count by fives.

Then work on twos. Then tens.

Do not introduce counting by any other numbers until the children can perform well on these.

14. As they become proficient at counting by fives, introduce tasks similar to those introduced in connection with counting by ones.

Have the children count to a given number: "Let's hear you count by fives to thirty."

Have them count from a given number: "Let's count by fives and start with fifteen. Fifteen . . ."

Have them indicate what comes after a given number when you count by fives: "When you count by fives, what comes after forty?"

15. Introduce a finger operation for counting by fives, twos, and tens.

Write this problem on the board:

$$5 \times 3 = m$$

"I can work this problem without even looking at the chart. What am I going to count by? . . . Five. I have to remember that. I'm going to count by fives. How many times am I going to count? . . . Three times. *So I hold up three fingers.* Here I go, counting by fives." Touch each finger as you count, "Five, ten, *fifteen.* I end up with fifteen." Have a child work the same problem on the chart to check your answer.

Give the children various problems that entail counting by fives, twos, and tens. At first have them count only two, three, or four times. As they become familiar with the operation, drop the cues.

The difficult part of the finger operation is to remember that the second number in the problem tells one how many fingers to hold up. Sometimes the children will read the first number in the problem and hold up that many fingers. For example, if the problem is $5 \times 4 = a$, the children may hold up five fingers. If they make this kind of mistake, introduce a series of problems in which the first number changes and the second remains constant:

$$5 \times 4 = c$$
$$2 \times 4 = r$$
$$10 \times 4 = n$$

This kind of series will help them to see the role of the second number. "How many times are we going to count in this first problem? . . . Four times. Let's see those fingers. . . ."

After the children have mastered the basic finger operation for counting two, three, and four times, have them count five, six, and seven times. Where the problem involves counting more than five times, instruct them to use both hands.

Present the children with individual worksheets, each with five to seven problems. Tell them to work the problems with their fingers. A typical sheet might look like this:

$$2 \times 6 = \square \qquad 5 \times 6 = \square$$
$$5 \times 2 = \square \qquad 10 \times 3 = \square$$
$$10 \times 7 = \square \qquad 2 \times 7 = \square$$

16. After the children have demonstrated that they can work the finger-operation problems without assistance, introduce algebraic problems.

Present them first as story problems: "Here's a story about Mary. Every time Mary is a good girl, she gets two dimes. Wow, two dimes!

And Mary is a good girl a lot of times. Here's how many dimes she has. . . . Fourteen dimes. She ends up with fourteen dimes."

"I wonder how many times she was a good girl. Let's find out. How many dimes did she get every time she was a good girl? . . . Two. So we have to count by twos. I can write that:

$2 \times$

"We count by twos. Do we know how many times we count? . . . No, that's what we have to figure out. So I have to put something that says I don't know how many times we count."

$2 \times c$

"Do we know how many dimes she ended up with? . . . Well, here they are. How many did she end up with? . . . Yes, fourteen. She ended up with fourteen. I can write that."

$2 \times c = 14$

Point to the symbols as you translate the problem. "We have to count by twos how many times to end up with fourteen? What do we have to do? . . . Count by twos, and we don't know how many times. But we know we're going to end up with fourteen."

To work the problem on the chart, have the child first find the number he's going to count by: "You're going to count by twos, so find the two." After the child finds the 2, say, "Now you've got to count until you end up with fourteen. Where is the fourteen?" Have the child put his other hand on the 14. "O.K., count until you end up with fourteen, and remember—you've got to tell me how many times you count." Do not let the child say simply "one, two, three . . ." as he points to the numbers in the 2 row on the chart. Insist that he say "one time, two times, three times . . . seven times." As soon as he has finished counting, say, "How many times? . . . Seven times." Erase the c in the problem and replace it with a seven:

$2 \times 7 = 14$

Relate the answer to the story problem: "How many times was Mary a good girl? . . . Seven times." Now refer to the group of circles. "Let's see if that's right. Every time Mary was a good girl she got two dimes." Draw a circle around the first group of dimes: "Here are two dimes. So she was a good girl one time." As you draw a circle around each group of dimes, count "two times . . . three times . . ."

Present similar problems every day.

17. Introduce algebra problems in connection with boxes.

Draw a large rectangle on the board and divide it as shown below. Write the number 12 inside the rectangle.

Count the divisions on the left side of the figure. "Look over on this side. There are two boxes on this side. That means we have to count by twos." Run your finger across the top of the rectangle. "We don't know how many times we're going to count, but look here." Point to the 12. "We know that there are twelve boxes. When we count all of the boxes, we'll end up with twelve."

Summarize: "We've got to count by twos how many times to end up with twelve? I can write that."

$$2 \times r = 12$$

Have the children work the problem on the chart by finding the 2 (the number they will count by). Then have them find the number they are going to end up with (12). Finally, have them count and indicate how many times they counted. "You counted six times, so I can erase the *r* and put a six."

$$2 \times 6 = 12$$

Check the answer by referring to the diagram. Run your finger across the top of the rectangle. "The chart says that we'll have six boxes up here. It says we've got to count six times." Draw in the vertical lines. Draw them quickly and do not let the children count with you. The reason is that to make six boxes across the top, you make only *five* vertical lines.

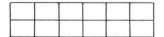

"Now, let's count the boxes and see if we end up with twelve boxes." After counting, say, "Well, the chart is right again."

18. Show the children how to use their fingers to solve problems that involve counting by twos, fives, and tens.

Introduce the operation with this problem:

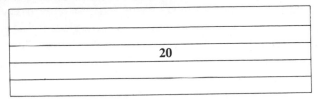

Count the divisions on the left side of the figure. "We're going to count by fives. We don't know how many times, but we know that we're going to end up with twenty. Let's count."

Every time you count, hold up a finger. "Five, ten, fifteen, twenty. Here's how many times we counted. Four times." Refer to the figure. "That means we have to have four boxes across the top."

$$5 \times 4 = 20$$

"Let's count them and see if the chart is right. . . . Yep, right again."

Present at least one problem of this kind every day until the children are solid.

19. Present problems that do not involve graphic representations.

First, introduce the problem $5 \times a = 15$. "What does it tell us to do? . . . Count by fives how many times to end up with fifteen."

If the children are shaky in interpreting the problem, point to the 5 and ask, "Do we know what to count by? . . . Yes." Point to the a and ask, "Do we know how many times? . . . No. That's what we have to figure out—how many times we count." Point to the 15. "Do we know how many we're going to end up with? How many?"

Have one of the children come up to the board and "show me what we don't know." When the child points to the a, say, "Yes, we don't know how . . ." and have the child complete the statement.

Repeat this procedure with a variety of similar problems.

Present problems in which the children will end up with relatively large numbers, even though they may not be able to read them. When reading a large number to the children (such as 81, 49, or 72), point to the first digit and read it in a dragged-out manner—"sevennnnty"—then pause before pointing to the second digit: "two." (The problem numbers are the 20s, 30s, 50s, and teens—which are read backward.)

At first concentrate on the regular numbers (sixties, seventies, forties, etc.) and do not introduce many teens or other irregulars.

Then begin to program irregulars. When a child is first exposed to irregulars, he may read 56 as "five-ty-six." Do not tell him that he is wrong, because he is simply generalizing a procedure that applies for other two-digit numbers. Tell him, "Yes, that's good, John, but we don't say five-ty; we say fifty. It's a funny number."

The teens are more difficult because if they were to be consistent with the other numbers, we would have to read 14 as "teen-four." Expect the children to have some difficulty with the teens, but do not allow this difficulty to delay learning of the regular two-digit numbers.

As the children become familiar with the operation of finding out how many times they have to count, start withdrawing the prompts used in the initial presentation.

20. After the children have learned to work with a minimum of prompting, present sheets that contain both regular and algebraic multiplication problems (a total of six to eight).

At first, group the algebraic problems together and the regular problems together. An initial sheet might look like this:

$$3 \times \square = 15 \qquad 7 \times 6 = \square$$
$$5 \times \square = 35 \qquad 9 \times 3 = \square$$
$$2 \times \square = 10 \qquad 10 \times 4 = \square$$

Remind the children, "Look at the problem and see what you have to find out. What do you have to find out in the first problem? . . . That's right, how many times. What do you have to find out in the last problem? . . . That's right, how many you end up with. O.K., work them."

After the children have learned to handle these problems, start to mix the regular and algebraic problems in the sheets. Try to include on each sheet a problem that involves counting by twos, one that involves counting by fives, and one that involves counting by tens.

21. Introduce algebra problems in which there is no times sign. If this convention is presented properly, the children should have no trouble with it.

326

Write this problem on the board:

$$6c = 12$$

"This is a tricky problem. If you want to work it, you have to pretend; you have to pretend there's a little bitty times sign right here." Make a small dot between the 6 and the *c:*

$$6 \cdot c = 12$$

"That times sign is so small you can't even see it. But you know it's there. When you see two things stuck together like this six and this *c*, there's a little bitty times sign in there. O.K., what does it tell you to do? . . . That's right—count by six how many times to end up with twelve. Let's do it on the chart. . . . How many times do you count? Two times. So I erase the *c* and put a two."

$$6 \cdot 2 = 12$$

"Oh, we'd better make that times sign bigger or this answer will be silly. Someone might think it's a sixty-two. Does sixty-two equal twelve? . . . No, six times two equals twelve."

$$6 \times 2 = 12$$

Present various problems without the times sign. Include problems of this type on the children's daily worksheets:

$$6a = 24 \qquad a =$$
$$7 \times 9 = a \qquad a =$$
$$4a = 24 \qquad a =$$
$$10a = 70 \qquad a =$$

Have the children specify what the unknown equals by completing the statement to the right of each problem. They should have no trouble with this operation. They will use it in tasks that are to come.

22. Introduce story problems that can be written as problems without signs.

Begin with this problem: "A man walks into a store and he says to the storekeeper, 'I want to buy a candy bar.' The storekeeper says, 'O.K., five candy bars cost thirty cents.' What did he say? Listen big: Five candy bars cost thirty cents. The man says, 'But I don't want to buy five candy bars. I want to buy one candy bar.' How much does one candy bar cost? Let's figure it out. What do we know? We know that

327

five candy bars cost thirty cents. Let's write that."

$$5c = 30$$

"Remember, we've got to pretend that there's a little bitty times sign after the five. Let's work it. . . . Yes, c (or candy bar) equals six. So I can erase the c and put a six."

$$5 \times 6 = 30 \qquad c = 6\cent$$

Introduce a variety of similar problems. Concentrate on examples that involve buying: "A girl wants to buy one orange. There's a sign in the store. The sign says, 'Six oranges cost forty-two cents.' The girl says, 'I don't want to buy six oranges. I want to buy one orange.' "

At first help the children through each step of the problem. After they have worked with various examples, make them increasingly responsible for setting the problem up: "What do I write?" If the children can't answer, say, "O.K., listen to the problem again. Listen good, because you'll have to tell me what to write." Later, call on one child to write out the problem and another child to work it. Also have the children work some of these word problems from the verbal presentation: "Let's see if you can work this problem without writing it down. Listen big. Henry wants a bottle of pop, but the man in the store tells him that ten bottles of pop cost ninety cents. Ten bottles cost ninety cents. What does one bottle cost?" After the children have worked the problem, write it on the board: "Let's see if your answer is correct. What do I write?"

$$10B = 90$$

"Count by tens how many times to end up with ninety. . . . We count nine times. So B equals nine."

Present word problems on daily worksheets. Keep the wording simple. Give them four to six problems on a sheet:

Five balls cost 35¢. What does one ball cost?
Two shoes cost $10. What does one shoe cost?
Ten cans of beans cost 70¢. What does one can of beans cost?
Two dogs cost $14. What does one dog cost?

Multiplication facts

As the children demonstrate that they can handle the various types of problems outlined above, devote about two minutes at the beginning of each period to a drill on multiplication facts.

1. For the first drill, write these three facts on the board:

$$5 \times 1 = 5$$
$$5 \times 2 = 10$$
$$5 \times 3 = 15$$

Have the children read each statement several times. Prepare them for a race: "You better really remember these, because I know them and I could beat you in a race."

After they have indicated that they think they have learned the facts, race with them. (Draw a box on the board; then present questions: "What's five times three? . . . What's five times one? . . .") Repeat those facts that give the children the most trouble. Work on the first three facts every day until the children have mastered them.

2. Present new facts. Begin with two new facts in the fives series, mixing them with the old facts. Continue in this manner until the children have learned all the five facts.

Then present the twos, adding two new facts at a time.

After the twos have been mastered, introduce the other numbers in this order: tens, nines, threes, sixes, fours, sevens, eights.

Consolidation problems

From time to time, give the children sheets that contain a variety of problem types they have studied. They should encounter every type of problem they have worked at least once a week. If they have difficulty with any of the older problems, don't be surprised. They have a number of different forms they must keep straight. Show them how to work the troublesome problems, and then concentrate on similar ones for a few days. A typical consolidation sheet might look like this:

$$4 + \square = 9 \qquad\qquad 2 - 5 = \square$$
$$\sim6 + \square = 0 \qquad\qquad 5 \times \square = 40$$
$$8 + 6 = \square \qquad\qquad 8 - \square = 0$$
$$6 - 5 = \square \qquad\qquad 6 - \square = \sim3$$
$$7 \times 4 = \square \qquad\qquad 9 \times 5 = \square$$

Consolidation sheets of this type help you direct your efforts to the trouble spots that may be developing. These sheets are powerful diagnostic tools if you make use of them. When children are able to handle all the problems on sheets similar to the one above (which tests all of the operations presented), they are ready to move on to fractions and more complicated problem-solving operations.

7 Arithmetic for the More Advanced Child

The preceding chapter outlined procedures for teaching the basic operations of addition, subtraction, and multiplication, with emphasis on how these operations relate to counting. The present chapter takes the child into more advanced operations—column addition (and carrying), column subtraction (and borrowing), and a variety of fraction operations. These operations build on those outlined in the preceding chapter, which means that a child must know the basic operational procedures before he can handle the complex tasks presented in this chapter.

The most economical means of placing children who seem to be proficient in arithmetic is to start them on the tasks presented in this chapter. If they have difficulty with a particular task, back up and teach the basic operations they have not mastered (referring to the preceding chapter); then proceed with other tasks in this chapter. If you find yourself dropping back repeatedly, the children are not ready for the tasks in this chapter.

Structure the arithmetic period so that the children are spending about half their time on one set of exercises and half on another. A workable procedure is to start on column addition below and fractions (p. 344) at about the same time. Proceed with the tasks outlined in each section. Spend a few minutes each day on fact learning. Review when necessary, making sure that the children make use of the operations they have been taught.

Column Addition and Subtraction

Column addition

Children can be taught column addition very quickly. The secret is to demonstrate that every element in the in-line statement is preserved in the column statement.

1. Present this statement on the board:

$$5 + 3 = 8$$

Have the children check the statement to make sure that it is true. "Is that right? Is five plus three the same as eight?" Have the children read the statement several times. Then tell them, "I'm going to show you a new way to write this problem. This is tough, so you'll have to watch carefully." Erase the 5 and put it above the 3:

$$\begin{array}{r} 5 \\ + 3 = 8 \end{array}$$

"Let's read it." Touch each symbol as you read. "Five plus three equals eight." Call on one or two of the children to read the statement and point as they read.

Erase the equals sign and draw a line under the 3. "Look what's happened to the equals. Here it is. It turned into a line."

Move the 8 below the line:

$$\begin{array}{r} 5 \\ + 3 \\ \hline 8 \end{array}$$

"Who thinks he can read this problem now?" The chances are that most of the children in the group will be able to read it. As they do, make sure that they touch each of the symbols: "John, you didn't touch this. What is it? . . . Equals. This is the equals sign."

2. Present the problem

$$\begin{array}{r} 4 \\ + 3 \\ \hline 7 \end{array}$$

and have the children read it. Present several other complete statements before proceeding to the next task.

3. Present the problem

$$\begin{array}{r} 9 \\ + 1 \\ \hline r \end{array}$$

and have the children read it. Then say, "O.K., what does nine plus one equal? . . . Yes, ten." Erase the r and replace it with a 10.

Present several other problems that the children can answer without actually adding the two numbers.

Next, present several more difficult problems:

$$
\begin{array}{r}
8 \\
+\ 13 \\
\hline
s
\end{array}
$$

Call on one of the children to do what it says. Make the tally marks to the right of the problem:

$$
\begin{array}{r}
8 \\
+\ 13 \\
\hline
21
\end{array}
$$

"We have twenty-one lines on this side of the equals sign"—point above the line—"so we'll have twenty-one lines on this side of the equals sign. Twenty-one equals twenty-one."

4. Present longer problems such as this:

$$
\begin{array}{r}
4 \\
+\ 6 \\
+\ 3 \\
+\ 5 \\
\hline
m
\end{array}
$$

Put a plus sign in front of each number, so that the children will know what operation is called for with each number.

After the children have worked on problems like this for several days, present problems in which only one plus sign appears:

$$
\begin{array}{r}
8 \\
2 \\
5 \\
+\ 3 \\
\hline
\end{array}
$$

"Look at this problem. There's only one plus sign. Do you know what that tells you? That tells you that all these numbers are plussed. You do the same thing with every number."

Present four to six of these problems every day. The children should be able to work them on individual sheets within two days after the new problem form has been introduced. A sheet should contain both short and long problems:

6	4	5	7	2
1	1	+ 8	1	2
+ 5	1		2	2
	3		1	2
	6		+ 3	2
	+ 2			+ 2

Carrying

Carrying is not difficult to demonstrate.

1. First, show the children how to add two-digit numbers.
Write the following column of numbers on the board:

1
2
3
4
5

Have the children read each of the numbers. Then draw a vertical
line to the right of the numbers:

1 |
2 |
3 |
4 |
5 |

Point to the 1. "Here's a rule. When you see a one on this side of
the line, it's not a one. It's a ten." Point to the 2. "When you see a two
on this side of the line, it's not a two. It's a twenty." Continue in the
same manner with 3, 4, and 5.

Form two-digit numbers out of each of the numbers in the column
by adding zeros on the right side of the vertical line:

1 | 0
2 | 0
3 | 0
4 | 0
5 | 0

Point to the 1. "Remember—when it's on this side of the line, it's
not a one; it's a . . . That's right. A ten. What's ten"—point to the zero
—"plus zero? . . . *Ten.* That's what this number is."

Point to the 2. "Remember—when it's over here, it's a twenty. What's twenty plus zero?" Point to the zero. "Twenty."

Continue through the remaining numbers in this manner. Review the numbers several times. Encourage the children to give the addition statement as you point. They should say "ten" as you point to the first digit, "plus zero" as you point to the second, and "equals ten" as you run your finger from left to right under the two-digit number.

Erase the zeros and replace them with 1s:

1 | 1
2 | 1
3 | 1
4 | 1
5 | 1

Point to the first digit in 11. "Remember—when it's on this side of the line, it's a . . . O.K., what's ten"—point to the second digit— "plus one? . . . Eleven. That's what this number is." Point to the first digit in 21. "Remember—this is a what? Is it a two? . . . It's a twenty. That's right. And what's twenty . . . plus one?" Run your finger from left to right under the number. "Twenty-one."

Go through all the numbers in this manner. Review all numbers several times with the children. Then erase the 1s and replace them with 2s:

1 | 2
2 | 2
3 | 2
4 | 2
5 | 2

Point to the digits in the first number and ask, "What's ten plus two? . . . Twelve." Point to the digits in the second number and ask, "What's twenty plus two? . . . Twenty-two."

Repeat this demonstration on two or three days, cutting down on the cueing and making the children increasingly responsible for identifying the numbers that are to the left of the vertical line as ten or twenty rather than one or two. Also, hold them responsible for the addition statement that is implied by the two-digit number.

2. After the children have demonstrated that they understand the kind of addition statement that is implied by two-digit numbers, present a more random group of two-digit numbers and have the children interpret them. Make sure that they are exposed to many ones, both to the right and to the left of the dividing line. Every group of numbers should include 11:

```
6 | 4
1 | 5
1 | 1
8 | 1
3 | 7
```

"O.K., let's add up the first number. Is that a six? . . . No. That's right, a sixty. Sixty plus four equals sixty-four. Look at this next number. Is that a one? . . . No, a ten. Ten plus five equals fifteen."

From time to time, demonstrate that these statements are true: "Let's see if ten plus five does equal fifteen." Hold up your fist. "I've got ten in here. And I'm going to plus five. . . . Ten, eleven, twelve, thirteen, fourteen, fifteen. It's true. Let's do the first problem. Let's see if sixty plus four equals sixty-four. I've got sixty in here and I'm going to plus four. Go. Sixty . . . sixty-one . . ."

3. Before introducing carrying, remind the children of the rule. Write the number 11 on the board. Refer to the left digit. "Remember —if it's over here, it's a ten. And if it's a ten it has to be over here." Point to the second digit in 11. "Can this be a ten? . . . No. When it's over here, it's a one."

Write this problem:

```
    1 | 8
  + | 3
    ┼
```

"I'm going to show you a tricky way to work this problem." Point to each digit and ask, "What's this?" The answers should be ten, eight, and three. "Remember the rule, now. If it's a ten, where does it have to go?" Slap the left side of the dividing line. "Over here. We can't have a ten on this side [the right], can we? What's eight plus three? . . . Figure it out? . . . Eleven. So I just write eleven down here."

```
    1 | 8
  + | 3
    ┼──
    | 11
```

"Trouble. We've got trouble. Look down there. I see a ten and he's on the wrong side of the line. Ten, what are you doing over there?" Erase the first digit of the 11. "Where do tens go? . . . Over on this side. Here you go, ten—over where you belong."

```
1 |
1 | 8
+ | 3
——|——
  | 1
```

"Now the tens are together. What's ten plus ten?" If the children have trouble, ask, "What's one plus one?" Put a 2 below the line:

```
1 |
1 | 8
+   | 3
——|——
2 | 1
```

"So ten plus ten equals—when it's over here it's not a two, it's a . . . So ten plus ten equals twenty." Refer to the answer to the problem. "What's twenty plus one? . . . Twenty-one. Eighteen plus three equals twenty-one."

Present similar problems. At first, introduce problems in which one of the numbers to be added is a teen number. The reason for working with teens initially is to help solidify the rule that the tens are to the left of the dividing line. If the children have trouble figuring out where a misplaced ten should go, you can tell them: "You better put him over here with the other ten."

4. As the children become increasingly proficient with the basic problems, introduce problems with three numbers to be added:

```
1 | 6
1 | 3
+ 2 | 2
——|——
```

First have the children add each of the numbers in the column: "Let's add this first number. Ten plus six equals . . ." Next, remind them of the rule: "If it's a ten, where does it have to go? . . . And if it's a one, where does it have to go? . . . Good." Now work the problem. "Remember that we start over here with the little numbers." Point to the right side of the dividing line. "What's six plus three? Figure it out." After the children have arrived at the correct answer, strike out the 6 and the 3 and write a 9:

```
  1 | 6
  1 | 3   9
+ 2 | 2
```

"We're done with these guys. They equal nine. What do we have left to add? . . . A nine and a two. What's nine plus two? . . . Eleven." Cross out the 9 and the 2. "We've got eleven above the equals sign, so how many do we have to have below the equals sign? . . . Eleven. So I just write an eleven down here."

At this time the children will probably be up in arms, objecting that the ten is on the wrong side of the line. "Right. Eleven is really ten . . . plus one. And ten, you can't be over here. Wait a minute. I forget where I should put him. Who can help me out?" One of the children will probably come to your rescue.

"We've got a whole bunch of tens over here. How many do we have? . . . Three—ten, twenty, *thirty*. Hey, that's just like counting by tens." Cross out the three tens and write a 3. "What's thirty plus twenty? What's three plus two? Figure it out. . . . Five. So thirty plus twenty equals . . ."

```
    x |
  3 x | 6
    x | 3   9
+ 2   | 2
  ────────
  5 | 1
```

"Look at the answer. We've got a fifty plus one. That's . . . Yes, fifty-one. We figured it out."

When the opportunity arises in working these problems, call attention to the relation between adding a group of tens and counting by tens. Structure problems so that the children get a great deal of exposure to this relation. During a session you might present the following problems that involve carrying.

$$
\begin{array}{c|c}
1 & 7 \\
1 & 3 \\
1 & 1 \\
+ & 3 \\
\hline
\end{array}
\qquad
\begin{array}{c|c}
1 & 9 \\
2 & 2 \\
4 & 1 \\
+1 & 1 \\
\hline
\end{array}
\qquad
\begin{array}{c|c}
 & 6 \\
1 & 4 \\
1 & 2 \\
+1 & 2 \\
\hline
\end{array}
$$

When the tens are separated as they are in the left-hand problem above, show the children that they can add them up and then move on to the other numbers in that column as long as they remember to cross out every number that is added: "How many tens do I have over here? . . . Three—ten, twenty, thirty. Let's cross them out to show that we've counted them and put a thirty in place of them."

Do not introduce problems that involve carrying more than ten.

Borrowing

Borrowing involves the reverse of the operation the children have learned in adding tens. They have learned that four tens is equal to forty. When they borrow, they will break down forty into four tens.

1. Acquaint the children with subtraction problems written in column form. Since they have already been introduced to column addition, it is usually necessary only to write a column subtraction problem on the board and to ask them to read it.

Present this problem:

$$
\begin{array}{r}
9 \\
- 1 \\
\hline
r
\end{array}
$$

"Mary, read that for me. . . . Good reading. Can you tell me what nine minus one equals? . . . Good. So I can erase the r and put an eight in its place."

2. After the children have worked three or four similar problems, introduce problems that involve two-digit numbers:

$$
\begin{array}{c|c}
1 & 4 \\
- & 7 \\
\hline
 & m
\end{array}
$$

"Let's all read this problem together: fourteen minus seven equals how many. Who knows? . . . Fourteen minus seven equals seven."

Present other problems that involve the facts the children will use in borrowing problems. These are the primary facts for which they will be responsible:

$$
\begin{array}{r|r} 1 & 8 \\ - & 9 \\ \hline \end{array}
\quad
\begin{array}{r|r} 1 & 6 \\ - & 8 \\ \hline \end{array}
\quad
\begin{array}{r|r} 1 & 6 \\ - & 9 \\ \hline \end{array}
\quad
\begin{array}{r|r} 1 & 4 \\ - & 7 \\ \hline \end{array}
\quad
\begin{array}{r|r} 1 & 4 \\ - & 8 \\ \hline \end{array}
$$

$$
\begin{array}{r|r} 1 & 2 \\ - & 6 \\ \hline \end{array}
\quad
\begin{array}{r|r} 1 & 2 \\ - & 7 \\ \hline \end{array}
\quad
\begin{array}{r|r} 1 & 0 \\ - & 5 \\ \hline \end{array}
\quad
\begin{array}{r|r} 1 & 0 \\ - & 6 \\ \hline \end{array}
$$

Present these problems until the children know the answers without having to figure them out. Work first on the pairs:

$$
\begin{array}{r|r} 1 & 8 \\ - & 9 \\ \hline \end{array}
\quad
\begin{array}{r|r} 1 & 6 \\ - & 8 \\ \hline \end{array}
\quad
\begin{array}{r|r} 1 & 4 \\ - & 7 \\ \hline \end{array}
\quad
\begin{array}{r|r} 1 & 2 \\ - & 6 \\ \hline \end{array}
\quad
\begin{array}{r|r} 1 & 0 \\ - & 5 \\ \hline \end{array}
$$

Then introduce the problems in which one more is minused. As the children are learning these facts, present problems that involve large numbers but that do not involve borrowing. During a session you might present these problems (in addition to the fact learning):

$$
\begin{array}{r|r} 2 & 6 \\ - 1 & 1 \\ \hline \end{array}
\quad
\begin{array}{r|r} 4 & 8 \\ - & 3 \\ \hline \end{array}
\quad
\begin{array}{r|r} 7 & 2 \\ - 6 & 2 \\ \hline \end{array}
\quad
\begin{array}{r|r} 8 & 6 \\ - 7 & 2 \\ \hline \end{array}
\quad
\begin{array}{r|r} 4 & 7 \\ - & 3 \\ \hline \end{array}
\quad
\begin{array}{r|r} 3 & 6 \\ - 1 & 5 \\ \hline \end{array}
$$

3. Next, demonstrate the borrowing operation. Show the children why there is a need to borrow.

Present this problem:

$$
\begin{array}{r|r} 3 & 4 \\ - & 7 \\ \hline \end{array}
$$

"What's thirty-four minus seven? I don't know, so let's work this problem another way. Let's start over here with the smaller numbers, not with the thirty. That's too big. What does four minus seven equal?" If the children give the answer in terms of negative numbers, say, "That's good. But we're going to have trouble with negative numbers. I wonder if there isn't a way we can come up with a regular number." Ponder the problem a minute. "I've got it." Point to the 3. "What is this? . . . Yes, thirty. And I know another way to write thirty: three tens." Hold up three fingers. "Ten, twenty, thirty. We can erase this thirty and put three tens, because three tens is the same as thirty." Write one of the tens where the 3 was. Write the others above it:

```
1 |
1 |
1 | 4
- | 7
——+——
  |
```

Count up the tens: "Ten, twenty, thirty. We've still got thirty over here. This number is still thirty plus four. It's still thirty-four. That's what we started out with, and that's what we've got now." Draw an imaginary line with your finger under 14. "Hey, look at this. Ten plus four. Fourteen. Fourteen minus seven; I know what that is. What is it? . . . Seven." Write a 7 below the equals sign. "Let's cross out the numbers we've used up so we can see what we haven't used."

```
1 |
1 |
1̶ | 4
- | 7̶
——+——
  | 7
```

"All we've got is a ten and a ten. What's that? . . . Twenty. What's twenty minus zero? . . . Twenty."

```
1 |
1 |
1̶ | 4̶
- | 7̶
——+——
2 | 7
```

"Look what we end up with: twenty plus seven. Twenty-seven."

Present a number of similar problems (two digits on top, one digit on the bottom). Always break the number from which you wish to borrow into tens. The children can use all the practice they can get at breaking these numbers down and then recombining the tens to form a new number.

4. Present a new way of writing the number from which you borrow after the children are solid on the borrowing operation above.

```
3 | 8
- | 9
——+——
  |
```

Have the children read the problem and indicate where they are going to start working. "That's right, over here with the smaller numbers. What's eight minus nine? . . . We're in trouble. I wonder what we can do? . . . Turn the thirty into tens? O.K., let's do it. But wait. I think I've got an idea. How many tens are we going to have? . . . Three. O.K., I need one of them here. . . ."

$$\begin{array}{c|c} 1 & 8 \\ \hline - & 9 \\ \hline \end{array}$$

"How many other tens are there? I started out with three and I used used one of them. . . . Two. Two tens. What's that? . . . Yes, twenty. So instead of writing two tens, I'll just write twenty."

$$\begin{array}{c|c} 2 & \\ 1 & 8 \\ \hline - & 9 \\ \hline \end{array}$$

Complete the problem quickly. "What's eighteen minus nine? . . . Nine. Let's cross out the numbers we've used. . . . What's twenty minus zero? . . . Twenty."

$$\begin{array}{c|c} 2 & \\ \cancel{1} & \cancel{8} \\ \hline - & \cancel{9} \\ \hline 2 & 9 \\ \end{array}$$

If the children have trouble seeing the relation between thirty and twenty plus ten, give them a series of worksheet exercises on problems like these:

$$80 = 10 + \square$$
$$70 = 10 + \square$$
$$40 = 10 + \square$$
$$20 = 10 + \square$$
$$90 = 10 + \square$$

(Actually, these sheets are valuable even for children who have a relatively firm intuitive understanding of the operation by which a number is broken down into ten plus another number.) Present a sheet with five to seven problems on it every day until the children can work them almost as quickly as they can write.

Drill them orally on the operation: "Forty. Forty equals ten plus how many? . . . Good. Here's another number: seventy. Seventy equals ten plus how many? . . . Good." When the children have demonstrated that they understand thoroughly, return to the borrowing operation.

Present this problem:

$$
\begin{array}{c|c}
6 & 4 \\
- & 8 \\
\hline
\end{array}
$$

"Here we go again. What's four minus eight? . . . Can't do it without getting a negative number. So what are we going to do? . . . Change the sixty into ten plus something. Sixty equals ten plus how many? . . . Yes, plus fifty. So we can erase the sixty and put ten plus fifty."

$$
\begin{array}{c|c}
5 & \\
1 & 4 \\
- & 8 \\
\hline
\end{array}
$$

"Now we can work it. What's fourteen minus eight? . . . Six. Good. Cross it out. What's fifty minus zero? . . . Fifty. We end up with fifty-six."

5. After the children have worked many problems of this kind and learned to handle the operation without much cueing (that is, when they are able to work the problems on the board—starting in the right place, changing the number into ten plus something, and carrying out the subtraction operation), introduce worksheets. Set the problems up with the dividing line. A typical sheet might look like this:

$$
\begin{array}{c|c}
6 & 4 \\
- & 7 \\
\hline
\end{array}
\qquad
\begin{array}{c|c}
3 & 8 \\
- & 9 \\
\hline
\end{array}
\qquad
\begin{array}{c|c}
4 & 6 \\
- & 9 \\
\hline
\end{array}
\qquad
\begin{array}{c|c}
9 & 2 \\
- & 7 \\
\hline
\end{array}
\qquad
\begin{array}{c|c}
2 & 2 \\
- & 6 \\
\hline
\end{array}
$$

Repeat problems that give the children trouble.

6. Drop the dividing line in both column addition and column subtraction problems after the children have reached this point in the program. First present a problem on the board with the dividing line: "Do you want to see how smart I am? I can work these problems without putting the line in." Erase the line. "I'm probably the only one here who can do this. But I don't even need that line. I still remember how to work these problems."

$$
\begin{array}{r}
34 \\
- 8 \\
\hline
\end{array}
$$

The children will probably demonstrate that they too can handle the problems without the line. If not, make a joke out of it and brag about your ability from time to time. Before very long the children will be able to deflate you. When they show that they can work the problems, act disappointed: "Gee, I didn't think you guys could do that. You're really smart. I'll have to think of something else to fool you on."

7. Introduce borrowing problems in which a two-digit number is subtracted from another two-digit number.

Present this problem:

$$\begin{array}{r} 42 \\ -\ 27 \\ \hline \end{array}$$

The children may have no trouble with this. First they try to take seven from two and find that they can't do it without getting into negative numbers. So they change the forty into ten plus something: "Ten plus thirty." They erase the forty and write a ten and a thirty in its place:

$$\begin{array}{r} 3 \\ 12 \\ -\ 27 \\ \hline \end{array}$$

Then they take seven from twelve. They cross out the numbers they have used. Now there are a three and a two in the left column. "What's thirty minus twenty?" If the children can't answer, ask, "Well, what's three minus two? . . . One." Write a 1 below the line. "So thirty minus twenty equals"—point to the 1—"ten."

$$\begin{array}{r} 3 \\ \cancel{12} \\ -\ \cancel{27} \\ \hline 15 \end{array}$$

"Look at the answer. Ten plus five. Fifteen. We end up with fifteen."

The only new operation in this problem is processing two numbers in the left column.

Once the children have seen the procedure demonstrated with several problems, they should have no trouble with the operation and should be ready to handle worksheets. Again, make the number from which the children will borrow very small. As the children learn new subtraction facts, include these in the problems:

46	24	35	88	94
− 18	− 19	− 26	− 79	− 47

Present worksheet problems of this kind until all the children understand the borrowing operation.

Fractions

Fractions can be introduced after the children have learned basic addition, subtraction, and multiplication. They do not have to finish column addition and subtraction before starting on fractions.

1. Introduce the fraction $\frac{1}{4}$ and explain to the children how to work with it. Read the fraction not as one-fourth, but as one over four: "This is a fraction. Let's read it. One over four. Let's read it again. . . ."

Point to the 4. "Do you know what this fraction tells you? It tells you that each group has four parts." Draw two circles. Divide each into four parts:

Count the parts in each circle with the children. "Here's a group of four . . . and here's a group of four. We can make as many groups of four as we want, but each group has to have how many parts? . . . Four." Refer to the fraction again. "The *four* tells us that each group has four parts. The *one* tells us how many parts we have. How many parts do we have? . . . One." Shade in one part of the left circle:

Erase the original fraction (not the diagram) and replace it with the fraction $\frac{3}{4}$. Point to the 4. "This tells us that each group has four parts." Point to the top number. "This tells us how many parts we have. How many parts do we have? . . . Three. So I color in three parts. I've already got one." Color in the two remaining parts. "This is a picture of three over four."

Erase the fraction and replace it with the fraction $\frac{4}{4}$. "What does this bottom number tell us? . . . That each group has four parts. What does this top number tell us? . . . It tells us how many parts we have. How many parts do we have? . . . Four. So I color in four. I've already got one, two, three. So I color in one more. . . . There's a picture of

344

four over four. Look, that's one whole group. Four over four is the same as one whole group."

Erase the fraction and write the fraction $\frac{9}{4}$. Point to the 4. "This tells me that each group has how many parts? . . . Four." Point to the top number. "This tells me that I have how many parts? . . . Nine. O.K., I've got four." Shade in the parts of the second circle, counting as you do. . . . "I've only got eight parts. But the fraction tells me I should have nine parts. I need more circles." Draw two more circles and divide each into four parts. Shade in the ninth part on the third circle. "There. That's a picture of nine over four."

Erase the fraction and the diagram. Put this fraction on the board: $\frac{5}{2}$. Point to the bottom number. "What does this tell me? . . . It tells me that each group has how many parts? . . . Two. That means every circle has to have how many parts? . . . Two." Draw two circles on the board. Divide each into two parts:

Point to the bottom number of the fraction again. "What does this tell me? . . . I can't hear you. . . . Yes, each group has two parts." Point to the top number of the fraction. "What does this number tell me? . . . It tells me that I have five parts." Call on a child to make five parts. After he has colored in four parts, he will probably stop. "You colored four parts. But the fraction tells you to color five parts. What are you going to do?" If none of the children are able to give the answer, point to the bottom number and say, "We'll just make more groups. How many parts does each group have? . . . Two." Call on a child to make some more circles. Then have the child finish the problem. When he has finished, remind him of the relation between the diagram and the fraction. "Yes, John made a picture of what? . . . A picture of five over two." Then call the children's attention to the number of whole groups.

345

"Look—five over two makes one, two whole groups and part of another group." Don't discuss halves or fourths at this time.

2. Demonstrate the relation between fractions and diagrams with other fractions. Concentrate on halves, thirds, and fourths (because these are easier to draw than fractions with larger denominators). The procedure is always the same. The bottom number tells you the number in each group. Drop out the cues as the children become more reliable in working on their own. Introduce many fractions that are greater than one. Later you will tie in multiplication with fractions. The children should have a solid understanding of fractions larger than one if the tie is to be firm.

3. Have the children make fractions from diagrams.

Draw two circles on the board. Divide each into two parts. "Each group has how many parts? . . . Two. So what number do I put at the bottom of the fraction? . . . Two." Write $\frac{}{2}$.

Shade in one of the parts:

"What do I write at the top of the fraction? . . . How many parts do I have colored? . . . One. So I put a one at the top of the fraction."

Erase the circles and draw two circles, each divided into four parts. "Each group has how many parts? . . . Four. So tell me what to do. . . . That's right. Put a four at the bottom of the fraction."

Shade in two parts:

"What number do I put at the top of the fraction? . . . Yes, two."

Present other diagrams and have the children specify the fraction that is to be written for each one. At this stage, continue to make the circles and have the children specify the number that is to go at the bottom of the fraction before you shade in some of the parts. Present diagrams of $\frac{4}{6}$, $\frac{2}{3}$, $\frac{3}{2}$. Repeat tasks if necessary.

As the children demonstrate that they can handle the tasks when they see the circles being divided and then shaded, begin presenting problems in which you present the circles already drawn, divided, and shaded:

346

"Tell me what to write." Insist that the children tell you the bottom number first: "First you have to tell me what to put at the bottom of the fraction. . . . O.K. Now you can tell me what to put at the top."

As a final set of tasks, present diagrams in which the circles are already divided and shaded. Call on individual children to write the appropriate fractions. In connection with this task, present worksheets on which different groups appear. Have the children write the appropriate fraction next to each group. Provide a box in which they are to write—the box to be divided into a top part and a bottom part:

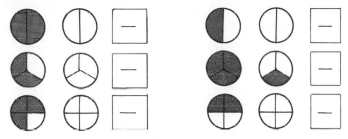

4. Demonstrate how to make fractions that are equal to one. Present the verbal rule.

First the demonstration: "I want to make a fraction that is equal to one whole group." Write $\frac{}{4}$ on the board. "What does this tell you?

That each group has four parts." Draw two circles on the board and divide each into four parts.

Circle the first circle with your finger. "This is one whole group." Circle the second circle. "This is another whole group. Now how many parts do I have to have for one whole group?"

If the children have trouble, point to one of the circles and ask, "Well, how many parts are there in this whole group? . . . Four. So if I wanted one whole group, I would have to have how many parts? . . . Four." Shade in four parts as you count. Then complete the fraction $\frac{4}{4}$. "Look at this fraction. It is the same as one whole group. Four over four equals one whole group. Let's all say that: 'Four over four equals one whole group.' Is four over four less than one whole group? . . . No. It is one whole group. Is four over four more than one whole group? . . . No. It is one whole group. Now remember that—four over four equals one whole group."

347

Draw two circles on the board. Divide each into two parts. "I want to make another fraction that's equal to one whole group. Tell me how to write that fraction." If the children have trouble, lead them through the problem. First ask what number you should put at the bottom of the fraction. Then ask what number goes at the top. If they have trouble with this question, remind them how many parts are in a group: "Look—there are two parts in this group. . . . And there are two parts in this group. . . . So if I wanted to make a whole group, how many parts would I have to have? . . . Yes, two." Write $\frac{2}{2}$.

"Two over two equals one whole group. Is two over two more than one whole group? . . . No. Is two over two equal to one whole group? . . . Yes. Is two over two less than one whole group? . . . No, two over two *is* one whole group."

Use the procedure outlined above to demonstrate that three over three equals one whole group. Draw two circles. Divide each into three parts. Tell the children that you want to write a fraction that is equal to one whole group. "Tell me what to write." After they have indicated the correct fraction, have them repeat the statement: "Three over three equals one whole group."

Compare the statements on the board:

$$\frac{4}{4} = 1 \qquad\qquad \frac{2}{2} = 1 \qquad\qquad \frac{3}{3} = 1$$

"Look at the ways we can write a fraction that equals one whole group. If we're talking about groups of four, we have to have four parts. If we're talking about groups of two, we have to have two parts. If we're talking about groups of three, we have to have three parts. So four over four equals one whole; two over two equals one whole; three over three equals one whole. I wonder what seven over seven equals? . . . What about nine over nine? . . . What about one over one? . . . ten over ten? . . ."

5. Review fractions that equal one whole every day until the children understand them thoroughly. Spend about three minutes at the beginning of each period working on the tasks outlined above. As the children become able to identify fractions equal to one, say, "Tell me some fractions that equal one whole group." Encourage novel responses, such as thirty-six over thirty-six: "Oh! that's a good fraction that's equal to one whole."

6. Present tasks in which the children must indicate whether a fraction is equal to one whole, is greater than one whole, or is less than

one whole. At first, structure the task so that they can compare various fractions with a fraction that is equal to a whole.

Write $\frac{}{3}$ on the board. Tell the children, "I want to make this fraction equal to one whole group." Write 3 above the fraction bar. "Yes, this fraction equals one whole group." Point to the bottom number. "Look, here's how many are in the group. How many? . . . Three." Point to the top. "And here's how many parts we've got. Three. We've got a whole group. We've got three."

Explain the task: "I'm going to write some fractions on the board and you have to tell me whether they're bigger than a whole group or smaller than a whole group. Here goes." Write the fraction $\frac{2}{3}$ next to $\frac{3}{3}$. "Is this fraction bigger than a whole group or smaller than a whole group?" If the children have trouble, point to the 3 in $\frac{2}{3}$ and say, "Well, here's how many are in the group. Do you have that many?" Point to the top. "No, you don't. Do you have more than three or less than three? . . . Less than three. So you have less than one whole group."

Erase the fraction and write $\frac{4}{3}$. "Is this fraction more than one whole group or less than one whole group?" Again, if the children have trouble, refer them to the bottom number: "Look down here. This number tells you how many are in a group. Do you have that many? . . . No, you don't have three. Do you have more than three or less than three? . . . More than three. So four over three is more than one whole."

Erase the fraction and replace it with the fraction $\frac{5}{3}$. "Is this fraction more than one whole group or less than one whole group?"

Write the fraction $\frac{2}{2}$ and next to it $\frac{1}{2}$. Refer to $\frac{2}{2}$. "Is this fraction more than one whole or less than one whole? . . . Yes, that's right. It *is* one whole. There are two in each group. And we've got two. So we've got one whole group." Refer to one-half. "Is this fraction more than one whole or less than one whole?"

7. Present more-or-less-than-one-whole tasks every day until the children can handle fractions involving large numbers—$\frac{13}{10}$, $\frac{18}{19}$, and so forth—without much hesitation. Give them worksheets that present more-or-less problems:

If the fraction is more than one, circle MORE.

If the fraction is less than one, circle LESS.

$\frac{1}{2}$	MORE	LESS	$\frac{2}{3}$	MORE	LESS	$\frac{5}{3}$	MORE	LESS
$\frac{9}{4}$	MORE	LESS	$\frac{5}{4}$	MORE	LESS	$\frac{8}{9}$	MORE	LESS
$\frac{6}{7}$	MORE	LESS	$\frac{10}{11}$	MORE	LESS	$\frac{1}{3}$	MORE	LESS

8. Demonstrate that every counting number can be written as a fraction over one.

Draw two circles on the board. Shade in both circles:

"O.K., let's write the fraction." The children will probably not be able to specify the fraction $\frac{2}{1}$. Point to the left circle. "How many parts?" The children may say zero. "No, it looks like a zero, but it has one part. See—the whole circle is colored. The whole thing is a part." Write $\frac{}{1}$. "O.K., that *one* tells us that each group has one part. How many groups do we have? . . . Two." Complete the fraction.

"How many circles do we have? . . . Two. Two over one is the same as two. Each group has one part and you have two parts. That means you have two whole groups."

Add two more circles. Shade them:

"Let's write the fraction. Each group has how many parts? One." Write $\frac{}{1}$. "How many parts do we have? . . . Four." Complete the fraction: $\frac{4}{1}$. Summarize: "Four over one equals four."

Add another circle and repeat the demonstration. Keep adding circles until you have ten. Write the fraction for each presentation.

Give the children worksheets on which they are to write the fraction that describes the groups:

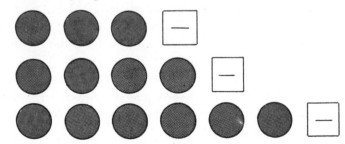

Include larger fractions: $\frac{7}{1}$, $\frac{8}{1}$, and so forth.

After the children have demonstrated that they can handle a variety of problems similar to those above, present the rule about the relation between counting numbers and fractions. (If the children perform adequately on the first sheet, there is probably no need to present other

350

sheets. You may want to give them the same sheet to work again, which should require only a few minutes.)

"Listen big. Here's the rule. Any number is a fraction. Four is a fraction—four over one. Seven is a fraction—seven over one. Nine is a fraction. What fraction? . . . Twenty-six is a fraction. What fraction? . . . Thirty-four is a fraction. What fraction? . . . One thousand is a fraction. What fraction?" Repeat a drill of this sort every day until the children thoroughly understand the rule. They must understand the rule without having to derive it every time they need it.

9. Demonstrate how any fraction can be changed into one.

Present the fraction $\frac{1}{5}$ on the board. "Is one-fifth equal to one whole group? . . . Is it less than one or more than one? Do you want to see a funny trick? I'll show you how to change one-fifth into one. Do you know how we do it? Turn this fraction upside down and multiply."

$$\frac{1}{5} \times \frac{5}{1} =$$

"Here's the rule. When we multiply fractions, we have to go straight across the top and straight across the bottom." Draw a faint line through the numbers on the bottom and the numbers on the top. Extend the lines past the equals sign:

$$\frac{1}{5} \times \frac{5}{1} =$$

"O.K., let's multiply across the top. One times five. Count by ones five times. . . . Five." Write 5 on the right of the equals sign. "Now let's go across the bottom. What's five times one? . . . Five."

$$\frac{1}{5} \times \frac{5}{1} = \frac{5}{5}$$

"Is five over five more than one whole or less than one whole? . . . It *is* one whole. Five over five equals one."

$$\frac{1}{5} \times \frac{5}{1} = \frac{5}{5} = 1$$

Summarize: "Look—I changed one over five into one. How did I do it? I turned one over five upside down and multiplied."

Write $\frac{2}{3}$ on the board. "I wonder how I would change two over three into one whole. . . . Same way. I'd turn it upside down and multiply. Here goes. . . ."

$$\frac{2}{3} \times \frac{3}{2} = \frac{6}{6} = 1$$

Remind the children that when you multiply you have to go straight across the top and straight across the bottom. "How did I change two over three into one? I turned it upside down and multiplied. Do you know what you call it when you turn a fraction upside down and multiply? This is hard and you'll never remember it. It's called multiplying by the reciprocal. Who can say that? . . . Good talking. How do you turn one over five into one? . . . You multiply by the reciprocal. How do you turn two over three into one? . . . You multiply by the reciprocal. I wonder how you turn three over five into one? . . . That's it—you multiply by the reciprocal."

$$\frac{3}{5} \times \frac{5}{3} = \frac{15}{15} = 1$$

"Yes, fifteen over fifteen is just another way of saying one whole group. Each group has fifteen parts and you color fifteen parts. You color the whole group."

Present various examples. Withdraw the cue as the children begin to become firm in the operation. Stop drawing in the lines across the numbers on the top and the bottom. Call on children to perform the multiplication operation. As they perform, reinforce the rule: "Look at John go. He remembers to multiply straight across the top and straight across the bottom."

Ask the children to make up fractions and test the rule: "Mary, tell me what fraction to write down. Any fraction. Let's see if the rule works." If the children specify fractions that involve numbers larger than ten, tell them that you can't work them on the chart.

From time to time, start with a fraction that is equal to one: $\frac{8}{8}$. "Oh, this is silly! Eight over eight is already equal to one. But let's see if the rule works. What do we do to change this fraction into one? . . . Multiply by the reciprocal. O.K., so we turn it over and multiply by . . ."

$$\frac{8}{8} \times \frac{8}{8} =$$

Also demonstrate that the rule holds for whole numbers. Write a number on the board and say, "How do I change six into one?" If the children have trouble, remind them, "Every number is a fraction. Six is really a fraction. What fraction? . . . Yes, six over one. So what do we do? . . . Multiply six over one by its reciprocal.

$$\frac{6}{1} \times \frac{1}{6} = \frac{6}{6} = 1$$

"Boy, we can turn anything into one, can't we? Just multiply by the reciprocal."

352

After the children have worked on reciprocals during one or two sessions, present worksheets. (NOTE: The children should start to show a considerable increase in the rate at which they learn new concepts. You may be able to introduce multiplication by reciprocals and present the worksheets in a ten-minute segment of the period.)

$$\tfrac{2}{5}(\quad) = \square = 1 \qquad\qquad \tfrac{4}{3}(\quad) = \square = 1$$
$$7(\quad) = \square = 1 \qquad\qquad 3(\quad) = \square = 1$$
$$\tfrac{5}{5}(\quad) = \square = 1 \qquad\qquad \tfrac{9}{9}(\quad) = \square = 1$$

Present worksheets until the children have overlearned the procedure. The parentheses on the worksheets anticipate problems in which parentheses will replace the times sign. In these exercises the children should write the times sign within the parentheses. The answer for the first problem, for example, is $\tfrac{2}{5}(\times \tfrac{5}{2}) = \tfrac{10}{10} = 1$.

Changing a Number into Zero

The ability to change a given number into zero is very important in working complex multiplication problems as well as in working complex addition problems.

1. To introduce the procedure, write the number 7 on the board. "What do I do if I want to change this number into one? . . . That's right. Multiply by the reciprocal of seven over one, which is one over seven. But what do I do if I want to change seven into zero? How do I do that? It's pretty easy. Watch." Write -7 after the number:

$$7 - 7$$

"What does seven minus seven equal? . . . Zero." Write the number 8 on the board. "What do I do to change eight into zero? . . . That's right. Minus eight."

$$8 - 8 = 0$$

Present several examples. Ask the children for numbers: "Come on—try to find a number the rule doesn't work for." Demonstrate that the procedure works for fractions as well as for whole numbers.

2. Present discrimination exercises in which you ask the children to change a number either into one or into zero.

Begin with verbal exercises: "Now you have to listen big or I'll catch you. How do you change seven into one? . . . Yes, multiply by

353

the reciprocal of seven. O.K., how do you change seven into zero? . . . Minus seven."

After presenting quick verbal exercises for a few days, present worksheet problems.

Change these numbers into zero:

$\frac{1}{3}$ 81   5   23   1 $\frac{7}{2}$

Change these numbers into 1:

$\frac{1}{4}$ 5   7 $\frac{10}{3}$ 10

Rules of Equations

Rule 1: If you change one side, you have to change the other.

1. At this point the children know what fractions are. They know whether a fraction is one whole, is more than a whole, or is less than a whole. They know how to change numbers into fractions and they know how to change any fraction into one. Finally, they know how to change a number into zero. Before they can proceed, however, they must learn this rule: When you change one side of the equation, you must change the other side in the same way if the equality is to be maintained.

Present the statement $7 = 7$ on the chalkboard. Then give the rule before proceeding: "I can change this side of the statement"—point to the 7 on the left of the equals sign—"or I can change this side of the statement"—point to the right side of the equation. "But the rule is this: What I do to one side of the equals sign, I have to do to the other side. Let's say that together: What I do to one side of the equals sign, I have to do to the other side. Watch what I can do to one side of the equals sign." Add 3 to the left side, in front of the 7:

$$3 + 7 = 7$$

"Is that equal? No, because I've changed it. How can I make it equal?" Some of the children may suggest erasing the 3. "Good thinking. That would make it equal. Another way to make it equal is to add three to the other side of the statement."

$$3 + 7 = 7 + 3$$

Have the children check to make sure there is ten on each side of the equals sign. "That's the rule. What you do to one side of the statement, you have to do to the other side of the statement. Let's keep going."

Add 1 to the left side of the equation:

$$1 + 3 + 7 = 7 + 3$$

"I changed the equation. I did something to this side of the equals sign. What did I do to this side of the equals sign? . . . I added one. What's the rule? What you do to one side of the equals sign, you have to do to the other side. So what do I have to do to the other side to make it equal? . . . Add one to the other side."

$$1 + 3 + 7 = 7 + 3 + 1$$

Have the children check to make sure that both sides add up to the same number. "Eleven on this side and eleven on that side. Eleven equals eleven." Then say, "I can do this without looking. It's hard, but I can do it. One plus three plus seven equals seven plus three plus one." Have the children try to say it. Don't be disturbed if they have trouble. Proceed to the next problem after they have tried several times. Don't expect them to master the concept at this time. Instead, have them repeat statements of this sort from time to time. They will learn not only how to sequence the numbers, but also something about the commutative law of addition (that one plus three equals three plus one).

Present several problems in which you start out with a simple statement of equality such as $3 = 3$ or $5 = 5$ and then add a number to one side of the equation. Don't always add to the left side of the equation. As soon as you add the number, inform the children that you "changed it" and ask them, "So what do I do now?" Ask for the rule. "What you do to one side of the equals sign, you have to do to the other side." Ask the children, "What did I do to this side of the equals sign?" and "So what do I do to the other side?"

Give the children worksheet problems that require the application of the rule:

$$9 + 8 = 8 + 9 \qquad 6 = 6 + 7 \qquad 7 + 1 = 1$$
$$2 + 4 = 4 \qquad 1 = 1 + 1 + 1 \qquad 3 = 3 + 2$$
$$4 = 3 \qquad\qquad\qquad 2 + 3 = 3$$

Have them complete each equation and check to make sure it balances.

2. Introduce problems in which you change one side of the equation by multiplying.

Write the equation $7 = 7$. Multiply the left side by three:

$$3 \times 7 = 7$$

"Oh, I'm going to fool you on this one! You'll never be able to work it." The children will probably be able to tell you what to do on the other side of the equation. If not, ask them, "Well, how did I change this side? . . . That's right. I multiplied by three. And what's the rule? . . . What you do to one side of the equation, you have to do to the other. So what do I have to do to the other side? . . . Yes, multiply by three."

$$3 \times 7 = 7 \times 3$$

"Hey! This says that three times seven is the same as seven times three. I don't believe it. Let's do it on the chart and see." After working the problem, say, "The chart is right again."

3. After the children have worked on similar problems, multiplying both sides by any number from one to ten, show them that the rule about multiplication holds even when a number in the problem is rewritten.

Write this equation: $10 = 10$.

Point to the 10 on the left of the equals sign. "I can write ten another way. Five plus five." Erase the 10 and replace it with $5 + 5$:

$$5 + 5 = 10$$

"Did I change the statement? Not really. There are still ten on this side . . . and ten on this side." Now multiply the right side of the equation by 2:

$$5 + 5 = 10 \times 2$$

Have the children recite the rule and apply it. Call on one of the children to write what should be done on the left side of the equation. The child will probably complete the equation this way:

$$2 \times 5 + 5 = 10 \times 2$$

Work the problem and point out the error: "Oh, oh! We have fifteen on this side of the equals sign." Point to the left side. "And twenty on this side. Maybe we did something wrong. Let's say the rule slowly and see if we did it the right way. What you do to one side of the equals sign you have to do to the other. I see what we did wrong.

We didn't multiply this whole side by two. We didn't do it to the whole side. We just multiplied the five by two." Erase the 2 × and write this:

$$2(5 + 5) = 10 \times 2$$

"Remember that five plus five is a number. It's ten. We have to multiply the whole ten by two. Now it tells us to count by twos five plus five times. What's five plus five times? . . . That's ten times. Let's do it. Count by twos ten times. . . ."

Present a series of similar problems. Remind the children, "We have to do it to the whole side." If they have any difficulty understanding the parenthesis and what it tells them to do, explain: "When you have one of these things—a parenthesis stuck next to a number—it tells you to multiply, to count by." Let the children suggest ways of changing a number—expressing it either as the sum of two numbers or as the product of two numbers. For example, the children may suggest writing 10 as 5 × 2:

$$10 = 5 \times 2$$

Multiply the 10 by 3:

$$3 \times 10 = 5 \times 2$$

"What's the rule? What you do to one side of the equals sign, you have to do to the other side. What did I do to this side of the statement? . . . I multiplied the whole side by three. So what do I have to do to the other side? . . . Show me how to do it. Remember—the whole side."

$$3 \times 10 - (5 \times 2)3$$

"Good. Now we're multiplying the whole five-times-two—that's ten—by three. It tells us to count by tens three times. . . ."

4. Introduce the distributive law. (Don't call it by name; simply show the children how it works and give them an operational understanding of it in the context of solving arithmetic problems.)

Present this statement: 10 = 10.

Change the left side to 5 + 5. Then multiply the right side by 4. The children should indicate that the left side must be changed to balance the equation:

$$4(5 + 5) = 10 \times 4$$

Refer to the left side. "Do you want to see another way of writing this?

357

We have to multiply this five by four and this five by four. The four belongs to both of these guys." Draw lines from the 4 to each 5:

$$\overset{\frown}{4(5} + 5) = 10 \times 4$$

"So we can put the four here. . . ."

$$\overset{\frown}{4(5)} + 5) = 10 \times 4$$

"And we can put the four here. . . ."

$$4(5) + 4(5) = 10 \times 4$$

"Let's check the answer. We have forty on this side. Let's see what we have on the other side. Four times five is twenty. We've got twenty and twenty. What's twenty plus twenty? . . . Forty."

Present exercises in which the children first multiply a number by two, five, or ten. Then have them repeat the operation when two, five, or ten is expressed as the sum of two numbers.

First write the number on the board: 3.

"Let's multiply this number by five."

$$3 \times 5 = 15$$

"Let's write five another way and see if we still come up with the same answer. What's another way to write five? . . . Four plus one."

$$3(4 + 1) =$$

"Now remember that four plus one is really five, and we've got to count by the whole four-plus-one, not just a part of it. The three goes with the four and the three goes with the one." Draw in lines to indicate the relationship:

$$\overset{\frown}{3(4} + 1) = 15$$

Rewrite the notation. "I can write it another way. I can leave the plus sign where it is and put the three with the four and the three with the one."

$$3(4) + 3(1) = 15$$

"Does it equal fifteen? Let's see. What's three times four? . . .

Twelve. What's three times one? . . . Three. We've got a twelve and a three. What's twelve plus three? . . . Fifteen. It works."

Present problems that relate addition to multiplication.

$$4 \times 10 = 40$$

"I'm going to write ten another way. Watch this."

$$4(1 + 1 + 1 + 1 + 1 + 1 + 1 + 1 + 1 + 1) = 40$$

"I'll bet that will never work. Let's see if it does." Remind the children of the rule. "Remember that all of this in here"—point to the parentheses—"is ten, so the four goes with all of it. That means the four goes with every par.." Multiply the four by each of the ones:

$$4(1) + 4(1) + 4(1) + 4(1) + 4(1) + 4(1) + 4(1) +$$
$$4(1) + 4(1) + 4(1) = 40$$

"Boy! Look at all the fours we have. Four plus four plus four . . . How many fours do we have? Ten of them." Either add up the fours or let the children multiply, counting by fours ten times.

Present many examples in which you break a number down into a number of ones that are added together. Repeat problems until the children see (1) that the regrouping procedure works if one breaks the number down into ones and (2) that it works if one breaks the number down into any other combination of numbers the sum of which is equal to the original number. From time to time, take a number and then demonstrate that there are various ways to express it and multiply it by a given number:

$$3 \times 5 = 15$$
$$3(4 + 1)$$
$$3(4) + 3(1) = 15$$

$$3(3 + 2)$$
$$3(3) + 3(2) = 15$$

$$3(3 + 1 + 1) = 15$$
$$3(3) + 3(1) + 3(1) = 15$$

$$3(2 + 2 + 1) = 15$$
$$3(2) + 3(2) + 3(1) = 15$$

When working these problems with the children, stress the point that you are *writing the number in different ways:* "Ask yourself: Do you have the same number in the parentheses that you did when you started out? Do you still have five in the parentheses? . . . Yes. Well, then you haven't changed the problem. You're still multiplying three times five." The second step—that of regrouping the elements—follows from the initial operation: "You know what three times five equals, don't you? . . . Yes, fifteen. Well, if you regroup the numbers and count by three with each of the numbers you will still end up with fifteen."

5. Give the children worksheet problems that involve regrouping:

$7 \times 2 =$ $\qquad$ $4 \times 5 =$

$7(\square + \square) =$ $\qquad$ $4(\square + \square) =$

$7(\ ) + 7(\ ) =$ $\qquad$ $4(\ ) + 4(\ ) =$

$6 \times 10 =$ $\qquad$ $4 \times 10 =$

$6(\square + \square) =$ $\qquad$ $4(\square + \square + \square) =$

$6(\ ) + 6(\ ) =$ $\qquad$ $4(\ ) + 4(\ ) + 4(\ ) =$

$6 \times 5 =$ $\qquad$ $2 \times 5 =$

$6(\square + \square + \square) =$ $\qquad$ $2(\square + \square + \square + \square + \square) =$

$6(\ ) + 6(\ ) + 6(\ ) =$ $\qquad$ $2(\ ) + 2(\ ) + 2(\ ) + 2(\ ) + 2(\ ) =$

Have the children check their work to make sure that at every step the statement they make is true: "Look what it says here, John. It says that six times eight plus six times two equals sixty. Does it? Let's see. What's six times eight? . . . Forty-eight. What's six times two? . . . Twelve. What's forty-eight plus twelve?" Write the problem out in column form and have the child add the numbers to see if they equal sixty. "It works. Forty-eight plus twelve equals sixty."

Rule 2: Multiplying by one does not change a number.

Demonstrate that if you multiply an equation (or a side of an equation) by one, you do not change its value.

1. Present this equation: $4 = 4$.

Multiply the left side by one:

$1 \times 4 = 4$

"Did I change this side of the equation?" The children may indicate that you multiplied by one. "Yes, but I wonder if I changed it. I wonder if this side still equals four. Let's see." Have the children multiply one by four: "Count by ones four times. . . . Yes, four. This side is four and this side is four."

Erase the problem and replace it with $3 = 3$.

"Let's see if we can multiply one side of this statement without changing it."

$$3 = 3 \times 1$$

"Count by threes one time. That's three. I've still got three on this side of the equation. I didn't change it."

Repeat the demonstration with several other equations suggested by the children. "Let's see if we can find an equation it doesn't work for. . . ." After working these equations, conclude, "If we multiply a side of an equation by one, we really don't change it."

2. Demonstrate that by multiplying a side of an equation by any number other than one, you change it: "Maybe we can multiply a side of an equation by any number without changing it. Let's see." Return to the original equation (4 = 4) and multiply one side of it by various numbers suggested by the children. After a number such as eight has been tried, conclude, "If you multiply by one, you don't change it; but if you multiply by eight, you sure change it." Remind the children of the rule about multiplying by one. This rule is critical for the problems that are to come. The children must understand it thoroughly.

3. Demonstrate that the side of an equation is not changed if it is multiplied by a fraction that is equal to one: "If we multiply one side of an equation by one, we don't change the equation. I wonder if we can multiply a side of an equation by a fraction that is equal to one."

Present this fraction: $\frac{3}{3}$. "Is this more than one whole group or less than one whole group? . . . It *is* one whole group."

Write the equation 4 = 4. "O.K., let's multiply one side of this equation by three over three."

$$\left(\tfrac{3}{3}\right)4 = 4$$

"Wait a minute. Before I can multiply, I'd better change four into a fraction. Any number is a fraction, right? What fraction is four? . . . Yes, four over one."

$$\left(\tfrac{3}{3}\right)\tfrac{4}{1} = 4$$

"Here's the rule when we multiply. We go straight across the top and straight across the bottom." Draw faint lines through the top numbers and the bottom numbers:

$$\overline{\left(\tfrac{3}{3}\right)\tfrac{4}{1}} \equiv 4$$

"What do we have at the top? Count by threes four times. . . . Twelve." Erase the top numbers and replace them with 12. "And what do we have at the bottom? Count by threes one time. . . . Three."

$$\frac{12}{3} = 4$$

"It says that twelve over three is the same as four whole groups. I wonder if that's right. Let's draw a picture and see. Each group has three parts and we color twelve parts."

"Look at that. Twelve over three does equal four whole groups. We multiplied this side by one and we didn't change it."

Return to the original equation (4 = 4) and demonstrate that you can multiply one side by other fractions equal to one without changing the equation.

"Is two over two more than one whole or less than one whole? . . . It is one whole. So let's multiply this side of the equation by two over two. Two over two is one, so it shouldn't change the equation."

$$(\tfrac{2}{2})4 = 4$$

"We better change four into a fraction so that we can multiply. What fraction does four equal? . . . Yes, four over one."

$$(\tfrac{2}{2})\tfrac{4}{1} = 4$$

"Remember the rule: when we multiply, we go straight across the top and straight across the bottom." Draw in faint lines:

$$\frac{(2)4}{(2)1} = 4$$

"What do we have at the top? . . . Eight. And what do we have at the bottom? . . . Two. I wonder if eight over two is the same as four. I wonder if they're equal. Let's make a picture."

"Look at that. There's a picture of eight over two. That's the same as four whole groups. Eight over two equals four. Same thing."

Return to the original equation (4 = 4) and demonstrate that you can multiply a side of the equation by $\tfrac{4}{4}$, $\tfrac{6}{6}$, $\tfrac{8}{8}$. After each demonstra-

362

tion, stress the conclusion: We multiplied the four by one and we didn't change it.

4. Demonstrate that multiplying by a fraction that is not equal to one changes the value of a side. Multiply one side of $4 = 4$ by $\frac{1}{2}, \frac{2}{3}, \frac{5}{8}$. After each demonstration, conclude, "Oh, oh! We changed it. Did we multiply by a fraction that is equal to one? . . . No. And we changed the four. When we multiply by one, we don't change the four. When we multiply by something that is not equal to one, we change the four."

5. Introduce the procedure for reducing such fractions as $\frac{12}{3}$ and $\frac{32}{4}$.

Multiply one side of the equation $4 = 4$ by $\frac{2}{2}$:

$$\frac{8}{2} = 4$$

"Do you want to see a quick way to see if eight over two is the same as four whole groups? Here we go. Each group has how many parts? . . . Two. There are two parts in each group. So we could find out how many groups we have by counting by twos until we end up with eight. Remember that every time we count, we make one whole group, so we want to see how many times we count. Two . . . four . . . six . . . eight. We counted four times. That means that we have four whole groups. Eight over two is the same as four."

Return to the original equation and multiply one side of it by $\frac{3}{3}$:

$$\frac{12}{3} = 4$$

"Let's do it the fast way. The bottom number tells us that each group has three parts. So all we have to do is see how many threes are in twelve. We count by threes and see how many times we count to end up with twelve. Three . . . six . . . nine . . . twelve. We counted four times, so twelve over three is the same as four wholes."

After demonstrating with several other problems, introduce a "mechanical" procedure. Write these fractions on the board:

$$\frac{12}{2} \qquad\qquad \frac{10}{5} \qquad\qquad \frac{20}{5} \qquad\qquad \frac{80}{8}$$

Point to the bottom number in the first fraction. "It's a two. Each group has two. That means we can count by twos how many times to end up with twelve? . . . Yes, six times. So twelve over two equals six wholes." Point to the bottom number in the second fraction. "This is a five. Each group has five. So we can count by fives how many times to end up with ten? . . . Two times. So ten over five equals two wholes."

Have the children give the sentences for the remaining fractions. Some children may say, "Count by fives twenty times" instead of "Count by fives how many times to end up with twenty?" Correct this error by pointing out, "No, we've got to see how many groups of five there are in twenty. We have to see how many times we count by five to end up with twenty."

Present worksheet problems:

Write how many wholes each fraction equals.

$\frac{20}{2} = \square$ $\frac{14}{2} = \square$ $\frac{16}{8} = \square$

$\frac{20}{4} = \square$ $\frac{8}{4} = \square$ $\frac{12}{4} = \square$

$\frac{20}{5} = \square$ $\frac{30}{6} = \square$ $\frac{15}{3} = \square$

$\frac{20}{10} = \square$ $\frac{72}{8} = \square$ $\frac{18}{6} = \square$

Present similar worksheets until the children are proficient at reducing any fraction that has no remainder. They should be able to finish a worksheet of twelve problems in five minutes or less. When they understand a concept, they can move very quickly. Conversely, if they spend a great deal of time pondering each problem, they do not clearly understand the procedure involved in reaching a solution.

Word problems using fraction skills

Begin with this problem: "Listen to this story. A man walks into a grocery store. He goes up to the storekeeper and says, 'I want to buy a can of beans.' The storekeeper says, 'That's good, because three cans of beans cost fifteen cents.' What did the storekeeper say? Let's hear it: Three cans of beans cost fifteen cents. The man says, 'But I don't want to buy three cans of beans. I want to buy one can of beans.' He's got problems. But I'll bet we can help him out. Who remembers what the storekeeper said about the beans? . . . Yes, three cans of beans cost fifteen cents. I can write that."

Write a 3 on the board.

"Now what should I write for beans? I know. I'll put a *b*."

3*b*

"And what did he say about three cans of beans? . . . Yes, they're fifteen cents."

3*b* = 15

"This tells about three cans of beans. But the man doesn't want to know about three cans of beans. He wants to know about one can of beans. We want to know what one b equals. I wonder how we could change this three into a one. . . . Multiply by the reciprocal. What's the reciprocal of three? . . . Yes, one over three."

$$(\tfrac{1}{3})\tfrac{3}{1}b = 15$$

"Oh, oh. We've got problems. Did we multiply this side of the equation by one? . . . No, we multiplied by one over three. We changed the three. We changed this side of the equation. So what do we have to do? . . . Good. If we change this side of the equation, we have to change the other side in the same way."

$$(\tfrac{1}{3})\tfrac{3}{1}b = \tfrac{15}{1}(\tfrac{1}{3})$$

"So now we know what one b equals. It equals fifteen over three. I wonder how many whole groups that is? . . . Yes, five whole groups."

$$1b = 5$$

"Now he knows how much one can of beans costs. Five cents."

Present a series of similar problems. Keep the form the same. The man (or girl, or boy) wants one, but the seller tells him what more than one costs: "A boy wants to buy a shoelace. He goes into the shoe store and tells the man, 'I want to buy a shoelace.' The man says, 'That's good, because four shoelaces cost twenty-four cents.' The boy says, 'But I don't want four shoelaces. I want one shoelace.' "

To write the problem on the board, refer to what the man said: "He said four shoelaces cost twenty-four cents. What should I write for shoelaces? . . . *Sh*. O.K."

$$4sh = 24$$

"This tells us about four *sh*. But we don't want four *sh*. We want one *sh*. How do we change the four into a one? . . . Yes, multiply by the reciprocal of four."

$$(\tfrac{1}{4})\tfrac{4}{1}sh = 24$$

"Did we multiply this equation by something that equals one? Does one over four equal one? . . . No. So we changed this side of the equation. What's the rule? . . . If you change one side of the equation, you have to change the other side in the same way. So what do I have to do on the other side of the equation? . . . Multiply by one over four."

$$(\tfrac{1}{4})\tfrac{4}{1}sh = 24(\tfrac{1}{4})$$

"How many wholes does twenty-four over four equal? . . . Yes, six. So . . ."

$$sh = 6$$

Stress the following points in working these problems:

1. The original equation does not tell what you want to know. You want to know what one b or one sh equals. However, the equation does not tell about one.

2. Therefore you have to do something to change the number that is given into one. How do you do this? You multiply by the reciprocal.

3. But when you multiply by the reciprocal, you are not multiplying by one. That means you are changing the equation. The equation no longer balances. To make it balance again, you have to multiply by the same number on the other side.

4. The answer will be expressed as a fraction. Reduce the fraction by finding how many times you have to count by the bottom number to get to the top number. This tells how many wholes there are.

The steps in solving the problem should be presented logically, so that the children can proceed from what is given in the original statement to a statement about one b or one sh. This is the goal to which all else leads. In order to reach the goal, you have to change the original statement. However, you can only change it according to the rules that have been set forth in the preceding sections. If the problems are presented so that each of the moves derives from the desire to change the statement into a statement about one b or one sh, the children will learn that the moves are not arbitrary and that they are introduced because the goal cannot be reached without making them.

Worksheets

Present worksheets with problems similar to the preceding problems. Do this after the children have demonstrated that they can (1) solve the problems (write down the original equation and take the steps necessary to arrive at a solution) and (2) tell why each step is taken: "Why did you multiply by one over three? . . . Yes, to turn the three into a one. Why did you multiply this other side of the equation by one over three? . . . Good. You changed that side of the equation, so you have to change this side the same way."

$$3a = 6 \qquad\qquad\qquad 10a = 40$$
$$a = \qquad\qquad\qquad\qquad a =$$

366

$2a = 6$	$10a = 70$
$a =$	$a =$
$5a = 15$	$10a = 90$
$a =$	$a =$
$7a = 42$	$10a = 20$
$a =$	$a =$

Present daily worksheets (each containing eight to ten problems) until the children have worked a wide variety of problems. Point out that the children can *check* each problem by using a procedure learned for handling basic algebra problems: "This problem says that three *a* equals six. Look at the three and the *a*. They're stuck together. That means that there's a little bitty times sign between them. So we count by threes how many times to end up with six? . . . Yes, two times. Our answer should be two." Require the children to *work* the problems using the procedure of multiplying by reciprocals, because the strategy involved in this procedure is basic to a variety of complex problems.

Using Equation Rules to Solve Problems

Word problems involving fractions

Introduce problems that are similar in form to those in the preceding section but that involve fractions.

1. Begin with this problem: "A man goes into a drugstore and says, 'I want to buy a bottle of medicine.' The druggist says, 'O.K. One-fourth bottle of medicine costs three dollars.' The man says, 'I don't want one-fourth bottle of medicine. I want one bottle of medicine.' Let's help him figure out what one bottle will cost. What did the druggist say? One-fourth bottle costs three dollars." The children have not been taught how to write one-fourth. They know $\frac{1}{4}$ only as "one over four." However, they should have little difficulty learning the conventional names for these fractions if you introduce fourths, sixths, sevenths, eighths, ninths, and tenths while at first avoiding halves, thirds, and fifths.

"How do we write one-fourth? That's one over four."

$$\tfrac{1}{4}b = 3$$

"Oh, oh! That tells about one-fourth bottle. But the man doesn't want one-fourth bottle. He wants one bottle. How do we change one-fourth into one? . . . Multiply by the reciprocal of one-fourth."

$$(\tfrac{4}{1})\tfrac{1}{4}\,b = 3$$

"We changed this side of the equation, because we didn't multiply by one. So what do we have to do? . . . Multiply the other side by four over one."

$$(\tfrac{4}{1})\tfrac{1}{4}b = \tfrac{3}{1}(\tfrac{4}{1})$$

"One bottle costs twelve over one. How many wholes is that? Twelve over one is the same as twelve. One bottle costs twelve dollars. Yikes, that's a lot of money!"

The strategy is the same as that used in working the preceding set of word problems. The only difference is that in these problems the price is given for less than one item rather than for more than one item.

2. Introduce a variety of fraction problems. Have the children write out the problems on paper as you tell them the story: "Now you have to listen big. A girl wants to buy pie. So she goes into a pie store and she walks up to the man and says, 'I want to buy a pie.' The man says, 'Well, one-sixth pie costs six cents.' Write it down."

$$\tfrac{1}{6}p = 6$$

"Good. Now figure out what one whole pie costs. Turn that one-sixth into one. How are you going to do that? . . . Good."

$$(\tfrac{6}{1})\tfrac{1}{6}p = \tfrac{6}{1}(\tfrac{6}{1})$$

"Yes, one whole pie costs thirty-six cents."

3. Work all problems out before presenting them, to make sure that they come out even (without a fraction remainder). An easy way to construct them is to make the number on the right of the equals sign the same as, or twice as big as, the top number on the left of the equals sign. However, don't use this formula for all the problems.

Statements about numbers other than one

The children have learned how to find the value of one unknown. The next step is to learn how to change an equation so that it makes a statement about a number smaller or larger than one.

"Listen to this story. A girl walks into a bakery and she says, 'I want to buy four pies.' The man says, 'O.K. One pie costs six cents.' "

$$1p = 6$$

"She says, 'I don't want one pie. I want four pies.' What does she have to do? . . . She has to change the one into a four. How do you change a one into a four? . . . You multiply by four."

$$(4)1p = 6$$

"Four times one. That's four. But I've changed this side of the equation. So what do I have to do? . . ."

$$(4)1p = 6(4)$$

"So four pies cost twenty-four cents."

The purpose of these problems is to demonstrate to the children that you have to understand your goal before you start working the problem. If your goal is to make a statement about one pie, you have to change the statement so that it tells about one pie. If your goal is to make a statement about four pies, you have to change the original statement so that it talks about four pies.

Problems in which one number must be changed to another

1. Introduce problems that involve changing *one* into another number:

"A boy wants to buy one-fourth of a sandpile. The man tells him, 'One sandpile costs eight dollars.' Write down the equation."

$$1s = 8$$

"The boy wants one-fourth sandpile, but this equation tells us about one sandpile. How can we change the one into one fourth? . . . Yes, multiply by one-fourth. If you have one-fourth one time, you have one-fourth."

$$(\tfrac{1}{4})1s = \tfrac{8}{1}(\tfrac{1}{4})$$

"One-fourth sandpile costs eight over four dollars. How many whole dollars is that? . . . Yes, two: *s* equals two."

2. After the children have become solid in converting *one* into any number (which involves multiplying by the desired number), present problems in which a statement is given about some quantity *other than one:*

"A boy wants to buy three wagons. He wants to be able to say . . ."

$$3w =$$

"But the man in the store doesn't tell him what three wagons cost.

He tells him that four wagons cost twenty-four dollars." Write the equation above $3w =$.

$$4w = 24$$
$$3w =$$

"Boy, this is tough! We've got to change four into three. I wonder how we can do that." Let the children ponder the question for a few moments. "I've got it. We can change the four into one. How do we do that? . . . Multiply by the reciprocal."

$$(\tfrac{1}{4})\tfrac{4}{1}w = 24$$

"Now we can multiply the one by three. That will give us the three we want."

$$(\tfrac{3}{1})(\tfrac{1}{4})\tfrac{4}{1}w = 24$$
$$3w =$$

"Look what we did to this side of the equation. We multiplied it by one over four and by three over one. That's what we did on this side of the equation, so that's what we have to do on the other side of the equation. Let's multiply by the one over four first."

$$3w = \tfrac{24}{1}(\tfrac{1}{4})$$

"That's six. So I can erase all of this and put six. . . . And then I've still got to multiply by three over one."

$$3w = 6(\tfrac{3}{1})$$
$$3w = 18$$

"If four wagons cost twenty-four dollars, three wagons cost eighteen dollars."

There are easier ways to work this problem, but the children will probably benefit most from the procedure outlined here. They must take these two steps:

• Change the four into a three. To do this, they change the four into a one and the one into a three.

• Multiply the two sides of the equation by the same amount.

Although these problems seem complicated, the children should have no trouble with them if they have learned the various component operations and rules.

Present worksheet problems:

$5P = 10$	$8R = 32$
$2P =$	$\frac{1}{2}R =$
$7R = 35$	$6B = 12$
$3R =$	$\frac{1}{2}B =$
$\frac{1}{2}A = 10$	$\frac{2}{3}B = 6$
$3A =$	$\frac{4}{2}B =$
$\frac{2}{3}B = 4$	$2A = 7$
$5B =$	$3A =$

After the children have worked on these problems for a few days, show them an easier way to solve them. Present the problem in which a man wants to buy four gloves and he is told that six gloves cost eighteen dollars:

$$6g = 18$$
$$4g =$$

"We have to change the six into a four. That means that we have to multiply by one over six . . . and then by four. Let's put those guys together in one parenthesis."

$$(\tfrac{1}{6} \cdot \tfrac{4}{1})$$

"See that little dot in there? That's a tiny times sign. If I don't have that in there, it will say fourteen over sixty-one. I sure don't want to say that, do I?"

The children now multiply the other side of the equation by $(\tfrac{1}{6} \cdot \tfrac{4}{1})$ and solve in the usual manner.

Problems involving transposing

Present this equation: $A - B = 0$.

"What are we ending up with? . . . Zero. We're taking away as many as we started out with. So what do we know about A and B? . . . Yes, they're the same size. They're equal." Below the original equation, write $A = B$:

$$A - B = 0$$
$$A = B$$

"Look at the B in the first equation. It's a minus B. When it goes across the equals sign, it's no longer a minus B. When it goes across the equals sign, it changes from a minus B to a regular B—to a plus B."

The children have not yet learned that when a number or letter does not have a sign it has a plus value. They will learn this convention in the present set of exercises.

1. Present various subtraction facts to demonstrate what happens when a minus number moves across the equals sign:

$$5 - 5 = 0$$

"These guys are the same size. So we can write . . ."

$$5 - 5 = 0$$
$$5 = 5$$

"When the minus five goes across the equals sign, it becomes a regular five."

2. After demonstrating the rule with a number of simple problems, demonstrate that the reverse operation works. Write $3 = 3$.

"Is that true? Does three equal three? . . . Sure it does. That means that if we have three and if we minus all three, we'll end up with zero. They're the same size, so we have to end up with zero."

$$3 = 3$$
$$3 - 3 = 0$$

Point to the 3 on the right of the equals sign in the top equation. "Look at this three. He goes across the equals sign and he becomes a minus three."

3. After the children have learned the rule and can verbalize it, present the next type of transposition:

$$5 - 4 = 1$$

"Is that true? Does five minus four equal one? . . . Well, figure it out if you're not sure. . . . Good. Five minus four equals one. Look at the four. Is it a regular four? Is it a plus four? . . . No, it's a minus four. What's the rule we learned? If a minus four goes across the equals sign, what will happen to it? . . . Yes, it will turn into a regular four—into a plus four. Let's see if it works."

$$5 - 4 = 1$$
$$5 = 14$$

"Oh, oh! I'm in trouble. It says five equals fourteen. I didn't want to say that. I wanted to say that five is the same as regular one plus regular four. Maybe I can put a sign in there to show that I mean regular four, or plus four."

$$5 - 4 = 1$$
$$5 = 1 + 4$$

"There. Is that true? Does five equal one plus four? . . . Yes, they're the same. The minus four went across the equals sign and became a plus four. Let's try another problem."

$$9 - 8 = 1$$

"Is that true? . . . Yes. O.K., then the rule says we can move the minus eight across the equals sign and it will become a regular eight—a plus eight."

$$9 - 8 = 1$$
$$9 = 1 + 8$$

"Is that true? . . Yes, it works. One plus eight is the same as nine."

Present a series of problems in this form. Then give the children worksheets:

$7 - 7 = 0$	$6 - 5 = 1$
$7 =$	$6 =$
$3 - 3 = 0$	$10 - 9 = 1$
$3 =$	$10 =$
$4 - 3 = 1$	$8 - 6 = 2$
$4 =$	$8 =$
$4 - 1 = 3$	$A - B = C$
$4 =$	$A =$

4. Present problems in which a plus number is converted into a minus number:

$$2 + 1 = 3$$

"Is that true? . . . Yes, it is. I wonder what would happen if we moved the plus one across the equals sign . . . Yes, the rule says it would become a minus one. Let's see."

$$2 + 1 = 3$$
$$2 = 3 - 1$$

"Is two the same as three minus one? . . . The rule works. Let's try another problem."

$$5 + 5 = 10$$

"Let's move the plus five across the equals sign. What do you think will happen to it? . . . Yes, it will become a minus five."

$$5 + 5 = 10$$
$$5 = 10 - 5$$

"Is that true? Is five the same as ten minus five? . . . Sure it is."

Let the children suggest addition statements that can be rewritten by moving the second term across the equals sign. Then present worksheets:

$$6 + 1 = 7 \qquad\qquad 4 + 1 = 5$$
$$6 = \qquad\qquad\qquad 4 =$$

$$6 + 2 = 8 \qquad\qquad 5 + 1 = 6$$
$$6 = \qquad\qquad\qquad 5 =$$

$$6 + 3 = 9 \qquad\qquad 8 + 1 = 9$$
$$6 = \qquad\qquad\qquad 8 =$$

$$6 + 6 = 12 \qquad\qquad A + B = C$$
$$6 = \qquad\qquad\qquad A =$$

5. Next introduce longer problems. Begin with

$$1 + 1 + 1 + 1 = 4$$

"Let's move all these ones except the first across the equals sign. What's going to happen to them? . . ."

$$1 + 1 + 1 + 1 = 4$$
$$1 = 4 - 1 - 1 - 1$$

"Work it out and see if it's true. We've got one on this side of the equals sign. See if we have one on this other side of the equals sign. . . . Good. Let's try a harder problem."

$$7 - 1 + 3 =$$

After the children give the answer, complete the statement:

$$7 - 1 + 3 = 9$$

"O.K., now let's move the minus one and the plus three across the equals sign. What's going to happen to the minus one? . . . Yes, it will become a plus one. And what will happen to the plus three? . . . It will become a minus three."

$$7 - 1 + 3 = 9$$
$$7 = 9 + 1 - 3$$

"Is that true? We've got seven on this side of the equals sign. If the rule is right we should have seven on the other side of the equals sign. Work it out and see. . . ."

Present similar problems that involve both plus and minus numbers. First have the children figure out how many they end up with. Then have them indicate what will happen to the signs of the numbers that are to be moved across the equals sign. Finally, have them check to see whether the equation balances.

Present worksheet problems such as these:

$$3 + 4 + 1 - 2 = 6 \qquad\qquad 8 - 2 + 1 + 1 = 8$$
$$3 = \qquad\qquad\qquad\qquad 8 =$$

$$A + B + C - D = F \qquad\qquad A + B + C + D + E = F$$
$$A = \qquad\qquad\qquad\qquad\qquad A =$$

$$9 - 1 - 1 - 1 = 6 \qquad\qquad A - B - C - D - E = F$$
$$9 = \qquad\qquad\qquad\qquad\qquad A =$$

$$A - B - C - D = E \qquad\qquad R + \square - CAT + 4 = K$$
$$A = \qquad\qquad\qquad\qquad\qquad R =$$

Set the problems up as indicated above. Keeping the second equals sign directly below the first in each pair of statements helps the children see which letters or numbers have to move across the equals sign.

6. Demonstrate how to solve these problems another way—by changing the numbers that are added or subtracted into zero.

$$a + 2 = 7$$

Introduce the new method: "O.K., let's find out what a equals. Do we want to know what $a + 2$ equals? . . . No, we want to know what a equals. Let's do it a new way. Let's change that plus two into zero. How do we change a plus two into zero? . . . We minus two."

$$a + 2 - 2 = 7$$

"Oh, oh! We changed this equation. We minused two on this side of the equals sign. What's the rule? . . . What you do to one side of the equals sign, you have to do to the other. So what do I have to do to the other side?"

$$a + 2 - 2 = 7 - 2$$

Simplify the statement. "What do we have on this side of the equals sign?" Point to the left side. "We have a. And what do we have on the other side? . . . Five. So a equals five."

Work the problem the other way (by moving the two across the equals sign) and demonstrate that you get the same answer.

7. Present a series of worksheet problems for the children to solve by reducing the undesired terms on the left of the equals sign to zero. Allow adequate space between the numbers for adding or subtracting:

$B + 3 = 2$	$B - 6 = 0$
$B =$	$B =$
$R + 3 = 4$	$A - 4 = 1$
$R =$	$A =$
$A - 3 = 5$	$A - 3 = -1$
$A =$	$A =$
$K + 7 = 6$	$B - 4 = -2$
$K =$	$B =$
$L + 6 = 2$	$A + B = C$
$L =$	$A =$

Present similar sheets until the children can work the problems quickly. Also present problems such as $B + 1 = 3$ verbally. Present two or three of these verbal problems a day after the children have worked problems on the worksheets.

Complex word problems

1. Introduce word problems in which the children must move terms across the equals sign before they can reach their goal of indicating what S or A equals:

"A guy goes into a bakery and says, 'I want to buy a pie.' The baker says, 'That's good, because one pie and two pennies cost fourteen cents.' The guy says, 'But I don't want to buy a pie and two pennies. I just want to buy a pie. You must be some kind of a nut, Mr. Baker.'

But the baker just says, 'One pie and two pennies cost fourteen cents.' Let's write down what he says."

$$1p + 2 = 14$$
$$1p =$$

"We want to end up with one *p*, not one *p* plus two. We'd better get rid of the plus two. How can we do that? . . . Move the plus two across the equals sign. What's going to happen to it? . . . Yes, it becomes a minus two."

$$1p + 2 = 14$$
$$1p = 14 - 2$$

"What's fourteen minus two? . . . Yes, twelve. So one pie costs twelve cents."

"Let's try another problem: A guy goes into the same store and he says, 'I want to buy a cake.' The crazy baker says, 'One cake and four pennies cost twenty-four cents.' There he goes again with that silly talk. What did he say? . . . One cake and four pennies cost twenty-four cents. And the guy says, 'But I don't want one cake and four pennies. I just want one cake. Forget the four pennies.' Let's help him out. What did the baker say? . . ."

$$1c + 4 = 24$$
$$1c =$$

"We want to end up with one *c*, not one *c* plus four. So what do we do? . . . Yes, get rid of that four. Move it across the equals sign. And what's going to happen to it? . . . It becomes a minus four. So . . ."

$$1c + 4 = 24$$
$$1c - 24 - 4$$

"So one *c* equals twenty cents."

2. Use the crazy baker to make up problems that involve both plus and minus numbers: "Do you want to hear a real silly story about the nutty baker? Well, a girl goes into the bakery and says, 'I want to buy a doughnut.' The baker says, 'One doughnut and minus three cents cost two cents.' The girl says, 'What are you saying? I just want to buy a doughnut. I don't want any minus cents. I don't even know what they are.' But the baker says, 'One doughnut and minus three cents cost two cents.' The girl doesn't know what to do, so we'll help her."

$$1d - 3 = 2$$
$$1d =$$

"We want to end up with one d. So what do we have to do? Move the minus three across the equals sign. And what's going to happen to it? . . . Yes, it will become a plus three. . . ."

$$1d - 3 = 2$$
$$1d = 2 + 3$$

"All right. Tell the girl how much one doughnut costs. . . ."

3. Work on similar problems until the children clearly understand the procedure of moving a number across the equals sign. Then give them worksheet problems:

$1R + 2 = 3$	$1R + 2 + 1 = 5$
$1R =$	$1R =$
$1A + 4 = 10$	$1A - 5 = 5$
$1A =$	$1A =$
$1B + 7 = 11$	$1A + 6 = 6$
$1B =$	$1A =$
$1B + 3 = 1$	$1A - 1 - 1 = 1$
$1B =$	$1A =$

4. Introduce word problems that involve all that they have learned about multiplying terms and moving them across the equals sign:

"A man walks into the crazy bakery and says, 'I want to buy a cake.' The baker says, 'That's good, because three cakes plus three pennies cost eighteen cents.' What did he say? . . . Yes, he must be some kind of a nut. Anyhow, the man says, 'I don't want three cakes and three pennies. I just want one cake.' Let's help him out."

$$3c + 3 = 18$$

"How are we going to work this problem? . . . Let's first find out what three c equals—not three c plus three. Then we can find out what one c equals. Remember—we want to find out about one c. We want to know what one cake costs."

$$3c + 3 = 18$$
$$3c =$$
$$1c =$$

"If we want to find out what three c equals, what do we have to do with the plus three? . . . Move it across the equals sign."

$$3c + 3 = 18$$
$$3c = 18 - 3$$

"So what does three c equal? . . . Yes, fifteen. So I can erase the eighteen-minus-three and write fifteen. . . . Now, how do we get one c? . . . Yes, we have to turn the three into a one. How do we do that? . . . Multiply by the reciprocal of three, which is what? . . ."

$$3c + 3 = 18$$
$$3c = 15$$
$$(\tfrac{1}{3})\tfrac{3\,c}{1} = \tfrac{15}{1}(\tfrac{1}{3})$$

"So one c equals five cents. That's what one cake costs. I wonder why that silly baker didn't say so in the first place."

5. Present a variety of similar problems. Construct them so that they involve moving both plus and minus numbers across the equals sign. Also introduce variations in which the crazy baker makes a statement that involves fractions:

"Tommy goes into that crazy bakery and says, 'I want to buy a loaf of bread.' The nutty baker says, 'One-half loaf of bread and four cents cost twelve cents.' Here we go again. Poor Tommy wants one loaf of bread and the baker tells him that one-half loaf of bread and four cents cost twelve cents."

$$\tfrac{1}{2}L + 4 = 12$$

"What should we do first? . . . Yes, let's find out what one-half loaf of bread costs. Then we can change the one-half into what? . . . Yes, one. We want to find out what one loaf of bread costs. Now what does one-half loaf of bread equal?"

$$\tfrac{1}{2}L = 12 - 4$$

"So one-half loaf equals eight. Now what can we do to take care of that one-half? . . ."

$$\tfrac{1}{2}L = 8$$
$$(\tfrac{2}{1})\tfrac{1}{2}L = \tfrac{8}{1}(\tfrac{2}{1})$$

"One loaf of bread costs sixteen cents. I wonder why that silly baker didn't just say that in the first place."

379

6. After the children have worked a number of these problems and are able to indicate which steps should be taken and why they are to be taken, present worksheets:

Tell what $1A$ equals in each problem.

$2A - 3 = 15$ $\qquad$ $\frac{1}{3}A + 2 = 3$
$1A =$ $\qquad\qquad\qquad$ $1A =$

$3A + 1 = 19$ $\qquad$ $\frac{2}{5}A + 1 = 3$
$1A =$ $\qquad\qquad\qquad$ $1A =$

$4A + 3 = 15$ $\qquad$ $\frac{3}{4}A + 1 = 10$
$1A =$ $\qquad\qquad\qquad$ $1A =$

Adding Fractions

The potential trouble spot in adding or subtracting fractions has to do with the denominators. When you multiply fractions, you go straight across the top and straight across the bottom. When you add, however, you operate *only at the top*. The bottom numbers simply tell you something about the kind of unit you are working with. Just as "three cats" tells you that you are working with units called cats, "three-fourths" tells you that you are working with units called fourths.

1. To teach the children this convention, begin with object problems. Draw two circles on the board. Next to them draw a group of four circles. "Let's add these up. What do I have here? . . ." Point to the group of two circles. "Yes, two circles. So I can write 'two *c*.' "

"What am I going to add to the two *c*? . . . Four *c*."

$2c + 4c =$

After the children have added up the circles, say, "So I end up with six *c*."

$2c + 4c = 6c$

"If I add two circles and four circles, I end up with six circles. Could I write this? . . ."

$2c + 4c = 6$ dogs

"Of course not. That's silly. If I'm adding circles, I end up with circles, not dogs." Refer to the circles on the chalkboard. "I didn't start with dogs, so I didn't end up with dogs."

380

2. Present several other examples. Stress the rule that when you're adding a particular kind of object, you end up with that kind of object.

3. Next draw two circles and four rectangles on the board. "Let's add these up. Tell me what to write."

$$2c + 4r =$$

"Can I say that we end up with six c? . . . No, because we don't end up with six c. Can I say that we end up with six r? . . . No, because we don't end up with six r. We end up with two c and four r. We can't add them up because we're not talking about the same thing."

Some of the children may object that you can count them. "Yes, but when you do, you're not calling them circles or rectangles. You're calling them things. Two things plus four things equals six things. But two circles plus four rectangles just equals two circles plus four rectangles. If I take the letters away, you can add them up. But when I have the letters in, you can't add unless you're talking about the same thing. You have to be talking about two circles and four circles or two rectangles and four rectangles."

4. Introduce examples until the children are comfortable with the letter convention. Introduce examples in which some of the things can be added but others can't. For example, draw a group of two circles on the board, a group of two rectangles, and a group of three circles:

$$2c + 2r + 3c =$$

"We can add up the c's because they're talking about the same thing. So what do we end up with?"

$$2c + 2r + 3c = 5c + 2r$$

"We end up with five circles and two rectangles."

5. Give the children worksheets that involve problems of this kind.

$$3M + 2C + 1M =$$
$$4A + 5A + 1B + 2B =$$
$$3B + 1A + 2B + 3A =$$
$$2A + 2C - 1A - 1C =$$
$$3B + 5B + 7C - 4C =$$
$$8R - 5R + 2D - 2D =$$

Tell the children to cross out the numbers as they do them. When the problem is completed, all the numbers should be crossed out.

6. Demonstrate that the same rule holds for adding fractions. Present this problem:

$$\tfrac{2}{3} + \tfrac{1}{3} =$$

"If you have two-thirds and you get one more third, how many thirds will you have?" If the children have trouble with the question, draw a circle, divide it into three parts, color two parts, and then color one more. "Two-thirds of a pie plus one more third equals three-thirds —the whole pie."

Introduce a new way of writing the problem. Draw a long horizontal line on the board. Write a 3 below the line:

$$\overline{}$$
$$3$$

"I'm going to make a fancy fraction. This tells us that we're talking about thirds. And this is how many we have. . . ."

$$\tfrac{2+1}{3} =$$

"We've got two of them and then we get one more."

Demonstrate the rewriting procedure with various circle problems. Then present worksheet problems:

$$\tfrac{4}{2} + \tfrac{2}{2} = \underline{} = \qquad \tfrac{1}{3} + \tfrac{5}{3} + \tfrac{3}{3} = \underline{} =$$
$$\tfrac{1}{5} + \tfrac{4}{5} = \underline{} = \qquad \tfrac{1}{3} + \tfrac{1}{3} + \tfrac{1}{3} = \underline{} =$$
$$\tfrac{2}{7} + \tfrac{12}{7} = \underline{} = \qquad \tfrac{2}{a} + \tfrac{3}{a} + \tfrac{b}{a} = \underline{} =$$
$$\tfrac{5}{6} + \tfrac{7}{6} = \underline{} = \qquad \tfrac{a}{b} + \tfrac{c}{b} + \tfrac{d}{b} = \underline{} =$$

In each blank the children are to rewrite the problem, using the same denominator. For example:

$$\tfrac{4}{2} + \tfrac{2}{2} = \tfrac{4+2}{2} = \tfrac{6}{2}$$

Do not require the children to reduce the answer.

7. Present problems in which the numerator is rewritten. As the children work the problems, remind them that the bottom tells them what they are talking about (fourths, or eighths) and the top tells them how many they have.

Write the fraction $\tfrac{3}{4}$ on the board.

"I'm going to make a fraction that is equal to this fraction. Watch. . . ."

$$\tfrac{3}{4} = \tfrac{2+1}{4}$$

"Are they the same? The first fraction tells me that I'm talking about fourths and that I have three of them. The second fraction tells me that I'm talking about fourths and that I have two plus one—that's three of them. They're the same. They're equal."

Demonstrate the procedure with several problems and then give the children worksheet problems:

$\frac{2}{3} =$ _____ $\frac{10}{b} =$ _____

$\frac{10}{2} =$ _____ $\frac{2}{rc} =$ _____

$\frac{6}{8} =$ _____ $\frac{3a}{1} =$ _____

$\frac{3}{a} =$ _____ $\frac{3a}{b} =$ _____

They may have trouble with the last two problems. Remind them of the rule: "You're talking about a's. That means you have to add up a's. Pretend that the a stands for an apple. Now how can you plus apples to get three apples?" If the child says "Two plus one," ask him, "Two what? Two elephants? . . . O.K., two apples. Then you have to say two a's."

$$\left(\frac{2a + 1a}{1}\right)$$

8. Present problems that involve fractions with unlike denominators:

$$\frac{1}{2} + \frac{6}{4} = \text{_____}$$

"We've got trouble. Look—this first fraction is talking about halves and this second fraction is talking about fourths. That's like talking about circles and rectangles. We can't add them up. I wonder what we can do?"

After the children have thought about the problem a moment, suggest, "I've got it. We can multiply this one-half by one. If we multiply by one we don't change it, do we? So we can multiply it by one. And we can multiply it by a fraction that's equal to one. We can multiply it by five over five or three over three. But we want to multiply it by a fraction that will change the two into a four. Two times how many equals four? . . . Two times two equals four."

$$\left(\frac{2}{2}\right)\frac{1}{2} + \frac{6}{4} = \text{_____}$$

"What will the bottom of this fraction be? . . . Four. Just like this other fraction. Then I can add them up."

$$\frac{2}{4} + \frac{6}{4} = \frac{\quad}{4}$$

"I'll be talking about fourths. And this is how many I'll have. . . ."

$$\frac{2}{4} + \frac{6}{4} = \frac{2+6}{4} = \frac{8}{4}$$

Make the point that you are not changing the fraction, since you are multiplying by one. The fraction-equal-to-one that you use is the fraction that makes the smaller denominator the same as that of the other fraction.

"Let's try another problem."

$$\frac{5}{2} + \frac{3}{6} = \underline{\hspace{3cm}}$$

"The first fraction is talking about halves and the second fraction is talking about sixths. I can't add them, because they're not talking about the same thing. Look at those bottoms. Which number is smaller —two or six? . . . Two. Can I count by twos to get to six? . . . Sure. How many times do I count? . . . Three times. So if I multiply two by three, I'll have six. . . ."

$$(_3)\frac{5}{2} + \frac{3}{6} = \underline{\hspace{3cm}}$$

"Oh, oh! I don't want to change five over two, so I'd better multiply by one. . . ."

$$(\frac{3}{3})\frac{5}{2} + \frac{3}{6} = \underline{\hspace{3cm}}$$

"I multiplied by three over three. Is that equal to one? . . . Yes. So I multiplied five over two by one. I didn't change it. This first fraction now has a six at the bottom, and this second fraction has a six at the bottom. I can add them."

$$\frac{15}{6} + \frac{3}{6} = \frac{}{6}$$

"How many sixths will I have? . . . Fifteen plus three. How many is that? . . . Eighteen. Good."

$$\frac{15}{6} + \frac{3}{6} = \frac{15+3}{6} = \frac{18}{6}$$

Work similar problems with denominators of 2 and 8, 3 and 6, 4 and 8, 4 and 12, and so on. When working these problems—

• Find the smallest number in the denominators.

• See if you can count by that number to reach the number in the denominator of the other fraction.

• Indicate how many times you count. Conclude that if the denominator of the smaller fraction is multiplied by the number of times

384

you must count to reach the other denominator, the denominators will be the same size.

• To keep from changing the fraction with the smaller denominator, multiply by a fraction that is equal to one ($\frac{2}{2}$, $\frac{3}{3}$, $\frac{4}{4}$, and so on).

• Add up the top numbers and write the sum over the common denominator.

Although the procedure may seem involved, it is important for the children to recognize that they are not changing the original fraction. They are simply multiplying it by one, which means that they can operate on one fraction without doing anything to the other fraction.

9. Introduce problems in which both fractions must be multiplied to find a common denominator:

$$\tfrac{1}{2} + \tfrac{1}{3} =$$

Have the children find the smallest number in the denominator and see if they can reach the other number by counting by it. "No, so what are we going to do? . . . Here's a good trick. We can multiply the first fraction by three and the second fraction by two."

$$(\tfrac{3}{3})\tfrac{1}{2} + \tfrac{1}{3}(\tfrac{2}{2}) = \frac{}{6}$$

"Now they both have six at the bottom. Let's figure out what they have at the top. . . ."

$$\tfrac{3}{6} + \tfrac{2}{6} = \frac{3 + 2}{6} = \tfrac{5}{6}$$

Present a number of similar problems until the children have caught on to the procedure. Then give them worksheet problems:

$\tfrac{1}{4} + \tfrac{1}{3} =$	$\tfrac{1}{2} + \tfrac{1}{3} + \tfrac{3}{2} =$
$\tfrac{2}{3} + \tfrac{1}{5} =$	$\tfrac{2}{3} + \tfrac{1}{4} + \tfrac{1}{3} =$
$\tfrac{2}{5} + \tfrac{1}{3} =$	$\tfrac{1}{a} + \tfrac{1}{b} =$
$\tfrac{1}{6} + \tfrac{1}{5} =$	$\tfrac{1}{c} + \tfrac{2}{d} =$

They may have some trouble with the last two problems. Demonstrate the procedure and then repeat the problems from time to time until the children have mastered them: "The number at the bottom will be a times b—ab. We'll multiply the a by b and the b by a. We don't want to multiply a fraction by anything but one, so we'll multiply the first fraction by b over b and the second fraction by a over a."

$$(\tfrac{b}{b})\tfrac{1}{a} + \tfrac{1}{b}(\tfrac{a}{a}) =$$
$$(\tfrac{b}{b})\tfrac{1}{a} + \tfrac{1}{b}(\tfrac{a}{a}) = \frac{b + a}{ba}$$

385

Factoring

The children should learn two methods of factoring—the more traditional method by which they find a common factor, and a second method in which they use a "mechanical" procedure.

Finding a common factor

1. Show that factoring involves multiplying a number by one.

Write the number 6 on the board and say, "Six is a fraction. What fraction is it? . . . Six over one. I'm going to multiply it by one. Will I change it? . . . No."

$$\frac{6}{1}\left(\frac{2}{2}\right) =$$

"Now, here comes the tricky part. I'm going to multiply the bottom numbers and put the answer under the six."

$$\frac{6}{2}(2) =$$

"Do you think that still equals six? Let's see. What's six over two? How many wholes? . . . Yes, three wholes. What's three times two? . . . Count by three two times. . . . Yes, it equals six."

$$\frac{6}{2}(2) = 6$$

2. Present a series of similar examples until the children are familiar with the steps. For example, write the fraction $\frac{8}{1}$ on the board.

"Now I'm going to multiply eight over one by one. Will I change it? . . . No, it will still equal eight."

$$\frac{8}{1}\left(\frac{4}{4}\right) =$$

"Multiply at the bottom and write the answer under the eight."

$$\frac{8}{4}(4) =$$

"How many wholes is eight over four? . . . Two wholes. Two times four? . . . It still equals eight."

3. After the children have learned the operation, give them worksheet problems:

$8\left(\frac{2}{2}\right) =$	$4\left(\frac{2}{2}\right) =$
$9\left(\frac{3}{3}\right) =$	$20\left(\frac{4}{4}\right) =$
$10\left(\frac{5}{5}\right) =$	$12\left(\frac{6}{6}\right) =$
$6\left(\frac{3}{3}\right) =$	$16\left(\frac{4}{4}\right) =$

4. Present more complex problems.

Write the expression $2a + 4b$ on the board. Point to the two and the four. "What number could we count by to get to both of these numbers? . . . I know the answer. We could count by twos. So watch what I'm going to do."

$$\tfrac{2}{2}(2a + 4b)$$

"Did I change two a plus four b? . . . No, because I multiplied it by one. Now I'm going to rewrite the fraction two over two. Watch. . . ."

$$2(\tfrac{2a}{2} + \tfrac{4b}{2})$$

"Can I do that? . . . Sure I can. That two belongs to both the two a and the four b. Let's see what we have inside the parentheses." Have the children reduce the fractions:

$$2(a + 2b)$$

"Look what we've got. We followed the rules, didn't we? That means this is the same as what we started out with—two a plus four b. Let's see if it is. Let's multiply and see if we end up with two a plus four b. Remember—that two goes with both a and b."

"Two times a, that's two a. Two times two b, that's four b."

If the children have trouble handling terms that involve both numbers and letters, remind them that there is a number in front of every letter. "If you don't see it, it's a one." The first term, for example, is $1a$. When you multiply, you multiply a number by a number—in this case, two times one.

5. Present a variety of simple factoring problems involving three or four terms:

$$10a + 5b + 20c$$

"O.K., what number could I count by to get to ten and five and twenty? . . . That's right, five. So I can multiply this whole thing by five over five."

$$\tfrac{5}{5}(10a + 5b + 20c)$$

"Did I change it? No, I multiplied by one. Now I can rewrite the fraction, so that the bottom part goes with each of these numbers."

$$5(\tfrac{10a}{5} + \tfrac{5b}{5} + \tfrac{20c}{5})$$

"Let's see what these numbers are inside the parenthesis."

$5(2a + 1b + 4c)$

Multiply the factors together and show that the product is the original expression:

$10a + 5b + 20c$

6. Present worksheet problems when the children have mastered the operation—that is, when they can tell you what to write when you present the problems on the board.

Factor:

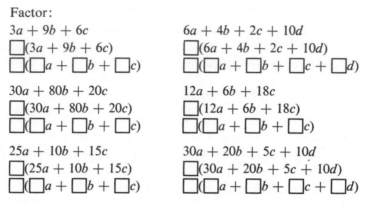

Work on similar problems until the children understand the operation.

General factoring procedure

1. Present this problem: $5(\ ) = 6$

"Look at that. It says that five times something equals six. I wonder what that something is. Do you want to see how to find it? . . . Watch. First I turn the five into a one. How do I do that? . . ."

$5(\frac{1}{5}) = 6$

"Now this whole thing says one equals six. That's silly. One times six equals six. So I'll have to put a six in there."

$5(\frac{1}{5} \cdot \frac{6}{1}) = 6$

"Now it says one times six equals six. And I've found the factor. I know what to multiply five by to get six. I multiply by six over five."

2. Work a variety of problems. Let the children make them up. A child may suggest the problem: $3(\ ) = 2$.

388

"We can do it. We can multiply three by something that will give us two. Let's find out what it is. First let's change the three into a one."

$$3(\tfrac{1}{3}) = 2$$

"But now it says that one equals two. That's silly. One times two equals two. So . . ."

$$3(\tfrac{1}{3} \cdot \tfrac{2}{1}) = 2$$

"And that's what we have to multiply three by to end up with two—two over three."

3. Introduce problems that involve fractions: $\tfrac{1}{2}(\;\;) = \tfrac{2}{3}$.

"Gosh, I wonder what I could multiply one-half by to end up with two-thirds. Who can help me out? John? . . . First, he changes the one-half into one."

$$\tfrac{1}{2}(\tfrac{2}{1}\;\;) = \tfrac{2}{3}$$

"But now it says that one equals two-thirds. That's silly. One times two-thirds equals two-thirds."

$$\tfrac{1}{2}(\tfrac{2}{1} \cdot \tfrac{2}{3}) = \tfrac{2}{3}$$

"So what do we have to multiply one-half by to end up with two-thirds? We have a four at the top and a three at the bottom. Four over three."

4. After the children have a firm understanding of the operation, present worksheet problems:

$$\tfrac{6}{1}(\;\;) = \tfrac{4}{1} \qquad\qquad \tfrac{5}{a}(\;\;) = \tfrac{1}{6}$$
$$\tfrac{1}{3}(\;\;) = \tfrac{3}{2} \qquad\qquad \tfrac{b}{3}(\;\;) = \tfrac{a}{5}$$
$$\tfrac{1}{4}(\;\;) = \tfrac{9}{4} \qquad\qquad \tfrac{a}{b}(\;\;) = \tfrac{c}{d}$$

Repeat the last problem from time to time. It gives the children the general rule for working any factoring problem of this type. It is worked just like the other problems. First turn $\tfrac{a}{b}$ into one. Then multiply by $\tfrac{c}{d}$ (since one times $\tfrac{c}{d}$ equals $\tfrac{c}{d}$).

More Fraction Operations

Reducing fractions

1. To reduce a fraction, you simply find two factors, *one of which is equal to one*.

Present the fraction $\frac{4}{8}$: "Do you want to see how to *reduce* this fraction? Here's how. What's the biggest number you can count by to get to the four and to the eight? . . . Yes, four."

$$\frac{4}{8}(\frac{4}{4})$$

Point to the denominator of $\frac{4}{4}$. "What do we have to multiply four by to end up with eight? How many times do we have to count by fours to get to eight? . . . Yes, two."

$$\frac{4}{8} = (\frac{4}{4})_2$$

Point to the numerators. "How many times do we have to count by fours to end up with four? . . . One time."

$$\frac{4}{8} = (\frac{4}{4})\frac{1}{2}$$

"So four over eight really equals one times one-half. Four over eight is really one-half."

Draw a picture of four over eight (a circle with eight parts, four shaded) and show that the picture is the same as that of one-half.

Demonstrate the procedure with other fractions. Write $\frac{10}{2}$.

"Let's work this problem the new way. What's the biggest number we can count by to get to both ten and two? . . . Two."

$$\frac{10}{2}(\frac{2}{2})$$

"How many times do we count by two to get to ten? . . . Five. So we have a five at the top. How many times do we count by twos to get to two? . . . One time. So we have a one at the bottom."

$$\frac{10}{2} = (\frac{2}{2})\frac{5}{1}$$

"So ten over two is the same as one times five. Ten over two equals five."

Work the problem the familiar way. "Count by twos how many times to end up with ten? . . . Five times." Draw the diagram.

2. After you have demonstrated the factoring procedure with a number of reducible fractions ($\frac{15}{3}$, $\frac{12}{4}$, $\frac{6}{3}$, $\frac{20}{5}$, $\frac{3}{12}$, $\frac{9}{36}$, $\frac{6}{24}$, $\frac{5}{30}$, and so on), present worksheet problems:

$$\frac{20}{4} = (\quad)\square \qquad \frac{7}{21} = (\quad)\square$$
$$\frac{30}{5} = (\quad)\square \qquad \frac{9}{27} = (\quad)\square$$
$$\frac{45}{9} = (\quad)\square \qquad \frac{6}{18} = (\quad)\square$$
$$\frac{12}{3} = (\quad)\square \qquad \frac{3}{15} = (\quad)\square$$

390

3. Demonstrate the reverse operation. Show the children how to manufacture fractions by multiplying a fraction by different fractions equal to one.

Start with the fraction $\frac{1}{3}$: "Let's make up some other fractions that equal one-third. How can we do that? . . . We can multiply one-third by one. That won't change it, will it? . . . Does two over two equal one? Yes, so we can multiply by two over two."

$$\tfrac{1}{3}(\tfrac{2}{2}) = \tfrac{2}{6}$$

"Two-sixths is the same as one-third. It has to be, because we multiplied one-third by one. Let's multiply one-third by another fraction that is equal to one—three-thirds."

$$\tfrac{1}{3}(\tfrac{2}{2}) = \tfrac{2}{6}$$
$$\tfrac{1}{3}(\tfrac{3}{3}) = \tfrac{3}{9}$$

Continue until you've multiplied the fraction by $\frac{10}{10}$. Repeat the demonstration with other simple fractions. Also work with whole numbers, such as $\frac{4}{1}$:

$$\tfrac{4}{1}(\tfrac{2}{2}) = \tfrac{8}{2}$$
$$\tfrac{4}{1}(\tfrac{3}{3}) = \tfrac{12}{3}$$
$$\tfrac{4}{1}(\tfrac{4}{4}) = \tfrac{16}{4}$$
$$\tfrac{4}{1}(\tfrac{5}{5}) = \tfrac{20}{5}$$

When working with whole numbers, stress the rule: "If the top is four times bigger than the bottom (if you count four times by the bottom number to get to the top number), the number is four. Four means that the top of the fraction is four times bigger than the bottom."

Clearing the denominator

This operation is the last to be discussed in the arithmetic section.

1. Present this problem:

$$\tfrac{1}{2}a + 1a = 2$$

Refer to the fraction $\frac{1}{2}$. "This tells me about one-half a. How could I change it into one a? . . . Yes, multiply by the reciprocal. But wait. Remember—I have to do it to the whole side of the equation, not just one part of it. What do we have on this side of the equation? . . . One-half a plus one a. I have to multiply that whole thing by two."

$$2(\tfrac{1}{2}a + 1a) = 2$$

Remind them of the rule about changing an equation: "What's the rule? . . . What you do on one side of the equals sign, you have to do on the other. So we have to multiply this other side by two."

$$2(\tfrac{1}{2}a + 1a) = 2 \times 2$$

Rewrite the left side of the equation: "Remember—the two belongs to both the one-half a and the one a. So we can write it . . ."

$$2(\tfrac{1}{2}a) + 2(1a) = 2 \times 2$$

Solve the problem:

$$1a + 2a = 4$$
$$3a = 4$$
$$a = \tfrac{4}{3}$$

2. Present other examples in the same form. For example:

$$\tfrac{1}{3}b + 4b = 1$$

Here are the steps involved in the solution:

• Turn the $\tfrac{1}{3}$ into a whole number by multiplying by 3, the number in the denominator.

• Multiply the entire side by this number:

$$3(\tfrac{1}{3}b + 4b) = 1$$

• Use the rule about changing both sides of an equation. Multiply the other side by 3:

$$3(\tfrac{1}{3}b + 4b) = 1 \times 3$$

• Rewrite the left side:

$$3(\tfrac{1}{3}b) + 3(4b) = 3$$

• Solve the equation for b:

$$1b + 12b = 3$$
$$13b = 3$$
$$b = \tfrac{3}{13}$$

Work on problems of this form until the children can handle them without prompting.

3. Introduce problems that contain two fractions:

$$\tfrac{1}{3}c + \tfrac{2}{3}c = 4$$

"Here's a hard problem." Point to the $\frac{1}{3}c$. "I want to change this one-third into one." Point to $\frac{2}{3}$. "And I want to change this two thirds into two. What could I multiply this side by? . . . Yes, I can multiply this side by three. That will get rid of the bottoms of these fractions."

$$3(\tfrac{1}{3}c + \tfrac{2}{3}c) = 4$$

"What we do on one side of the equals sign, we have to do on the other. . . ."

$$3(\tfrac{1}{3}c + \tfrac{2}{3}c) = 4 \times 3$$

"Let's rewrite and solve it."

$$3(\tfrac{1}{3}c) + 3(\tfrac{2}{3}c) = 4 \times 3$$
$$1c + 2c = 12$$
$$3c = 12$$
$$c = 4$$

Introduce similar problems in which the fractions have the same denominator. When working them, stress the idea that you are trying to find a number that will get rid of the denominator.

4. After the children have demonstrated that they can handle problems of this form without much coaching, present problems in which the fractions do not have the same denominator:

$$\tfrac{2}{3}b + \tfrac{1}{2}b = 1$$

Point to the fractions. "I want to change this two-thirds into two, and I want to change this one-half into one. What can I multiply this side by?"

Some of the children may suggest multiplying by three, while others may suggest multiplying by two. "Let's do both of them."

$$3 \cdot 2(\tfrac{2}{3}b + \tfrac{1}{2}b) = 1 \cdot 3 \cdot 2$$

Rewrite:

$$3 \cdot 2(\tfrac{2}{3}b) + 3 \cdot 2(\tfrac{1}{2}b) = 1 \cdot 3 \cdot 2$$

Cancel:

$$3 \cdot 2(\tfrac{2}{3}b) + 3 \cdot 2(\tfrac{1}{2}b) = 1 \cdot 3 \cdot 2$$

"See. I can just cross out that three over three because it equals one. And I can cross out the two over two because it equals one. Cross it out. And look what we have left. . . ."

$$4b + 3b = 6$$
$$7b = 6$$
$$b = \tfrac{6}{7}$$

5. Work on similar problems (presenting two or three a day on the board) until the children are familiar with the operation. Take these problems a step at a time:

Multiply the left side by the numbers in both of the denominators.
Multiply the right side of the equation by the same numbers.
Cancel out any fraction that is equal to one.
Solve for the unknown.

6. After the children have worked a variety of simple problems, present worksheets. Do not present more than four problems on a sheet.

At first, set the problems up so that the children are guided to take the proper steps:

$$\tfrac{1}{4}b + \tfrac{3}{5}b = 2$$
$$(\tfrac{1}{4}b + \tfrac{3}{5}b) = 2(\quad)$$
$$(\tfrac{1}{4}b) + (\tfrac{3}{5}b) = \square$$
$$\square b = \square$$
$$b = \square$$

$$\tfrac{2}{5}b + \tfrac{1}{3}b = 4$$
$$(\tfrac{2}{5}b + \tfrac{1}{3}b) = 4(\quad)$$
$$(\tfrac{2}{5}b) + (\tfrac{1}{3}b) = \square$$
$$\square b = \square$$
$$b = \square$$

$$\tfrac{1}{3}c + \tfrac{2}{7}c = 1$$
$$(\tfrac{1}{3}c + \tfrac{2}{7}c) = 1(\quad)$$
$$(\tfrac{1}{3}c) + (\tfrac{2}{7}c) = \square$$
$$\square c = \square$$
$$c = \square$$

$$\tfrac{3}{4}a + \tfrac{1}{3}a = 2$$
$$(\tfrac{3}{4}a + \tfrac{1}{3}a) = 2(\quad)$$
$$(\tfrac{3}{4}a) + (\tfrac{1}{3}a) = \square$$
$$\square a = \square$$
$$a = \square$$

After they have worked perhaps three or four sheets similar to the one above, drop out some of the steps. Require the children to take more and more of the initiative until they are able to write out all the steps that lead to the solution.

Further Arithmetic

The program outlined in this and the preceding chapter presents basic operations that can be applied to a wide range of problems—not all the operations needed in arithmetic, but only those that are perhaps most useful in solving basic problems, which is the focus of the program. Surprisingly, children can finish this program in much less time than a teacher might imagine. Some slow learners may finish it in less than two school years. The reason is that the various attacks on problems are reduced to a few fundamental rules about addition, multiplication, and fractions. The statements presented by the teacher are always the same. The operations are generalized, to demonstrate that they hold not only for numbers but also for letters.

The child who successfully completes the program outlined in these chapters should have a relatively solid foundation. He will not encounter many problems that cannot be reduced to the set of rules he has mastered. The operations that he will later learn (squaring, cubing, and so on) are related to operations that he has learned. These operations can therefore be presented in a meaningful manner, which simply means that they can be related to familiar operations. A child who finishes this program during his primary-grade years will be ahead in his operational understanding of arithmetic. He can remain ahead if his instruction continues to build on what he knows and to give understanding precedence over rote performance.

Notes

1. Eleanor P. Wolf and Leo Wolf, "Sociological Perspective on the Education of Culturally Deprived Children," in J. L. Frost and Glenn R. Hawkes (eds.), *The Disadvantaged Child: Issues and Innovations* (Boston: Houghton Mifflin, 1966), p. 69.
2. *Ibid.*, p. 73.
3. Helene M. Lloyd, "What's Ahead in Reading for the Disadvantaged?" in J. L. Frost and Glenn R. Hawkes (eds.), *The Disadvantaged Child: Issues and Innovations* (Boston: Houghton Mifflin, 1966), pp. 291–96.
4. Frank Riessman, "The Overlooked Positives of Disadvantaged Groups," in J. L. Frost and Glenn R. Hawkes (eds.), *The Disadvantaged Child: Issues and Innovations* (Boston: Houghton Mifflin, 1966), p. 52.
5. Jean Piaget, *The Origins of Intelligence in Children* (New York: International Universities Press, 1952).
6. W. C. Becker, C. H. Madsen, Jr., Carole R. Arnold, and D. R. Thomas, "The Contingent Use of Teacher Attention and Praise in Reducing Classroom Behavior Problems," *Journal of Special Education,* 1967, **I,** 287–307.
7. *Ibid.*, p. 303.
8. *Ibid.*
9. K. D. O'Leary and W. C. Becker, "Behavior Modification in an Adjustment Class: A Token Reinforcement Program," *Exceptional Children,* May 1967, 637–42.
10. *Ibid.*, p. 641.
11. D. R. Thomas, W. C. Becker, and Marianne Armstrong, "Production and Elimination of Disruptive Classroom Behavior by Systematically Varying Teacher's Behavior," *Journal of Applied Behavior Analysis,* 1968, **I,** 34–45.
12. *Ibid.*
13. C. H. Madsen, Jr., W. C. Becker, D. R. Thomas, Linda Koser, and Elaine Parker, "An Analysis of the Reinforcing Function of 'Sit Down' Commands," in R. K. Parker (ed.), *Readings in Educational Psychology* (Boston: Allyn & Bacon, in press).